Rhythms of Race

ENVISIONING CUBA
Louis A. Pérez Jr., editor

Envisioning Cuba publishes outstanding, innovative works in Cuban studies, drawn from diverse subjects and disciplines in the humanities and social sciences, from the colonial period through the post–Cold War era. Featuring innovative scholarship engaged with theoretical approaches and interpretive frameworks informed by social, cultural, and intellectual perspectives, the series highlights the exploration of historical and cultural circumstances and conditions related to the development of Cuban self-definition and national identity.

Rhythms of Race

Cuban Musicians and the Making of

Latino New York City and Miami, 1940–1960

CHRISTINA D. ABREU

The University of North Carolina Press / Chapel Hill

The paper in this book meets the guidelines for permanence and
durability of the Committee on Production Guidelines for Book Longevity
of the Council on Library Resources.

The University of North Carolina Press has been a member of
the Green Press Initiative since 2003.

Cover illustration: *La Musica,* painting by Dania Sierra, 2007.
www.sierrafineart.com. Used by permission of the artist.

Library of Congress Cataloging-in-Publication Data
Abreu, Christina D., author.
 Rhythms of race : Cuban musicians and the making of Latino New York City and
Miami, 1940–1960 / Christina D. Abreu.—1st edition.
      pages cm. — (Envisioning Cuba)
 Includes bibliographical references and index.
    ISBN 978-1-4696-2084-8 (pbk. : alk. paper)—ISBN 978-1-4696-2085-5 (ebook)
1. Music—Cuba—History and criticism.   2. Cuban Americans—New York (State)—
New York—Music—History and criticism.   3. Cuban Americans—Florida—
Miami—Music—History and criticism.   I. Title.
 ML480.A27 2015
 780.89'68729107471—dc23
                                                                          2014034895

For my parents,

Rosendo and Teresa Abreu,

for their unconditional love

Contents

Illustrations

Acknowledgments

I began this project with the support of a wonderful community of scholars and friends at the University of Michigan. Jesse Hoffnung-Garskof's thoughtful insights and critical reading of my work challenged me to write with more precision and clarity. His advice and example has made me a better writer and historian. Richard Lee Turits helped me realize that I had something important to say, and Yeidy M. Rivero and Anthony P. Mora offered helpful comments and suggestions. I also want to thank Rebecca J. Scott, James W. Cook, Philip J. Deloria, Kristin Hass, Matthew Lassiter, Susan Juster, and Sueann Caulfield for introducing me to fields, questions, and methodologies that informed my intellectual development. Alexander Olson and Erik Z. Morales offered feedback on parts of the manuscript, and the Rackham Graduate School and Department of American Culture provided generous funding for the early stages of research and writing.

Librarians, archivists, and fellow researchers at the various institutions I visited in New York and Florida proved essential. I am deeply indebted to Pedro Juan Hernández and the staff at the Centro de Estudios Puertorriqueños for permission to use the then-uncatalogued Carlos Ortiz Collection. It was also at the Centro that I met Aldo Lauria Santiago, and our brief conversations about my project and Cuban music led to his suggestion that I consult music journalist David Carp's collection of oral history interviews. That tip was priceless. Many thanks also to the archivists and staffs at the Schomburg Center for Research in Black Culture, the New York Public Library for the Performing Arts, the Bronx County Historical Society, the Historical Museum of Southern Florida, the Cuban Heritage Collection and the Otto Richter Library at the University of Miami, and the Interlibrary Loan departments at the University of Michigan and Purdue University.

I am forever grateful to those who put me in contact with their family and friends who were willing and eager to share their stories of migration and their love of Cuban music with me. A special thanks to Linda Radelat, Elsie Ferrara, Nicolette Bruner Olson, and Sarita Gantz. Mary Lynn Conejo and Vilma Rizo welcomed me into their homes and shared their family histories and photographs with me. Joe Conzo introduced me to dozens of musicians in the Bronx and treated me as someone who knew what she was talking about.

Very early on Raúl A. Fernández took an interest in my project. He read and commented on early drafts of the manuscript and shared research materials with me. I thank him for his guidance and generosity; his knowledge and encouragement have helped me and improved my work in countless ways. Many other people provided feedback on this project at conferences and seminars and through electronic correspondence. I appreciate the comments, suggestions, and support offered by Antonio López, Nancy Raquel Mirabal, George J. Sánchez, Anthony Macías, and Joel Dinerstein. I also extend my thanks to Geraldo Cadava, John Alba Cutler, Jason Ruiz, Sarah Cornell, Annette Rodríguez, Alex E. Chávez, and the many others who attended the Newberry Library Seminar on Borderlands and Latino Studies in April 2011.

I want to thank Johnathan O'Neill, Jonathan Bryant, Brian K. Feltman, Anastatia Sims, and Jeffrey Burson at Georgia Southern University for their sound advice and tremendous support and the Department of History for its funding of the images used in the book. I am also very grateful to my other GSU colleagues and friends, too many to name here, for their collegiality and encouragement. I would also like to thank Louis A. Pérez, Alison Shay, and, especially, Elaine Maisner at the University of North Carolina Press for their attentiveness and enthusiastic efforts on behalf of this project. A special shout out, too, goes to Dania Sierra (www.sierrafineart.com) for allowing me to use her beautiful artwork on the cover of the book.

Family and friends supported me as I worked to complete the manuscript. I thank the Hall and Espinal families and my aunt, Gilda Abreu, who provided housing in New Jersey and Florida so that I could visit archives. Katie Higgins and Brett Scipioni welcomed me and my writing companion—my Italian greyhound, Stuart Hall—into their apartments so that I could finish up some newspaper research at the Library of Congress in Washington, D.C. Carrie, Naomi, and Maxine Feltman offered daily reminders that short breaks for stories and laughter are totally worth it.

I dedicate this book to my loving and supportive parents, Rosendo and Teresa Abreu. Their tales of life in 1950s Cuba and their experiences adjusting to life in the United States set me on this path. It was their stories and my mother's special way of telling them—even the ones that seem to get embellished just a little more each time—that made me want to know more about Cuba and its history and culture. Thank you.

My deepest appreciation goes to my husband, best friend, and colleague Eric Hall. His endless confidence, optimism, and reassurances kept me going even on the toughest of writing days. I have learned so much from our daily conversations about history, race, and culture. I am incredibly thankful to have shared this intellectual journey with him and look forward to a lifetime of all sorts of adventures with such a loving, caring, and brilliant partner. I love you, today, tomorrow, *y para siempre.*

Rhythms of Race

INTRODUCTION

Almost twenty years after production of new episodes of *I Love Lucy* ended in 1957, an older, gray-haired but no less upbeat and dynamic Desi Arnaz took to the stage to host the fourteenth episode of the inaugural season of *Saturday Night Live*. As he had done countless times throughout his early musical career in the late 1930s and 1940s and on *I Love Lucy* in the 1950s, the Cuban entertainer had double duties that evening in 1976; he served not only as the show's host but also as the featured musical act. Backed by band members dressed in oversized bright red, orange, and yellow rumba sleeves, Arnaz performed an old favorite, the song "Cuban Pete," alongside a woman whose red lipstick, tropical fruit headdress, and maraca-shaking dance moves must have been intended to evoke comparisons with Carmen Miranda, the Portuguese-born singer, dancer, and actress from Brazil. He ended the show with his version of "Babalú," leading the cast and audience in an animated conga line throughout the studio. During the performance, Arnaz beat on a colorful conga drum, though less feverishly than he had on the Broadway stages of New York City, in the hotel ballrooms of Miami Beach, and on the small and big screens of Hollywood at the peak of his career. He then loosened his bowtie to signal impending disorder and wildness, a sort of cue that exotic revelry was on its way. In this act, Arnaz reproduced once more a kind of Cuban performance typical of the sort that had appealed (and continued to appeal) mostly, but not exclusively, to white North American audiences during the height of the Latin craze of the 1930s, 1940s, and 1950s. By doing so, Arnaz and other light-skinned charismatic musicians like him, including Xavier Cugat, Marco Rizo, and José Curbelo, participated in the production of images and stereotypes that emphasized Cubanness as nonblackness, tropical escape, and sanitized exoticism.

1

But this was not the only representation of Cubanness that circulated in the United States during the second half of the twentieth century. Just two years before Arnaz's hosting gig on *SNL*, black Cuban singer Celia Cruz made headlines when she traveled to Zaire with the Fania All-Stars to perform at a three-day music festival before the historic Rumble in the Jungle between African American boxers Muhammad Ali and George Foreman. Led by Dominican flute player Johnny Pacheco, Cruz and the Fania All-Stars performed "Guantanamera" and "Quimbara" for a stadium packed with Africans dancing in sync with the musical ensemble's fast-paced salsa beat. A popular entertainer since her days on the radio in Havana in the early 1950s, Cruz played a major role in the development and commercial success of the salsa music genre, which she described as "just a marketing term applied to what originally was Cuban music."[1] In this context, which was marketed and celebrated as a sort of "return to Africa," as performed by black Cuban entertainers such as Celia Cruz or Mario Bauzá, Machito, and Arsenio Rodríguez, national authenticity, musical innovation, and blackness marked the meaning of Cubanness.

On the one hand, it is not entirely surprising that Arnaz performed and had firmly in his repertoire a song like "Cuban Pete," with its mostly English-language lyrics and a "rumba beat" that makes everyone and everything go "chick chicky boom, chick chicky boom." It is also not too shocking that Cruz chose to perform the song "Quimbara," a quick-tempo *guaguancó* (a narrative song style based on the Afro-Cuban drumming and dance style that is also known as *guaguancó*, a popular subgenre of traditional rumba) with a chorus that repeats the Kimbundo word "quimbara." The word has no known English-language translation but nonetheless points to African origins. On the other hand, if we look more closely at the other two songs Arnaz and Cruz performed in these distinct settings, the apparent predictability of their musical selections becomes less clear. The song "Babalú" contains obvious Afro-Cuban themes, namely the hailing of the *orishas*[2] Babalú-Ayé and Changó and the use of Caribbean racial vocabulary with the word "*negra*" ("black woman") mixed with Spanish words like "*olé*," at least in the version of the song popularized by Arnaz.[3] "Guantanamera," which uses lyrics adapted from white Cuban patriot, intellectual, and poet José Martí's *Versos sencillos*, has generally been recognized as Cuba's most well-known song, the island's unofficial national anthem. In this particular version, Cruz accents her performance with the phrase "*dijo Martí*" ("said Martí") and her customary shouts of "*Azucar!*"[4] What these two examples illustrate is that the content and meaning of Cubanness changed as it was performed by black

What Black Cubans Represent

and white Cuban musicians and produced for different audiences, but [*Thesis?*] the choices these performers made were not always consistent or the ones that were expected or most obvious. As the context of these musical performances changed, so did their larger significance, particularly in relation to questions of racial and ethnic identity: Arnaz's performance of (Afro-)Cubanness shifted to one of Latinness, and Cruz's performance of Cubanness became one of Afro-Cubanness. [*]

Rhythms of Race takes as its premise that it is necessary to study these various modes of performance simultaneously and in dialogue in order to [*Purpose*] understand the role black and white Cuban musicians played in shaping Cuban ethnic and broader Hispano/a and Latino/a identity. It situates this relationship not in the post-1959 period that has until recently dominated Cuban American historical, cultural, and literary studies but rather in the [*Histo*] 1940s and 1950s, a period when the United States witnessed a boom in Cuban and Cuban American transnational cultural production. In these two decades before the Cuban Revolution of 1959, nearly 90,000 black and white Cubans migrated to New York and Florida, two of the most concentrated areas of Cuban settlement in the United States. This settlement pattern dates back to the late nineteenth century and held steady throughout the mid-twentieth century. Many of these migrants settled in New York City and Miami, where they encountered larger numbers of African Americans, Puerto Ricans, and other Latin American and Caribbean migrants, temporary visitors, and tourists. Consequently, Cuban [*Purpose*] and Cuban American cultural production in these two cities, specifically in relation to musicians' and audiences' interactions—positive and negative, real and imagined—in their Cuban and broader Latino/a communities, is key to understanding Cuban ethnic identity and its role in shaping lasting ideas and experiences of Latinidad and Afro-Latinidad.

Among the migrants who left Cuba to start new lives in the United States in the 1940s and 1950s were numerous musicians and entertainers, some of whom would emerge as well-known neighborhood celebrities and international stars. At social clubs, dance halls, and nightclubs in the South Bronx, East Harlem, and the southwest section of Miami and in the hotels, ballrooms, and nightclubs of Broadway and Miami Beach and on the Hollywood screen, black and white Cuban musicians and entertainers participated in the construction of multiple and contested representations of Cubanness, Afro-Cubanness, and Latinness. These Cubans and the representations they produced encountered Cuban, Puerto Rican, African American, and white North American audiences who brought their own sets of racial and cultural expectations to the dance floor. Some of the key

Music set the Racial Tone/attitude

Cuban participants in the Latin music scene of this period were musicians of color Mario Bauzá, Machito, Arsenio Rodríguez, and Miguelito Valdés and white entertainers Xavier Cugat, Desi Arnaz, José Curbelo, Marco Rizo, and Perucho Irigoyen.[5] Their stories and perspectives and those of other black and white Cuban musicians and entertainers reveal both shared understandings and significant differences in their migration experiences, their participation in the professional entertainment industries, and their construction of white, brown, and black racial identities. Oral histories and the Spanish-language newspapers of New York City and Miami are key sources of these stories and perspectives. It was in the pages of major newspapers such as *La Prensa* and *Diario las Américas* that Cuban and Latino/a musicians and migrants expressed and debated ideas and practices related to musical and cultural authenticity and commercialism, race and ethnicity, Cuban nationalism, and Hispano/a and Latino/a identity.

This book tells the story of Cuban and Cuban American cultural production in conversation with the largely untold narrative of Cuban community and identity development in New York City and Miami in the 1940s and 1950s. In what follows, I examine musicians, performances, and audiences in public spaces and markets and in the more private informal and formal spaces of Cuban and Latino/a social clubs, ethnic institutions, and community celebrations. Musicians, music, and performance are undoubtedly at the center of the story, and I hope to make the case for studying Cuban popular culture in both commercial and what I describe as ethnic or cultural contexts, though of course these were not mutually exclusive spaces. This story does not emerge in isolation; it emerges in relation to and as a critical component of what scholars have called the "Latinization" of New York City and Miami. Sociologist Agustín Laó-Montes defines Latinization as "the overall process of production of discourses of latinidad," which he argues should not be thought of "as a static or unified formation but as a flexible category that relates to a plurality of ideologies of identification, cultural expressions, and political and social agendas." More specifically, he explains that "Latinization can be produced around different axes of identification: at one end, in relationship to markers of identity/difference such as language, race, culture, or immigration resulting in self-identification by Latinos and, at the other end, as a result of practices of othering (classification and homogenization) racialized and ethnicized populations by governmental, corporative, and intellectual discourses." In the 1940s and 1950s, black and white Cuban migrants, including musicians and performers who were looking to "make it" in the world of enter-

[handwritten annotation: → Popular Latinos Made or Broke the Racialization of Latino Community]

tainment, were central to this two-sided process of Latinization. Those Cubans who gained prominence on the terrain of popular culture acquired the social, cultural, and symbolical capital to be at the forefront of the making of Latino/a New York City and Miami.[6]

Rhythms of Race examines the relationship between popular black and white Cuban entertainers and the growing Cuban communities and broader Latino/a publics of New York City and Miami in the 1940s and 1950s. It uses the stories told by some of the key Cuban participants in the Latin music scene of this period and the public discourse produced in widely disseminated Spanish-language newspapers as a window into a broader experience of Cuban ethnic identity. In both cities and, indeed, in the broader realm of popular culture, black and white Cuban musicians engaged in the construction of discourses of Hispano/a and Latino/a identity and community through their participation in music and cultural festivals, nightclubs, social clubs, and television and film productions. In New York City, Cuban migrants and musicians settled near and among much larger Puerto Rican and African American communities, mostly in Harlem and the South Bronx but also in lower Manhattan, and it was in these contexts, which were sometimes friendly, sometimes hostile, that black and white musicians engaged with ideas about their music, race, and national identity. In Miami, Cuban migrants and musicians lived and worked in the context of a tourism industry and political climate that encouraged and facilitated a massive back-and-forth movement between the United States and Cuba. Here, Cuban communities and Cuban ethnic identity took shape in relation to the racial boundaries of a Jim Crow city, island politics characterized by a seemingly constant cycle of reform and revolution, and increasingly dominant ideologies and racialized practices of Pan-Americanism (a term I use to refer to moments of inter-American cooperation that were supported and encouraged, separately and occasionally simultaneously, at the governmental, institutional, and local levels).[7]

[handwritten annotations in right margin: ✳ ; Diff Between NY & Miami.]

MUSIC, MIGRATION, AND RACE IN (AFRO-)CUBAN
AMERICAN HISTORIOGRAPHY

Like jazz, blues, and hip-hop in the United States, Cuban music demonstrates the all-too-familiar process by which popular music and cultural expressions with claims to blackness come to be accepted and adopted (albeit in an altered form) by the dominant society. Black popular music in general and Cuban music in particular, with its circuitous travels across national borders and national histories, complicates our understanding of the agency and influence of Cuban musicians of color and the relationship between race and mass cultural expression. Popular music and entertainment, even in their mainstream commercialized form, which some cultural studies scholars claim had become the "opiate of the masses," are seen here as the sites where conversations about race, ethnicity, nation, and social and political struggle took place.[8] Studying Cuban music and musicians offers us unique access to Cuba's national history, one that is as much about African and Spanish mixture and colonial legacies as it is about the influences of the United States.

In its emphasis on popular Cuban music and other forms of cultural production, this book is very much in conversation with the work of music historians, ethnomusicologists, literary studies, and cultural studies scholars such as John Storm Roberts, Gustavo Pérez-Firmat, Raúl A. Fernández, Robin Moore, and David F. García. Thanks to their efforts, we know a great deal about the development of the *son* (a blend of African and European dance music that originated in eastern Cuba at the end of the nineteenth century), rumba, conga, mambo, and cha-cha-chá as musical styles, both as international Latin dance phenomena and as cultural expressions of Afro-Cubanness. This book builds on this body of scholarship by elaborating not so much on the history of these specific musical styles or the Latin music genre in general—though perspectives expressed about these developments are very much a part of the story—but rather on the Cuban singers, musicians, dancers, and audiences who created, performed, and enjoyed those rhythms at nightclubs and social clubs and in cramped apartments all across New York City and Miami, two cities that have become centers of Latino/a America.[9]

Most scholars have long characterized the 1940s and 1950s as a time of fertile Cuban cultural production but little Cuban settlement in the United States. One of the goals of this study, therefore, is to uncover and examine Cubans in places and time periods that have previously been overshadowed by other migrant groups whose larger population size has come to overdetermine their relevance and significance to the Latino/a experience in the United States. By focusing on the experiences of Cuban entertainers *and* migrants in New York City and Miami in the 1940s and 1950s, this project bridges the gap between studies of Cuban migrants in late nineteenth- and early twentieth-century New York City and Tampa and narratives that define the Cuban Revolution of 1959 as *the* moment of origin for Cuban migration to the United States. Only a handful of studies challenge what historian Nancy Raquel Mirabal has called the "exile model," and historical and sociological studies of the migration and settlement of Cubans in the United States can be characterized as temporally disconnected and geographically polarized. Most studies of Cuban migration to the United States have focused on two seemingly disjointed and unrelated time periods: the relatively small migrations of Cubans that took place in the late nineteenth and early twentieth centuries and the more recent and massive waves of exiles who left the island following the Cuban Revolution of 1959. These studies have limited their examinations to four major areas of Cuban settlement: the early migrations to New York City and Tampa and the more recent migrations to Miami and Union City, New Jersey. Few of these studies have offered comparative analysis of the experiences of Cuban migrants in more than one of these areas of settlement.[10] *Rhythms of Race* seeks to counter this trend through a comparison, even if a somewhat uneven one, of the social and cultural worlds created by Cubans and Latino/as in New York City and Miami. The unevenness is not the result of choice but of reality, both historical and contemporary.

An early and important exception to the framework that is characteristic of the historiography of Cubans in the United States is anthropologist Susan Greenbaum's book *More Than Black: Afro-Cubans in Tampa*. Greenbaum recovers what she calls a "lost chapter in the Cuban American experience" through an examination of the Afro-Cuban community of Ybor City since its formation in the late nineteenth century. Her work challenges the traditional invisibility of blacks in the Cuban American experience and the popular beliefs that Cubans came to the United States only after 1959 and that they were always white and economically advantaged. She examines how Afro-Cubans in Tampa "defined and negotiated both blackness and Cubanness," concluding that these nineteenth- and early twentieth-century migrants were "black when with Cubans, and Cubans when with blacks." After the cigar industry collapsed in the 1930s, many Afro-Cubans moved north from Tampa to New York City. Those who remained forged tighter bonds with African Americans and the larger black community of Tampa, especially after World War II.[11] *Rhythms of Race* also aims to recover the presence and contributions of Cubans of color in the Cuban American experience, embarking on a trail mapped out but not pursued by Greenbaum. This book follows the thousands of Cubans who made their way from Tampa to New York City in the 1940s and 1950s and settled alongside newly arriving Cuban migrants, Puerto Ricans, and African Americans. It also begins to identify a pattern of migration by which Cubans left Tampa for Miami to continue working in the cigar industry or to pursue opportunities in the other developing industries of furniture-making, transportation, and tourism. By examining the experiences of these migrants in New York City together with the experiences of Cubans in Miami, this study recovers and deepens our understanding of a Cuban American experience that not only spans the entirety of the twentieth century but also as one that is not exclusive or confined to a single geographic area of the United States. Much like the cities of Havana and Santiago, Tampa remains ever-present in this story not only as a place of origin but as one of many sources of symbolic and material influences on race relations between black and white Cubans and among Cubans, Puerto Ricans, African Americans, ethnic whites, and other groups who lived, worked, and socialized alongside one another in New York City and Miami.

Similarly, this book is in dialogue with the more recent work of historian Frank Guridy and literary scholars Ricardo Ortíz and Antonio López, whose studies on Cuban and Afro-Cuban diasporic communities and cultural production have also helped accelerate this refocusing of the way scholars have periodized and geographically located the origins of (Afro-)Cuban America.[12] Guridy's historical study looks at Afro-Cuban and African American cultural and educational collaboration at the institutional level; Ortíz's literary study focuses on gender and sexuality in post-1959 Cuban American cultural identity in cities such as Los Angeles, Chicago, and New York; López examines Afro-Cuban writers' and performers' "unbecoming" relationship with U.S. black and mulatto identities. My project moves the conversation away from the mostly intellectual and cultural elite perspectives offered in these works and more toward the everyday ideas and experiences of both black and white Cuban and Latino/a popular musicians and migrants as expressed from within the Cuban and broader Latino/a communities of New York City and Miami. In its emphasis on comparative and relational understandings of race-making and Afro-diasporic and Latino/a framings, this book privileges the perspectives and experiences of well-known and not-so-well-known black and white Cuban musicians and migrants and Puerto Rican, African American, and other Latino/a performers, entertainment managers, journalists, and community leaders.

But any challenge to the post-1959 exile model also necessitates, at certain moments, taking a step back to consider the long history of political entanglement and cultural exchange between Cuba and the United States, as offered, most notably, by historian Louis A. Pérez in his book *On Becoming Cuban: Identity, Nationality, and Culture*. Pérez examines North American influences on Cuban national identity from the early 1850s to the late 1950s by looking specifically at the role of U.S. hegemony as a cultural condition and the ways Protestant missionaries, baseball and boxing,

> Explore how Music/Musicians influenced the construction of a Cuban Racial/Cultural identity

music and popular culture, and motion pictures shaped Cuban nationalism. Pérez focuses on an "interrelated constellation of factors and forces"
that formed and shaped Cuban encounters with North American influences in an effort to "understand the context and complexity of these
linkages as a totality, as a system, and to see how connections worked together, like the strands of a web."[13] My project builds on Pérez's work by
focusing on just one strand of the web, music and popular culture, in the
context of specific ideas about (self-)representation and performance, race
and ethnicity, and nationalism and transnationalism. This approach allows for closer examination of the ways the black and white Cuban migrants of the 1940s and 1950s, as individuals and as a community, responded to their encounters with North American culture, and more
importantly, how these encounters helped spur the development of (Afro-)
Cuban American cultural identity long before the massive post-1959 exodus of Cubans to the United States. However, this book is not about how
Cubans were exposed to North American ideas and values through various popular culture forms (though that is certainly a part of the story). Instead, at its core, this book is about how black and white Cuban musicians
and migrants perceived and participated in constructing and contesting
ideas and social practices that defined what it meant to be "Cuban," "Afro-
Cuban," "Hispano/a," and "Latino/a" in the United States.

Purpose

A NOTE ON FRAMEWORK AND TERMINOLOGY

Rhythms of Race focuses on three major and interrelated themes. First, I
examine the differences in experience between black and white Cuban musicians, specifically in terms of their engagement with nationalist discourses
about race, Afro-Cubanidad, and different modes of racialization practiced
in the United States and Cuba. Cuban musicians sometimes held fast to
the perspectives on their music, race, and culture that circulated in Cuba,
but they also frequently rethought the significance of their music, race, and
culture in terms of their migration. Each chapter in this book offers, to
varying extents, comparative analysis of the U.S. and Cuban racial systems
and contends that Cuban musicians and entertainers held multiple subject positions as celebrities, laborers, migrants, and racial and ethnic
pioneers.

Guridy observes that "people of African descent often did not see an
incompatibility between their national and racial self-understandings."
My book demonstrates that musical partnerships between Afro-Cubans,
Afro-Latino/as, and African Americans did not always result in shared

understandings and deliberate claims of blackness, especially because of limited opportunities for commercial visibility and marketing in the world of entertainment. *Rhythms of Race* explores instances when Cuban musicians of color accepted belonging in what López describes as a Cuban diaspora marked as "black, unsettling [the] memory, if not practice, of ideological postracial, *mestizaje*, and 'raceless' antirevolutionary nationalisms, now transnationalisms" and moments when they did not.[14] It moves the discussion of the choices made and perspectives offered by Cuban musicians of color in the United States into conversation with those of white Cuban musicians, positioning discourses of Cuban nationalism and racial and ethnic identity as self-reflexive, relational, and, at times, performative. The entertainment worlds and social spaces the black and white Cuban musicians of the 1940s and 1950s navigated often overlapped. The racial ideologies these musicians expressed are linked to their experiences within and beyond these worlds and spaces, which were, at various times and to various extents, fluid and contested, rigid and fixed, black and white, and Anglo and Latino/a. The story of the role black and white Cubans played in the making of (Afro-)Latino/a New York City and Miami emerges from their ideas about and lived experiences with migration, negotiation along a continuum of racial and ethnic inclusion and exclusion, and insertion into the Latin music scene.

It would be a mistake, however, to argue that U.S. racial discourses, which became familiar to Cubans through their encounters with colonial officials, U.S. businesses and employers, and tourists and through mediated encounters vis-à-vis popular culture, met with empty vessels. As shown by numerous historical studies that focus on Cuba's nineteenth-century struggle for independence from Spain, most notable among them historian Ada Ferrer's *Insurgent Cuba: Race, Nation, and Revolution, 1868-1898*, Cubans knew about and practiced racial discrimination long before U.S. intervention on the island. In the early 1890s, black and white Cuban revolutionary leaders and intellectuals forged a definition of Cuban nationhood and citizenship that envisioned an independent Cuba as a racially egalitarian society, a definition that directly challenged popular biological and cultural beliefs that people of color were inferior to whites. What U.S. occupation did to this vision shortly after the War of Cuban Independence was accelerate the growing tendency among white Cuban leaders to define civilization as "refinement, civility, and whiteness."[15] Beginning with the signing of the Platt Amendment and continuing throughout the first (1902-1933) and second (1933-1958) Cuban republics, the political and economic interests of the United States continued to prompt

Black/White/Cuban = Different in U.S.; how Did these Musicians help shape this identity?

interference and involvement in the island's domestic affairs. Emphasizing the role that state policies and social actors played in the development of Cuban race relations, historian Alejandro de la Fuente admits that "in the context of Cuba's imperial subordination, a modicum of independence could be maintained only at the expense of social justice."[16] Two points, therefore, deserve special attention. First, migrants from Cuba arrived in the United States with their own racial knowledge and sets of constructed and contested categories of racial identification. Their everyday experiences on the island included both the practice of and exposure to implicit and explicit forms of racial discrimination that shaped their mode of thinking. Second, for Cuban migrants, familiarity with the U.S. racial system prior to migration did not necessitate acquiescence to or rejection of either system in its entirety. In its focus on race and comparison between U.S. and Cuban racial systems, this book is in dialogue with historians of race in Cuba and with scholars such as Adrian Burgos Jr., *—Sources/* Laura Gómez, and Lilia Fernández, whose studies on race-making, racial *Histo* difference, and racialization have shown the various ways that Latino/a baseball players, Mexican Americans, and Mexicans and Puerto Ricans in Chicago navigated the color line in the United States.[17]

Cuban migration to the United States parallels other Latin American and Caribbean migrations of the nineteenth and twentieth centuries. The massive exodus of Cubans to the United States since 1959 has overshadowed the much longer process of migration as an element of a colonial relationship that began in earnest in the mid-nineteenth century and continued throughout the twentieth, playing itself out, in the Cuban case, on the terrain of popular culture. Cuban migrants to New York City and Miami in the 1940s and 1950s brought with them tastes and expectations shaped by decades of U.S. neocolonial rule on the island. In fact, Pérez has written extensively on the economic, political, and social "ties of singular intimacy" that have linked the United States and Cuba since the mid-nineteenth century. Cuban familiarity with U.S. culture and, conversely, U.S. familiarity with Cuban culture stretches back into this earlier period, and it is this reciprocity that underscores the complex and dynamic relationship between Cuban entertainers and Cuban, Latino/a, African American and white North American audiences in New York City and Miami, in the entertainment industry in Hollywood, and in local, national, and international relations.[18] This framework is key to understanding the Cuban migration of the 1940s and 1950s and drawing the necessary links between the earlier and later periods of migration and connections to other Latino/a migrations.

A second theme of this book concerns the differences between the music produced for and consumed by Cuban, Puerto Rican, and broader Latino/a audiences and in transnational circuits and music produced for popular consumption by white North American audiences. The boundaries between these two publics are, of course, fluid, given that in Cuba (and in Miami) the music industry was connected to international tourism and that musicians and musical styles oftentimes moved among these multiple audiences. Still, a notion of musical authenticity emerged, especially among Cuban musicians of color, that emphasized innovation over popularization and referenced the relationship between musician and audience, nationalism and rhythm, and blackness and Africanness. Both black and white Cuban musicians observed that light-skinned Cuban musicians, or at least those who "passed" as nonblack, performed a sort of Cubanness that targeted and appealed to a broad and mass audience by relying on simplified rhythms or gimmicks and costumes. These perspectives suggest that claims of musical talent and authenticity intersected with ideas about race and national identity and the realities experienced by those who sought entry into a commercial entertainment world that promised lucrative paydays beyond those that were possible in ethnic or cultural contexts.

Central to these debates about authenticity or, as we will see, the possibility of the performance of multiple authenticities is the complicated and contested term "Latin," particularly when applied to the variety of musical genres that musicians and bandleaders produced for Cuban, Latino/a, and North American audiences in the 1940s and 1950s. Many black and white Cuban musicians opposed descriptions of their music as "Latin," though it was the term most often used in the tourism and professional entertainment industries. Instead, they preferred the national and cultural terms "Cuban" and "Afro-Cuban." "Latin" continues to be used most commonly by the mainstream entertainment industries in the United States as a cultural marker and racial stereotype. As Latino/a Studies scholar Alberto Sandoval-Sánchez explains, "Being 'Latin' means to come from a Spanish-speaking country, to be an immigrant whose identity as 'Latin foreign other' is marked by, and anchored in, a Spanish accent and exotic looks. Such conceptions of the 'foreign other' are perpetuated by ready-made stereotypes: the Latin bombshell, the Latin lover, Latin music, Latin rhythm, Latin dance, Latin type, Latin temper, Latin time." Pérez offers a more specific definition of "Latin," one centered on a popular culture landscape dominated by the rhythms of the rumba, conga, mambo, and cha-cha-chá. He argues that "Latin" generally meant "Cuban" but points out that Cubanness was neither static nor immune to change, explaining that "commercial success on this scale, of course, could not have been achieved without sub-stantial adaptation of authentic rhythms and original phrasings."[19]

Third, I focus on ideas and constructions of Cubanidad, Hispanidad, and Latinidad, arguing that in the 1940s and 1950s, particularly in the realm of popular music, Cubanness and Afro-Cubanness played key roles in the developing collective conceptions of Hispano/a and Latino/a iden-tity and culture. The term Hispano/a, which has usually been understood to emphasize a romanticized Spanish past and minimize the acknowledg-ment of mixture with people of African or indigenous descent, was used most often during these decades, especially in New York City. The term Latino/a, defined as a pan-ethnic identity encompassing individuals from the Spanish-speaking Americas, was still common, however. At times, I use Hispano/a and Latino/a simultaneously, though not synonymously, to reflect that debates about the usefulness and accuracy of both terms were taking place in the Spanish-speaking communities of New York City and Miami. This strategy allows me to draw attention to the instability and contingency of racial and ethnic identification. In fact, a debate about which term best described the Spanish- and Portuguese-speaking peoples of the Americas erupted in the pages of *La Prensa* in the fall of 1944. Part of the discussion centered on the question of whether either category, in terms of both race and ethnicity, acknowledged or included "those [Spanish- and Portuguese-speaking] Americans that have African blood in their veins."[20]

Latino/a Studies scholars have for decades debated the use and useful-ness of the terms "Hispanic" and "Latino/a." Some critics charge that the ethnic label "Hispanic" "homogenizes the varied social and political expe-riences" of millions of people of "different races, classes, languages, national origins, genders, and religions" and fails to account for differences between self-identification and government-imposed terminology. Sandoval-Sánchez, for example, prefers the term "Latino/a" because it accounts for gender differences and "functions as a stratagem of/for political interven-tion, solidarity, and coalition." However, there are also critics of the eth-nic label "Latino/a." Latino/a Studies scholar Juan Flores argues that while a pan-ethnic concept such as "Latino/a" might offer "some significant stra-tegic advantages to [its] deployment in political movements for change," it "only holds up when qualified by the national-group angle or optic from which it is uttered. . . . Thus, what presents itself as a category of inclusion and compatibility functions as a tool of exclusion and internal 'othering.'" Sociologist Gabriel Haslip-Viera seemingly sidesteps these debates and uses the terms "Hispanic" and "Latino/a" interchangeably. For him, both terms simply "refer to all persons living in the United States whose origins can be traced to Spain and the Spanish-speaking countries of Latin America and the Caribbean. Included in this category are all U.S. immigrants who have come from these countries and their descendants who live in the United States, whether they are Spanish-speaking or not."[21]

More recently, "Afro-Latino/a" has emerged "as a way to signal racial, cultural, and socioeconomic contradictions within the overly vague idea of 'Latino/a.'" The term, according to Miriam Jiménez Román and Juan Flores, editors of the critical volume *The Afro-Latin@ Reader: History and Culture in the United States*, recognizes the presence of antiblack racism in the various Latino/a communities of the United States, including New York City and Miami. Jiménez Román and Flores argue that the term "Afro-Latino/a" articulates an understanding of "the transnational discourse or identity field linking Black Latin Americans and Latin@s across national and regional lines."[22] Several essays in their volume focus on the experiences of some of the very black Cuban musicians and social actors examined in this book, including Afro-Cuban performers Mario Bauzá, Arsenio Rodríguez, Graciela Pérez, and Melba Alvarado, one of the leaders of El Club Cubano Inter-Americano in the Bronx.

Among scholars working on Cuba, "Afro-Cuban" as a racial designation remains problematic. In Cuba and among the Cuban musicians and migrants examined in this book, "Afro-Cuban" had a specific cultural connotation that most active black intellectuals and politicians did not see as their own. More than a reference to skin color, Afro-Cubanness recognized and (in some instances) celebrated African influences in Cuban music, dance, and culture and claimed these as symbols of Cuban national identity.[23] As we will see, Afro-Cuban music—once marginalized but now nationalized and commercialized—played a critical and unique role in this process. It was one of the central fields of discourse in which both nationalism and race were articulated in Cuba beginning in the 1920s and 1930s, in intimate dialogue with the imperial gaze. Time and again, Cuban migrants and musicians reworked the familiar articulations of Cuba's history of racial mixture to suit new contexts, at times shifting seamlessly between critical and oppositional stories of race to discourses of musical nationalism and racial harmony. With Cuban music and musicians at the center, a relationship developed between national origin communities and nationalist cultural representations and an emerging public, often referred to as the *colonia hispana, colonia latina,* or *los nuestros,* that was defined by shared language, hemispheric and inter-American solidarity, and transnational culture. The term *nuestra raza* (our race), especially in descriptions of *nuestra música* (our music) or other popular cultural performances, sometimes stood in for these other terms. From Afro-Cuban music, whether it was performed and enjoyed in live and recorded settings or in public and private contexts, emerged multiple, dominant and subaltern, narratives of Cuban national history that not only represented the historical experiences of individuals but also contributed to the formation of a collective (Afro-)Latino/a identity.

Once in New York City or Miami, black and white Cuban musicians and migrants found ways to accept, reject, and modify the racialized discourses and practices that marked them as "Cuban," "Afro-Cuban," "Latin," "Negro/ Black," "Hispano/a," and "Latino/a." In tracing the ways these terms circulated in the Spanish-language press and the ways Cubans and other Latino/as used these terms and made sense of them, I emphasize their contested and socially constructed nature. Though my role as narrator oftentimes requires that I identify race, nationality, and ethnicity, my goal has not been to lay claim to or defend specific vocabulary. Rather, my aim has been to understand what it meant to be "Cuban," "Afro-Cuban," "Latin," "Negro/Black," "Hispano/a," and "Latino/a" on the stages, dance floors, television and movie screens, and crowded streets of New York City and Miami in the 1940s and 1950s.

A NOTE ON METHOD AND SOURCES

Rhythms of Race connects the methods of thick description, discourse analysis, and the examination of identity categories to public imagination and to the lived realities and central problematics of race and class.[24] I incorporate close readings of historical evidence from a wide range of primary source materials and theories of race and ethnicity, nationalism, identity, and popular culture. My project draws from major Spanish-language, U.S., and African American newspapers and magazines and archival materials housed in the Schomburg Center for Research in Black Culture, the New York Public Library for the Performing Arts, the Centro de Estudios Puertorriqueños, the Bronx County Historical Society, and the Cuban Heritage Collection.

One of the most significant contributions of this project is the use of documents and oral history interviews in the Carlos Ortiz Collection at the Centro de Estudios Puertorriqueños and the David Carp Collection of Latin Jazz at the Bronx County Historical Society, both of which have only recently become available to researchers. Both collections contain lengthy audio recordings and transcriptions of interviews with notable Cuban musicians and performers who have long since died and whose perspectives on race, nation, and popular culture have long been overlooked by historians interested in the relationship between cultural production and audience response. The perspectives of these entertainers, particularly those of Machito, Mario Bauzá, Marco Rizo, Arturo "Chico" O'Farrill, José Curbelo, Armando Sánchez, Armando Peraza, and Alberto Socarrás, considered simultaneously and in dialogue with one another, are critical to a deeper understanding of the relationship between cultural production, (self-)representation, and community belonging. This project also relies on oral history interviews I conducted with Cuban and Puerto Rican entertainers and migrants, records of El Club Cubano Inter-Americano, U.S. census information, and cultural texts, specifically song lyrics, musical performances, films, and episodes from the six seasons of *I Love Lucy*. Using this body of sources, this book contends that the rise in transnational Cuban and Cuban American cultural production in the 1940s and 1950s was inseparable from the smaller migrant stream that preceded the Cuban Revolution of 1959 by several decades.

AN OVERVIEW

Throughout the 1940s and 1950s, black and white Cuban musicians encountered complicated worlds of local celebrity and international fame shaped by different and inconsistent tastes and preferences. Cuban musicians and the popular culture they produced encountered a vast audience of Latino/as in New York City, a place that was both an urban center of cosmopolitanism and a place of racial segregation and ethnic divisiveness. In Miami, a city that belonged as much to the Jim Crow South as it did to tourism boosters and business officials who touted a formal, though racially ambivalent, agenda of Pan-Americanism, Cuban musicians performed for tens of thousands of Cuban, Latin American, and white North American tourists and a stable and growing community of Cuban, Puerto Rican, and Latin American residents. Thousands of Cuban, Puerto Rican, and Spanish migrants and smaller numbers of African Americans, Jewish Americans, and other ethnic whites crowded into nightclubs, ballrooms, and ethnic social clubs, forming publics that both embraced and rejected the cultural representations of Cubanness, Afro-Cubanness, and Latinness produced at these venues. *Rhythms of Race* examines these publics and the ways these representations helped set the racial, ethnic, and political terms by which Cuban migrants came to define themselves during this period. Through the use of oral history interviews, reports in Spanish- and English-language newspapers and magazines, and the meeting minutes, publications, and social calendars of Cuban social clubs in New York City and Miami, this study shows that many of the popular black and white Cuban performers of the 1940s and 1950s participated in the production of public discourses and private debates that were central to ideas and broader experiences of Cuban ethnic identity. Additionally, this book demonstrates the significant role that Cuban performers and migrants played in the making of Latino/a New York City and Miami through their cooperation with institutions such as newspapers, festivals, nightclubs, and social clubs.

Chapter 1 examines the musical and cultural contributions that black Cuban trumpet player Mario Bauzá, white Cuban pianist Marco Rizo, and many other black and white Cuban musicians made to the Cuban ethnic and broader Latino/a communities that were developing in New York City during the 1940s and 1950s. Though many regard Xavier Cugat as the archetypal "Latin" bandleader of the period, this chapter offers a look at how Bauzá's, Rizo's, and other Cuban musicians' understandings of the intersections of race, nationalism, and popular culture created the possibility of multiple authenticities and disrupted "Cuban" and "Latin" as static or singular identity categories. In the process, I pay close attention to the role *Thick Description* of race and class in shaping the stories these musicians told about their migration, their participation in the entertainment industries, and their sense of racial and ethnic identity.

Chapters 2 and 3 center on the associational life of Cubans in New York City. El Club Cubano Inter-Americano and the Ateneo Cubano de Nueva York were two of the more active and well-organized Cuban social clubs in New York City during the 1940s and 1950s. Whereas most Cuban social clubs such as the Ateneo Cubano denied membership to Cubans of color, El Club Cubano opened its doors and extended memberships to Cubans of color and to Puerto Ricans, Dominicans, Jamaicans, Haitians, and African Americans. Chapter 2 focuses on several of the popular Cuban musicians and performers affiliated with and hired to perform at events sponsored by these social clubs, especially Generoso Montesino, Alberto Socarrás, Marcelino Guerra, and Arsenio Rodríguez. Chapter 3 looks more closely at the events themselves, particularly those marked as Cuban patriotic celebrations such as José Martí's birthday and Cuban Independence Day and inter-American festivities such as Día de la Raza and Pan-American Day. In both chapters, examination of club records and announcements and advertisements published in the Spanish-language press reveals moments of cross-racial and cross-ethnic collaboration and tension, the irony of black exclusion in the context of Afro-Cuban celebration, and instances of musicians navigating their professional careers in cultural and commercial contexts. These two chapters detail how black and white Cubans managed their multiple identities as Cubans of the diaspora united in a *colonia cubana* and as Cubans who were also part of the *colonia hispana* and *colonia latina*.

Chapter 4 examines the musical popularity contests and fund-raising musical showcases sponsored by *La Prensa*, New York City's largest and longest-running Spanish-language daily newspaper, from 1941 to 1959. Black and white Cuban singers, musicians, and dancers figured prominently in the contests and festivals, and this chapter analyzes that presence as a critical component of Hispano/a and Latino/a identity and community during this period. In particular, I argue that these contests and festivals serve as early examples of the role Cuban musicians and Cuban ethnic identity played in the development and broadcasting of Hispano/a and Latino/a identity that was both local and hemispheric.

Chapter 5 considers how the lived realities of Cuban migrants and musicians intersected with symbolic, mass-mediated representations of Cubanness and Latinness. Millions of viewers across the United States gathered around their television sets in the 1950s to watch Ricky Ricardo, their favorite Cuban bandleader, on *I Love Lucy*. This chapter juxtaposes the lived experiences of Cuban musicians and Latino/a audiences at New York City nightclubs and dance halls with the fictionalized narratives Desi Arnaz presented on the popular CBS sitcom. In doing so, I provide a comparison of the professional experiences of well-known black and white Cuban performers such as Machito, Miguelito Valdés, and Perucho Irigoyen with those of Desi Arnaz and the semi-autobiographical character he played on television, Ricky Ricardo.

Chapter 6 moves the narrative to Miami. The city's newly established nightclubs and hotels drew tourists from across the United States and Latin America, including thousands of Cuban visitors, but not everyone saw Miami as a temporary destination or a vacationer's tropical paradise. This chapter discusses the role of Cubans and Cuban popular culture in the city long before it became a refuge for the hundreds of thousands of Cuban exiles who fled the island after 1959. Cubans in Miami in the 1940s and 1950s formed social clubs such as the Círculo Cubano and Juventud Cubana and attended dances, musical performances, and other social events at hotels and nightclubs such as the Tropicana and Barra Guys and Dolls. What follows is the story of the early emergence of Cuban Miami in the context of the ideology and racialized practices of Pan-Americanism, in relation to the large number of Puerto Ricans in the city, and in dialogue with political happenings on the island.

Finally, the book concludes with a brief account of what became of the musicians, social clubs, ethnic institutions, and other opportunities for cultural expression of the 1940s and 1950s in the 1960s and beyond. The two examples that open this introduction demonstrate, as this entire book intends to show, that the cultural productions and racialized expectations of the 1940s and 1950s shaped future claims of belonging and modes of (self-)identification as (Afro-)Cuban and (Afro-)Latino/a. It also considers how post-1965 Latin American and Caribbean migration and the Cold War–era politics of Cuban exiles in the United States since 1959 have conditioned popular memory and historiography toward an all-too-easy dismissal of the similarities and links between Cuban migration during the twentieth century and that of Puerto Ricans, Mexicans, and other Latino/a groups. This book argues against a certain kind of Cuban and Cuban American exceptionalism, symbolized as whiteness, upward mobility, and political conservatism. But it puts forth an exceptionalism of another sort in making the case that Cuban musicians and migrants, both black and white, shaped the development of a collective cultural consciousness of Latinidad, albeit a Latinidad that was contested and, though it usually celebrated African influences, was not always tolerant or inclusive of people of color.

Thesis!

- How the experiences + Actions of White + Black Cuban Musicians shaped a unique cultural identity in the United States

- Thick Description?!

1

RACE AND THE ROOTS/ROUTES TRACED

BY LATIN MUSICIANS

At first glance, Mario Bauzá and Marco Rizo had many things in common. Both musicians came from wealthy, well-connected families, both had received musical training in some of the best conservatories in Cuba, and both had left their homeland for New York City, determined to make it as professional musicians. Once in the city of their hopes and dreams, both musicians soon began making significant contributions to what was considered Latin music during the 1940s and 1950s: Bauzá as a trumpet player and arranger for Machito y sus Afro-Cubans and Rizo as pianist and arranger for the Desi Arnaz Orchestra and the *I Love Lucy* television program. They also shared a more dubious distinction. Throughout their professional careers, both Bauzá and Rizo achieved less celebrity than their more popular and widely recognized musical collaborators. Bauzá remained largely in the shadows of his more charismatic brother-in-law Machito, and Rizo never saw anywhere near the same level of stardom as his more business-savvy childhood friend Desi Arnaz.

A closer look at the personal experiences and professional careers of these two Cuban musicians suggests that, for the most part, the similarities end here. Soon after their arrival in New York City, their racial experiences and alliances, musical preferences, and personal friendships took them in quite different directions. Bauzá was an Afro-Cuban from Havana. He left Cuba in 1930, moving to Harlem, where he used his formal training and ear for music to emerge as a top trumpet player in African American jazz circles, playing alongside the likes of Cab Calloway, Dizzy Gillespie, and Chick Webb. Later, he and Machito formed one of the most popular Afro-Cuban/Latin jazz bands of the 1940s and 1950s, Machito y

Micro-Narrative of Rizo + Bauza to Compare Black + white Cuban experiences

sus Afro-Cubans. Rizo was a white Cuban from Santiago. He came to New York City in 1940 and moved into his aunt's midtown Manhattan apartment while he attended the Juilliard School. After a brief stint in the U.S. Army during World War II, Rizo agreed to work as the pianist and principal arranger for Desi Arnaz's new band. Within a few years, Rizo moved to Hollywood where he continued in this position during the six-season run of *I Love Lucy*, one of television's most popular situation comedies.

Bauzá and Rizo belonged to a remarkably large and diverse cohort of black and white Cuban musicians who lived, worked, and performed in New York City in the 1940s and 1950s. These musicians' personal and professional lives offer a better understanding of key moments of racial negotiation, ethnic identity formation, and musical development that took place within the city's *colonia cubana* and *colonia hispana*. Self-narration is one of the key texts this book analyzes: the stories told by well-known and not-so-well-known black and white Cuban musicians and entertainers reveal that skin color produced significant differences in perspectives and experiences. In particular, this chapter explores these differences as expressed by these musicians and entertainers through their experiences in Cuba, their stories of migration, their insertion into the music scene in New York City (and Hollywood), and the production of racialized discourses and practices. Of course, skin color alone did not dictate the trajectory of the professional careers of the many Cuban performers who migrated to New York City. Social networks, intra- and interracial and ethnic tensions and alliances, and the politics of the mass culture industries also played key roles in shaping competing representations of Cubanness and Latinness in the 1940s and 1950s.[1]

Discussions about musical innovation, authenticity, and commercialism often took place among the many musicians who left Cuba for New York City at midcentury, and these debates disrupted "Cuban," "Afro-Cuban," and "Latin" as static or singular musical genres and identity categories. Racial ideas and practices and cultural traditions and expectations informed these conversations and, quite significantly, prompted individual and collective desires for social mobility and racial equality, especially among Cuban musicians of color. As we will see, the long-standing cultural hierarchy dividing classical music and highbrow tastes from popular music and lowbrow tastes not only reflected the social and racial divides of Cuban society before 1960 but also played a direct role in pushing musicians and entertainers, both black and white, to migrate to the United States in search of performance opportunities, artistic growth, and a secure livelihood. Historian Raúl A. Fernández argues that "as musicians

Black + white had Very Different Experiences

"High brow vs. Low Brow" Tastes Reflected Racially!

Source

traveled and sometimes settled outside of Cuba, they established 'bases' of Cuban music outside the island, even 'colonized' extensive territories." New York City became one of these bases of Cuban music, and it was in downtown hotels and ballrooms before mostly white audiences and in up-town nightclubs and neighborhood joints before mostly Afro-Cuban, Puerto Rican, African American, and Jewish audiences that the lines be-tween "popular" and "serious" music became less and less well defined as creative processes of innovation, borrowing, and co-optation produced musical styles and performers dubbed "Cuban," "Afro-Cuban," and "Latin."[2]

XAVIER CUGAT AND THE LATIN MUSIC MODEL

Racial ideologies and the boundaries of social class affected the cultural production and profitability of both black and white Cuban musicians throughout the first half of the twentieth century. As rumba rhythms and colorful conga lines gained international fandom, opportunities to perform and profit increased for musicians. This was the era dominated by Xavier Cugat, and Latin musicians, especially those who wanted to get paid, played Latin music, not jazz, and certainly not classical music. Cugat, a formally trained violinist born in Barcelona, Spain, in 1900 but raised in Havana until he left for the United States in the late 1920s, failed to make a name for himself on the concert stage with the Los Angeles Philharmonic. He found work instead as a cartoonist for newspapers and magazines in San Francisco and Los Angeles but eventually returned to music in 1928 at the height of the jazz era. "No jazzman, Cugat realized that he could not com-pete with Afro-Saxons on their own ground. So," a report in *Time* explained, "he bravely cultivated a little Afro-Latin plot of his own." Cugat abandoned his initial preference for the violin and classical music for what he saw as the more financially lucrative opportunity to perform Afro-Cuban popu-lar music. By 1942, the bandleader was earning an estimated $500,000 a year performing Afro-Cuban music and other Latin rhythms such as tango for mostly white, middle- and upper-class North American audiences. Four years later, his annual income from record sales and radio, film, and night-club performances had nearly doubled to a million dollars.[3]

Cugat frequently reflected on what he considered to be a demotion from classical to popular forms of music. He emphasized his role as a creative and innovative marketer and admitted to focusing on performance and excitement rather than technique and precision: "I knew that the Ameri-can people was polite to an artist but crazy for a personality, so I decided to become a personality," he told a reporter for *Time* in 1946, concluding,

"I'd rather play Chiquita Banana tonight and have my swimming pool than play Bach and starve." That the Chiquita Banana act, which featured deliberate mispronunciations and two sidemen dressed in banana costumes, might seem foolish mattered little to Cugat because the novelty made him money. A reviewer for *Billboard* characterized Cugat's role in popularizing Latin music similarly: "Take three parts showmanship, add two parts imaginative arrangements and one part good (but still second stature) instrumentalists, shake well to a rumba beat."[4] His many interviews in the popular press indicate that he resolved whatever ambivalence he may have felt about his Latin performance, especially given his self-concept as a classical virtuoso, by counting the dollars in his bank account. In the process, he created a performance of Latin that shaped ethnic experience and musical opportunity for others.

At the Waldorf Astoria in New York City, Cugat's group first appeared as the Latin relief band, but by 1942, his eleventh season at the luxury hotel, his was "the main band, and the Latin name band of the nation." Reports in newspapers and magazines noted that Cugat was the top performer of Latin music in the United States, focusing on the appeal and spectacle of his "tropicalized" performances. Cugat's success rested "not so much in the importing as in the processing of his hip-cajoling products," and that "processing" included dressing his band in "lustrous Cuban silks and colored lights" and producing numbers with "just enough subtle tropical pounding and gourd rattling to give it pith, not enough to ruffle the polite suavity of an expensive hot spot." Nicknamed the "The King of Rhumba," Cugat presented audiences with the "fast and furious" rhythms of rumba, mambo, and tango as the front man for a band he "dressed in colorful garb of the South Americas." A review of the Xavier Cugat Orchestra in *Billboard* summarized the band's widespread appeal: "And the band dishes out a please-everybody variety of show tunes, standards, pops, waltzes, tangos, rumbas and sambas. Cugat, too, makes sure his Latin rhythms are easy-for-dancing, without permitting them to lose that air of authenticity."[5]

During World War II, Cugat's recordings such as "Mexico" and "Viva Roosevelt!" carried messages laden with "good neighborly incentives," and this patriotic positioning also played a role in popularizing his music among North American audiences familiar with the rhetoric and practices of hemispheric solidarity. Using the conga line as a metaphor, the English-language lyrics of Cugat's "Viva Roosevelt!" urged listeners and, by extension, the twenty-one nations of the Americas to come together in support of President Franklin D. Roosevelt and the war effort: "Viva Roosevelt! Viva Roosevelt! / Oh what a señor! / Ladies and Gents, get in the conga

Must accentuate stereotypes and sensationalize to succeed in Latin Music

Cugat Makes music For $ & white People

line of defense / Come on and follow this leader, give him a vote of confidence." The festive conga line transformed into a "line of liberty" as the dance itself shifted from a "conga" to a "Panamericonga." Part of what made "Viva Roosevelt!" and other songs that came out of Tin Pan Alley during the war years popular was the overt message of Pan-American solidarity. In this particular example, Cugat's performance of (Afro-)Cubanness, by way of the conga line, becomes representative of a certain kind of Latinness, one that is intentionally inter-American, patriotic, and optimistic.[6]

RACE, *SABOR*, AND THE LATIN MUSIC MODEL

For Latin rhythms to triumph on Broadway, in Hollywood, and elsewhere in the United States, especially in the early 1940s among white audiences, the personality had to be nonblack. Sociologist Vernon Boggs explains the process by which Cugat and other light-skinned performers like him were racialized as nonblack: "Cugat wasn't seen as black. Both Carmen Miranda and Desi Arnaz, well-known Hispanic musical performers of the time, were known to be Hispanic, but their antics on stage made the public tolerate their ethnic affiliation." Afro-Cuban musicians such as Arsenio Rodríguez and Alberto Socarrás, however, "did not please the racial sensitivities of the time." Fernández makes a similar argument: "During the 1930s and 1940s, some musicians faced not only the travails of the poor but the obstacles set down by a society where the local racial codes separated people not so much into blood-based 'white' and 'nonwhite' categories as into perceived 'nonblack' and 'black' skin pigmentation."[7]

Though historian Adrian Burgos Jr. focuses on Latino baseball players in the United States throughout the twentieth century, he offers an important model for understanding how migrants from the Spanish-speaking Americas experienced race in the United States. Like Latino baseball players, Cuban musicians "did not enter the U.S. playing field as simply black or white. Rather, most occupied a position between the poles of white (inclusion) and black (exclusion)." Lighter skin, European physical features, class status, and education in U.S. schools helped well-known Cuban musicians such as Cugat and Arnaz and, as we will see, lesser-known performers such as Rizo, José Curbelo, Arturo "Chico" O'Farrill, and Horacio Riambau gain entry into nightclubs, hotels, and ballrooms that initially excluded their darker-skinned compatriots. These practices were not entirely unknown to these Cuban musicians, Burgos argues, because "by Cuban tradition, social class and wealth combined to effectively lighten how others perceived an individual's skin color and racial status." Inclusion, however, did not mean that musicians such as Cugat and Rizo were accepted as fellow whites, nor did it guarantee equality.[8]

This process of racialization is perhaps made more complicated when seen in a broader Cuban context and from the perspective of these Cuban performers. Throughout the early part of the twentieth century, Afro-Cuban popular culture, in the form of *comparsas* (carnival street bands), *sones*, and rumbas, gradually achieved acceptance among whites in Cuba and became central symbols of Cuban national identity. Ethnomusicologist Robin Moore has argued that whites and middle-class blacks in Cuba initially tried to limit and repress black popular expression. The increasing popularity of Afro-Cuban popular music abroad and among North American tourists in the hotels and nightclubs of Havana, however, allowed these forms to move from the cultural margins to become the central symbols of authentic Cuban nationalism. This "nationalized blackness" suggests that the point is not simply that black and white musicians received different treatment.[9] Rather, they conceived of themselves as playing black music and received different treatment while doing it. Among Anglo audiences in the United States, it was Cugat's nonwhiteness that lent him authenticity as he performed Afro-Cubanness. At the same time, it was his nonblackness that allowed his performance of Afro-Cubanness to be seen as Latinness. What was once considered vulgar, sinful, and degrading by polite, white society in Cuba and the United States, now took top billing at "ultra-swank places" such as the Waldorf Astoria, thanks to Cugat and novelties such as the Chiquita Banana act, rumba sleeves, and the exaggerated conga drum.

African American writers and artists noticed the disparity between the welcome white audiences gave to the performance of black music and the small number of black musicians given the opportunity to perform on stage. Cugat, whose band members came from Puerto Rico, Cuba, and the Philippines, told a reporter for the *Chicago Defender* that "under the American standards my band would be considered a mixed ork [slang for orchestra] for the members therein vary in complexions" and admitted that "a large percentage of my materials are Negro composed and arranged." He promised that he would "include at least one colored performer in his appearance in theatres throughout the country" in the hope of convincing Broadway producers to present "mixed" productions. He even stated that "given an opportunity to present themselves before the entertainment public[,] Negro artists, in many instances, excel white artists." One writer for the *Baltimore Afro-American* complained, however, that Cugat and other nonblack musicians made a "fabulous salary" because of this "cold-blooded exploitation," while "the black man can't follow his stuff and collect the gravy."[10] Here was an early mention of the contrast perceived between innovation and popularization as a matter of racial difference.

As a result of Cugat's effective marketing, his popularity was related in many ways to his Cubanness. Described by both Spanish- and English-language newspapers in New York City as Cuban, American, Catalán, and Catalán-Cuban, the Spanish-born Cugat did little to clarify his national origin. Instead, he often spoke of his passion for Cuba, noting that he "loved the land of sugar, tobacco, rum, and above all else, land of rumba," for it was there that he had learned "that musical style, that energizing and elegant rhythm that has given him so many triumphs." On his first visit to New York City in 1942, Cuban president Fulgencio Batista "made three specific requests: To visit the Empire State Building, Rockefeller Plaza and hear Cugat's music." The Cuban government appreciated Cugat's efforts so much that in 1942 it awarded the "salesman" and "ambassador of culture" the title of Commander in the Order of Honor and Merit of the Cuban Red Cross.[11]

Writers for *La Prensa* also took notice and credited "the popular musical director" for what they described as "the big boom of tropical rhythms in the United States." Within the *colonia hispana*, reports suggest that Cugat enjoyed an admiring public throughout the 1940s and 1950s. In 1957, when he was past the prime of his professional career, Cugat performed at the Domingo de Pascuas (Easter Sunday) festival at the Manhattan Center not only "at the request of the hispanic public of New York" but as an "idol of our hispanic publics." The event also featured performances from Tito Rodríguez and Conjunto Cibao. As one report explained, "Few times in the history of nuestra colonia has a group of true interpreters of nuestra música hispana been brought together." As anticipation for the event increased in the pages of *La Prensa* and, presumably, the *colonia hispana* as well, readers and potential attendees learned that Cugat would perform a "vast repertoire of tropical music heard few times in this city" because of the "warm reception that the hispanic public has been giving him." One year later, a reporter declared that "Cugat is an 'institution' in the popular music camp in the United States" and reminded readers that the "Catalán" had "once abandoned Cuba to conquer the world with Cuban music."[12]

In a column written for the Spanish-language newspaper *Pueblos Hispanos* as a response to a young man who was upset that he had been called a "spic" and a "greaser," Puerto Rican writer and community activist Jesús Colón noted the various ways that Latin bandleaders Xavier Cugat, Enric Madriguera, Juanito Sanabria, Alberto Iznaga, and Noro Morales, among others, had contributed to the dissemination of Latin American culture in the United States. Colón reasoned that these Hispanic bands "have taken hispanic popular music from the most refined cabaret to the little house in Long Way," and for that the young man should be proud.[13] What stands out in addition to Colón's use of popular cultural expression as a marker of progress and defense of racial prejudice, a move that stands as evidence of the significance of cultural citizenship as a sort of substitute for political citizenship, is that this dark-skinned, working-class migrant gave as examples mostly Spanish and light-skinned Cuban and Puerto Rican musicians. At one level, his choices suggest that only certain types of "Latin" bandleaders could secure the type of social mobility he described. On another, Colón seems to be deploying a notion of a unified Latino/a race that downplays the significant differences of experience based on color within Latino/a communities and in the United States at large.[14] Quite significantly, both perspectives are suggestive of the critical role that musicians who could follow Cugat's Latin music model, a mode of performance that was characterized as much by its musical stylings as its nonblackness, would play in shaping, in relational and oppositional terms, Latino/a identity and culture.

Many black and white Cuban musicians acknowledged that without Cugat "the American people would have been deaf to Latin music."[15] Complaints about Cugat's musical abilities did not stop musicians such as Bauzá, Machito, and Miguelito Valdés from performing alongside him early in their professional careers. In fact, Bauzá claimed that he had helped promote Cugat within the *colonia hispana*, explaining, "I'm the guy that brought Cugat to play for the Latins up there in the Hunts Point Palace." He was likely referring to the Latin American Fiesta, a dance held in 1943 at the Hunts Point Palace, located at 153rd Street and Southern Boulevard in the Bronx, that featured both Cugat and Machito y sus Afro-Cubans. In anticipation of the event, one reporter announced that "without a doubt this is one of the most attractive festivals presented in New York, because it features in it two of the hispanic orchestras considered the most popular and artists with the most fame in our colonia."[16]

Although they respected his role in popularizing Latin music, especially among North American audiences, many Cuban musicians and Latino/a fans saw Cugat's performance as inauthentic. Bauzá charged that Cugat didn't play *música típica* (traditional or "authentic" music) and that his music was not "de sabor cubana," but reasoned that what he did play he played well. The concept of *sabor* (literally flavor or taste) has been discussed at length by scholars and musicologists interested in questions of

Cugat "sells out," not playing authentic Cuban music

national identity and Cuban popular music, particularly salsa. Fernández succinctly argues that it is "the sine qua non of Cuban musicianship: a musician who does not play with sabor cannot play Cuban music well."[17] A poll conducted by *Revista Teatral* in 1947 revealed that Latino/a audiences believed that non-Cuban musicians—Spaniards such as Cugat and Enric Madriguera—lacked *sabor*: these musicians "miss[ed] the real feel of this music . . . that only Cuban musicians are able to get." Afro-Cuban flute player Alberto Socarrás applauded Cugat's business skills but complained, probably unfairly given his formal musical training, that "he could not read music and much less conduct." But his criticisms of Cugat went beyond his musicianship. In an interview with music historian and journalist Max Salazar, Socarrás supported the claims made by *Downbeat Magazine* that Cugat's popularity in the United States outraged Cubans on the island who believed that he passed off his music as authentic. Yet when Cugat returned from Havana, where he performed with his orchestra in 1951, he told a reporter for *La Prensa* only of the warm reception that greeted him throughout his visit: "In truth, I was more than well-received. The Cuban people are a serious thing. I've returned overjoyed."[18] This contradictory evidence suggests not simply the possibility of Cugat's misguided self-concept or Socarrás's personal disdain of the bandleader, but rather a general ambivalence toward Cugat generated by his marketing savvy, on the one hand, and his lack of *sabor*, on the other. It is not surprising that those who attended his performances on the island, most likely middle- and upper-class white Cubans (and North American tourists), would have greeted Cugat with enthusiasm and excitement, while others, specifically those Cubans excluded from his performances at nightclubs and hotels because of race and class, would be less celebratory of his musical talents and style.

By the late 1940s and early 1950s, perhaps as a result of the space Cugat had opened for other musicians, musicians who were perceived to have more *sabor*, critics and reviewers began to portray Cugat's formula as antiquated. One reviewer wrote that Cugat had "long since fallen out of favor with the real rhumba bugs. . . . Compared to more authentic efforts, there's not much beat. . . . In fact, it's more like dinner music." Another reviewer noted that "musically, the band is tailored for Yankee tastes. But, of course, Cugat is playing for a well-defined audience and his version of Latin-American music has a sound, commercial basis," especially among those "who aren't finicky about authenticity."[19] This shift in preferences signaled not only the emergence of new artists but also demographic changes within the *colonia hispana* as more and more migrants from Cuba and Puerto

Rico arrived each day. These new migrants became an audience for a different style of Latin music pioneered by Bauzá and Machito y sus Afro-Cubans. Not an "overnight" development, as some have argued, the merging of Afro-Cuban music and jazz in the mid- to late 1940s was best described by Puerto Rican saxophonist Ray Santos as "two revolutions going on at the same time, one in the Afro-Cuban music and one going on in jazz, and they both like met head on and absorbed each other."[20] Cuban trumpet player Arturo "Chico" O'Farrill described the 1940s as the era of Latin musicians such as Cugat and Enric Madriguera. But eventually, he explained, "people became hipper because they heard Machito, they heard some of the other bands that were not so commercially oriented and there was a change of mind in that sense."[21] In other words, this shift in preferences produced a complex set of discourses of authenticity that also suggested notions of progress and modernity.

MARCO RIZO AND THE CUBAN CONTEXT

Another white Cuban musician followed a professional trajectory quite similar to that of Cugat. Born in Santiago de Cuba, Marco Rizo Ayala started his musical training at an early age, thanks, in part, to his father's post as conductor of the city's symphony orchestra. Rizo recalled "a good, nice living" in Santiago and positioned his family as middle class, noting that "we weren't rich people, of course, not either very poor."[22] Cross-racial interactions, according to Rizo, were very common in Santiago despite what he described as the "very unjust" prejudices of "the high people," suggesting a nuanced understanding that differences in social class shaped notions and practices of racial inclusion and exclusion. When pressed for more details on the interactions of Cubans across class and racial lines, however, he clarified that the only time he saw white Cubans "mix with the blacks and the mulattoes and Chinese and so on, that was in carnival time." Only during carnival time in Santiago, he explained, did "they all get together and at the time they forget about the racial barrier, you know, that 'you are white, I am black,' all that stuff." Rizo attributed racial mixture during carnival to the island's proximity to Haiti, in terms of both musical influences and the presence of a large black population.[23]

This understanding of the relationship between race and class reflects the colonial legacies of the late nineteenth- and early twentieth-century struggles for Cuban independence and racial equality. During the War of Independence from Spain, Cuban revolutionary leader José Martí put forth a nationalist ideology "that proclaimed all Cubans to be equal." As historian

Alejandro de la Fuente summarizes, "The existence of 'races' was seen as a social reality, but within an encompassing notion of Cubanness that was supposed to subsume, and eventually erase, racial identities." Though universal male suffrage guaranteed by the Constitutional Convention of 1901 stood as evidence of Cuba's commitment to racial equality, participation in electoral politics did not mean representation for Cubans of color in government, despite the efforts of the Afro-Cuban organization the Partido Independiente de Color. Tensions came to a head during the much-debated "race war" of 1912. What began as a political protest against the Morúa law, which banned political parties that were organized along racial lines, escalated into Afro-Cubans in Oriente burning and plundering foreign-owned cane fields, sugar mills, stores, and other properties. However, the events of 1912 had numerous other causes and had major implications for the role race would play in Cuban society. Historian Louis A. Pérez argues that the events of 1912 should be understood as an uprising by peasants, farmers, and rural workers (not just Afro-Cubans) who were frustrated by the loss of land to foreign companies. He contends that Cuban elites constructed the events as a race war because it divided the peasantry along racial lines, a strategy that unified whites and facilitated the repression of black Cubans. Historian Aline Helg, however, insists that the uprising came about because "race still dominated many aspects of the political and socioeconomic relations in Cuba" after independence. Cuban elites constructed stereotypes that portrayed Afro-Cubans as a threat to whites and the Cuban nation, and this ideology of white supremacy "justified the collective and individual repression of Afro-Cubans by whites." Indeed, the uprising resulted in the indiscriminate killing of black Cubans by the Cuban Army in the eastern part of the island.[24]

Deemed un-Cuban, opportunities for racially based mobilization became scarce. Since the 1880s, however, key Afro-Cuban thinkers had looked to education as a means of climbing the social ladder. Afro-Cubans had access to a desegregated public school system and saw formal schooling "as a prerequisite to social advancement." According to De la Fuente, "The result was the formation of a sizeable group of black and mulatto professionals who, given the precariousness of their recently acquired status, sought to distance themselves, socially and culturally, from the masses of black manual workers." Afro-Cuban percussionist Armando Peraza, who together with Mongo Santamaría formed the duo Los Diamantes Negros, confirmed the efforts that some members of the Afro-Cuban middle class made to distance themselves from Afro-Cubans of the lower class: "You find a black person with good intellectual capacity and good economic

Class Struggle Supersedes Race in Cuba.

capacity, he no wanna socialize with a poor black man from the ghetto."
Afro-Cuban *conguero* (conga player) Luis Miranda, who grew up in the
barrios of Havana, believed that among the lower classes, racial prejudice
mattered little: "I mean the poor people don't have that much prejudice—
because you have nothing, the other guy has nothing either, that's it." What
these contradictory statements confirm is the centrality of race and class
to ideas about Cuban nationhood and identity, and in the 1920s and 1930s
the ideology of *afrocubanismo*, which "proudly proclaimed miscegenation
to be the very essence of the nation—a mulatto 'Cuban race,'" gained mo-
mentum. As De la Fuente explains, "Cuba was definitely not white—but
was only one step short of claiming that there was no racial problem in
the island, merely an economic one. Racial inequality was thus increasingly perceived [by Afro-Cuban intellectuals] as a by-product of class
inequities."[25]

Returning now to the contrasting remarks Rizo made about cross-racial
interactions and prejudice, the point is made clearer: race was a social reality. The perspectives offered by Rizo, Peraza, and Miranda illustrate that
race had distinct modes of operation in different cities (Havana and Santiago), especially at different social strata. Significant discourses of racial
equality and harmony and black civilization operated at the national level
and were reproduced locally, including in the stories told by black and white
Cuban musicians. These discourses were not consistent, reflecting a gap
between expressions of racial unity and practices of racial exclusion and
separation that were sometimes inconsistent in maintaining boundaries
between black and white Cubans.

MIGRATION AND A PROFESSIONAL CAREER
IN POPULAR MUSIC

After studying at the Conservatory of Santiago, Rizo soon left for Havana
"looking for bigger horizons in music." That musical quest took him to the
Havana Philharmonic Orchestra, where he occupied the post of official pianist from 1937 to 1940. His musical education in Cuba included private
lessons with three pioneers in Cuban music education and composition,
Tomás Planas, César Pérez Sentenat, and Pedro Sanjuan, and performances
alongside Ernesto Lecuona, probably the most famous composer of the
time and a key white participant in the Afro-Cubanist movement. While
in Havana, Rizo also met and performed for jazz musicians and classical
artists from the United States, and it was during these cultural encounters that his desire to leave Cuba reached its peak. His motivation to

migrate to the United States developed as a dual mission of cultural and personal significance: "To expose what [I] had to offer this country [and] to improve also my musicianship . . . I going to be long enough here in Havana to do what I have to do to make the jump to New York."[26] His account reveals that he lived in a world in which a generalized assumption existed that going to New York City was a key step in becoming a top musician. Here, Rizo makes a rhetorical leap as well, suggesting that his musical style, defined in national terms, would contribute to U.S. culture and society.

Rizo had first experimented with jazz as teenager. He formed his first jazz band in Santiago, explaining that "my father told me, said 'You would like to be a pianist of a jazz band, orchestra, so we can play dances, you know, parties and things like that?'" To that question, the answer was a resounding "yes." With his father, uncles, and other family and friends recruited as band members and his aunt in New York City sending him sheet music and the latest records, Rizo began making arrangements for the Jazz Band Rizo-Ayala. The band's musical repertoire included *son*, *danzones* (instrumental music typically danced to by couples that emerged in Matanzas during the late nineteenth century), polkas, fox trots, and ballads for a dancing public: Cuban and American music, according to the pianist.[27]

Rizo was not the only musician with classical training whose family supported and joined his ventures into popular music. José Curbelo, born in Havana in 1917 to an American-born father and Cuban mother, came from what one reporter described as a "family of musicians that dates back to various generations." His "musical heritage" could be traced back to his grandfather, who had fought in the Cuban War of Independence and later performed with the Havana Philharmonic Orchestra. His father, José Curbelo Sr., was a "fine violinist" who also played with the Havana Philharmonic Orchestra and hoped that his son would follow in the family's musical footsteps. Early on, Curbelo received training in piano and composition from Pedro Menéndez, and he eventually graduated from the Havana Municipal Conservatory. Curbelo took a break from music when he enrolled at the Universidad de La Habana to study medicine. It wasn't until he and some friends formed a dance band that he decided to abandon a career as a doctor and pursue a career in popular, not classical, music. One reporter surmised that "what the medical profession lost is 'music's' gain." After forming the Orquesta Riverside in Havana, Curbelo left Cuba in 1939 "to try his luck in the United States." Other family members, including Nilo, Fausto, and Heriberto Curbelo, had already left for New York City, where the latter two had established themselves as bandleaders "very well-known on the continent." Soon, his father joined his son's band as the bass player;

Micro Narrative / Micro - history

one reporter concluded that "Dad figured that he might as well be handy and add valuable experience and background to the talents of his son." His decision makes sense, given that the senior Curbelo had performed "the most typical Cuban music" with his own band at *academias de bailes* (working-class dance halls) and famous nightclubs in Havana such as the Sans Souci. Curbelo's love of popular music, which developed at an early age, drew on the musical influences of jazz: "But I was always a fan, and my favorite music always has been jazz. Even that I love my own music, Cuban music, my native music."[28]

That Rizo and Curbelo's families not only supported but participated in their experimentations with popular music contrasts with the response Arturo "Chico" O'Farrill got from his family when he first told them he wanted to pursue a musical career. O'Farrill's father worked as a lawyer for the Cuban government, and his family sent him to study at Riverside Military Academy in Gainesville, Georgia, expecting that after that he would train for a professional career in architecture or law. He returned to Havana in 1940 and enrolled in the Universidad de La Habana to study law, but after some "fooling around" at a jazz club in the city, he decided that his real passion was for music. His family "flipped," he recalled: "In those days in Cuba to be a musician in popular music was one of the lowest forms of employment that you can have, was almost similar to servants. . . . So they were scandalized that I was gonna become a musician." With race and class defining who should study and perform particular genres of music, his family's objection referred specifically to his preference for Afro-Cuban popular music and jazz instead of classical music. O'Farrill's grandmother offered him the following condition: "If you're gonna become a musician, remember, be a good musician, be like Mozart." He didn't quite listen to her advice. Though he did receive formal training in classical music, he continued to perform with local bands at various social events, hoping that the "society people" in the audience wouldn't notice him. When he arrived in New York City in 1948, he spent the $300 he had saved for the journey hanging out at nightclubs listening to Dizzy Gillespie and Machito y sus Afro-Cubans.[29] It seems that he saw becoming a musician as an attraction to the Afro-Cuban.

Blacks and mulattos in Cuba generally regarded being a musician as a relatively high-status occupation. O'Farrill's grandmother's aversion to his choice of a career in black popular music likely suggests that there was a racial component to this rejection expressed as class. But there might have been more to it than this. A career in music was unpredictable, and even the families of black Cubans expressed a degree of skepticism about that choice. Bauzá's white godparents had initial misgivings about his decision to pursue a career in popular music, and it is well known that the father of Afro-Cuban singer Celia Cruz rejected her secret foray into performing on the radio in Havana.[30] Machito's father hoped that his son would eventually lose interest in music, going so far as to buy him a restaurant "to take music out of my head." At his father's insistence, he agreed to work in the family business in exchange for a new radio set, which he used to catch live broadcasts from hotels in Havana and stations along the East Coast of the United States. He hoped to one day meet Duke Ellington, Fletcher Henderson, and the other jazz musicians he listened to on the radio. Then, in 1937, he and Bauzá exchanged letters and agreed that Machito would join him in New York City so the two could put together a new band, one that would be more successful than the bands they had formed in Cuba. Machito offered another explanation for his family's skepticism: "I wasn't imported here. I came here with my money and wasn't announced to anybody. So it is very hard to have the respect of the people you are talking with, that you have been a professional over there."[31] Machito chose to make it on his own when he left for New York City without a contract with a U.S. record company in his pocket. It was not until he returned to Havana as an established musician with his bandmates that he was able to prove his success and legitimize his career choice. In other words, the contrast Machito made between being an "imported" celebrity and a self-made one suggests that the discourses these musicians produced are not only about race but also about the entertainment industries in Cuba and the United States.

RIZO'S ARRIVAL

Though Rizo's professional ambitions centered on establishing himself as a classical musician, he explained that "while I was in Havana also I start playing jazz, because of the proximity of Miami and the radio station." After three years in Havana, in 1940 he decided to leave for the United States to study classical piano. Once in New York City, he enrolled in the Juilliard School under the tutelage of Josef and Rosina Lhevinne, and on 27 September 1940, the "Cuban pianist-composer" made his public debut at Town Hall in midtown Manhattan playing classical pieces and "Cuban music by composers such as [Ignacio Cervantes] and Lecuona, Amadeo Roldán, all those wonderful composers from Cuba." Rizo's professional ambitions were soon put on hold by the onset of World War II and his decision to enlist in the U.S. Army, a decision he framed in both legalistic and nationalist terms: "I could have refused because I wasn't a citizen at the time. But since my aim was to stay here, I was already a resident, you know, legally here in this country, so I went to the Army." He completed his basic training at Fort Bragg in North Carolina and transferred to the Second Army headquarters in Memphis, Tennessee, to perform with and arrange for the jazz band at the base. Rizo played the glockenspiel and cymbals in the marching band but returned to the piano when the jazz band traveled to perform at benefits, hospitals, and other sites across the United States and overseas in Europe with the USO. After his honorable discharge from the army on 18 October 1945, Rizo went back to New York City to pursue his professional career as a classical musician.[32]

Upon his return to civilian life, Rizo worked as a pianist for Voice of America, playing what he described as "music of the Americas," compositions by Argentine composer Alberto Ginastera, Brazilian composer Heitor Villa Lobos, and Mexican composers Silvestre Revueltas and Carlos Chávez. The radio program also featured him as a soloist performing classical pieces by Lecuona. Then, at three o'clock in the morning one night late in 1945, Rizo received a phone call from his longtime friend Desi Arnaz. Arnaz planned to start his own band, and he wanted Rizo to join him for an upcoming engagement at Ciro's in Hollywood. As one columnist for a Spanish-language newspaper put it, Rizo "accepted the call from Hollywood made by his countryman and schoolmate" and joined the Orquesta de Desi Arnaz as it "toured the United States with success." The columnist reasoned that in accepting the invitation, Rizo hoped to burst into the "artistic environment of the nation, occupying a place among the 'quotables' in popular art," as Arnaz had.[33]

Rizo missed the first engagement at Ciro's but met up with the band for a nearly four-month engagement at the Copacabana, located at 10 East 60th Street in New York City, assuming the roles of pianist, arranger, and musical director. The band moved on from the "aristocratic" nightclub for a coast-to-coast tour of one-nighters at some of the most popular nightclubs, theaters, and radio stations in cities across the United States, including Cleveland, Columbus, Chicago, Milwaukee, Omaha, and Los Angeles. One reviewer of the band's performance at the Avadon Ballroom in Los Angeles praised "the duo piano work of René Touzet and Marco Rizo," noting that "whether ivory pilots are flying solo on a Latin standard such as Malagueña or backing up the ork with a rocking beat, they are much in evidence thruout sessions." Another reviewer for a Spanish-language newspaper framed the band's performance and extensive touring schedule as a sort of cross-cultural encounter that had diplomatic significance, arguing that "this magnificent orchestra was introducing our genuine rhythms and melodies in all of the United States."[34] As we have seen, introducing new musical styles to the United States, in the discourse of Jesús Colón, Bauzá, and the white musicians themselves, is typically the role assigned to white performers. Not viewed as innovators, these white performers are credited for packaging Afro-Cuban music and performances in ways that accommodate and appeal to Anglo audiences.

Back in New York City in the late 1940s, the Arnaz band performed at the Paramount, Roxy, Capitol, and Strand Theaters. The "attraction" featured jugglers, acrobats, dancers, and Arnaz's popular rendition of "Babalú" (a song in the new Afro-Cuban style that represented Afro-Cuban spiritual practices but drew on stage traditions that included *son* and minstrel performance), which ended with a conga line parading throughout the nightclub.[35] In 1949, Rizo was settled in the city and living with his family. That year Arnaz called on his musical expertise again. This time, he asked Rizo to move to Hollywood permanently to work as his musical director on *I Love Lucy*. Rizo couldn't resist the opportunity, and once in California he enrolled at the University of California, Los Angeles, where he studied with Igor Stravinsky and Mario Tedesco-Castelnuovo, earning a master of arts degree in 1953. This formal musical training and association with "good quality musicians" on the show helped Rizo accept the fact that he never quite got the "promotion and the credit that [he] deserved" for his musical contributions to *I Love Lucy*, particularly his composition of the show's theme song. As a member of the American Society of Composers, Authors and Publishers (ASCAP), which he had joined in 1952, Rizo received his share of the royalties for the songs he composed as musical director of the show, but he never attained the celebrity status or public acclaim he felt he had earned.[36]

After the show's run ended, Rizo stayed on to work as a staff musician for CBS and emphasized that because of his technique and versatility as a musician, even though he was categorized as "Latin," he managed to secure work in the radio, television, and film industries: "So in that way I don't think I was discriminated in a way, you know, by being just Latin, you know what I mean? I did a lot of Latin assignments, yes, I did. But also they were very impressed by my sight-reading."[37] As a relatively wealthy, light-skinned Cuban, it is not entirely surprising that this remark stands as Rizo's only discussion of the possibility that he might have been discriminated against because he was "Latin." Rizo's light skin, class, and musical style afforded him opportunities for social mobility that were not avail-

Rizo succeeds b/c he is light skinned, Middle Class & Educated

able to the majority of Cuban musicians, particularly those of color or lower socioeconomic status.

Rizo's privileged experiences were not entirely unique but were rather characteristic of the generalized process by which white Cubans became Afro-Cuban performers in the United States. The experiences of rumba dancer and mambo instructor Horacio Riambau offer a case in point. Born to a German mother and French father in Havana on 26 December 1927, Riambau was raised by a woman he affectionately called *abuela* (grandmother), a former slave on his grandfather's sugar plantation. She spoke a mixture of Spanish and Carabalí, a language spoken by the Abakuá peoples from the Cross River region of Africa. Abakuá formed mutual aid and, later, male-only secret societies in nineteenth-century Cuba and are noted for their contributions to Cuban popular music. According to writer Josephine Powell, Riambau's *abuela* exposed him to African rituals, ceremonies, and dances that took place at the many *solares* (urban apartment buildings housing lower- and working-class residents, usually built around a shared patio) scattered throughout Havana. This relationship also points to the presence and labor of black Cuban women as real and surrogate mothers in white Cuban families.[38]

In New York City, Riambau and his various dance partners performed at downtown clubs and theaters, reportedly earning up to $350 a week to perform at the Havana-Madrid Club, located at 1650 Broadway, in the early 1940s. He also gave dance lessons at an Arthur Murray Studio and danced in film shorts with Noro Morales and José Curbelo. A light-skinned, fair-haired son of a plantation owner, Riambau believed that in Cuba "we don't have no race." He explained that only when he arrived in the United States did he "feel this thing about the races" and argued that racial consciousness among Cubans of color living in the United States developed because of formal segregation and public protests against racial discrimination. This perspective suggests that the threat of political mobilization based on race had largely been diffused since 1912 and that the Afro-Cubanist movement of the 1920s and 1930s, which touted the ideology of *mestizaje*, had helped realize the ideal of a racially egalitarian Cuban nation. But racial discrimination had not ended and calls for racial equality had not been silenced in Cuba, especially among the members of the black working class and from within the ranks of the Communist Party. For Riambau, however, it was the migration experience and exposure to rigid racial codes and race-based organizing in New York City that prompted Afro-Cubans to question the island's posturing as a

handwritten margin note (right): Its only Socially Acceptable For white Americans to get their Latin/Black Music through white Performers

handwritten note (bottom): White Cuba = much More racially integrated than U.S.; Artists See Racial Divides only when they come to the States

racial paradise and develop a racial consciousness that was distinct though not entirely separate from their Cubanness.[39]

It is useful to note how easily white performers such as Rizo and Riambau reproduced claims of transracial unity in Cuba, contrasting them with less peaceful race relations in the United States. As we will see, black Cubans often preserved a different memory. Yet it would be a mistake to see the claims of white performers as simple pretext. They did see differences between racial experience in the United States and in Cuba, and given the particularities of their position as white Cubans and near-white Latinos, it was possible for them to interpret these differences as a contrast between a society with race and a society without race.

A MUSICAL PARTNERSHIP

Rizo spoke at length about his experiences in the music business and entertainment industry. Many of his public comments and private reflections on his personal and professional relationship with Arnaz suggest an uneasy ambivalence, specifically in terms of Arnaz's abilities as a technical musician, on the one hand, and his status as an international celebrity, on the other. Rizo implied on several occasions that Arnaz depended on his musical expertise and technical abilities, stating plainly that "he wasn't a musician, you know." He described Arnaz as a "good businessman [but] as far as music is concerned he didn't have the background as we all know." Arnaz managed the business aspects of the music industry expertly, Rizo argued, because "he knew what he wanted" and had a clear idea of the kinds of arrangements that would be commercially successful. Those successful arrangements, however, were not always Cuban or authentic or, as Rizo put it, "our music." More specifically, he revealed, "Sometimes [Desi] couldn't explain it musically, but he knew what he wanted. He asked me to tell him what the best new numbers were, because he said, 'I want to form my own new band. . . . I have learned from [Cugat] what it takes to be commercial and at the same time to have my own sound, my own individuality.'"[40] Here, then, was the crux of the musical tradition (and by the mid-1940s it was tradition) that Rizo helped popularize: a watered-down, commercial Afro-Cuban music for North American audiences of the sort popularized by Cugat. "Our music," in this case, signaled African and Spanish mixture, but only from a safe distance, far enough away from direct exposure to or encounters with blacks or Africanness.

What many of his more positive remarks emphasize, however, is a sense of gratitude toward Arnaz for exposing North American audiences to

[handwritten margin notes, left side top: "Black Cubans saw Racial Divide in Cuba."]

[handwritten margin notes, left side bottom: "White Cubans made a 'watered down' version of Black Cuban music for white Americans"]

Cuban music and culture. For example, Rizo wholeheartedly agreed with a reporter from *Prensa Libre* in Havana who asked why the Cuban government had not yet honored Arnaz and his wife, Lucille Ball, with La Orden Nacional de Mérito Carlos Manuel de Céspedes, the award of highest distinction presented by the Cuban government to individuals engaged in diplomatic work on behalf of the homeland: "Has anyone calculated what it signifies that sixteen million people—more than twice the population of Cuba—listen to our music once a week by way of such prestigious ambassadors?" At times, Rizo even praised Arnaz's musicianship, citing a strong connection between their musical preferences and his memories of carnival in Santiago. Rizo recalled a childhood memory of carnival when he "saw two very white hands among the black ones, waving at me from the comparsa crowd in the street." He soon realized that "it was Desi." Rizo stood on the sidelines, observing the revelry in the streets before him, while Arnaz took a more active role as an engaged participant in the festivities. Rizo traced Arnaz's reliance on his musical expertise back to Santiago and argued that what began as childhood experimentation evolved into a partnership that made its way into the musical worlds of New York City and Hollywood. And this partnership produced within Rizo an understanding of "our music" that was defined by its Afro-Cuban roots but was meant to reach audiences beyond the island and its carnival traditions.[41]

Though he lived in Hollywood throughout much of the 1950s, Rizo hoped to stay relevant and maintain a following within Cuban circles using his association with Arnaz and his identity as a Cuban to elevate his own celebrity status. On one occasion, a Spanish-language newspaper, most likely published in Havana, reported that Rizo, "the famous orchestra director," had sent along a photograph of himself and "our compatriot" Desi Arnaz "so that our readers are convinced that these native celebrities, despite being at the pinnacle of glory, do not forget their own." As he reflected on his professional career, Rizo also recalled performing and developing relationships with other popular Cuban entertainers in New York City, including Machito, José Curbelo, and Xavier Cugat. His claims of friendship with other Cuban musicians did more than confirm a sense of camaraderie based on musical preferences and ethnic loyalties. By offering evidence of close ties—whether personal or professional—with other Cuban musicians who played more active and prominent roles in the *colonia cubana* and *colonia hispana*, Rizo aimed to establish his relevance and importance within the Cuban ethnic and broader Latino/a communities of New York City.[42]

Rizo's return to New York City in the late 1950s reveals a symbolic root-edness in the city's *colonia cubana* and *colonia hispana*. Soon he became involved with El Club Cubano, though the full extent of his association with the club during the 1940s and 1950s remains unclear. In 1959, the mostly Afro-Cuban social club honored "the great Cuban pianist" with a banquet at its clubhouse simply because "this institution is always on alert to honor those who deserve it." That same year, the club organized an event honoring Cuban concert pianist Jorge Bolet and announced that it would be donating a piano, which Rizo, Cuban singer-pianist Bola de Nieve, and Puerto Rican pianist and bandleader Charlie Palmieri had once played, to the Fernando Ortiz Foundation. Rizo also seems to have developed a following among the city's broader Latino/a audiences. In 1958, he emerged as a winner in *La Prensa*'s musical popularity contest, and the newspaper boasted that "the fine Cuban composer . . . would interpret some of his compositions of authentic Cuban and Hispanic American flavor" at its upcoming fund-raising festival. He remained engaged in the city's cultural life in other ways, too. The following year, he joined Polly Rogers, Aida Pujol, Alberto Socarrás, and George Boreland to help direct the Festival Antillano (Antillean Festival), a musical revue sponsored by La Federación de Sociedades Hispanas that featured bands and performers from Cuba, Puerto Rico, the Dominican Republic, Haiti, and Jamaica.[43]

Rizo also returned to the task of establishing himself as a classical musician and concert pianist. In 1958, he performed an entire concert at Carnegie Hall. One review in the *New York Times* described Rizo as a "native of Cuba" and an "arranger, composer and pianist in radio, movies, and television." The review characterized his musical offerings as "brief, unpretentious works, thoroughly pianistic and in an authentic-sounding Hispano-Cuban idiom." He performed his own compositions in the traditions of *afrocubanismo* and nationalist folklore, including "Rapsodia Cubana," "Ñañigo," "Suite Española," and "Suite Campesina." He also performed "fluent and effective transcriptions of works by Rodgers, Ravel, Scott, Lara, Baxter, Marquina, Provost and Grieg." Rizo performed another concert at Carnegie Hall the following year. One review noted that he delighted the audience with Cuban compositions and "fluent works that unite a Latin American melodic idiom with a keyboard style derived from the European romantic era."[44]

Reviews of some of Rizo's musical recordings from the late 1950s suggest that his musical versatility, marketing strategies, and commercial

White Cuban Rizo Trying to Re-establish "his ethnic Roots after "selling out"

Latin = Derogatory b/c it is white
Afro-Cuban = authentic!

expectations stand in contrast to his eventual rejection of "Latin" as a defining category of musical and self-representation. Despite industry categorizations and racial constructions that marked him and his music as "Latin," Rizo, like Bauzá and many other Cuban musicians, rejected that mode of cultural representation: "I don't know why they call it Latin jazz. What I play and what Mario plays, I am sure, it was Afro-Cuban, that's what it is. . . . Cuban music, man, it comes from the *son*, it comes from, that's the roots." The "Latin" label, however, was hard to shake. In 1958, his album *That Latin Touch* received positive reviews as "a broad range of instrumental material, including many facets of Latin music—Afro-Cuban, Mariachi, cha, cha, cha, etc., as well as a touch of classical."[45] For nearly a decade, Rizo played what might be described as commercial, popular Latin music as he toured the country with Arnaz's band and performed for radio, television, and film.

Throughout his professional career, Rizo's musical compositions—whether popular, classical, or "serious" music—drew from a folkloric Cuban musical tradition, what he described as "nothing more than two great influences, African and Spanish." In his discussion of the formation of the Cuban American Music Group in 1945, a writer for the *New York Times* also argued that African and Spanish influences had contributed to both Cuban popular and classical music but cautioned that "in Cuba, however, there is no fundamental difference between popular and 'classical' music. The ingredients of popular music produce symphonic music of good taste and strong appeal when mixed by the master hands of Cuba's serious composers." No matter what genre of music he played, whether *son* or jazz, Rizo insisted that his improvisations and technique reflected his "Cuban style." Rizo's musical versatility and classical training did not undermine his Cubanness, and he consistently presented himself as "authentic": "I am so proud to be Cuban and I am so proud to be able to expose all my life. . . . You know, that's what I've been doing, playing our music. I love classical music, of course, but first my music, my roots, what I am, what I am." Rizo articulates here what Fernández has described as "the *criollo* [native] attitude toward music making . . . in which musicians, in every moment of their construction of a people's musicalia, are at the same time performing their *cubania* (Cubanness)."[46]

Vilma Rizo, the pianist's younger sister and the trustee of her brother's musical legacy, speaks of a dual sense of camaraderie and competition within Cuban musical circles. I interviewed her three floors above the very apartment on 38th Street and Lexington Avenue in New York City, where Rizo lived and composed music until his death in 1998. Vilma constructed

From left to right: Mario Bauzá, Marco Rizo, and Dizzy Gillespie.
Courtesy of Vilma Rizo.

a narrative that positioned Marco's musical innovations as intellectually parallel to though geographically isolated from developments that have been more commonly attributed to Bauzá and other Cuban musicians of color. Vilma described Bauzá as "the brain behind the fame" and credited him with developing Latin jazz on Broadway in New York City. This is not a unique perspective. Bauzá is often seen as the key innovator in Afro-Cuban music, a characteristic that is different from being marked as authentic raw material. Vilma argued, however, that Marco had made similar innovations in Santiago with the Jazz Band Rizo-Ayala. For her, "these were two separate worlds," a framing that helps her construct a narrative that elevates her brother's role in the development of Afro-Cuban/Latin jazz. Of course, it also reminds us of the much longer process of development of this musical genre. Her analysis is in line with Fernández's contention that "the histories of Cuban and American music, while parallel and separate, intersected much earlier."[47]

A CRITIQUE OF CUBAN RACE RELATIONS

Mario Bauzá grew up during "the cosmopolitan 1920s in Havana," raised by a godmother he described as white and godfather he described as *criollo.*

These wealthy Spanish godparents provided him with an excellent music
education after his mother and his father, a cigar manufacturer, died
when he was five years old. That Bauzá was raised by white godparents
and Riambau by a black woman shows the inconsistency of racial boundaries in Cuba compared to the rigidity of such boundaries in the United
States. Bauzá studied at the Municipal Academy of Cuba and was playing
clarinet for the Havana Philharmonic Orchestra by the time he was nine
years old. His godparents hoped he would remain a classical musician, but
life in Havana offered him the opportunity to perform and experiment with
popular dance bands and exposed him to American jazz music via shortwave radio and recordings that made their way onto the island. On his first
visit to the United States in 1927, a fifteen-day trip to record with Antonio María Romeu's orchestra, he stayed in Harlem. That short trip radi-
cally altered Bauzá's perspective: "I fell in love with [Harlem], I say, 'I gotta
come back to live in this country, because I can live here, don't worry about
what color my skin [is]. I'm a black, I gon' be right along with these other
black, we all black.'" During that trip, he heard Frankie Trumbauer of the
Paul Whiteman orchestra perform at the Paramount Theater, and that inspiration prompted him to drop the clarinet and classical music and pick
up the saxophone and popular music.[48]

Not only had Bauzá fallen in love with Harlem and jazz, but he also reasoned that as "a colored man, and from Cuba, in symphony music, and clarinet, too," his chance for success "all over the world" seemed unlikely.[49] But
not every Afro-Cuban musician had this pessimistic outlook. Afro-Cuban
percussionist Armando Peraza, for example, offered a less racially defined
or ethnic-specific understanding of a career as a professional musician by
juxtaposing popular and classical music as beyond racial barriers: "Music
is music, music is no, have no color. . . . It's like, you wanna tell a black man
'You can't play no violin.' He can play the violin, see, he going to Jap—, see,
he going to Vienna or into any conservatory. You understand what I mean,
it's a culture. . . . This no have to be nothing with a pigmentation of your
skin."[50] Though Peraza's philosophy is not a description of social conditions,
it nonetheless offers an alternative mode of understanding racial prejudice and the possibility of social mobility for performers of color within
the world of music.

Despite his formal education and privileged upbringing as a young boy
in Havana, Bauzá recalled being denied membership into the Centro Asturiano, a whites-only social club, because he was black. All across the island, informal racial segregation prevented Cubans of color from entering
designated areas of public parks and certain barbershops, for example,

Music as a Form of Social Mobility

Racism/Seg in Cuba

ited them from participating in or becoming members of the
clubs and fraternal organizations as whites. Afro-Cuban con-
Miranda explained, "Well, at that time the black go to the
and the white was going to the white dance. . . . Some white
were raised together with the black people and those guys could
get in, in the black dance . . . but a black guy could not get into one of those
white dances."[51] Bauzá argued that black and white Cubans created separate *ambientes* (scenes, environments, or spaces) for themselves and that
this social distancing prevented a sense of fraternity from developing among
the races. The fraternity to which he refers harkens back to notions of
Cuban nationhood presented by Cuban independence leaders and black
Cuban organizations of the 1890s whereby, as historian Ada Ferrer explains, "racial transcendence and national unity were forged in manly union
during war."[52]

Bauzá's memory of race in Cuba centered on his belief that "that country is no different than Mississippi." He recalled that after a performance
at a club in the upscale neighborhood of Marianao, he was falsely accused
of raping a woman and escaped charges only because the chief of police
was also a man of color, perhaps revealing that Cuba was also very different from Mississippi. His remarks indicate that stereotypes of black men
raping white women contributed to a fear of Afro-Cuban sexuality. He
blamed racial mixing in general, and women in particular, for the racial
problems he experienced on the island: "But the trouble with my country
is so much mixture of people. Because, after all, how the Cuban race was
produced? By Spaniard with African womens. And the mulatto, it was a
mulatto race. But then, if the Spaniard had a mulatto daughter, he don't
want that daughter to be with a black man, he had to be another white
man, so there was lighter the race."[53] This critique of Cuban race relations
from the perspective of a black man who posits that there was no difference between Cuba and Mississippi highlights two fundamental differences
in the kind, if not the degree, of racism practiced on the island: the existence of black and brown police and the existence of intermediate racial
categories between black and white.

It is helpful to compare Bauzá's account with that of Chico O'Farrill,
who grew up in Vedado, an upper-middle-class neighborhood in Havana
in the 1920s and 1930s. Though he admitted that some public areas and
institutions were off limits to black Cubans, he described segregation in
Cuba as "more subtle" than the lynchings and "horrible things" that happened in the United States. Formal segregation was unnecessary in Cuba,
he explained, because blacks and whites "knew their place [and] nobody

trespassed on each other's territory." Just as Bauzá's argument that Cuba was no different from Mississippi was in some ways qualified by his own account of his experience in Cuba, O'Farrill's notion that Cuban segregation was somehow less violent left open the question of how Cubans came to "know their place" and what happened to them if they did not. Not only do these somewhat contradictory remarks illustrate the different ways that light- and dark-skinned Cubans experienced cross-racial interactions, but they also confirm De la Fuente's contention that "neither unqualified racial integration nor linear exclusion characterizes the history of Cuba as an independent nation. . . . Ambiguity is what best defines the evolution of race relations in twentieth-century Cuba." It was this ambiguity that Cuban migrants would use to make sense of the new social order they encountered on the stage and in the streets of New York City.[54]

THE MOVE TO HARLEM

Bauzá's account is fascinating as much for its depiction of Cuba as for its vision of Harlem. Just before he made the move from Havana to Harlem in 1930, he explained to his godfather, who thought he was crazy for making the move during such poor economic times, the reasons for his decision: "I want to be where the people is like me. I want to know what it is to be a black man in a black country. There is my roots. It has to be there. Let me find them. Because here I have no identity." Bauzá believed that he could create for himself a national cultural identity defined by his racial identity among other blacks in Harlem, a position that falls in line with cultural studies scholar Stuart Hall's contention that "identity is not in the past to be found, but in the future to be constructed." Bauzá's embrace of the black world of Harlem contrasts with the ideas expressed by Afro-Cuban poet, writer, and intellectual Nicolás Guillén in his 1929 essay "El Camino de Harlem." Guillén described Harlem as a sort of "black ghetto," an example of segregated, second-class space in cities and towns, and, more broadly, as evidence of North American race relations that, he warned, "those of us who have the color of Martí and those of us who have the color of Maceo must work to avoid." Though Guillén's perspective reflects how some Cubans interpreted the black-white racial system of the United States, for Bauzá and other black Cubans, Harlem offered a gathering place for a collective black diaspora made up of Cubans and Puerto Ricans of color, African Americans, and West Indians.[55]

Musicologist Jairo Moreno has focused specifically on Bauzá's musical partnerships with African American musicians, his mobility within the jazz community of Harlem, and his black racial identity. He contends that "evaluation of Bauzá's agency in the articulation of Latin/Jazz needs to consider his negotiation between material conditions (sociomusical and economic factors) and ideal processes (subjective poetics of self-construction)." Moreno follows this argument with an analysis of Bauzá's "rhetoric of homeland" and understanding of this negotiation as romance or marriage.[56] My project widens the lens of historical inquiry to include the perspectives of Cuban and Latino/a audiences and positions Bauzá not simply as a musician of color who found relief from intraethnic racial discrimination among fellow black artists in Harlem but also as an individual, ordinary migrant, and musician who negotiated the double bind of his race and ethnicity without ever losing hold of either his Cubanness or his blackness. The objective here is not to substitute one mode of identification for another or to position race as exclusively more meaningful than ethnicity or vice versa but rather to understand the set of circumstances that contributed to the ways in which racial and ethnic identities, tensions, and alliances were negotiated at particular historical moments and for particular gains.

In New York City, Bauzá met up with Antonio Machín, a black Cuban singer who was fronting one of the key white Cuban bands of the 1930s, the Orquesta de Don Azpiazu. Machín had coincidentally been on the same boat that had brought Bauzá from Havana to the United States. His band's trumpet player had suddenly left and returned to Cuba, and, according to Bauzá, "he couldn't find no Latin that played that stuff on the trumpet like he wanted." Bauzá listened in on a few of the band's rehearsals and, as he and legend tell it, he told Machín that "if you buy me a trumpet I think I can do that job." He "fell in love with the trumpet," and after a successful stint with Cab Calloway's band, he reasoned, "I gotta get me a Latin band with the same sound, the same idea as this big jazz orchestra." Bauzá "started fooling around with putting together the two music [Afro-Cuban and jazz] and prove to the world it could be done . . . what they calling today Latin Jazz." This historical reconstruction, of course, recalls the development of Afro-Cuban/Latin jazz as an "overnight," uninterrupted process, a description that scholars such as Fernández have long dismissed as too simple.[57] Artists' narratives oftentimes emphasized this kind of sudden inspiration and novelty, but we know that contact between musicians and experimentation with different kinds of music had been happening for a long time.

From the time he arrived in New York City in the 1930s, Bauzá worked solely as a professional musician. In contrast, many of the other Cuban musicians around him, especially those who had no formal training, had to piece together a living by working as wage laborers in construction, factories, restaurants, barbershops, *bodegas* (small neighborhood grocery stores), and other industries.[58] Afro-Cuban bass player Cresencio Gutierrez of Oriental Cubana, for example, earned a more steady paycheck as a typographer for *Diario de Nueva York* than he did as a musician. Afro-Cuban percussionist Luis Miranda worked as both a musician and dock worker throughout the 1940s and 1950s. He had returned to New York City in the late 1940s specifically to work with his father as a longshoreman. He attended school in the evenings, hoping to learn English and eventually pursue a career in law. However, his father had been friends with Machito in Cuba and because of this association, Miranda decided to drop his books, but not his job on the docks, shortly after his arrival in the city in favor of the conga drum.[59]

According to Bauzá, very few Cubans lived in New York City in the 1930s and 1940s. Most of them were cigar makers, he said. His reference to cigar makers suggests that most of these were Cubans of color. Just as Bauzá had done, many Afro-Cubans chose to live among African Americans in Harlem, north of 110th Street, rather than among Puerto Ricans in El Barrio, or Spanish Harlem, located between 110th and 96th Streets. Bauzá recalled that he preferred living among blacks in Harlem because he felt free to do whatever he wanted in that world. There, he said, he could distance himself from what he called the inferiority complexes of other Latino/as and the racism he had seen develop in Cuba.[60]

Bauzá was not the only Afro-Cuban musician living in Harlem. He could count Alberto Iznaga, Alberto Socarrás, Generoso Montesino, and others among his mostly black neighbors.[61] One such neighbor was percussionist Armando Sánchez, who left Cuba in 1945 to volunteer in the U.S. Army with a group of friends from the Universidad de La Habana. Born into what he described as a middle-class family in Cuba, Sánchez grew up around music and dance: his mother, of Spanish origin, and his father, "mulatto and mixed, from Indian, black, and white," met as performers in Europe in the early 1920s. In New York City, Sánchez could not convince landlords in Spanish Harlem, the supposed "refuge beyond the ghettos of the Lower East Side, Washington Heights, Brooklyn, and the South Bronx," to rent him a room. His sister, who was already performing at the Teatro Hispano, advised him to meet up with some of their old friends from Cuba at the Arte Renovación barbershop on 116th Street and Fifth Avenue. The owner of the barbershop, he recalled, played trombone in Marcelino Guerra's orchestra. As he moved deeper and deeper into Harlem, the surroundings shocked him: "I never saw so many black people together. I say, 'God, this is Harlem and it must not be here.'" But he was in the right place, and it was in Harlem where he finally managed to rent a room on 120th Street and Madison Avenue for $3 a week.[62]

When Afro-Cuban flute player Alberto Socarrás first stepped off the Seventh Avenue subway onto 125th Street on his way to meet up with Puerto Rican bandleader Augusto Coen, the shock of so many black faces moving around him led him to think he had accidentally stumbled upon a "festival by negroes." Socarrás left Cuba in 1928 to escape from racial discrimination, not because he saw the United States as a racial paradise. In fact, he reasoned that his privileged position as an in-demand professional musician limited his exposure to practices of racial exclusion: "That's why in United States I never saw any racism here, and I believe because I was a musician. I play with white musician, with black, with every kind of musician." When Armando Peraza arrived in New York City in 1948, he soon met up with Machito at the Palladium, and Machito immediately invited him, as he did for "any newcomer comin' from Cuba," to perform with the band. Peraza had left Cuba because he shared in the idea that the United States "was the dreamland for everybody." Unable to find a room in El Barrio, he rented one in Harlem on 135th Street between Seventh and Eighth Avenues.[63] The case can be made that many of these Afro-Cuban musicians experienced the best of both worlds, the freedom to operate a private life in an all-black setting free of white racism but also a public and professional life where Cubanness and Latinness shielded them somewhat from antiblack racism. As we will see, however, this mobility did not mean that these musicians did not also experience the same racial discrimination outside Harlem as did the African Americans who lived beside them, nor did it prevent them from having to contend with the particular racial biases of white Cubans and other light-skinned Latino/as.

What many of the Cuban musicians who left the island knew of life in the United States through encounters with American tourists and radio programs, music recordings, and film hardly prepared them for what surrounded them on the streets of New York City. The realities of life brushed up against the idealized and romantic notions of many black Cuban musicians, including Bauzá. The initial reactions of many Cuban musicians to Harlem, for example, reveal that they knew very little about the existence of the mostly black neighborhood or how to navigate the racial segregation and racial politics of the city. It is important, of course, not to essentialize Harlem's black community. Native-born African Americans, including hundreds of thousands who migrated north from the southern

United States both before and after World War II, and tens of thousands of Caribbean migrants from Cuba, Puerto Rico, and the West Indies settled in the neighborhood throughout this period. Blacks in New York City faced discrimination in housing, employment, and places of leisure and recreation. They also contended with police brutality, limited political representation, and inadequate schools and other public services. Historian Martha Biondi argues that "black labor became a dynamic source of social struggle, race leadership, and democratic ideas," and this was true for most Afro-Cuban musicians who were racialized as nonwhite, were prohibited from performing in certain venues, and were offered lower pay than their lighter-skinned compatriots.[64]

[handwritten margin note: Black Cuban experience]

THE (IM)POSSIBILITIES OF LATINO/A HARMONY

Bauzá described a complex racial negotiation among the Latino/as living in New York City in the 1930s and 1940s: light-skinned Latino/as rarely interacted with or wanted any association with darker-skinned Latino/as and African Americans.[65] Not only did the city's racial codes dictate where a person lived, socialized, and worked, but for Afro-Cuban musicians such as Bauzá much of the racism they encountered occurred within the *colonia hispana*. Tensions between Puerto Ricans and Cubans in New York City intensified in the mid-1930s due to "competition for housing, employment, and political identity." Immigration laws also worked to aggravate relations between the two ethnic groups. Many Cubans grew resentful of Puerto Ricans, who as U.S. citizens could travel freely between the island and the mainland, while Cubans who remained in the United States for more than twenty-nine days without a visa risked arrest and deportation.[66] Bauzá recalled that before he formed Machito y sus Afro-Cubans, Puerto Rican and African American musicians often ridiculed Cuban music, referring to the sound as "hillbilly." Others judged his abilities based on his ethnic background, making such statements as "You play jazz, yeah, but you don't play jazz like a Negro musician play."[67] It is somewhat surprising that Bauzá would recall such criticism from Puerto Rican musicians, given that he recorded and performed alongside many Puerto Ricans throughout his career. The apparent contradiction between his past actions and preserved memory is perhaps an example of a musician working to elevate his own reputation and contributions, as is often the case in the music business. Afro-Cuban musicians also often partnered with African American musicians and found work in jazz musical circles, though we can see that these relationships, too, had their own sets of biases and tensions.

Noting that in the late 1930s and 1940s "the Latin colony here was very small," Bauzá insisted that a "whole lot of Puerto Rican people reject[ed] my music," mainly because of his use of the bongo, an instrument that symbolized Africa and *ñañigos* (Abakuá members) music. Boggs reasoned that "Afro-Cuban music not only suffered from the disdain held for it by Puerto Ricans and the popularity of the Tango, but the omnipresence of racialism in New York City. . . . In spite of the fact that racist ideology had prevented Afro-Cuban musicians from gaining credence as serious practitioners of music, racism, it appears, frequently made it necessary for them to join Afro-American bands to earn a living." Boggs's argument seems to simplify Puerto Ricans' rejection of Afro-Cuban music as exclusively a matter of racial prejudice. This is not entirely unfounded. Tango was a popular genre that offered a white, modern, urban expression of Latinness as opposed to one that was "African," on the one hand, or "tropicalized," on the other, by the likes of Cugat, Arnaz, Rizo, or Carmen Miranda. Historian Ruth Glasser's study of Puerto Rican musicians in New York City demonstrates that Puerto Ricans' rejection of African influences, however, was not limited to Afro-Cuban music. In fact, Puerto Ricans routinely "argued about whether the *plena*, of black 'lowlife' origins, was a fitting national music." Puerto Ricans' attitudes about race were shaped by their past experiences on the island and new experiences with North American biracial classifications, and both factors contributed to practices of racial exclusion within Puerto Rican communities in New York City. Glasser also contends that "the production of Puerto Rican music in New York was inextricably bound up with *boricuas*' [Puerto Ricans'] desire to maintain cultural boundaries where social and political ones were ambiguous." Puerto Rican musicians, she argues, incorporated some aspects of Cuban music while rejecting others, as when composers such as "Rafael Hernández and Pedro Flores grafted intensely nationalistic Puerto Rican words onto commercially acceptable Cuban forms." Puerto Ricans' initial rejection of Afro-Cuban music, therefore, had as much to do with race and race relations as it did with a contrast between Puerto Rican and Cuban nationalism and ethnic identity.[68]

A MUSICAL AND RACIAL PIONEER

Bauzá relied on metaphor to explain not only how he developed his own sound and style as a jazz musician but also how he overcame criticism to forge relationships between jazz and Afro-Cuban music and with African American, Cuban, Puerto Rican, Filipino, and Anglo musicians. He used

language as a metaphor, positioning himself as both a cultural r
and racial pioneer who negotiated difference not in terms of n
ethnic identity but through his musical accents and phrasing. Fe¹
pet and saxophone player Benny Carter offered him some impu.
vice: "You, all you gotta do, adapt yourself to some of this language of jazz.
It's a different language, you know. When you really find out or learn the
language of our music, I don't think you have no problem." For Bauzá, the
"language of our music" was not English or Spanish or even Cuban or
American; rather, it was *African.* He constructed Africa as the source of
both jazz and Cuban music, and he insisted that his new band would carry
the "Afro-Cuban" modifier: "This here name of the band, gon' use it, otherwise I don't want to have no band, period. Why, I say why, because my
music, the Cuban music from Africa, man, and my race is African. So I'm
representing my music and my race, that's all." Ray Santos, who played saxophone for the Afro-Cubans from 1956 to 1960, revealed that among Bauzá,
Machito, and featured singer Graciela "there was a, always like 'race talk'
going on," an indication that race and discussions of race relations were
central to the band's identity.[69]

Naming the band "Afro-Cuban," however, was hardly an innovation in
the way that U.S. musicologists and even Bauzá and Machito liked to pre-
tend. *Afro-sones* (songs with themes that centered on an African and slave
past) had become very popular in Cuba in the late 1930s, and other bands,
including the Sexteto Afrocubano, had already included the modifier "Afro-
Cuban" in their names as early as 1936. *Afrocubanismo* was a major artistic and intellectual movement in Cuba during this period, and this name
constituted a reclaiming more than an innovation. José Curbelo, who eventually led the second band at La Conga after Bauzá recommended him,
expressed a notion of Afro-Cubanness that was very much in vogue in Cuba
in the 1930s. He defined Cuban music as Afro-Cuban music "because the
negro slaves that came from Cuba, they brought the rhythm. And in Cuba
they put the voicings out, the melody and the harmony, et cetera. But that
was—still is, the real Cuban music should be called not salsa—Afro-Cuban
music."[70] Similarly, Bauzá's reading of race through Africanness seems to
enable a diasporic musical collaboration, albeit in strategically essentialist ways. It must have reflected and used as resources notions of Africanness that were very popular in Cuba at the time and came to be reproduced,
at least in a derivative form, in New York City.

As much as the adjective "Afro" referred to Bauzá's African roots, the
"Cubanos" portion of the name, the subject, served to temper what might
have been perceived as an aggressively racialized and unmarketable

musical product. Indeed, what was called Cuban or Latin was easily recognized back home as a version, however watered down, of Afro-Cuban. The term "Latin," though fluid and negotiable, in many ways also carried a heavy burden, for it worked to describe both light-skinned musicians such as Cugat, Arnaz, and Rizo and Cubans of color such as Bauzá, Machito, and Socarrás. Burgos made the point well when he argued that Latino baseball players—and here I make a similar case for Latino/a musicians—"learned that others perceived Latinos as people of color (nonwhite) yet differentiated them from African Americans primarily due to their different cultural practices."[71]

These criticisms notwithstanding, Bauzá's role as a music pioneer and antiracist remain largely uncontested. According to Salazar, when Bauzá's "rumba, jazz, and classical sound started demolishing ethnic barriers in 1939, it was the beginning of his tacit war against racial discrimination." With Cugat as the most notable exception, in the early 1940s, most Latin bands performed in the *colonia hispana* in nightclubs and ballrooms such as the Park Palace, Club Obrero Español, the Odd Fellows Temple (a black Cuban club dating back to the 1870s), Club Tampa, Borinquen Hall, Club Ponceño, Laurel Gardens, Carlton Hall, the American Legion Hall, and the Cubanacán in Spanish Harlem and the Tropicana and the Hunts Point Palace in the South Bronx.[72] But racial exclusion did not stop Bauzá and his newly formed band, Machito y sus Afro-Cubans, from working below the 96th Street color line in nightclubs and venues where other dark and light-skinned Latino/as initially questioned their potential for sustained success. Bauzá credited the support of Jewish audiences who made the trek uptown to dance at the Park Plaza on 110th Street and Fifth Avenue for bringing Machito y sus Afro-Cubans to the attention of the owners of downtown clubs such as the Havana-Madrid and La Conga at 290 West 51st Street. The band first worked as a replacement band for the Anselmo Sacasas Orchestra at La Conga, but Bauzá soon convinced the owner to make Machito y sus Afro-Cubans the nightclub's headliner. It was the first time a Latin band held the featured position in a "swanky" downtown nightclub or hotel. The Afro-Cubans worked as the house band there from 1942 to 1945.[73]

Bauzá embraced his role as a racial pioneer because of a past episode with other Latino/a musicians in New York City. He attended a meeting organized by Latino/a musicians who were upset by the fact that Latin bands were hired only as relief bands and those that were hired for downtown clubs had to be white or very light-skinned. What frustrated and annoyed Bauzá was not the discrimination that had been experienced by those at the meeting but his realization that he was the only dark-skinned musician who had been invited to attend. He reasoned that these musicians included him in the meeting only because of his success as a professional musician, which had come about early in his career partly through his connections with African American musicians. They also hoped that he might hire some of them to perform with his new band. Of this particular incident, Glasser states, "The bandleaders had failed to organize themselves along cultural lines. The net result, according to Bauzá, was a weakening of both their musical and their economic bargaining positions."[74]

Throughout the 1940s and 1950s, performance reviews listed Bauzá as a trumpet player and arranger and consistently linked him to his associations with popular African American jazz musicians, a relational framing that positioned him as a sort of cultural mediator between Cuban and African American musical circles. A *Billboard* review of Machito y sus Afro-Cubans at the Palladium credited "the expert musicianship of Mario Bauzá" for the band's sound and polish. This public acknowledgement cautioned, however, that "this specialized musical excitement . . . ain't too good from a commercial viewpoint."[75] In this case, commercial success seemed to be measured in terms of whether or not the band could cross over and appeal to Anglo audiences.

Most news reports offered little more than casual mention of Bauzá as the musical director of the Afro-Cubans. When Machito y sus Afro-Cubans won *La Prensa*'s musical popularity contest in 1952, the newspaper presented contrasting images of Bauzá and Machito (who was also black), relying on exaggerated stereotypes to describe the latter. Bauzá earned praise as a "genius Cuban musician" and "as a serious man, quiet," while the newspaper portrayed Machito as "the real Cuban, happy, *cumbanchero* [slang term for someone who likes to have fun], noisy."[76] Although here being a "real Cuban" is an ambivalent compliment, the article nonetheless reveals contemporary expectations of Cubanness. One exception to this familiar framing occurred in 1951, when a debate on the origins of the mambo erupted in the pages of *La Prensa*, fueled largely by Arsenio Rodríguez's contention that Pérez Prado, also a Cuban of color, should be considered an interpreter, not the creator, of the mambo. Bauzá emerged as an expert figure; the newspaper asserted that within the *colonia hispana* "he is considered one of the best musicians in all senses." Asked to provide his perspective on the debate, Bauzá concluded that "the true creator of the mambo is none other than Arsenio Rodríguez," and with that final declaration the newspaper, too, ended its discussion on the matter. As we will see in the next chapter, however, statements about the origins of the mambo cannot be taken at face value.

Bauzá's experiences with racial exclusion as a young man in Cuba and as a professional musician within the *colonia hispana* likely influenced what might be described as his restrained Cubanness. He generally rejected the appropriation of his musical accomplishments as symbolic or representative of Cuban national identity, arguing instead that his hard work and persistence defined him more than his national or ethnic identity: "I don't embrace myself with my flag. My flag is my dignity. I made my flag." Bauzá's rejection of the notion that his individual accomplishments should be co-opted by or deemed symbolic of Cuban nationhood pushes back against Fernández's contention that Cuban musicians "in every moment of their construction of a people's musicalia, are at the same time performing their *cubania*." This is not to say that Bauzá denied or rejected his Cubanness but rather that for him his musical innovations illustrated his role as a social agent who was operating in conditions that often marginalized and excluded him and other musicians of color as full members of both the Cuban nation and the *colonia hispana*. Glasser argues that for Puerto Ricans in New York City, especially in the 1930s, their music took on patriotic and political significance. Music became a site of contestation for Cuban musicians as well, but Bauzá believed that it was not the musical product itself that mattered so much as the actual laboring to produce that musical product.[77] Bauzá reclaimed the music that nationalism had laid claim to, emphasizing the role of the individual musician as an innovator and rejecting the notion that music arises out of or reflects national spirit.

The popularity of Machito y sus Afro-Cubans within the *colonia hispana* initially surprised Bauzá, mostly because of the criticisms his music had received from Puerto Ricans. These criticisms help explain Bauzá's rejection of the term "Latin jazz": "Because it's Afro-Cuban rhythm in the bottom with jazz in the top, it's nothing else. . . . When you say Latin, how about the other 21 republics, they supposed to, they got their own music, they got their own rhythm." Here, Bauzá adopts a national perspective on rhythm: "Rhythm is a folklore, a rhythm is like a ground in any country. . . . The notes don't belong to us, so therefore melodies ain't got no nationality if you want to talk about, but rhythm do." With these remarks, Bauzá emphasized the centrality of Afro-Cubanness to what has been called or marked as Latin. He explained, "What they talking about, what's I begin with? 21 republic[s], and each one of them got a different r different expression. And what I play, there's no similarity to that stuff. So please—respect my, the name I give to my daughter whe.. . _ . tize her—Afro-Cuban jazz."[78] That Bauzá was able to ascribe nationality to rhythm, though he resisted the general notion of music as national expression, suggests that at times making nationalist claims served a purpose. His purpose here was to reject Latinness, marking Cuban innovations, especially contributions by Cubans of color, as unique and distinct from the musical contributions of other Latino/a musicians.

■ This chapter began with a comparison of the personal life histories and professional trajectories of Marco Rizo and Mario Bauzá, and it seems only fair to return to this analytic pairing in closing, for it reminds us, as Fernández has argued, that "the compensation and recognition received by the majority of Cuban professional popular musicians for most of the twentieth century seems inversely related to their contribution to the Cuban *musicalia*." Rizo and Bauzá both illustrate this point. As musicians in the shadows of Arnaz and Machito—and all four musicians had in some way or another to contend with the Cugat archetype—they helped frame the production of racialized discourses and musical practices in the context of the broader demands of the U.S. entertainment industry. In subtle and not-so-subtle ways, Rizo seemed to have realized that he shared the shadow with Bauzá. That shadow had followed Rizo since childhood: Arnaz "knew a few chords on the guitar and he used to go to my home and he used to say 'Marco, play that,' you know. And he tried to catch up with me." Rizo acknowledged that like him, Bauzá carved out a career as a musician in the shadow of a less-talented colleague. He said that "[Machito y sus Afro-Cubans] was Mario's band. . . . Machito was the personality, the front man. . . . But Mario was the musician."[79]

2

CUBAN MUSICIANS AND NEW YORK CITY'S

CUBAN SOCIAL CLUBS

One evening in September 1941, Machito y sus Afro-Cubans took the stage for a performance at the Audubon Ballroom, located at the edge of Harlem on the corner of 165th Street and Broadway. The popular band had been hired by Victor Alonso, president of the Hispano-American Club. Outside the ballroom, a reporter for the *Amsterdam Star-News* explained that "two prominent young white women, an African prince of great culture and a young colored girl" sought entry into the "public dance" they had purchased tickets for. It was likely Louise Crane, the daughter of a former governor of Massachusetts and one of the white women in the group, who suggested they attend the event, as she was known to be "intensely interested in swing music and Negro musicians." The man at the door, however, reportedly told the "mixed group" that "negra gente" [*sic*] ("black people") could not be admitted into the ballroom. Crane told the newspaper that the man at the door insisted that this "was a 'private' dance and that the club reserved the right to choose its own guests." The group left after receiving a refund and spent the night at the Famous Door, a "swank Swing Street night spot," where they had "absolutely no trouble." Morris Spencer, owner of the Audubon Ballroom, argued that if he had been present he "would have taken a stand in the matter," given his "policy of discrimination to no one because of race, creed or color." Writers for the newspaper attempted to contact Alonso for an explanation, even going so far as to visit one of the businesses he reportedly managed near 114th Street and Madison Avenue, but to no avail.[1]

The reception that this "mixed group" received as they tried to enter an event sponsored by a Hispanic social club was not uncommon in the *colo-*

nia hispana and *colonia cubana* of New York City in the 1940s and 1950s. Cubans, Puerto Ricans, and other Latino/as of color were also refused admittance into social events, including dances and celebrations headlined by Cuban musicians of color performing Afro-Cuban music. Whether the "negra gente" in question were denied entry to the dance because they were not of the Spanish-speaking world or simply because of the color of their skin is not entirely clear. It is evident, however, that racial and ethnic boundaries existed and that these boundaries were often tested, reinforced, and crossed at social events and cultural activities that (somewhat ironically) featured Afro-Cuban popular music and musicians. This suggests that the construction of Cuban and Latino/a racial and ethnic identities took place on the terrain of popular culture as it was negotiated and confronted by musicians and their various audiences.

This chapter and the next are not intended to provide an extensive and elaborate history of all or even the most prominent Cuban social clubs and ethnic organizations that were active in New York City in the 1940s and 1950s. Rather, the goal is to examine the discursive elements and processes of racial and ethnic negotiation that characterized the Cuban New York experience before the massive exodus of Cubans to the United States after 1959. Together, these two chapters detail the Cuban American cultural landscape that took shape in New York City in relation to the relatively small but significant number of Cubans who were living, working, and socializing in the city at midcentury. These chapters examine the role of race in shaping the discourses expressed and the practices sanctioned by the various Cuban social clubs and pan-ethnic institutions of New York City during this period. In this chapter, I focus on popular Afro-Cuban musicians and performers that were affiliated with and hired to perform at events sponsored by the city's Cuban social clubs and pan-ethnic institutions. Much of the spotlight turns to the mission and musicians of the racially inclusive El Club Cubano Inter-Americano, though attention is also given to Cuban and pan-ethnic organizations and events that were marked as racially exclusive, Hispano/a and Latino/a, or inter-American, categories that are not always clearly defined or delineated. Through their involvement in these various activities, Cuban musicians of color participated in the development of Cuban and Afro-Cuban consciousness and community. Given the range of their musical performances, from those hosted in the private spaces of the clubhouse to those that took place in more public commercial contexts such as hotel ballrooms and nightclubs, these Afro-Cuban musicians also helped construct broader Hispano/a and Latino/a identity. The marketing of these musicians and events and an awareness of the ways the developing mass culture industries affected socialization in and beyond the clubhouse was central to this process. Members and leaders of Cuban social clubs thought about their self-presentation and sought to engage the broader Spanish-speaking public of New York City in cooperation with the city's Spanish-language press. In doing so, black and white Cubans of the city gained the symbolic and cultural capital that would position Cubanness and Afro-Cubanness as central to Hispanidad and Latinidad.

A BRIEF HISTORY

Throughout the nineteenth and early twentieth centuries, Cuban migration to the United States remained small but constant. Historian Louis A. Pérez surmises that "Cubans went precisely because they had always done so."[2] During the revolutionary nation-building wars of the late nineteenth century, some Cubans traveled north across the Florida Straits to escape political insurrection while others came to secure employment in the booming cigar industries of Key West and (later) Tampa. In the first half of the twentieth century, wealthy Cubans sent their children north to attend prestigious schools and universities, and professionals who worked for U.S. corporations often traveled abroad for advanced training and instruction. By the late 1920s, thousands of black and white Cuban migrants from all socioeconomic backgrounds had formed mutual aid societies in Tampa, such as El Círculo Cubano and La Union Martí-Maceo, and had built theaters and dance halls that offered black and white Cubans separate spaces for leisure and recreation. The Great Depression, however, devastated the cigar industry that had employed many of the Cubans living in Tampa and forced workers to look elsewhere for employment. Many of these older Cubans and their families chose to retire and stay in Tampa. As we will see in chapter 6, some simply relocated a few hours south to Miami, where an expanding tourism industry offered jobs and other opportunities. Some of the younger generation chose to return to Cuba, while many others looked north to New York City as a refuge from the racism of the Jim Crow South and as a place with more economic advantages.[3]

The steadily growing presence of Cubans in New York City throughout the 1940s and 1950s was the result of both international migration from Cuba and this domestic migration from Tampa and other parts of Florida. This migration allowed a modestly sized *colonia cubana* to develop in New York City. The 1940 U.S. census indicates that 7,410 Cubans (defined as those who were born in Cuba or who had a mother or father who was born in Cuba) lived in New York. Of those born in Cuba, just over 5,000 were racially classified as "white," while only 600 were designated as "black." Historian Jesse Hoffnung-Garskof has noted that before 1960, U.S. census takers ascribed color and racial identification to the individuals they surveyed "based on the physical appearance of the individual but probably also influenced by other factors such as dress, speech, family members, and neighborhood." Hoffnung-Garskof explains, "Rather than recording the color and racial identities of these early settlers as they perceived themselves, census enumeration reflected shifting national ideas about race, codified by the color categories that Congress included in the forms: White, Black, and mulatto."[4] By 1950, the Cuban population in New York had more than doubled. The 1950 U.S. census reported that 16,895 Cubans lived in the state and that 12,272 of the Cuban-born individuals were assigned a racial classification of "white" and 1,291 were categorized as "black." Economic uncertainty and political instability escalated in Cuba throughout the 1950s, and many more Cubans migrated to the United States during this decade. The 1960 U.S. census indicates that 41,262 Cubans lived in New York, though it is unclear exactly how many of those Cubans arrived immediately after the Cuban Revolution. According to one report, only 3,000 Cubans left the island for the United States in 1959, and many of those early émigrés chose to remain in Miami, expecting Fidel Castro's regime to be short lived. This evidence suggests that the majority of Cubans living in New York in 1960 had migrated before the Cuban Revolution. Of the 41,262 Cubans who were in New York by 1960, an estimated 28,000 had been born in Cuba. More than 25,000 were classified as "white," while nearly 3,000 were classified as "black."[5] These numbers reveal, at least from the perspective of census enumerators, that New York City's *colonia cubana* was predominantly "white." These findings are significant because they suggest that Cubans had "become white" in the United States well before the popular post-1959 image of Cubans as mostly white and almost always middle and upper class had solidified. In the case of Cubans in the United States, however, race as constructed and imposed from above did little to diminish the cultural presence and social relevance of "black" Cubans in and beyond the *colonia cubana*.

Though Cubans accounted for a relatively smaller number of migrants compared to the hundreds of thousands of Puerto Ricans in New York City or Mexicans in the southwestern United States, these numbers do not reflect the presence and contributions of temporary Cuban visitors and tourists to New York City. Nor do they account for Cubans who overstayed their visa permits and settled for an extended period or permanently in the city.

Cubans who wanted to travel to the United States after the Immigration Act of 1924 did not need a visa to enter the country. Instead, when they reached Key West or Miami, the two most common points of entry, Cuban travelers could apply for a B-29 visa that allowed them to remain in the United States for twenty-nine days. Self-reported anecdotal evidence suggests that during this period it was common for Cubans who arrived in the United States as visitors to overstay their tourist permits. Cuban comedian Guillermo Álvarez Guedes, for example, recalled that he first came to New York City in 1946 on a B-29 visa to pursue a career in theater. When detected by immigration officials, he chose formal deportation to avoid having to pay his own transportation costs back to the island.[6]

At times, Cuban laws and regulations made migration challenging for artists. In 1953, artists drew the attention of Cuban government officials. One news report explained that any individual who requested a passport and claimed to be an artist required a contract that was approved by the Sociedad de Artistas and official certification from the society that confirmed "not only his status as a member but also the status of his morals." This change came as a result of charges that "people of questionable morality have left Cuba with an artist's identification card," possibly a veiled mode of referring to Cubans of color. Speaking about the relationship between race and changes in migration laws, Afro-Cuban percussionist Armando Sánchez explained, "At that time it was very hard for black people to get a visa. You have to have more papers than a white guy would. That's the way it was, it was a reality." Despite these types of claims, Cuban foreign minister Miguel Ángel de la Campa argued that the change aimed to guarantee that Cuban artists abroad "receive the same treatment that Cuba offers to foreigners" and that Cuban president Fulgencio Batista "has particular interest in defending the legitimate interests of the Cuban artistic class."[7]

Ethnomusicologist David F. García estimates that the Cuban population of New York City increased by 84 percent over two decades, from nearly 23,124 in 1940 to 42,694 in 1960. However, in the same period, the Puerto Rican population increased nearly 600 percent, from 61,500 to 612,574. García concludes that "Cubans in New York did not form an identifiable core of settlement. Instead, they resided primarily in Puerto Rican sections, although class and race dictated in which neighborhood Cubans settled." The conclusion that Cubans "did not form an identifiable core of settlement" because of their small numbers too easily obscures the significance of Cubans living in New York City (and elsewhere) during this period and constitutes a hierarchy of importance based solely on population size. I argue that Cuban migrants did, in fact, create an identifiable *colonia cubana* for themselves, one with a considerable amount of symbolic and cultural capital that became an undeniable presence in New York City in the 1940s and 1950s, particularly in the realm of popular culture. This project not only destabilizes hierarchies of significance relative to population that seem to dominate the field of Latino/a Studies but also contributes to the field's growing commitment to the recovery of Latino/as in "new" or "unexpected" places and time periods.[8]

Throughout the 1940s and 1950s, the Spanish-language press in New York City recognized the growing Cuban presence in the region. A multi-part story that appeared in *La Prensa* in 1943 directly discussed the "problem of Latin American minorities in the United States." The "problem," the story argued, concerned Cubans and natives of the West Indies in Florida, New York, and New Jersey; Central and South Americans in California, Illinois, Louisiana, Massachusetts, New Jersey, New York, and Pennsylvania; and Mexicans in Arizona, California, Illinois, Michigan, New Mexico, New York, and Texas. While some foreigners enjoyed generous scholarships and other forms of support from government and private institutions thanks to the Office of the Coordinator of Inter-American Affairs, countless others "are an isolated population . . . whose presence is considered a charge, a problem, a bother." Even more to the point, the article explained that "blacks of foreign extraction . . . retained their status as minorities for long periods."[9] The story here was not one of good neighborly relations but one of racial and ethnic exclusion and inequalities, evidence that the inter-American interests of the period could have obvious limitations, especially for Afro-Cubans and Afro-Latino/as.

CUBAN SOCIAL CLUBS IN NEW YORK CITY

El Club Cubano Inter-Americano and the Ateneo Cubano de Nueva York played key roles in establishing the Cuban presence in the city. Most historians agree that El Club Cubano emerged in New York City in September 1945 when a group of Afro-Cubans, many of whom had migrated north from Tampa in the late 1930s and early 1940s, planned a centennial celebration in honor of Antonio Maceo, the beloved Afro-Cuban general whose leadership contributed to the success of the nineteenth-century Cuban War of Independence. The event netted a profit of $200, which organizers used to form the new club. Anthropologist Susan Greenbaum explains that the impetus for the celebration and, by extension, the formation of the new club, came from the mayor of Havana, who contacted former members of the Mella Club, a political social club for both black and white Cubans in New York City that disbanded before 1933, to commemorate Maceo's birthday. This origin story makes sense, given the seemingly close relationship the club maintained with Cuban government officials in the years that followed. Though El Club Cubano was not founded on the basis of race or color, Greenbaum reasoned that it "became black by default and 'inter-American' by necessity." Existing and recently formed Cuban social clubs such as the Círculo Cubano and the Ateneo Cubano denied membership to Cubans of color, an act of racial exclusion that forced Afro-Cubans to create for themselves what longtime club member and president (1957–1958) Melba Alvarado called a "safe space for 'la gente negra'" in the *colonia cubana*. Cubans of color found refuge at El Club Cubano on Prospect Avenue in the Bronx, where club leaders also extended membership to Puerto Ricans, African Americans, Dominicans, Jamaicans, and Haitians. Most club members were skilled men and women from middle- and working-class backgrounds who lived in the Bronx within walking distance to the clubhouse, but some also rode the subway from East Harlem and other parts of Manhattan to attend club meetings and participate in social and cultural events.[10]

Newspapers and magazines present a rich variety of information on the kinds of social activities and cultural events sponsored by the Ateneo Cubano. The historical record offers fewer details about the origins and development of the club, which was located at 2824 Broadway between 109th and 110th Streets. In fact, much of what I have uncovered about the membership and policies of the Ateneo Cubano comes from comparisons and oppositional references made by Afro-Cuban musicians and members of El Club Cubano. From these piecemeal historical reconstructions, the Ateneo Cubano emerges as a much less racially inclusive and much more closed organization than El Club Cubano. Though leaders of the Ateneo Cubano were willing to hire and promote Afro-Cubans such as Arsenio Rodríguez and Eusebia Cosme to perform at club events, they seem to have denied ordinary Cubans of color admittance into their social spaces. The club, which was founded in 1941 and was open to both men and women, routinely excluded Cubans of color from participating in club affairs, sometimes through direct confrontation at the door and sometimes through "misinformation and deliberate silences." The club welcomed white non-members at its events, but Alvarado recalled that Cubans of color who sought entry were routinely met with the racially marked phrase "we reserve the right to admission." She also remembered that she and other members of El Club Cubano would often learn that a white Cuban social club such as the Ateneo Cubano had organized an event only after the fact.[11]

THE MISSION AND MUSICIANS OF EL CLUB CUBANO INTER-AMERICANO

On 11 November 1945, Generoso Pedroso, Narciso Saavedra, Julio Cardenal, Mario Alfonso, and José J. León gave final approval to the mission statement that would come to define the ideals and principles of El Club Cubano.[12] That statement revealed a social and cultural club that aimed to "maintain the fraternity that should exist in the colonia cubana and the other Latin American countries . . . separating itself from any association with partisan politics or religion." Early club leaders established *fraternidad* as a primary goal of the new social institution, a choice of words that suggests not simply a borrowing of language but also a borrowing of ideology from Cuba's nineteenth-century revolutionary struggles for independence from Spain. Historian Ada Ferrer has shown that Cuban patriot-intellectuals offered black slaves and free persons of color the promise of a free Cuban nation based on equal rights, liberty, and brotherhood, hoping to recruit them to the insurgent cause. Rebel leaders such as José Martí extended to Cubans of color citizenship in a Cuban nation constructed as "transracial." Renewed calls for fraternity in the *colonia cubana* by Afro-Cubans who were often denied entry into white Cuban social clubs in New York City and were all too familiar with acts of formal and informal racial exclusion in Cuba and the United States confirms that these nineteenth-century promises remained unfilled in the 1940s and 1950s. By drawing on this legacy of (unfulfilled) Cuban brotherhood and community based on equality and freedom from racial divisiveness, these early club leaders positioned El Club Cubano as a proponent of racial change and progress.[13]

El Club Cubano's founding mission statement declared that the organization would first and foremost "disseminate culture in all its forms, for the purposes of which it will celebrate conferences, talks, art exhibitions, inter-American commemorations, [and] . . . promote social acts, etc., etc."[14] Club leaders did not have to look very far to find the talent and celebrity they needed to host crowd-pleasing musical and dance events. Popular Afro-Cuban bandleaders Generoso Montesino, Alberto Socarrás, and Marcelino Guerra were listed as founding members of the club.[15] The club eventually counted Arsenio Rodríguez as an active member and Machito, Miguelito Valdés, and nearly a dozen other Cuban bands and solo

Members of El Club Cubano Inter-Americano, ca. 1960. Courtesy of Justo A. Martí,
Justo A. Martí Photograph Collection, Archives of the Puerto Rican Diaspora,
Centro de Estudios Puertorriqueños, Hunter College, City University of New York.

performers of color as frequent supporters of and participants in club events. One club leader argued that "people won't show up to dance to records but they will come to dance to live music," demonstrating El Club Cubano's belief that live musical attractions would increase the success and profitability of its social and cultural activities.[16] One suspects, however, that many of the professional musicians that formally joined or informally allied with El Club Cubano did so not entirely out of a commitment to the mission of the organization but also to increase their odds of being hired to perform at the club's social and cultural events. Musicians rarely turned down an opportunity to perform, and Cuban musicians were no exception. They crossed ethnic lines routinely and purposefully throughout this period, motivated by economic need, familial obligations, dreams of fame and fortune, and, at the very least, an understanding of, if not a genuine appreciation for, the profitability and pragmatism of developing a pan-Latino/a and Pan-American musical repertoire and reputation.

Music was a major element of the social and cultural events El Club Cubano and the many other Cuban and Latino/a social and cultural clubs of New York City sponsored. Montesino, Socarrás, Guerra, and Rodríguez are just four of the most well-known examples from a cohort of Afro-Cuban musicians who joined and participated in club events. These Afro-Cuban musicians not only helped confirm El Club Cubano's commitment to racial and ethnic openness but also, through their involvement with other Latino/a social events, revealed the extent to which the construction of a "transracial" pan-Latino/a identity took place by way of popular music generally and within the Cuban American cultural landscape specifically. Cuban musicians of color navigated and negotiated not only race (blackness) and culture (Cubanness) but also Afro-Cubanness and (Afro-)Latinidad. It was this process, which sometimes was fluid, sometimes less so, that both facilitated and reflected the growing centrality of Cubanness and Afro-Cuban musicians and music to the coming together and socialization of the Spanish-speaking community of New York City in the 1940s and 1950s.

GENEROSO MONTESINO

Afro-Cuban percussionist Generoso Montesino joined El Club Cubano as one of its founding members in 1946. His membership in the club came toward the latter portion of a professional musical career marked by pan-ethnic and Pan-American sensibilities, and the club's inter-American mission and marketing likely appealed to the aging musician. Montesino was popular in the *colonia hispana* and among white ethnic audiences, and his early membership in the club demonstrates the centrality of Afro-Cuban musicians to the construction of a "transracial" pan-Latino/a identity. The "real Cuban and Habanero to the core" left Cuba in 1925 with no formal musical training or dreams of a career as a professional musician. But Montesino soon observed the "popularity that criollo music was gaining among the Hispanic and North American elements" and decided to give the music business a chance. The pan-ethnic and crossover appeal of Afro-Cuban music and his performances at numerous pan-Latino/a social and cultural events facilitated his success as a musician in New York City in the 1940s.[17] Most notably, in 1946, Montesino y su Conjunto del Ritmo performed at a dance in honor of Día de la Raza at the Embassy Ballroom in the Bronx. Each October, numerous social clubs and cultural associations in the *colonia hispana*, including El Club Cubano and the Ateneo Cubano, came together to celebrate Día de la Raza with a dance and parade. While Anglos and ethnic whites celebrated Columbus Day, the city's Latino/as gathered in honor of Día de la Raza, which served, according to one commentator, as a "tribute to the motherland and reaffirmation of our condition as nations united in brotherhood by race, religion, and language."[18] Montesino's participation in this cultural and (at least implicitly) political celebration indicates just one of the ways that Afro-Cubanness became central to the construction of *nuestra raza* in the 1940s and 1950s.

Montesino's Los Happy Boys appealed early on to white audiences. It was one of the first bands to attract Jewish and Italian teenagers to venture into Spanish Harlem. Machito credited the band for helping to integrate nightclubs and ballrooms across the city or, as he put it, "start[ing] the whole thing" at the Park Palace on 110th and Fifth Avenue. As one of many "local neighborhood orchestras," Los Happy Boys developed a following in the broader Latino/a community. In 1940, at an event organized by El Habana Social Club at the Grand Plaza in the Bronx, the band performed alongside Casino de Ponce and Casino Dominicano.[19] In addition to Los Happy Boys, two of the other featured bands, by name and likely by their musical offerings, signified Puerto Rican and Dominican national origins, suggesting one of the ways transnational culture and hemispheric solidarity developed among an emerging Spanish-speaking public. By 1942, the band's popularity seemed on the rise; one report concluded that Montesino's band "count[ed] on a great deal of popularity in the Hispanic-New Yorker element."[20]

Billed throughout this period as both Los Happy Boys and El Conjunto del Ritmo, the former considered more English-friendly, the latter more "barrio-centric," Montesino's band performed at the annual fund-raising gala sponsored by *La Prensa* in 1941 and returned as winner of the newspaper's annual musical popularity contest in 1942. Both Los Happy Boys and El Conjunto del Ritmo earned votes in *La Prensa's* musical popularity contest, demonstrating that even fans in the *colonia hispana* and *colonia cubana* seemed confused about the band's official name. It is not clear whether the band's racial or ethnic makeup changed significantly according to billing or venue, but I have found no evidence to suggest that this was ever the case. The band's name may have changed, but its leader remained Montesino, a Cuban of color. This naming irregularity (or perhaps strategy) suggests that public recognition as Los Happy Boys helped Montesino and, by extension, event promoters attract and develop a following among non-Spanish-speaking audiences in the 1940s. Moreover, the rather generic name El Conjunto del Ritmo, though it targeted a Spanish-speaking public, would not have explicitly marked the band as Cuban or Afro-Cuban, and this would have allowed Latino/as, regardless of national origins, to claim the band as their own.

In 1946, El Club Cubano also welcomed Alberto Socarrás as a founding member. Born in Manzanillo, Cuba, on 18 September 1908, the Afro-Cuban, classically trained flutist was a man of many firsts. He traveled throughout Europe and the Caribbean as the arranger for the all-female Cuban band Anacaona in the 1930s.[21] Socarrás later recounted that he faced racial discrimination at the outset of his musical training in Havana. Socarrás said that after his white flute teacher refused to get up from a nap to meet him, he had no choice but to find himself a black flute teacher, resolving to be a great flutist, all before he was seven years old. Indeed, he recalled that racial discrimination in the blossoming music and entertainment industries of Havana was part of the impetus for his move to New York City. Noticing that U.S.-owned nightclubs and hotels in Cuba hired only light-skinned or white musicians, he reasoned, "Well, I have to get out of here. This is my country, I was born here, and I don't want to be discriminated here. If I'm discriminated in the United States, that means I'm no American. I'm no American, but in my own country to be discriminated because I was black, I don't want to get into that." Socarrás believed that migration to New York City simply made him Cuban and that whatever discrimination he might face would be based on his foreignness rather than on the color of his skin. Many Afro-Cuban migrants faced the difficult task of negotiating what historian Adrian Burgos Jr. has described as "the double bind of cultural difference and racial standing in the United States." Yet Socarrás seemed much more concerned about avoiding exposure to the racial prejudices and exclusionary practices of white Cubans. After he arrived in New York in 1928, his status as a professional musician allowed him to limit his contact with white Cubans and create partnerships with the many African Americans he met while working in the city's jazz circles. In fact, he claimed to never have experienced racial discrimination in the United States, a point of view that seems to have been shaped by his privileged position as a professional musician.[22]

Socarrás set out to form a new band that was not restricted by barriers of race, ethnicity, or musical genre. He wanted his band to be skilled musically and also remain friendly and appealing to white North American audiences: "But I don't want all Cubans . . . because I see many Puerto Ricans here, and they are Latin. So I want to organize a GOOD band here

Cuban Musicians and New York Social Clubs / 67

playing Cuban music, because the American likes Cuban music very much." But his band played what can best be described as one of many variations of Cuban music that popped up across New York City in the 1930s and 1940s. He explained: "So what I did, I took American music, jazz, and put it Cuban rhythms [*sic*]. . . . Make jazz, American jazz, with Cuban rhythm. So I was the first one to bring bongo and the, all those things to American music." Here we see again a black musician claiming the role of musical innovator, and it seems that other musicians agreed with him. Socarrás played at the Cotton Club on 66th Street and Broadway and worked as director of the house band at the Cubanacán at 114th Street and Lenox Avenue for nearly four years, prompting many other Afro-Cuban musicians, including Mario Bauzá, to recognize his band as one of the few "playing authentic Latin music both up and downtown."[23]

For Socarrás (and Montesino), formal membership in El Club Cubano did not result in a monopolizing presence as a featured performer at club events. But Socarrás was popular among club members, and his professional achievements beyond the clubhouse earned him recognition. The year 1952 marked the fiftieth anniversary of Cuban independence, and celebrations associated with this historic date revealed a deep appreciation of Cuban musicians and their role in disseminating Cuban culture abroad. In February, El Club Cubano received a letter from a club member suggesting that the club organize a "café" at its clubhouse in honor of Socarrás, describing him as a "notable Cuban musician who has recently earned various honors." His popularity extended beyond the clubhouse; after *La Prensa*'s musical popularity contest and fund-raising gala that year, the newspaper described Socarrás as "the doctor in music."[24]

Though he was busy performing at social and cultural events across the city, Socarrás often returned to Spanish Harlem. Throughout the 1950s, Socarrás participated in the annual festival for poor students held at Benjamin Franklin High School on 116th Street and Pleasant Avenue. Organized by Cuban journalist Babby Quintero and sponsored by *Diario de Nueva York*, this community event raised funds for the poor, mostly Puerto Rican, students in the area and featured several other notable Cuban performers, including musicians Fausto Curbelo, Miguelito Valdés, Machito, Graciela, Juanito Sanabria, and Arsenio Rodríguez and poetry reciter Eusebia Cosme, poet Eulogio Peraza, and entertainers Perucho Irigoyen and Willie Chevalier. Participation in this event, which *La Prensa* described as having "extraordinary importance for the hispanic population of the city," reflected a commitment to the local community regardless of national origins or ethnic and racial divisiveness.[25] For that reason alone, it makes sense that Socarrás was among those who were involved.

MARCELINO GUERRA

Marcelino Guerra was a founding member of El Club Cubano in 1946. He frequently participated in the social and cultural events sponsored by the club, much more often than Montesino and Socarrás.[26] His unique position as a club member and professional musician led to negotiations over club dues and performance fees that benefited both parties. In 1949, for example, Guerra agreed to waive his $50 fee and perform at no cost at an upcoming club event. Club records indicate that Guerra donated his talents because the club had received complaints from many of the *excursionistas* (visitors from the island on an arranged trip overseas) who had attended a dance held in their honor at the Hotel Diplomat, located in midtown between Broadway and Avenue of the Americas. It is unclear if Guerra's band had performed at the disappointing event and he was attempting to build goodwill after a lackluster performance or if he was simply being generous to improve the club's standing as a source of quality entertainment. Because of the singer's reputation, the latter scenario seems more likely. Guerra was a favorite among his peers; one musician said that he was more friendly and popular than Machito. The leaders of El Club Cubano repeatedly discussed the possibility of hiring Guerra and his orchestra to perform at club events to ensure that all who attended would be entertained and satisfied. Longtime membership and participation in club events proved advantageous to Guerra in 1958, when club leaders unanimously agreed to forgive the musician's debts and accept his late dues.[27]

Guerra caught what was arguably the biggest break of his musical career thanks, in many ways, to Machito and Mario Bauzá. After Machito left the band to serve in the U.S. Army during World War II, Bauzá organized the Second Afro-Cubans with Guerra as singer and Luis Varona as bandleader. Machito and Guerra often performed on the same billing, and though some in the listening public suspected that a rivalry had developed between the singers, a rumor that was likely encouraged by savvy concert promoters, in reality a "strong camaraderie" and "strong friendship" existed between the two bandleaders. For weeks, advertisements presented a 1950 concert at the Manhattan Center that featured the two bands as a sort of battle of the bands, and reporters concluded that the billing "produced a great deal of enthusiasm among the hispanic youth."[28]

Guerra's membership in El Club Cubano did not restrict his performance schedule or limit his ability to perform at events sponsored by other Latino/a social clubs, cultural organizations, and commercial venues such as the Hunts Point Palace.[29] One musician recalled that he was "a favorite band of that era, excellent Cuban singer with a real strong, true, projecting type voice."[30] In 1947, Guerra's orchestra and Machito y sus Afro-Cubans performed at a dance sponsored by Juventud Panamericana to celebrate Pan-American Day. In honor of the occasion, the organization decorated the main ballroom of the Hotel Diplomat with the flags of the twenty-one republics of the Americas and invited what one reporter described as "diplomatic hispanos" to attend the festival.[31] A few years later, in 1950, the Manhattan Center hosted a "grand Antillean carnival" that featured performances by three orchestras: Esy Morales representing Puerto Rico, Marcelino Guerra with Gilberto Ayala at the piano defending "the 'rhythmic colors' of beautiful little Cuba," and Josecito Roman's Orquesta Quisqueya representing the Dominican Republic.[32] That many of the events featuring Guerra were organized as pan-Latino/a celebrations again suggests one of the ways Afro-Cubanness figured as a core element of Hispanidad and Latinidad.

Guerra's professional career reached a high point in 1954, when his band won *La Prensa*'s annual musical popularity contest. Reports described the band as "a grouping of rhythm and native music justly applauded and in demand," and the newspaper hired Guerra to perform at its fund-raising gala that year, professing no doubt that "dance lovers would receive the news with enthusiasm." The "famous director's" band returned the next year to perform once again at the newspaper's festival, earning praise as "distinguished exporters of mambo and creole music" and "one of the most popular in the colonia." This evidence confirms that Guerra's career extended well into the 1950s, though some scholars have argued otherwise. Music scholar John Storm Roberts, for example, has stated that Guerra left the music scene in 1947, after joining the merchant marine. Music historian and journalist Max Salazar has argued that Guerra retired from music in 1954 because he could no longer tolerate "his sidemen's problems with drugs and alcohol and the racism of some midtown club owners who thought his sidemen were 'too black.'" Whatever the timing and the reasons for his retirement from music, an unfinished song penned by the bandleader reveals a profound attachment to New York City, where his relationship with El Club Cubano and the commercial entertainment industry undoubtedly shaped his life experiences: "New York, New York / City where I was so happy / New York, on your ground I did also suffer / Someday I will die / And I hope it is here / Beloved New York."[33]

ARSENIO RODRÍGUEZ

Perhaps no professional musician benefited from his affiliation and membership in El Club Cubano more than blind Afro-Cuban *tres* player Arsenio Rodríguez. Born in Matanzas in 1911 to a black working-class family, Rodríguez lost his eyesight when he was a young boy after a mule kicked him in the head. Rodríguez's musical repertoire drew on his early exposure to *santería* and *palo monte*[34] and to African-derived musical instruments such as the *marímbula* (a wooden box with metal strips across the sound hole that are plucked), the *botija* (an earthenware jug that is blown into and used as a bass instrument), and the *tres* (a three-stringed instrument very similar to the guitar). By 1940, Rodríguez had developed his own *son montuno* style (sub-genre of *son* with slower tempo that incorporated the use of the conga drum) and was recording and performing at popular cabarets and nightclubs in Havana as the leader of and composer for his band, Arsenio Rodríguez y Su Conjunto. Rodríguez made frequent trips to New York City from 1947 to 1952, but it was not until the latter date, motivated by his brother Kiki's criminal history, the promise of better pay for musicians, and the deteriorating political situation in Cuba, that his stay became permanent. According to García, when he arrived in New York City, Rodríguez immediately and consistently asserted that he alone was the creator of the mambo, specifically "claiming authorship of the underlying rhythmic approach that linked the otherwise idiomatic styles of [Tito] Puente, Pérez Prado, Machito, and others."[35]

The date of Rodríguez's initial membership in El Club Cubano is unclear, but he was apparently reinstated as a member on 14 March 1957, likely after losing his membership for failing to pay club dues or because he was away from New York City for an extended period of time. The club hired him to perform at many of its social and cultural events throughout the 1950s, ranging from small cocktail events held at the clubhouse to larger events such as a costume party held in honor of Cuban heavyweight boxer Nino Valdés.[36] Authenticity mattered to El Club Cubano and seems to have helped increase attendance at club events, including those organized in honor of the *excursionistas*. In 1951, for example, Arsenio y su Conjunto de Estrellas performed at a dance held to celebrate the visitors' arrival in the grand ballroom of the Hotel Diplomat. In 1959, a club newsletter advertising its latest dance for the *excursionistas* at the Statler Hotel described Rodríguez's *conjunto* (smaller *son* dance band that included the addition of the conga drum) as "the only band that has the real and true Cuban *sabor*. Arsenio's music is authentic."[37] Among Cubans on the island, Cuban New Yorkers, and others in the *colonia hispana*, Rodríguez's style "engendered at once a sense of nostalgia for their respective homelands and cultural resistance to 'modern' or Americanized Latin music styles."[38] This combination of nostalgia and resistance to watered-down commercial Latin styles, like those popularized by Xavier Cugat and Desi Arnaz, solidified Rodríguez's popularity among Cuban and Latino/a audiences.

Rodríguez's style offered less showmanship and spectacle than other Cuban mambo performers, which limited his crossover appeal among white North American and international audiences. Bauzá noted the apparent drawbacks to his style, explaining that Rodríguez "played with a tempo that to follow it you had to be Cuban, a dancer, and on top of that black, because it was very slow."[39] Most white audiences preferred the "showtime" exhibitionism of the more exuberant Pérez Prado. But Rodríguez's stiff performance style was only one reason why he failed to achieve international stardom like that of his Afro-Cuban contemporaries such as Pérez Prado, Machito, and Miguelito Valdés. His repertoire of songs engaged Africanness and the realities of racial inequality, the perils of colonialism and imperialism, Cuban patriotism, and life in El Barrio and the Bronx. These racial and political themes likely resonated with members of El Club Cubano but did little to generate a following among broader audiences.

One of his earliest and most popular compositions, "Bruca maniguá," features *bozal* speech ("Africanized" Spanish) and a slave denouncing the mistreatment and abuses he has suffered at the hands of his white owner. Other songs firmly locate Rodríguez as a member of the *colonia hispana*. "Fuego en el 23" tells the story of a fire breaking out at an apartment building, number 23 on 110th Street, the boundary between Harlem and Central Park. In "El elemento del Bronx" and "Como se goza en el Barrio," Rodríguez celebrates local neighborhood music and cultural tastes. With lyrics such as "the people of the Bronx / dance mambo and danzón / they like dancing cha cha chá / they like dancing guaguancó / the people of the Bronx / they like to dance rock 'n' roll / they dance mambo and danzón" and "the barrio is for dancing / the barrio is for having fun," these songs positioned the uptown scene as *the* place for music and dancing. In "Pasó en Tampa," Rodríguez recounts the story of his short stay in Tampa on his way to New York City in 1947 because of a problem with his visa.

While walking around the city looking for a place to eat, he is met with the phrases "what you said?" and "speak English." It is not until he meets a local Cuban (presumably of color since he was staying in the black section of Tampa) who helps him with the translations that he can order a cup of coffee. He sings that he "will never forget about what I suffered" there.[40]

Songs such as "El elemento del Bronx," "Como se goza en el Barrio," and "Pasó en Tampa" made Rodríguez a favorite among the black and white Cuban audiences of his generation and in the broader *colonia hispana*. It is important to note that many of Rodríguez's compositions, including those that assertively reclaimed Africanness through language or imagery ("Bruca maniguá," "Fufuñando," and "Adios Africa," for example), were recorded and popularized among white audiences by lighter-skinned and white Cuban musicians and orchestras in Cuba and in the United States, namely Casino de la Playa, Miguelito Valdés, and Xavier Cugat. The point is not just to acknowledge the familiar process of black innovation and white commercialization but also to emphasize that these songs took on different meanings when performed by different kinds of musicians and before different kinds of audiences. As performed by Rodríguez, a dark-skinned black Cuban, songs written in *bozal* speech about racial inequality or those about street life in El Barrio elicited a sort of empathy and identification that was not entirely possible when these same songs were performed by Cugat and even, in certain instances, Valdés in different kinds of venues and to different kinds of audiences. Unfamiliar with *santería* and *palo monte* and disconnected from the legacies of slavery and experiences with racial discrimination, the audiences of the latter performers likely missed the cues and symbolism present in the song lyrics. The process was repeated over and over again, as we will see: Afro-Cubanness shifted toward Cubanness and Latinness when performed by white musicians and remained Afro-Cuban when performed by black and dark-skinned musicians. In Rodríguez's case, particularly because of his ties to El Club Cubano and the *colonia hispana*, Afro-Cubanness also took on a broader meaning that allowed other Latino/as of color to make claims on it, at least culturally, as a sort of transnational diasporic blackness.

Club records reveal mutual cooperation and appreciation between El Club Cubano and Rodríguez. In 1950, for example, the club honored Rodríguez and his musical talents by presenting him and film star Cesar Romero with honorary diplomas at a ceremony held in their clubhouse.[41] Club leaders counted on Rodríguez's musical appeal to their constituents, and in 1951, they agreed to move the date of the dance in honor of Cuban independence only after consulting with the bandleader, whose only request was that the club not schedule the dance for 19 May, the date of José Martí's death.[42] Later that year, Rodríguez performed at El Club Cubano's Ritmos de Otoño (Fall Rhythms) festival at Audubon Hall. He agreed to split either the losses or profits from the event with the club, a risky business decision that suggests both poor management skills and a confident spirit of generosity. By 1952, however, Rodríguez's lack of business savvy had taken its toll on relations with club leaders. In March, club president José J. Leon commissioned Narciso Saavedra and Pablo Soublet to investigate and seek repayment for a debt of $200 that Rodríguez owed to the club. It is unclear whether this debt came as the result of the contract he had made with the club to perform at the Ritmos de Otoño festival, but the evidence suggests at least some connection. The special commission met with Rodríguez in June to discuss the debt and reported to the board of directors that the bandleader believed his debt to be only $120 and that he had agreed to split that amount evenly with the club. Club leaders approved of this arrangement and closed the case, satisfied that they had resolved the matter.[43]

For the most part, Rodríguez and El Club Cubano enjoyed a strong and mutually beneficial relationship. At a general meeting he attended in July 1953, a report of club finances revealed less than positive projections for the club's future. Rodríguez immediately suggested that the club organize a dance to raise money for the treasury and offered his band at no cost, explaining that "this is the only Cuban organization and it shouldn't be allowed to fold."[44] The meaningfulness of Rodríguez's remark should not go unnoticed, particularly because it is quite clear that he knew about and even performed at events sponsored by other Cuban social clubs. In the city's *colonia cubana*, the fact that he positioned El Club Cubano as "the only Cuban organization" signifies the club's unique policy of racial and ethnic inclusiveness. More broadly, the club's openness and embrace of Cubans and Latino/as of color also stood as one of the only manifestations of the ideal of the Cuban nation as "transracial." In other words, perhaps what Rodríguez meant was that "this is the only Cuban organization" that includes and welcomes into its membership *all* Cubans, including Cubans of color such as himself.

Rodríguez performed for social events organized by other Cuban social clubs and managed to book engagements at commercial venues across the city. He was a fixture in the local neighborhood music scene, performing at events sponsored by Cuban social clubs and cultural organizations and many of the prominent Latin dance halls in New York City such as the Manhattan Center, the Palladium, and the Hunts Point Palace.[45] Rodríguez also performed at events sponsored by the Ateneo Cubano throughout the mid-1950s. In 1954, for instance, club leaders invited Gilberto Valdés and many of the other musicians performing in a mambo concert at Carnegie Hall to an informal gathering at their clubhouse. Among those who were invited were Rodríguez, José Curbelo, Tito Puente, and Noro Morales.[46] Members of the Ateneo Cubano were reportedly "overjoyed" that the club had once again hired Rodríguez, "who was so well-liked," to perform at an upcoming dance, a rather unexpected announcement given the club's reputation as less than friendly to and inclusive of Cubans of color, including musicians. Yet the decision to hire him is not so surprising, since his style and the tastes of those in attendance were "better suited for social and not exhibition dancing." As García has argued, Rodríguez represented a traditional Cuban style that Cuban audiences preferred, and it was not uncommon for social clubs with racially exclusive policies to enjoy Afro-Cuban popular music, especially because in these contexts it was likely framed and promoted as "Cuban" rather than "Afro-Cuban."[47]

Rodríguez's popularity was not limited to the *colonia cubana*. He also performed at events that targeted Puerto Rican, broader Latino/a, and black audiences. In 1954, for example, Rodríguez and Vicentico Valdés performed for El Morel Campos Social Club at its annual Miss Puerto Rico pageant held at the Manhattan Center. The Pan American Merchants Benevolent Association hired Rodríguez's *conjunto* in 1957 to perform at its annual banquet at the Hotel St. George, confidently concluding that "all of our community admires it."[48] Rodríguez also performed at the Palladium almost exclusively on Sundays. Whether because there was more room to dance or because of cheaper admission costs, Sundays at the Palladium drew a decidedly more working-class and African American, Afro-Cuban, and Afro-Puerto Rican clientele.[49] In 1952, Rodríguez performed at the dance hall's Una Noche en Habana (A Night in Havana), which featured "a parade of comparsas," a sort of nod to an Afro-Cuban spiritual past. He performed Afro-Cuban music and other Latin rhythms, including merengue, which likely helped him draw a broader Latino/a audience. At the Palladium's Carnaval de Oro (Carnival of Gold), he provided the music for the dance contest, which reportedly generated a great deal of anticipation among Hispanic dancers of merengue, mambo, and cha-cha-chá. One reporter alerted dancing patrons that Rodríguez's band would provide "pure rhythm."[50]

Like Socarrás, Rodríguez performed at the annual festival for poor Puerto Rican students held at Benjamin Franklin High School in 1951. Rodríguez's participation in this event initiated commentary that not only established him as a musician who was respected among his peers but also credited him as both an authentic and pioneering figure in the creation of Cuban music. A report in *La Prensa* noted that "Arsenio Rodríguez, whom Cuban musicians consider the true originator of mambo, will be seen and heard with his tres, giving the public a true demonstration of what is today called mambo, but was earlier known as capetillo and then son montuno."[51] "The well-known authority on folkloric Cuban music" spoke at length to another reporter about the origins of the mambo, tracing its history back to early 1940s Cuba and noting the influences of Afro-Cuban religious traditions. Though Rodríguez conceded that Cuban bandleaders should appreciate Pérez Prado for "facilitating for the American musician the interpretation in a certain way of Cuban music," he also insisted that Pérez Prado (who was also a Cuban of color but had much lighter skin and whose father was of Portuguese-Jewish background) had played no role in its creation. He framed his remarks as a matter of public record: "I make these clarifications with profound sentiment, because I don't like criticizing my fellow artists, especially my compatriots. But, I think this is the right time to do it, so that the public recognizes how history is written."[52] Many Cuban musicians, including Bauzá, Socarrás, Graciela, and Armando Sánchez, have agreed and have reproduced Rodríguez's history lesson in oral history interviews, acknowledging and valuing his innovations to Cuban music more than the widespread popularity and commercial successes of other more processed and packaged performers, even if those performers also happened to be black.[53]

Some music scholars and other musicians, however, have been less willing to accept Rodríguez's origin story, which far too easily dismisses Pérez Prado's role as a musical innovator. Cuban musicologist and historian Helio Orovio, for example, notes the early contributions of the *sones* of Rodríguez and the *danzones* of Israel "Cachao" López and Orestes "Macho" López to the development of the mambo. He concludes, however, that "the mambo as a form, as a structure, as a complete piece from top to bottom, he molds it into his works, instrumentations and piano, [Pérez Prado,] the mulatto from Matanzas." As early as 1945, trade magazines in Cuba reported that musicians and singers hailed Pérez Prado as "The Mambo King."[54] And in 1950, Afro-Cuban singer Beny Moré released "Locas por el Mambo," a dance hit that asked about the origins of the mambo with the lyrics "who invented the mambo / that drives the women crazy / that makes women blush?" The answer comes in the final line of the song, which declares unequivocally that the inventor is "a short, chubby guy with a seal face," a reference to the nickname that friends had given to Pérez Prado.

The point of this discussion is not to take sides or reach a consensus. The different memories that musicians and scholars have preserved and constructed about the origins of the mambo demonstrate, once more, that musical innovations do not happen overnight or in isolation.[55] The mambo that reached its peak of popularity in the early 1950s evolved from the influences of various musical contemporaries, including Rodríguez, Israel "Cachao" López, and Peréz Prado. As a musical style, it circulated in the United States, Cuba, Mexico, and elsewhere, and whether it "belonged" to Rodríguez or Peréz Prado, it was quite clearly (and perhaps not enough credit has been given to it as such) a form of black popular music that multiple and overlapping audiences enjoyed and identified as Cuban and Latin. It is not entirely surprising, then, that in 1946 José Curbelo recorded a song titled "El Rey del Mambo," which featured Tito Rodríguez as singer, and that the New York City and Miami press often referred to Curbelo (and other musicians, too) as "The Mambo King" throughout the 1950s.[56] In many ways, this sort of competition between performers was good for business. No matter how contrived such rivalries were, they got people on the dance floor and netted venue owners, record companies, concert promoters, and musicians larger profits. Given these advantages, it makes sense that Rodríguez and Pérez Prado and other musicians took part in "battle of the bands" concerts. In 1952, Rodríguez and Pérez Prado squared off at the Saint Nicholas Ballroom for an event that was billed as "one of the best musical battles of the year," an event that pitted "the creator of the mambo," Rodríguez, against its "most faithful exporter," Pérez Prado.[57]

Much has been written about Rodriguez's inability to secure lucrative earnings or to achieve crossover celebrity status throughout his musical career. Poor marketing, the fact that he acted as his own agent in negotiations with record producers, and generational taste differences precipitated by population changes and by the emergence of the salsa music industry all share part of the blame. Still, Bauzá cautioned one oral historian against reproducing the myth that the *tres* player died "poor and forgotten." He insisted that Rodríguez did not die in poverty and that he received sufficient royalties from his compositions to "live well."[58] Whatever his financial misfortunes and limited commercial appeal among white North American and international audiences, the Afro-Cuban composer enjoyed the respect and support of his fellow musicians. In 1947, a group of musicians and friends organized a festival in Rodríguez's honor at the Hotel Diplomat. The event featured performances by Rodríguez and many other popular entertainers, including Machito, Marcelino Guerra, Bobby Capó, Miguelito Valdés, Noro Morales, Olga Guillot, and Sexteto Puerto Rico.[59]

Ten years later, Puerto Rican event promoter Federico Pagani, who was a member of El Club Cubano, organized a birthday celebration for Rodríguez at Club Las Tres Antillas. More than 700 people attended what a reporter described as "one of the most affectionate manifestations of love offered to a musician." Pagani's membership in El Club Cubano suggests that affiliation with the club had some advantages in the entertainment world, including access to popular Cuban musicians and an already targeted network of potential consumers.[60]

THE MAKING OF A SPANISH-SPEAKING PUBLIC SPHERE

El Club Cubano and other Cuban cultural organizations in the city turned to the print and mass culture industries to publicize social events and musical performances, many of which featured Cuban musicians of color who were also club members. Pamphlets and bulletins printed and distributed by social clubs and organizations and advertisements and announcements published in the Spanish-language press contributed to a growing sense of Cubanidad that was particular to the residents of Cuban New York.[61] Leaders and members of El Club Cubano, recognizing the need for effective marketing, established a Comisión de Prensa y Propaganda (Committee for Press and Advertising) and publicized many of their social and cultural events in both *La Prensa* and *Diario de Nueva York* and on the radio in New York City. Often when planning their social and cultural events, club leaders discussed "the imperious need for double propaganda on radio and in the press." Problems and complaints about advertising sometimes developed into matters of contentious debate at club meetings. In 1949, one club member complained that the newspaper advertisement announcing an upcoming dance had appeared only the day before the event. The president of the Comisión de Prensa y Propaganda countered that a radio advertisement had aired for several days and argued that those are "more effective than newspaper ones."

But El Club Cubano did not rely exclusively on mass media outlets to advertise its events. The club also hung signs and posters and distributed small leaflets, or throwaways, throughout the city to publicize upcoming activities. El Club Cubano hoped that printing posters and throwaways in both Spanish and English would attract attendees from within and beyond the *colonia hispana*, and that included members of the non-Spanish-speaking world. Discussions about publicity for the Ritmos de Otoño dance, which featured Arsenio Rodríguez, resulted in the following advertising strategy: "Make one hundred posters in English and two hundred in Spanish. And the throwaways should be English on one side and Spanish on the other. . . . Let's advertise the dance in the newspapers *La Prensa* and *Diario de Nueva York* and on the radio."[62]

The Spanish-language newspapers of the city benefited financially from their relationships with Cuban social clubs such as El Club Cubano and the Ateneo Cubano. At a board of directors meeting in April 1958, leaders of El Club Cubano responded to an inquiry from *Diario de Nueva York* about the club's interest in placing an advertisement in a souvenir pamphlet for one of the newspaper's upcoming events. After a short discussion, club leaders agreed to place a $15 half-page advertisement. The relationship between the Spanish-language press and the Cuban social clubs of the city appears to have been mutually beneficial. Club records reveal that at that same meeting, members received complimentary tickets to the newspaper's annual spring dance.[63] That the relationship between El Club Cubano and *Diario de Nueva York* was interconnected is demonstrated by the fact that the club placed an advertisement congratulating the newspaper on its second anniversary and inviting the *colonia hispana* to its clubhouse in the Bronx to celebrate its fifth anniversary.[64]

Newspapers did more than profit directly from advertising revenues, though that was a critical component of the relationship. Both *La Prensa* and *Diario de Nueva York* wrote to El Club Cubano to confirm that the club would be placing its annual holiday greetings in the newspapers. Both newspapers hoped to become informational resources for club members and potential attendees at club events and activities. Other newspapers sought such relationships, too. For example, *Ecos de Nueva York* wrote to El Club Cubano in 1952 offering to put "at our disposal its pages and asking for our cooperation so that they can print on them our weekly social activities."[65] The social clubs of the city advertised their upcoming events and activities not only to ensure that club members stay informed but also as a means of recruiting new members and supporters from the *colonia cubana* and throughout the *colonia hispana*. In short, the Cuban social clubs and Spanish-language newspapers of New York City interacted to create and document a public sphere that reflected the ways club members specifically and the *colonia cubana* and *colonia hispana* more generally spent their leisure time. The associational life of the city emphasized entertainment and dancing, close relationships with Afro-Cuban musical performers, and, as we will see in the next chapter, the continued observance of Cuban national holidays. Advertisements in these newspapers indicate the rich variety of events and activities available to the *colonia hispana* and suggest that rivalry existed among the various Cuban clubs of the city: many of the clubs competed for audiences for events hosted on the same days and for similar purposes.

The relationship between the Spanish-language newspapers and Cuban social clubs of the city extended beyond finances and crossed over into shared involvement in social and cultural events. In 1949, *Diario de Nueva York* invited a member of El Club Cubano's leadership to be a juror at its upcoming beauty pageant. Meeting minutes indicate that Mrs. De La Paz agreed to participate in the newspaper's fund-raising event. That same year, the Comisión de Prensa y Propaganda organized a dinner-dance in honor of Afro-Cuban boxer Kid Gavilán and the Spanish-language newspapers of the city. A change to Kid Gavilán's fight schedule forced club leaders to postpone the event and place announcements in "the daily press" alerting potential guests of the cancellation. El Club Cubano, however, resolved to keep the social hall open and prepared to receive guests and offer dancing "with the victrola [record player]."[66]

Music and musical performances became the most visible public expressions and outward manifestations of socialization among club members and the *colonia hispana*. No less important to club life were the more private gatherings that took place in front of the television. Club leaders recognized the growing centrality of television in the everyday lives of its club members and in U.S. society.[67] They discussed purchasing a television set for the clubhouse at great length in the spring of 1950. The process of purchasing the club's television set was so well documented that it reveals the degree to which access to popular culture mattered to the success of the club and the satisfaction of its club members. The process was fraught with fund-raising issues and concerns about the cost of "such an expensive appliance." The Comisión de Actos Sociales (Social Activities Committee) organized a dance to raise money to purchase the television to avoid having to ask club members for direct contributions. The dance succeeded in raising a considerable amount of money, and the club's monthly newsletter announced that "soon we will hear everyone's happy exclamations because of the purchase of the television." Club member Alberto Baños suggested that the club purchase the television set at a store where he had been offered a 20 percent discount. Club leaders charged a five-member committee with the task of making a recommendation to the president about which television set to purchase. After its product research, the committee determined that the club should purchase a 16" Emerson television from La Casa Sigue [*sic*] at the price of $311.50, and by the summer of 1950 club leaders had installed the set in the clubhouse.[68] Eight years later, the club wanted an upgrade. Though fund-raising efforts began in June 1958, a dance held in the fall of that year failed to raise enough money and forced the club to use funds in its treasury to purchase its much-desired 27" television set.[69]

The public face of El Club Cubano, as represented by the social and cultural events it hosted that featured Afro-Cuban music and musicians, mattered in terms of helping shape club members' identities and constituting the city's broader Cuban American cultural landscape. Given its racial and ethnic inclusiveness, it also worked to make Afro-Cuban music and musicians and Cubanness and Afro-Cubanness central elements of a broader Hispano/a and Latino/a identity. These public events and activities were also the means to the more private end of facilitating members' socialization among each other, in this case to watch television. Members of El Club Cubano likely gathered around their newly purchased television set to watch professional boxing matches and baseball games. These televised sporting events featured the participation of a relatively large number of Cubans of color, and Afro-Cuban boxers such as Kid Gavilán and Nino Valdés often attended club events held in their honor.[70] Socialization in the private space of the club and principally among club members mattered, and both radio and television helped encourage this mode of engagement. In 1952, club leaders also raised funds to buy a record player for the clubhouse. At a dance held in honor of the *excursionistas*, the club managed to raise $102, a good sum of money but not enough to purchase the record player, according to Melba Alvarado, who suggested that they pay the remainder in installments. The next month, the club organized a dance at the Tropicana in the Bronx; proceeds went toward the purchase of an RCA Radiola radio.[71] In many ways, live musical performances, the print media, and radio and television, which eventually became the preferred mode of entertainment and source of information, helped forge a Spanish-speaking public. The next chapter looks at particular moments when that public came together and instances when the possibility of doing so proved more difficult.

3

A PLACE FOR NATION IN THE DIASPORA

Afro-Cuban singer Graciela Pérez, a lead vocalist for Machito y sus Afro-Cubans, recalled that the Ateneo Cubano denied Cubans of color entry into club events and charged that the club's members did not attend the band's performances. She reasoned that "we have no reason to be grateful to the [white] Cubans."[1] For the most part, the black and white Cuban social clubs of New York City maintained independent memberships and hosted separate events and activities, a coexistence that racially divided the Cuban American cultural landscape. That El Club Cubano, the Ateneo Cubano, and other Cuban social clubs offered black and white Cuban New Yorkers separate physical and discursive spaces to come together as members of the *colonia cubana* does not mean that moments of collaboration and cross-racial unity did not also take place in the 1940s and 1950s. There were moments of cooperation and solidarity, but there were also instances when racial, class, and political differences threatened to fracture the *colonia cubana* and the relationships forged with other Latino/as in the *colonia hispana*. Afro-Cuban popular music and musicians played important roles in these contexts, as did local city officials and representatives of the Cuban government, who, motivated by diplomatic and inter-American interests, intervened at key moments to make instances of cultural encounter and cross-ethnic exchange possible.

This chapter continues its focus on El Club Cubano and the Ateneo Cubano, but it expands its coverage to examine some of the lesser-known Cuban social clubs and Hispanic ethnic institutions in the city, offering close readings of key social and cultural events that were presented as Cuban patriotic celebrations and other events that were marked as pan-Latino/a festivities. As with the Ateneo Cubano, much of what I have uncovered about these seemingly less prominent Cuban social clubs—Club

Social Cuba, La Sociedad Maceo y Martí, and Logia Isla de Cuba, as just three examples—is limited to event announcements and advertisements in the city's Spanish-language newspapers and magazines. The absence of organizational records or meeting minutes for most of these clubs leaves the story of Cuban associational life somewhat incomplete. But this silence allows us to consider how Cuban and broader Hispano/a and Latino/a identity took shape, in part, by way of the Spanish-language press, which placed Cubanness and Afro-Cubanness on center stage for readers from a range of national origin groups.[2]

Cultural celebrations and nationalist commemorations took place in the private spaces of the Cuban social clubs and Hispanic ethnic institutions of New York City and in more public settings, including dance halls, nightclubs, and public parks. Both contexts should be understood as literal and symbolic spaces where the *colonia cubana* and *colonia hispana* came together. Social and cultural events that honored Cuban national holidays, diplomatic exchanges between Cuba and the United States, failed plans to erect a public memorial in honor of José Martí and Antonio Maceo, and responses to increased migration due to political turmoil on the island all reveal the social, cultural, and (a)political agendas of the city's various Cuban and Hispanic social clubs and organizations. These events and agendas illustrate more than the simple presence of Cubans or the complexity of the Cuban New York experience. This portrait also demonstrates the various ways the black and white Cubans of New York City negotiated their national identities on the terrain of popular culture from within two distinct, though sometimes overlapping, points of view: first, as Cubans of the diaspora who were negotiating ties to the island as they established roots in the city as a *colonia cubana*, and, second, as Cubans of the *colonia hispana*, which during this period took into account notions of inter-American and hemispheric unity and identity.

CUBAN SOCIAL CLUBS AND PATRIOTIC CELEBRATIONS

The thousands of Cubans living in New York City during the 1940s and 1950s came together at various points throughout the calendar year to observe Cuban national holidays and honor their national heroes. The Cuban American cultural landscape flourished as a space of patriotic symbolism and celebration. Social clubs and cultural organizations across the city offered their members numerous opportunities to attend poetry readings, lectures, conferences, musical performances, and dance events commemorating important dates and figures in Cuba's national history. These events, which included celebrations in honor of José Martí's birthday and commemorations of El Grito de Baire, El Grito de Yara, and Cuban independence, allowed Cuban New Yorkers to reconnect with the island and with each other through cultural practices that were marked by an essentialized and sanitized Cuban past. Whether these events were solemn remembrances or festive dance parties, they reflect the rich and varied presence of Cuban migrants and culture in the city and point toward a Cubanness framed by a transnational reality. However, despite the national and cultural unity such events suggest, the boundaries of politics, race, and class that led to the development of so many disparate Cuban social clubs did not quite fall to the wayside on these dates. Though now settled and, in many cases, flourishing in New York City, the black and white Cubans who participated in these patriotic celebrations engaged in a process of historical (mis)remembering that allowed them to look back nostalgically at the departed homeland, reflect critically on the island's struggles against Spanish colonialism, and demonstrate an ambivalence toward the closeness of U.S.-Cuba political, economic, social, and cultural relations.

On or about 28 January each year, Cuban social clubs such as El Club Cubano and the Ateneo Cubano invited members, family, and friends to join them in remembering the birth of José Martí. Historians interested in Cuban national identity have long focused on Martí's political leadership and national symbolism during and after Cuba's nineteenth-century struggle for independence, especially the anticolonial writer's declarations on slavery, race, and inter-Americanism.[3] El Club Cubano hosted events such as the annual Cena Martiana (Martí's Dinner Party) which offered guests a festive meal priced affordably at $2 per plate. The club also organized other commemorative events that gestured more toward symbolism and metaphor. In 1951, for example, members of the club visited the Cuban consulate in downtown New York City for the purpose of placing a single white rose at the entrance of the building, an obvious reference to Martí's "Cultivo una rosa blanca," one of the writer's most famous poems in which the white rose symbolizes friendship in both good and bad times. By performing the main action of the poem outside the embassy, club members signified the close (albeit not always positive) ties between Cuba and the United States generally and El Club Cubano and consular and diplomatic officials more specifically.[4] More than a simple act of cultural diplomacy, this sort of deliberate display of patriotic sentiment might also be seen as a reminder to Cuban government officials that Cubans of color expected to be considered and treated as equal and full members of the Cuban nation both on the island and abroad as members of the Cuban diasporic community of New York City.

Alongside officials from the Cuban consulate, the Cuban social clubs of New York City also celebrated the Grito de Yara on or about 10 October to commemorate the beginning of the Ten Years' War in 1868. Led by sugar planter, slaveholder, poet, and lawyer Carlos Manuel de Céspedes in Manzanillo in the eastern part of the island, the Grito de Yara was an armed insurrection that touched off the first war for Cuban independence from Spanish rule. Significantly, Céspedes freed the slaves on his sugar mill at the outset of the rebellion, "invit[ing] them to help 'conquer liberty and independence' for Cuba."[5] In 1946, the Cuban consul-general and his wife asked members of El Club Cubano to join them for a celebration of the anniversary of the Grito de Yara in NBC's Studio 8-H at 30 Rockefeller Plaza. The event featured musical compositions by Emma Otero, Ernesto Lecuona, Zoraida Marrero, Luis A. Bas Molina, and Ángel Reyes.[6] That the consul-general chose to invite members of El Club Cubano to this event makes sense given the date's significance, but his showcasing of music in the European classical tradition rather than Afro-Cuban popular music may have served to whiten and elevate the proceedings and, by extension, the Cuban diaspora.

Nineteen forty eight marked the eightieth anniversary of the Grito de Yara, and the various Cuban social clubs of the city made sure to commemorate the "patriotic date that the colonia cubana of this country celebrates with great animation." Afro-Cuban popular music was at the core of their celebrations. With "great enthusiasm spreading among the Cuban families and those of other colonias of this city," El Club Cubano invited guests to what one reporter for *Diario de Nueva York* described as "an elegant soiree" at the Embassy Ballroom. Club leaders decorated the ballroom with the flags of the United States and Cuba, and the event featured the "happy música típica" of Frank García's orchestra and the Conjunto Puerto Rico.[7] Club Social Cuba hosted a dance in its social hall that featured live music from the orchestra of Roberto Pérez, "offering an atmosphere of sincere cordiality for the prosperity of the Cuban republic."[8] Members and friends of the Ateneo Cubano, which the Spanish-language press described as a "refined Cuban entity" that was always attentive to its mission of presenting events of "sincere patriotism," attended one of the "better social events" of the weekend. The club hosted a dance at the Hotel Taft that promised "an atmosphere of fraternity and diversion of authentic Cubanidad." Guests enjoyed the "Antillean rhythms" provided by Orquesta Renovación and

Young girls performing at a Cuban cultural presentation hosted by the Ateneo Cubano de Nueva York, 1957. Courtesy of Justo A. Martí, Justo A. Martí Photograph Collection, Archives of the Puerto Rican Diaspora, Centro de Estudios Puertorriqueños, Hunter College, City University of New York.

paused briefly at midnight to observe the playing of both the U.S. and Cuban national anthems.[9]

Year after year, the city's Cuban social clubs also hosted musical and dance events to commemorate the Grito de Baire on or about 24 February in honor of the start of the War of Independence in 1895. Organized by Martí's Cuban Revolutionary Party, the Grito de Baire was the first time that rebels took up arms for the cause of Cuban independence in both the eastern and western provinces.[10] Since its founding in 1933, El Círculo Cubano, "the oldest Cuban society of this city" which was known to include only white Cubans, had celebrated the Grito de Baire as it did in 1940 with a dance at its club headquarters on 160th Street and Amsterdam Avenue.[11] In 1945, the Cuban society Maceo y Martí hosted a dance at the Grand Plaza in the Bronx that featured the "most criollo rhythms" of Machito and Graciela, Casino Tropical, and Toñito and his Conjunto Cubanacán.[12] In 1947, El Club Cubano invited members of the "colonia cubana and others of our language" to an evening event at the New York City Center in honor of the Grito de Baire and Cuban consul-general Reinaldo Fernández Rebull. The event, which was open to the entire *colonia hispana*, also marked the club's first attempt to raise funds for the Monumento Martí-Maceo.[13] In 1950 and 1951, El Club Cubano hosted "brilliant" dances that celebrated both the Grito de Baire and Washington's and Lincoln's Birthdays. The fact that U.S. and Cuban national holidays were jointly celebrated suggests not only the transnational loyalties, Pan-American sensibilities, and inter-American interests of club leaders and members, particularly with Cuban consul Mario León as guest of honor, but also the continued development of a Cuban American identity.[14]

The Ateneo Cubano, which one reporter described as a "progressive society, integrated by the Cuban individuals of this metropolis," celebrated the Grito de Baire in 1950 with a dance that featured the Tropical Knights. That same year, Club Social Cuba, which the press referred to as "the club of Amsterdam Avenue," hosted its own dance headlined by Orquesta Renovación; it was attended by "a large representation of the Cuban and Hispano-American sector of this neighborhood."[15] These characterizations suggest that some Cuban social clubs such as the Ateneo Cubano drew in Cubans from all across New York City, whereas others, such as Club Social Cuba, had a more limited, neighborhood-based appeal. Advertisements and news reports in the Spanish-language press positioned the Ateneo Cubano as "refined" and as hosting some of the "better social events" that were organized in the *colonia hispana*. The characterization is not entirely surprising, given the club's reputation of excluding Cubans and other persons of color from its membership and club spaces. More puzzling, particularly when compared to the more racially and ethnically inclusive practices of, for example, El Club Cubano, is that advertisements and news reports also framed the Ateneo Cubano as "progressive" and as creating "an atmosphere of fraternity." There is little evidence to suggest that the Ateneo Cubano acted as an agent of racial progress or fraternity, especially in terms of the ideology of the nineteenth-century Cuban independence movement. What these (self-)descriptions might suggest, however, is that the very practice of racial exclusion served to allow the Ateneo Cubano to claim a "refined" and "progressive" identity, one that relied on a sort of ritualized whitening of its Cubanness. It also shows the role, as we saw in chapter 2, of the Spanish-language press in enabling these clubs to fashion a public image and identity.

More than any other Cuban national holiday, Cuban Independence Day seemed to generate the greatest amount of interest among the city's Cubans in the 1940s and 1950s. Cuba had achieved its independence from Spain in 1898, but U.S. intervention and the signing of the Platt Amendment meant, as historian Louis A. Pérez reminds us, that "Cubans had achieved self-government without self-determination and independence without sovereignty. . . . Foreigners again ruled Cuba, again in the name of Cubans, but, as before, for their own ends." On 20 May 1902, U.S. military occupation of the island ended, and Tomás Estrada Palma became the republic's first elected president.[16] The Cuban social clubs of the city hosted some of their grandest events of the year to commemorate this date, offering club members, family, and friends a wide array of social and cultural events that included presentations by some of the most distinguished Cuban and Latin American intellectuals and poets in the city and performances by some of the most popular Cuban bands of the period.

The Ateneo Cubano hosted a variety of events in honor of Cuban independence.[17] Just a year after the club's founding in 1941, members and guests celebrated the anniversary of Cuban independence with two events that were broadcast via shortwave radio on NBC and were attended by the Cuban consuls in New York City. The first was a concert that featured the singing of the U.S. and Cuban national anthems and readings by Afro-Cuban reciter Eusebia Cosme, and the second was a dance held at the Hotel Vanderbilt that featured the music of José Curbelo. Interestingly, in these two cases, consular officials attended events sponsored by a white Cuban social club that featured an Afro-Cuban performer and Afro-Cuban popular music. In certain contexts, as we have seen, expressions of black popular culture could be rendered "Cuban" rather than "Afro-Cuban." Again in 1946, the Ateneo Cubano organized a dance at the Hotel Park Lane attended by "a select group of Cubans and those from other Hispanic nationalities." Juanito Sanabria's orchestra played dance music and performed the U.S., Cuban, and Puerto Rican national anthems. Cuban consul Luis A. Bas Molina, Inspector General Ramón San Román, and a representative from Argentina attended what one report deemed as this club's "best event yet." Reviews of the Ateneo Cubano's 1947 Cuban independence celebration described the event at the Hotel Biltmore in midtown as a "formal" and "elegant" dance that was accompanied by the orchestra of Enrique Navarro and noted that "a select group of Cuban residents enjoyed hours of exquisite dancing."[18]

Frequent descriptions and (self-)representations such as "select" and "elegant" indicate that the Ateneo Cubano had and hoped to maintain its reputation as a club for white and light-skinned members of the *colonia cubana* and *colonia hispana*, a characterization that is supported by evidence of the club's practices of racial exclusion and discrimination. "Select" and "elegant" should be understood as coded words that reflected the club's racial and class biases. The club's decision to hire Afro-Cuban performers such as Eusebia Cosme and Arsenio Rodríguez does little to counter these realities. It does, however, confirm elements of the historical processes by which upper-class whites appropriated and eventually repackaged black popular culture for middle-class consumption.[19]

El Club Cubano inaugurated its clubhouse and held its first public social event on 20 May 1946. The celebrations held each year on this date commemorated both the anniversary of Cuban independence and the anniversary of the founding of the club, merging in the imaginary of club members and Cubans across the city a date of dual significance.[20] El Club Cubano organized a variety of joint celebrations, including a 1947 "artistic-cultural program" that featured poetry, speeches, music, and a buffet dinner and a 1950 dance at the Park Garden that featured club members and bandleaders Marcelino Guerra and Arsenio Rodríguez.[21] At the joint celebration in 1957, club leaders presented Cuban performers Panchito Riset, Machito, and Vicentico Valdés with honorary diplomas. The event also featured poetry readings by Eusebia Cosme and the debut of Arsenio Rodríguez's most famous patriotic song, "Adórenla como Martí." The song recalled many of the most important fighters for Cuban independence, leaders such as Roberto Bermudez López, Ignacio Agramonte, Quintín Bandera, Carlos Manuel de Céspedes, Francisco Vicente Aguilera, Guillermo Moncada, Antonio Maceo, and José Martí. In calling by name white Cubans and Cubans of color who fought and died for an independent Cuba, a nation that promised transracial unity and freedom to all Cubans, the song, as ethnomusicologist David F. García explains, "appeals to all Cubans to resolve their differences in peace and love and to unite the country so that the sacrifices of the Cuban independence patriots would not have been in vain."[22] That Rodríguez would debut this song at El Club Cubano makes sense, given the fact that he had once praised the club as "the only Cuban organization." The following year, El Club Cubano again presented honorary diplomas to "distinguished exponents of música criolla," praising these musicians for "disseminat[ing] Cuban music in this country." The "very crowded" event, held at the club's social hall, honored Puerto Rican bandleader Noro Morales and Afro-Cuban musicians Gilberto Valdés, Mario Bauzá, Arsenio Rodríguez, and Alberto Socarrás.[23] At this event, club leaders celebrated Afro-Cuban musicians (and a Puerto Rican bandleader known for performing Afro-Cuban music) for popularizing Cuban music among audiences in the United States. This acknowledgment suggests how in certain settings—not surprisingly, as we see here, in one dominated by Cubans of color—black Cuban musicians could be credited as cultural agents of Cubanness, not just of Afro-Cubanness.

Though the Cuban social clubs and cultural organizations of New York City hosted and advertised separate events, members of the *colonia cubana* and *colonia hispana* sometimes came together to commemorate Cuban patriotic holidays. Beginning in the mid-1940s, celebrations in honor of Cuban independence brought together the city's various associations and Cuban New Yorkers who had yet to be affiliated with particular clubs or groups. In 1945, Agrupación Social Cubana, Club Continental, and the Centro Social Puertorriqueño cohosted a dance at the Hotel Diplomat that featured the orchestras of Noro Morales and Cuban bandleader Luis Varona. Reports before the event boasted that the parade of artists on stage would represent Cuba, Puerto Rico, the Dominican Republic, and Mexico, a marketing strategy that marked this event as both Cuban and pan-Latino/a.[24] This sort of event that represented the greater Spanish-speaking Americas must have resonated with audiences, just as Cubanness was becoming more and more central to Hispanidad and Latinidad.

Independent celebrations also took place. In 1946, several Cuban families in New York City, led by Cuban journalist José M. de Poo, met for the purpose of forming a "society that represents Cuba abroad." One of their first goals was to organize an event to celebrate the founding of the Cuban republic. A few days after that initial planning session, this "select group of Cuban families" met once again at El Fundador restaurant to commemorate Cuban independence and strategize further about establishing the new society. In another part of the city, passersby likely noticed the Cuban flags adorning the Rinconcito Criollo restaurant, where Cuban families gathered more informally to commemorate the holiday.[25] Cuban New Yorkers made it clear that there was certainly a place for nation in the diaspora.

Patriotic commemorations oftentimes merged with celebrations of commercial popularity and achievement, generating the participation of well-known and sought-after Cuban musicians and entertainers and securing endorsement from some of the city's most popular Latin nightclubs. La Sociedad Maceo y Martí hosted a dance at the Audubon Ballroom in 1945 not only in honor of Cuban Independence Day but also to congratulate Machito and his orchestra for completing their third successful year as the house band at La Conga. The event featured performances by Machito, Luis Varona, Marcelino Guerra, and Carlos Varela. The following year, La Conga hosted its own celebration in honor of Cuban independence that featured Miguelito Valdés and "a group of Cuban and Hispanic-

American personalities."[26] Nationalist sentiments, intra- and interethnic cooperation, and popular entertainment intersected in meaningful ways during many of the independence day celebrations organized throughout the 1940s and 1950s. It seems likely, of course, that commercial celebrations of Cuban patriotism took place because there was money to be made in these types of festivities. In 1951, promoters at the Palladium organized a dance dedicated to Cuban independence headlined by the bands of Marcelino Guerra, Arsenio Rodríguez, Tito Puente, and Tito Rodríguez, "four popular orchestras specializing in Antillean and Hispanic-American rhythms." The following year was the fiftieth anniversary of Cuban independence, and the Palladium once again hosted an event that was both an authentic patriotic celebration and a "grand" commercial affair. The event featured "twenty-five Cuban artists of the theater, movie screen, and television in this metropolis," including Miguelito Valdés, Arsenio Rodríguez, Mario Bauzá, and Machito. Those in attendance enjoyed hours of live music and dancing and the opportunity to express their Cubanidad in a setting that extended beyond the private confines of the social clubs.[27]

THE POLITICS OF CUBAN AND LATINO/A COLLABORATION

On 11 March 1946, more than two months before its first official meeting, El Club Cubano joined with five other Cuban social clubs, organizations, and associations in the city to offer words of support and encouragement for Cuban president Ramón Grau San Martín. Grau had led the Cuban government for 100 days in 1933 and returned to the nation's top post from 1944 to 1948. He had been elected in 1944 on a platform of continued constitutional reforms, though by the end of his term, these promises had been betrayed by government corruption, mismanagement, and public disillusionment. The joint letter the clubs drafted, which was signed by Generoso Pedroso of El Club Cubano, Francisco de Peña of the Ateneo Cubano and the presidents of the Centro Artesanos Cubano, Club Social Cuba, Logia Isla de Cuba, and Club Habana, suggests the potential for cross-racial and cross-class Cuban unity through engagement with island politics. Transracial unity across class could sometimes be achieved in a Cuban national context that was imagined from within the diaspora. Interestingly, the fact that one of its earliest acts as a social and cultural club was, in effect, a political endorsement seemed to have been lost on the leaders and members of El Club Cubano, who maintained that the club lacked formal political interests. Though historians have emphasized that the racial legacies of Spanish colonialism limited interactions between white Cubans and Cubans of color and led Afro-Cubans to associate more often with African Americans, a collective sense of Cubanidad trumped racial divisions and class biases at critical moments during the 1940s and 1950s.[28]

Cubans in New York City had, in fact, already proven their ability to come together in 1944 as they worked to raise money for the island's recovery from a devastating Category Three hurricane. The Comité Pro Ayuda a Cuba, backed by the Cuban consul and the Ateneo Cubano, responded to this tragedy by sponsoring a fund-raising event at the Essex House. Organizers decorated the ballroom with the flags of Cuba, the United States, and the Red Cross and promised performances by Miguelito Valdés and other Broadway artists and a dance with music by Alberto Iznaga's La Siboney and Isla de Cuba de Montes de Oca. The "colonia hispana responded generously" to this fund-raising campaign, as did diplomatic officials and members of the *colonia hispana* of Washington, D.C., who traveled to New York City to attend the event. The following month, the Comité Pro Ayuda a Cuba organized another fund-raising event at the Manhattan Center that featured "Cuban artists of well-deserved fame" and music by "two good hispanic orchestras of the city," Isla de Cuba and Los Segundo Afro Cubanos de Varona.[29]

The push for unity in the *colonia cubana* resonated with the calls for hemispheric unity across national borders that were common in the 1940s and 1950s. Motivated by the spirit of good neighborliness and the ideologies and everyday practices of Pan-Americanism that marked this period, local politicians and Cuban diplomats often helped commemorate Cuban independence and reflect positively on the history of U.S.-Cuba relations.[30] The year 1950 marked the one hundredth anniversary of the flying of the Cuban flag from the top of the Sun Building in downtown Manhattan, and this historic date prompted New York City mayor William O'Dwyer to send a telegram to Cuban president Carlos Prío Socarrás offering congratulations to the people of Cuba: "The ties that have existed between our two countries have always been very close, but because the flag of your republic was first raised in this city we New Yorkers consider it a privilege to unite ourselves with you in these celebrations."[31] On 19 May, Cuban Flag Day, Cuban flags flew all across the city in honor of Cuban independence. One reporter found Cuban flags hoisted atop city landmarks, hotels, and the homes of distinguished New York businessmen, and a flag and enormous billboard with a greeting for the Cuban people stood on the corner of 34th Street and Broadway, "the most walked on corner in the world."[32] This commemoration allowed all New Yorkers, Cubans and others alike, to make claims on the legacy of U.S.-Cuba relations, a move that simultaneously evoked the early twentieth-century development of the *colonia cubana* in the city and whitewashed the less than positive results of U.S. involvement on the island. For Cuban New Yorkers of this period, what might have been regarded as part of Cuban national history could now be framed as equally relevant to and part of U.S. national history.

Through advertisements and announcements placed in the pages of the Spanish-language press, Cuban consular officials played key roles in shaping Cuban ethnic identity and broadcasting the presence of the Cuban diasporic community within the broader *colonia hispana*. These officials routinely attended many of the social and cultural events sponsored by El Club Cubano and the Ateneo Cubano, and several times during the 1950s, they placed announcements in *La Prensa* that addressed the entire *colonia cubana* on the date of Cuban independence. In many ways, these statements served to unite the *colonia cubana* using nationalist sentiment, reminding them, as one such statement declared, of the "prosperity of our nation on this glorious date as a reaffirmation of our freedoms."[33] Cuban consular officials thus played an important role in shaping the social and cultural identities of Cubans living abroad by emphasizing the significance of the homeland in the diaspora. This task included working to maintain positive relations with local officials in New York City. In 1951, for example, Cuban ambassador Luis Machado presented New York City mayor Vincent R. Impellitteri with La Orden Nacional de Mérito Carlos Manuel de Céspedes in recognition of his "interamerican good neighborliness and solidarity in peace and in war." The mayor responded kindly, promising: "I will be a friend of the Cubans as both the mayor of New York and as a mere citizen. Cuba has a place in my heart."[34]

Diplomatic exchanges between Cubans living in New York City and visitors from the island also took place in the 1940s and 1950s, and many involved musical performances by popular Cuban entertainers. El Club Cubano routinely welcomed *excursionistas* and hosted musical events and dances in their honor. A 1947 club newsletter detailed how the *excursionistas* were welcomed with a "magnificent dance reception" that sought "to strengthen the ties between Latin American residents in this city and visitors." Other dances in their honor featured Alberto Iznaga, and Arsenio Rodríguez offered a memorable performance in 1951 that included the introduction of a new dance known as "El Pinguino."[35]

Historian Frank Guridy has noted the rise in Afro-Cuban travel to the United States in the late 1940s and early 1950s thanks to tourist excursions arranged by the Cuban-American Good-will Association, which he described as an "obscure organization . . . that promoted cultural exchanges between Afro-Cubans and African Americans." Under the leadership of Sergio "Henry" Grillo and Pedro Portuondo Calá, a Havana-based journalist and writer for *El País*, the Cuban-American Good-will Association coordinated travel for Afro-Cuban visitors and seems to have been "an attempt to profit from the emerging market in black tourism."[36] In August 1950, a writer for the *Atlanta Daily World* reported that "about 40 members of the Cuban-American Good-will Association" visited Washington, D.C. "to get a close-up view of the operation of the U.S. government and to obtain first-hand knowledge of the social, economic and political life of American citizens, especially the minority groups." During this fourth annual trip, the Cuban delegation participated in ceremonies at Howard University, a Franciscan monastery, and various foreign embassies and "had dinner at the Club Cubano Interamericano Club house and attended the Cleveland-Washington baseball game."[37] It is not clear exactly what sort of formal connections El Club Cubano had with the Cuban-American Good-will Association, but at the very least an informal relationship and mutual interest in facilitating tourist exchanges and Afro-Cuban travel seems evident. El Club Cubano organized trips for club members and *excursionistas* to other parts of the United States, including Washington, D.C., and Bridgeport, Connecticut, and even to Niagara Falls in Canada.[38] To commemorate the anniversary of Cuban independence in May 1951, for example, members of El Club Cubano traveled to Washington, D.C., where they visited the Capitol Building and stopped for a short time at Howard University to place flowers before the busts of Martí and Maceo (which perhaps also served as further motivation for club members to work toward erecting a similar public memorial in New York City). Later that evening, they attended a banquet hosted in their honor by members of the Club Cubano Inter-Americano of Washington, D.C., which seems to have been distinct from the Comité Cubano de Washington Guridy has identified. Ambassador Luis Machado had notified club leaders that those traveling to the capital city would also be received at a reception at the Cuban embassy there.[39]

Despite moments of cross-racial and cross-class collaboration and manifestations of friendship between Cuban New Yorkers, Cuban visitors from the island, and Cubans settled elsewhere in the United States, maintaining these alliances sometimes proved a difficult task, even at the local level. A few days after its first official club event, founders of El Club Cubano explained that they had organized the club "to promote the coming together of the social life of all the Cuban residents in this city, who for diverse reasons remain inexplicably distant from one another." Hinting at ethnic, racial, and political divisions in the *colonia cubana* and *colonia hispana* of the city, the founding members of the club aimed to establish harmonious relationships with "all of our brothers that form part of the diverse colonias hispanas of this metropolis."[40]

The Liga Internacional de Acción Bolivariana, also known as the Good Neighbors Center of New York, did its part to bring together the disparate Cubans and Cuban social clubs of the city. In 1950, this civic organization coordinated a meeting with "personalities representing the New York's colonia cubana and leaders of Cuban organizations such as the Ateneo Cubano, Club Social Cuba and Club Cubano Interamericano." The meeting resulted in a resolution to celebrate a joint act to honor the Cuban flag at the Teatro Rivoli.[41] Two years later, Acción Bolivariana invited leaders and members of El Club Cubano to participate in a parade to celebrate Cuban Independence Day. Ángel Ramón Ruiz, president of Acción Bolivariana, attended El Club Cubano's board of directors meeting on 14 April, which (perhaps intentionally) was held on Pan-American Day. Ruiz hoped to convince club leaders that the parade "had no connection whatsoever with anything political or partisan, that it was solely a demonstration from New York's colonia hispana to the Cuban people." His insistence that the parade had no political undertones suggests that the *colonia cubana* might have been at odds on political matters and that El Club Cubano had successfully publicized its mission as apolitical. Club president Narciso Saavedra responded that "since its foundation the club has lent its cooperation at all times to the civic and social acts of the colonia hispana" and agreed to ask club members to participate in the parade. News coverage of this event confirmed that Acción Bolivariana did indeed organize "a program of apolitical acts." For El Club Cubano, it seems that its "apolitical" agenda had very little to do with formal affiliations with U.S. or Cuban political parties and much more to do with maintaining the inclusiveness and openness, regardless of a person's race, ethnicity, politics, and religion, that came to define the club in this period. Any sort of political association or mobilization by members of a social club and cultural organization made up mostly of Afro-Cubans could have been interpreted by others in the *colonia cubana* and *colonia hispana* as both radical and potentially threatening to the community's safety and status quo. By rejecting politics, broadly understood, members of El Club Cubano likely hoped to avoid these (mis)characterizations. In doing so, club leaders demonstrated, as historian Nancy Raquel Mirabal has argued, an implicit understanding that political mobilization by Afro-Cubans specifically or on the basis of race more generally, as had been the case in late nineteenth- and early twentieth-century Cuba, often yielded increased repression and limited social mobility.[42]

Yet this lack of formal political involvement in local city affairs was not entirely unique to Afro-Cubans or members of El Club Cubano. For many Cuban New Yorkers, political involvement as long-term residents of New York City and concern for political events on the island were fundamentally distinct and separate things. One Cuban hinted that lack of engagement could be blamed on limited political representation: "In my country I was only involved and paid attention to political matters but here I've never been interested in it. . . . I'd like to see more hispanics involved in politics. We have a right to it. We are a great majority among the minorities." Another Cuban noted divisions in the *colonia hispana*, explaining, "We lack interest in the affairs of nuestra colonia. This general apathy is harmful for everyone. Before anything else we need to come together, not do so much harm to one another. And above all cooperate in our affairs."[43] Remarks such as these indicate the extent to which some Cuban migrants self-identified not only as Cubans but also as Hispanos.

Each spring throughout the 1940s and 1950s, Acción Bolivariana took the lead in organizing a week of Pan-American celebrations in New York City that culminated with a parade on 14 April. According to a reporter for *La Prensa*, Pan-American Day celebrated "the ideal of inter-American solidarity that was one of the most prized objectives of the liberator Simón Bolívar."[44] Cuban participation in Pan-American celebrations peaked in 1950, when Juanito Sanabria's orchestra performed at a formal dance hosted by Acción Bolivariana at the Manhattan Center, Cuban soldiers marched in the Pan-American Day parade, and the Ateneo Cubano asked that all of its members who had served in the U.S. armed forces wear their military medals when they walked in the parade as representatives of the club.[45] The following year, the Ateneo Cubano selected nearly 150 young women to ride on floats and in cars during the Pan-American Day parade and hosted a dance at its social hall that featured Orquesta Renovación and "distinguished Cuban families."[46] In contrast to the eager participation of the Ateneo Cubano, some members of El Club Cubano expressed less enthusiasm. In 1951, the club received an invitation from Acción Bolivariana to participate in its annual Pan-American Day parade. Club member Alberto Baños objected to club participation, charging that Acción Bolivariana had sponsored activities in the past and had not invited the club, a reference, perhaps, to the kind of silent but deliberate racial exclusion Melba Alvardo described. Despite this protest, club leaders eventually agreed to participate.[47]

There were numerous instances of debate among El Club Cubano members about whether they should collaborate with other Cuban and pan-Latino/a associations. In 1951 and 1952, the club received letters from the Union Martí-Maceo in Tampa requesting financial help with funding for the construction of its clubhouse and inviting club members to an assembly in its social hall. Records do not indicate what the club finally decided on the matter, although the requests touched off significant discussion.[48] Also in 1952, Félix Navarro, president of the Comité Hispano Americano del Bronx, attended the board of directors meeting to discuss the upcoming Semana Hispano Americano del Bronx (Bronx Hispanic American Week). Navarro, who seemed to be aware of El Club Cubano's public stance against politics or political affiliations, insisted that his organization was "not political even though it is usually branded that way" and complained that the club "had never lent its sought-after cooperation." Navarro wanted club leaders to explain the reason for their distance, especially since the committee worked to improve the social life of the *colonia hispana* in the Bronx. He charged that "El Club Cubano is the only institution based in this district that has not, at any time, cooperated." Club leaders responded that they had not received the organization's previous solicitations for help and promised that they would participate in the future.[49]

Though members of El Club Cubano seemed to be keenly aware of the club's mission to avoid political or religious expression, they found ways to negotiate, circumvent, and ignore these expectations. In 1957, for example, El Club Cubano hosted a dance on 8 September in honor of the women in the club named Caridad, affectionately known as "Cachitas."[50] By referencing Cuba's patron saint and nationalist symbol the Virgen de la Caridad del Cobre (Our Lady of Charity), who also shared the "Cachita" nickname, the club's celebration had, at the very least, veiled religious connotations. The event was held on the same date as the saint's Catholic feast day, and most in the *colonia cubana* would have made the connection. Although El Club Cubano seems to have wanted to prevent any direct association with Afro-Cuban religious practices that might draw criticisms from white Cubans, by masking the event as a simple celebration of women in the club named Caridad, club leaders engaged in a process of erasure, disassociating themselves and the club from the Virgen de la Caridad as the incarnation of Ochún (the *orisha* who represents love, femininity, and beauty) and themselves as believers in and practitioners of *santería* and other Afro-Cuban spiritual traditions.[51] The following year, the board of directors agreed to place a statue of the Virgen de la Caridad in the club office, noting that it was a gift donated by Silvio Hernández. Club member

Cesar Telles cautiously agreed that the club could accept the statue "so long as the rules of the rule book are met, that this Club is neither political nor religious." He worried that placing the statue on club property threatened to blur the boundaries between religion and politics, on the one hand, and social life and culture, on the other. By insisting that the club's intentions in this instance were neither political nor religious, members believed that they were still operating within the rules and expectations set forth in the mission statement.[52]

Most other Cuban social clubs celebrated the feast of the patron saint of Cuba with little concern that the musical events they sponsored merged religious and cultural expressions with nationalist sentiment. One report revealed the collective enthusiasm of the *colonia cubana*: "Día de la Virgencita prieta. . . . In all of Cuba and everywhere that Cubans who have faith in the Virgencita del Cobre reside, this date will be celebrated, and in many homes in New York. . . . The Virgen de la Caridad counts on thousands of devotees, not just Cubans but those of all nationalities."[53] This report described the patron saint as "the little dark-skinned Virgin," suggesting an awareness of the competing origin myths surrounding the figure's appearance. In the most widely accepted and familiar legend, the Virgin figure appeared to three fishermen, one black, one white, and one Indian, on the shores of eastern Cuba. A less well-known version of the legend, one that was first produced by Juan Moreno at El Cobre, a copper-mining community of royal slaves, claims instead that the Virgin appeared to two Indian and one black fishermen. The slaves at El Cobre paid direct tribute to the Spanish Crown without the direct control of overseers or masters, a unique mode of slavery that shared more in common with the indigenous system of exploitation practiced in parts of South America than with the familiar patterns of plantation life in the Caribbean. Though historian María Elena Díaz has argued that for eighteenth-century royal slaves in El Cobre the Virgin symbolized local roots and the local community, by the late nineteenth and early twentieth centuries the figure and apparition story had assumed national significance. Cuban New Yorkers and others in the *colonia hispana* continued to reproduce these stories in perhaps a modified form. By marking the "little Virgin" as "prieta" rather than "negra," as dark-skinned and visibly nonwhite but not quite "black," the description suggests a process of racialization that exchanged the blackness of Juan Moreno's legend for a racial mixture that would include the white fisherman of the more dominant and enduring origin myth.[54]

Devotion to the Virgen de la Caridad prompted even Cubans who rarely participated in activities sponsored by the city's Cuban organizations to join in the commemorations. Mary Lynn Conejo, whose mother settled in New York City in 1946 because of health problems and whose father arrived in 1949 after he lost his job working on trolley cars in Cuba, remembered that her family attended mass each year on the patron saint's feast day.[55] In 1943, the Comité Cubano organized a dance at the Palm Garden that featured musical performances by Alberto Socarrás and poetry recitations by Eusebia Cosme. Proceeds from this event benefited the "hispanic" Iglesia de Nuestra Señora de la Milagrosa (Church of Our Lady of the Miraculous Medal), located on 114th Street and Seventh Avenue. Cuban promoter Fernando Luis acted as host, and reviews of the event noted that "the flute solos of Socarrás were without a doubt the best artistic detail of the night." The next day Cuban priest Father P. Manuel Mendiola celebrated mass at the church in honor of the Virgen de la Caridad. Cuban consul-general Cayetano de Quesada attended, and the celebration featured the singing of the Cuban national anthem and a salute to the Cuban flag. The mass in honor of Cuba's patron saint at the Milagrosa Catholic church became a tradition that continued throughout the 1940s and 1950s.[56] The Ateneo Cubano also organized dances in honor of the Virgen de la Caridad and celebrated the saint's feast day at its clubhouse by placing flowers on an altar in her honor.[57] That the predominantly whites-only Ateneo Cubano hosted private and public events to commemorate the Virgen de la Caridad also indicates the whitening or creation of a *mestizo* apparition story that served to deemphasize the blackness of the national symbol.

THE CAMPAIGN FOR A MONUMENTO MARTÍ-MACEO

If the number and variety of celebrations organized in New York City in honor of Cuban independence are any indication of local regard for national symbolism and national heroes, then it should come as no surprise that throughout the 1940s and 1950s leaders and members of El Club Cubano devoted themselves to the cause of erecting a monument in New York City to commemorate both José Martí and Antonio Maceo. These Afro-Cubans united the significance of Martí and Maceo in their private and public memories, revealing some of the competing (albeit sometimes silent) discourses about race, nation, and identity that circulated within the *colonia cubana*. Cubans had long recognized Martí as a national hero who was responsible for uniting black and white Cubans in the cause of Cuban independence from Spain. In his oft-cited political essay "Mi Raza," Martí explained, "In Cuba, there is no fear of a racial war. Men are more than whites, mulattos, or Negroes. Cubans are more than whites, mulattos, or Negroes. On the field of battle, dying for Cuba, the souls of whites and Negroes have risen together into the air." Historian Ada Ferrer argues that Martí "professed the equality of all races . . . boldly asserting that there was no such thing as race." This understanding of racelessness, or rather of Cubanness over race, she explains, "was less the product of miscegenation than of masculine heroism and will" that left "intact racial categories like white and black" and "exclud[ed] women from the symbolic birth of the nation," though these critiques were not openly acknowledged by Cuban New Yorkers.[58]

Known as "the Bronze Titan," Maceo was a Cuban of color who joined the Cuban independence movement in 1868 as a foot soldier and eventually rose to the rank of general under the guidance of Máximo Gómez, the Dominican-born commander of Cuba's revolutionary forces during the War of Independence. Maceo's leadership won him the respect of black and white men. However, Ferrer explains that unlike white leaders, Maceo "always accorded the questions of emancipation and racial equality the same importance as the question of political independence." During the Ten Years' War, rumors circulated that Maceo wanted to establish a black republic with himself as absolute ruler. He refuted these accusations and warned that the rebel cause would suffer because of "the politics of selfishness and racism," a prediction that seemed to presage the reasons for El Club Cubano's eventual inability to secure a public memorial for the black general.[59]

That the leaders and members of El Club Cubano sought to erect a public memorial in honor of *both* Martí and Maceo confirmed the club's vision of racial inclusion and openness. Discussions and debates about the monument, however, never mentioned Maceo's blackness. In fact, no reference to his color ever made it into club records. But the link between Martí and Maceo can be traced to the colonial legacies of African and Spanish mixture on the island. When asked what he missed most about his homeland, a Cuban journalist named Gonzalo de Palacio who now lived in New York City noted that Cubans are "proud of the Spanish and African heritage and have a sense of justice for those who founded their nation."[60] The desire for a statue to honor Martí and Maceo reflected the cross-racial ideals of the revolutionary movement of nineteenth-century Cuba, but for the leaders and members of El Club Cubano it also reflected contemporary and everyday concerns about racial discrimination, exclusion, and erasure. It makes sense that the club remained so committed to realizing its plans for a Monumento Martí-Maceo.

The club organized countless social and fund-raising events to achieve this goal and solicited the support and involvement of consular and local political officials in New York City and Cuba. To say that club affairs and morale hinged on the successful erection of a Monumento Martí-Maceo would be no overstatement.[61] Just a few months after El Club Cubano's founding, club leaders began their efforts to secure a memorial for Martí and Maceo. A 1946 memorandum from the president of the Sección de Asuntos Económicos (Department of Economic Affairs) to the board of directors about an event organized to honor the consul-general reveals some of the inner workings of the club's event-planning agenda. The guidelines that committee members who were organizing this celebration established demonstrate the interconnectedness of popular culture, Pan-Americanism, and symbolic nationalism: "Said event should be in a first-class place, preferably downtown. . . . The artists that participate should be professionals. . . . Two speakers with well-known influence in the Inter-American opinion should be invited. . . . The entrance fee will go toward covering expenses and the remainder will be the initial funds for the monuments. . . . At said event the plans for the monuments should be revealed but there should not be a special collection."[62] The following year, El Club Cubano organized a musical event at the Audubon Ballroom that featured Miguelito Valdés as host and performances by "well-known artists" such as Olga Guillot, Chano Pozo, and Marcelino Guerra. Reports announced that proceeds from the event would go toward the monument for Martí and Maceo and projected that "given the character of the party and the work put in by the organizers, a large crowd is expected to attend." That month's club newsletter offered appreciative remarks to "our great Babalú" and to Mr. Vincent Michael Lee of Theater, Inc., who "without being from our homeland" helped choreograph the fund-raiser. But with that statement of thanks also came a forceful admonishment: "It's a good time to mention Mr. Lee's gesture so that it may serve as a lesson to many Cubans mad with patriotism, but of no action . . . [especially] those who boast about contributing and those that wish to have their image printed in newspapers just for show."[63] Club leaders called members to action and asked that they abandon patriotic rhetoric as a means of personal gain.

Leaders and members of El Club Cubano were determined to secure a public memorial to honor Martí and Maceo's heroism and recognize the roles both men played in the founding of the Cuban republic. In the private space of its clubhouse, El Club Cubano managed to procure smaller, but no less loved and protected, statues of the two patriots. In 1950, one club member complained that the bust of Maceo had been placed "in a very bad spot" in the social hall. In response, those present at the meeting "promised to correct the mistake." A bust of Martí also adorned the club's social hall thanks to a gift donated by Cuba's secretary of education in 1951.[64]

The project of erecting the Monumento Martí-Maceo mattered to both Cuban New Yorkers and Cubans on the island. The project took on diplomatic significance as numerous government officials in Cuba indicated their interest in the memorial. Words of support and encouragement from consular officials and local government officials in Cuba poured in throughout the club's long campaign for the monument. In November 1947, El Club Cubano received a letter from Cuban consul-general Reinaldo Fernández Rebull pledging his cooperation with the club's initial goal of erecting a bust of Maceo in a public place in the city.[65] The club also received letters from several members of the Cuban Senate and House of Representatives, each letter expressing "great interest in such a patriotic and noble desire" and echoing themes of "cooperation and affection for the [Martí-Maceo] project."[66] Francisco Orue, mayor of Marianao, wrote to club president Narciso Saavedra in May 1951: "I pray that success meets the labor of your members and that the monument to Martí and Maceo in that city will soon be a reality, like an eternal public exhibition, of the democratic relations that unite the countries of the Americas."[67]

Throughout the 1940s and 1950s, diplomatic excursions to and from Cuba were specifically aimed at raising support for the monument. Members of El Club Cubano led the patriotic cause. In 1948, El Club Cubano hosted Cuban journalist Portuondo Calá during his visit to New York City, where he planned to meet with Mayor O'Dwyer on behalf of Havana mayor Nicolás Castellanos. He also hoped to participate in "activities related to the project of erecting a monument in this city in honor of the leaders of Cuban independence José Martí and Antonio Maceo." The club organized a "magnificent buffet" in honor of Calá's visit, and in his remarks at the dinner he noted the various activities taking place in Cuba on behalf of the memorial.[68] In 1949, members of the Comité Pro Monumento a Martí-Maceo of New York City and Havana formed a joint commission and met at the offices of the American embassy in Havana to discuss with the ambassador the plans to build the monument in "perpetual memory" of both men. El Club Cubano member and Puerto Rican activist Francisca Cardenal, who seemed to take the lead on these excursions to Cuba, was part of the commission, as were Cuban delegates Coronel Eliseo Figueroa, Captain Rosendo Campos Marquetti, Delia Vizcaino, Pablo Almeida, and Ramón Cabrera Torres. One report explained that Mayor O'Dwyer "promised utmost cooperation in achieving this patriotic desire."[69]

Two years later, in May 1951, Cardenal traveled to Cuba on a "patriotic pilgrimage" to discuss with Cuban government officials the possibility of erecting a monument in honor of Martí and Maceo for the purposes "of fostering tourism between the social sectors in Cuba and New York."[70] A month later, Narciso Saavedra traveled to Cuba on an official visit as president of El Club Cubano. While on the island, he visited the Senate to monitor the progress of the proposed Ley del Monumento Pro Martí-Maceo (Law for the Martí-Maceo Monument) and inquired about the club's eligibility for La Orden Nacional de Mérito Carlos Manuel de Céspedes. When progress on acquiring the memorial stalled in 1952, club leaders discussed the possibility of once again sending a delegation to Cuba to solicit a special credit from the Cuban government to cover the cost of the Martí-Maceo monument. Club member Alberto Baños objected to the idea, suggesting instead that they contact an individual close to the government to determine the best moment to approach Cuban officials. Baños's advice went unheeded, and the club voted to send a delegation led by Cardenal to Cuba, using funds for the monument to pay the cost of the trip.[71]

Citywide efforts to erect a public memorial persisted throughout the 1950s, although the members of El Club Cubano did not entirely approve of the results, nor were they representative of the efforts club members made. In a lengthy article that appeared in *La Prensa* on the hundredth anniversary of Martí's death, Havana-based journalist Félix Lizaso reflected on the great need for a monument of the poet and political leader in New York City. Lizaso explained that Cuban New Yorkers had wanted a statue of Martí since 1948, but he credited the Ateneo Cubano rather than El Club Cubano for making this project a public cause and bringing it to the attention of Cubans on the island. He made no mention of Maceo or of the campaign for the Monumento Martí-Maceo. Lizaso argued that the statue would be best placed in the Plaza de las Américas at the end of the Avenue of the Americas between the already existing statues of Simón Bolívar and José de San Martín. In this configuration, (white) Cubanness would, quite literally, be at the center of Hispanidad and Latinidad in New York City. His plan to bring to New York City a much-deserved memorial in honor of Martí included the suggestion that Cubans on the island provide the statue and that the United States provide the location of the monument and the granite base on which it would stand. To this end, the Ateneo Cubano celebrated an event at its clubhouse in honor of Martí's birthday that not only "took the first steps toward the construction of a monument in honor of Martí in New York" but also became "a continental event" that featured representatives from the United States, Mexico,

Chile, and other countries coming together to give the project "hemispheric flavor."[72]

Finally, in 1956, Martí got his statue at the head of the Avenue of the Americas, but the announcement in *La Prensa* intimated disappointment on the part of members of El Club Cubano: "Dr. Narciso Saavedra as well as other leaders of the Club Cubano Interamericano of the Bronx . . . [have] patriotically put aside whatever differences may have existed in honor of the homeland and the unique figure that symbolizes it." It is likely that the disagreement concerned the club's mission to erect a monument in honor of Martí *and* Maceo, a project that would have been representative of the black and white leaders and soldiers of Cuba's nineteenth-century cross-racial revolutionary movement. With few other options at hand, club leaders hoped that the New York City Art Commission would consider placing bas-reliefs of Maceo and Máximo Gómez on the pedestal of the existing statue. El Club Cubano celebrated Maceo separately from Martí, and this homage continued into the late 1950s, perhaps as a response to Maceo's removal from the monument.[73] These acts notwithstanding, here is perhaps the clearest example of the club's avoidance of direct confrontation or protest on the basis of color or racial discrimination. As in the early republic period in Cuba, when political mobilization on the basis of race came under attack as unpatriotic and "un-Cuban," leaders of El Club Cubano became "patriotic" by acquiescing to the preferences of white Cubans and quietly abandoning their pursuit of a dual memorial that would have been more representative of all Cubans.[74]

TURMOIL ON THE ISLAND, CONFUSION IN THE CLUBS

Migration from Cuba to the United States increased steadily throughout the 1950s. For Cubans, the United States had become "the new 'land of promise,'" according to one reporter who detailed the status of fifty-eight Cubans who had recently sought exile in various foreign embassies because of political differences with the government. In 1952, nearly 3,500 Cubans obtained permanent resident visas to the United States. In 1954, that number rose to just over 4,000, a 13.4 percent increase. In 1952, over 33,000 Cubans registered for temporary travel visas, which usually remained valid for two years, and another 40,000 registered for the same type of visa the following year, a 17.5 percent increase. The reporter calculated that "during the past year daily migration to the U.S., in one form or another, stands at 121 Cubans" and estimated that "many of the temporary migrants remain illegally in this country."[75]

What had begun as a slow trickle in the early 1950s had by 1954 become a steady stream of permanent and temporary migration to the United States, mostly due to political instability and a worsening economic crisis on the island. In 1952, Fulgencio Batista seized power through a military coup, ousting Carlos Prío Socarrás, a member of the Auténtico Party, from the presidency. The coup disrupted elections, including elections in which Fidel Castro had campaigned for a seat in the House of Representatives as a member of the Ortodoxo Party. The following year, on 26 July 1953, Castro and other young armed revolutionaries opposed to Batista led an attack on the Moncada barracks in Santiago. The attack failed, and Castro and other survivors received fifteen-year prison terms for their participation. With the Auténtico and Ortodoxo parties leaderless and disorganized, Batista ran unopposed and was elected to a four-year term as president in 1954. He had the support of the U.S. government and U.S.-owned businesses, which is not surprising; these companies controlled a majority of the land and utilities in Cuba. The Cuban people, however, had become increasingly frustrated with Batista's encouragement of gambling, his acquiescence to U.S. interests over Cuban needs, and the widespread poverty and unemployment that wracked the island in the 1950s. In May 1954, Batista released Castro and other revolutionaries involved in the Moncada attack from prison in a general amnesty, and they soon departed for Mexico. As early as 1955, Castro began to reorganize his 26 of July Movement and plan for a second attempt at armed resistance against Batista.[76]

Revolution on the island was brewing, and Cubans on and off the island, including those in New York City (and Miami), took notice. In 1955, the Comité Obrero Democrático de Exilados y Emigrados Cubanos, which had offices in Brooklyn, organized an event described as "an affair of unity and reaffirmation of Cuban democracy" at the White Hall Hotel on Broadway and 100th Street. An announcement explained that the event would feature speeches by Cuban and American democrats. In 1957, members of the 26 of July Movement in New York City, a local branch of Castro's revolutionary organization that had headquarters on 70th Street and Amsterdam Avenue, gathered at the Palm Garden for an afternoon event commemorating Cuban independence. Other group members traveled to Washington, D.C., to march in front of the White House to protest U.S. aid to the Batista regime. By 1958, the 26 of July Movement was regularly sponsoring political acts of solidarity, though most were described in the press as mere "patriotic events."[77]

Some Cuban New Yorkers chose to distance themselves from Cubans who had come to New York City because of the island's political instability.

Even before the Revolution of 1959, *exile* had become a marker of differ-ence in the *colonia cubana*. Mary Lynn Conejo revealed that her parents distinguished themselves from Cubans who came to the United States be-cause of Castro: "They would say, 'We didn't come because of politics.' It wasn't a prejudice but a distinction. It was important for them to not be a part of that." When asked by a reporter for *Diario de Nueva York* to ex-plain why they migrated to New York City in 1952, none of the Cubans who were surveyed mentioned political motivations. Enrique Varona said that he had been in the city since 1923 with the intention of working there for just a few years but that he had stayed on longer to make more money. An-other respondent, Tomás Rodríguez, had reasoned that he was "descended from adventurers" and had taken to the sea, landing in this country and finding work as a paper exporter.[78]

As more and more Cubans arrived in New York City every day in the late 1950s, Cuban social clubs began to see changes in their memberships and club agendas. El Club Cubano responded to the increased Cuban pres-ence in 1957 by organizing a Comité de Orientación (Orientation Commit-tee) "so that we can give information to those who arrive in this country." Even though club leaders hoped to distance themselves from the protests and violence on the island, political differences among club members seemed to infiltrate club events. In 1957, when a disturbance broke out at a costume dance the club had organized, club leaders responded by set-ting up a commission to investigate the club members who were involved in the incident. While meeting minutes do not reveal the exact cause of the disorder, that its intensity prompted club leaders to hire a private po-lice service to supervise its next dance and to send a letter to Batista no-tifying him of the incident suggests that it was both violent and politically motivated. Two club members, Juan Oleno and Miguel Ángel Suarez, ac-cepted blame for the incident, and club president Melba Alvarado warned that "this matter cannot be forgotten."[79] The Ateneo Cubano, for its part, welcomed a number of Cuban migrants from Puerto Padre into its club during a "mass inscription ceremony." The club even celebrated a recep-tion to honor Aristides Labrada, who was "beloved and distinguished in the colonia de habla española de Nueva York, especially in la cubana and even more especially in the one of Puerto Padre."[80]

Social and cultural events sometimes led to disorder, and New York City officials responded by making it more difficult for social clubs to receive assembly permits. Stricter enforcement of these rules directly affected El Club Cubano in 1958, and leaders discussed the possibility of acquiring a larger club space for dances and events. Other issues surfaced in the late

1950s, including skepticism about the club's dedication to its inter-American mission. Many of the club's events and activities featured Cuban performers and celebrations of Cuban patriotic holidays, but the club's almost sudden recommitment to its inter-American roots suggests a purposeful repositioning in order to continue to appeal to a public that had likely grown accustomed to the centrality of (Afro-)Cubans and (Afro-)Cubanness to Hispano/a and Latino/a identity. In 1958, Melba Alvarado recommended that the club "purchase the 21 flags of the 21 republics because this club is called Club Cubano Inter-Americano and because of this it's important to actually represent it." That year, another club leader proposed that the club invite all of the Latin American consuls in the city to an event at the club "since the club is, after all, inter-american."[81] One wonders if this renewed emphasis on the club's inter-American roots might also have stemmed from an interest in distancing the club from negative associations with the political violence in Cuba and protest organizations such as the 26 of July Movement, which by 1957 had developed a controversial presence in the city. At least until the mid-1950s, most Cubans and others in New York City had a relatively favorable impression of Batista, and social clubs such as El Club Cubano often invited him to their larger events.[82]

Toward the end of 1958 and into the first few weeks of 1959, many of the city's Cuban associations suspended their activities and postponed holiday events in light of the civil unrest and violence that was taking place across the island. Some clubs such as Casa Cuba, located at 691 Columbus Avenue between 93rd and 94th Streets, explained the decision with vague references to the "Cuban situation." The Ateneo Cubano cancelled its end-of-year festivities and declared that it was entering a period of mourning as a result of "the spilling of Cuban blood and the horrible tragedy that our homeland is living." The public notice, signed by club president Diego Díaz and secretary Fabio Valdéz, ended with a hopeful call for "peace and cordiality among all Cubans" and promised that "once peace and happiness returns to the Cuban soul so too will the happy end-of-year celebrations." The "Cuban situation" did not stop El Club Cubano from going ahead with its customary celebrations, and members and guests welcomed the New Year with a festive dance at the clubhouse complete with "classic party hats." Whether the event serves as testimony to the club's apolitical agenda or an implicit celebration of Castro's victory, however, is not clear.[83]

A few short but tense days after Castro's victory in January 1959, the Cuban social clubs of New York City ended their moratorium on hosting events. One of the first events the Ateneo Cubano sponsored was its traditional Cena Martiana in honor of Martí's birthday, and its Comité de Damas (Ladies' Committee) announced that it had prepared two *canastillas martianas* (Martí's baskets, or arrangements of blankets, bottles, and other baby necessities), which they promised to present to the first two children born on 28 January. Casa Cuba also offered a Cena Martiana that featured recitations by orator Eulogio Peraza and a lecture by Aristides de Llanos on the significance of libertarianism in Martí's thinking and its influence on Castro. The 26 of July Movement, for its part, promised to "cooperate in putting forth a brilliant event in [Martí's] honor." Cuban social clubs also hosted traditional celebrations in honor of Cuban independence. But, unlike past years, celebrations in 1959 reflected more on recent history and conditions than on the nineteenth-century legacies of Martí. The Ateneo Cubano, for example, hosted a dance with music by Rodolfo Curbelo, noting that "this year, with more happiness than ever and with a truly independent Cuba, this will be a social event."[84] This remark signaled support for the Cuban Revolution and was a sharp critique of decades of U.S. involvement in Cuban affairs.

In an undeniable sign of tension and conflict in the Cuban community of New York City, several clubs and organizations popped up in 1959 with the intention, at least in name, of bringing about Cuban unity. Club Unidad Cubana sponsored a dance at the Broadway Casino to commemorate Cuban independence and "honor a variety of personalities from the social, civic, and cultural world of the Latin American community of New York." The Federación Cultural de Sociedades Cubanas, of which the Ateneo Cubano was a member, hosted a "grand act" at the Community Center on 35th Street between Sixth and Seventh Avenues. In addition to musical performances, the event featured speeches by journalist José M. de Poo, Cuban consul Luis A. Baral, and Manuel Bisbe, Cuban ambassador to the United Nations. In December 1959, in what was likely a response to the political changes taking place on the island and the subsequent factionalism developing in the *colonia cubana*, the Federación Cultural de Sociedades Cubanas held a meeting at the Broadway Casino "to discuss issues of vital importance to the Cuban community of New York."[85]

But perhaps no event revealed the convergence of popular culture and the current Cuban political drama more than the Reina de *La Prensa* (Queen of *La Prensa*) beauty pageant of 1959. As social clubs, cultural organizations, and other groups across the *colonia hispana* chose a young woman from within their ranks as their representative in the contest, the pageant reportedly generated "a great deal of enthusiasm from all of New York society."[86] The newspaper named Gladys Feijoo of the Ateneo Cubano winner of the contest, and the young woman's victory brought her more than a crown, flowers, and the admiration of her fellow club members. The coronation ceremony coincided with Castro's first visit to New York City since his rise to power, and the newspaper wasted no time in trying to secure his attendance at the event. Photos show Feijoo presenting the bearded Cuban leader with a ticket to the coronation ceremony, which was held that year at the Manhattan Center and featured musical performances by Tito Rodríguez, Arsenio Rodríguez, and Los Chavales de España. One reporter indicated that Castro would be attending the event after he finished delivering an evening speech in Central Park. Not only would the event honor Feijoo, it would also celebrate Castro. The "tremendous welcoming" would be "a manifestation of affection on the part of all the admirers who have not had the chance to be close to him."[87] Reports never confirmed whether or not Castro attended the event, but the ambiguity hardly soured his relationship with the newspaper. Less than a month after his visit, a photo spread appeared on Cuban Independence Day showing Castro reading *La Prensa* and offering praise for the newspaper's "editorials in favor of the Revolution and in defense of the acting Cuban government."[88]

4

LA PRENSA'S MUSICAL POPULARITY

CONTESTS AND FUND-RAISING FESTIVALS

In 1941, *La Prensa*, the largest and longest-running Spanish-language daily newspaper in New York City, announced that it would be sponsoring an annual Concurso de Popularidad de Artistas y Orquestas Hispanos de Nueva York, a musical popularity contest that culminated in a Gran Festival Pro Fondo de Caridad, a fund-raising festival that sought to raise money for those most in need in the *colonia hispana*. Though the newspaper had organized its first musical popularity contest in 1933, it was not until 1941 that the Concurso de Popularidad and Gran Festival reportedly "sparked such interest among the colonias de habla española" that they became annual events. In 1941, after weeks of counting votes, the newspaper announced that Consuelo Moreno, Don Arres, and Xavier Cugat had emerged as the contest winners. After the contest, the newspaper focused its energies on the fund-raising festival, a showcase where the winners and runners-up in each of the contest's categories would be presented with trophies and allotted time in the program to perform on stage before a packed audience. Following these presentations and performances, which started in the early afternoon, popular bands hired by *La Prensa* would alternate on stage, inviting audience members to hit the dance floor until the wee hours of the morning. For the inaugural gala, organizers hired two Cuban-led bands, Anselmo Sacasas's Havana Royal and Generoso Montesino's Conjunto del Ritmo, to perform for the dancing public. One review boasted that never before had the *colonia hispana* been presented with a show that featured such a large group of splendid performers "on the same stage, on the same date, and at such affordable prices!"[1]

Each spring from 1941 to 1957 and in the fall of 1958 and 1959, a quick glance at the newspaper's headlines would make it seem as though the entire *colonia hispana*, the entire city, even audiences across the United States and throughout Latin America and the Caribbean, had stopped to take notice of the winners and participants in the musical popularity contests and fund-raising festivals. Daily coverage in the pages of *La Prensa* would alert even the most casual readers that "the best of the best performers of Spanish and Hispanoamerican art," in the spirit of "genuine disinterest," were collaborating with an enthusiastic public to celebrate the contest winners and runners-up and raise money for the newspaper's Charity Fund.[2] Black and white Cuban singers, musicians, and performers figured prominently among the long lists of winners, runners-up, and participants in the contests and festivals throughout the 1940s and 1950s. Their presence and the presence of Afro-Cuban music became critical components of the newspaper's notion of Hispanidad during this period. Cuban musicians—from Machito, Marcelino Guerra, and Miguelito Valdés to Xavier Cugat and José Curbelo—generally performed at nightclubs, dance halls, and social clubs that drew crowds that were often defined and restricted by informal practices and formal policies of racial inclusion and exclusion. In this case, however, the newspaper and its readers (at least those who voted in the contest and attended the showcase) claimed these black and white performers of Afro-Cuban music as both Cuban and Hispano/a, not limited by the boundaries of race, national origin, class, or entertainment industry squabbles about musical authenticity and commercialism.

The musical popularity contests and fund-raising festivals serve as early examples of the development and broadcasting of a pan-Latino/a identity that was both local and hemispheric. I am not so interested in the determinants of local popularity or international celebrity as I am in examining these contests and festivals as events that produced a complex and sometimes contradictory set of discourses about transnationalism, local politics, and Hispanidad and Latinidad. An examination of these discourses not only offers insight into the relationship between print culture and the imagined community hailed by the newspaper as the *colonia hispana* but also demonstrates modes of collaboration between the newspaper and the entertainment industries of the 1940s and 1950s. As we saw in the two previous chapters, newspapers played an important role in helping structure the associational life of Cubans and Latino/as in New York City. This chapter turns its attention to *La Prensa* as an ethnic institution that shaped ideas and practices related to (Afro-)Cubanness and

Hispanidad by way of its annual musical popularity contests and fund-raising festivals.

By the late 1950s, casual and everyday readers of *La Prensa* had likely grown accustomed to headlines that promised spectacular entertainment and charitable spirit. For months each spring dating back to 1941, *La Prensa* filled its pages with articles, editorials, and advertisements announcing its Concurso de Popularidad and inviting readers to attend the Gran Festival. But before any contest winners could be announced or any tickets to the fund-raising gala could be sold, readers had to know and follow the rules. Printed next to each write-in ballot in the newspaper was a long set of rules explaining key elements of the voting process to readers. In addition to more mundane rules such as the dates of the voting period and the expectation that each person submit a ballot by mail or in person at the offices of *La Prensa*, located at 245 Canal Street, only once each day, the newspaper gave readers specific information about eligibility requirements, category definitions, ticket sale locations, and the behavior expected of those attending the Gran Festival.

The contest rules defined an "artist" as a "singer or dancer or solo instrumentalist or orator of any and all genres." Throughout the 1940s, the contest rules simply stated that votes had to be cast for a Hispanic artist or orchestra. To be considered eligible to receive votes, an artist also had to be over the age of fourteen and have worked in a local Hispanic theater or cabaret or performed on the radio in New York in a professional capacity. Contest and festival organizers initially required that participating artists and musicians be residents of New York City, a clear objection to the importation of performers from Spain, Latin America, and the Caribbean. This rule suggests a preference for local talent, likely at the behest of local entertainment industry insiders. The same restrictions applied to orchestras and *conjuntos*, though the rules in this category allowed votes for those bands that "having been properly organized, have been livening up the festivals of well-known hispanic societies." These rules were apparently enforced. In 1941, the Comisión de Escrutinio, the committee responsible for establishing the contest rules and voting practices, disqualified Miguelito Valdés (who received 11,545 votes) and the Sacasas Orquesta (which received 8,835 votes) for not meeting the one-year residency requirement.[3]

Some of these rules changed over time. In 1949, organizers lifted the residency requirement and expanded the rules to include artists that had performed on television in New York City. Artists, orchestras, and *conjuntos* had to have performed in New York City or the surrounding area only during the year before the start of that year's contest. The contest evolved again in 1950, when the rules specified that "any hispanic artist, or artist of hispanic origin, regardless of nationality" was eligible. The label "Hispanic" and the clause "regardless of nationality" rendered neutral any distinctions based on country of origin or ancestry within the *colonia hispana*. That same year, the guidelines changed in another way: only a "professional artist . . . that receives remuneration for his work" was eligible for votes.[4] This stipulation likely sought to maintain the reputability of the contest and exclude amateur performers and impromptu bands that formed to play at informal neighborhood events such as house parties and family gatherings. This clause also suggests an interest in establishing the legitimacy of the contest by certifying its participants as professionals, a standard that probably mattered most to entertainment industry insiders. It is possible that some of the entertainers cared about this, too, especially those who would not achieve celebrity beyond the newspaper's readership but who had nonetheless worked hard to move up from amateur status and struggled to make their livelihoods as professional artists.

As a steady influx of tens of thousands of Puerto Rican migrants added to an already substantial presence of migrants from Puerto Rico, Cuba, Spain, Mexico, and other parts of Central and South America, it is not entirely surprising that tensions and divisions had started to develop in the *colonia hispana* in the late 1940s and early 1950s.[5] Changes to the contest rules reflect the newspaper's role, though probably inadvertent at first, in defining the boundaries of this rapidly growing community. A relaxation of the residency requirements of the early contests, a move that was likely protested by "resident" artists and bands, probably came about as a result of pressure from managers, nightclub owners, recording executives, and even the "foreign" artists. More than a reflection of the newspaper's perceived interest in inclusiveness or acquiescence to external pressure, the rule change reflects the demands of a professional entertainment industry that required its artists to tour frequently and suggests that for those in the *colonia hispana* popularity did not necessitate residency. For fans and voters in the contest, some of whom were now long-term residents of New York City while others had just recently settled in the area, the *colonia hispana* the newspaper hailed was not bound by rigid geographic borders but was instead defined by a mode of seeing mediated by local realities and longing for the homeland. After this change, the contest allowed Hispanic performers to participate regardless of their national origins and residency status. The change illustrates that the cultural preferences and musical horizons of the newspaper's readership, fans, and voters in the contest can best be described as transnational; they cared little if their favorite act was in Havana, Mexico City, or Madrid instead of New York City for most of the year.

Anthropologist Nina Glick Schiller has argued that migrants do not automatically shift their loyalty and involvement from one country to another. Instead, they engage in long-distance nationalism, what she defines as a claim to membership in a country of origin that generates emotional attachments and concern about how the actions of migrants will influence the reputation of the home country.[6] *La Prensa* seems to have recognized that its readers voted and bought records and attended live performances based on emotional attachments rather than on where the artists lived. In other words, members of the *colonia hispana* who voted in the musical popularity contests and attended the fund-raising festivals engaged in a lived transnational social practice that simultaneously fulfilled the needs of their constructed transnational social imaginary.

Within the field of Latino/a Studies, the concept of transnationalism has often been used to explain why Latino/a migrants have not fully assimilated into mainstream society in the United States. Scholars have conceptualized transnationalism, understood broadly as alliances among individuals, groups, or communities that span two or more nation-states, as a complicated response to international migration shaped by global capitalism, experiences with racism in the United States, and the nation-building endeavors of the home country. Many of these studies have examined transnationalism as a social practice and a symbolic social field. As a social practice, transnationalism refers to activities such as speaking two languages in the home, sending remittances to family or organizations in the home country, building and supporting bi-national businesses, and traveling back and forth between the sending and receiving countries. The transnational social field, however, does not require physical movement. Instead, the mass media, especially electronic media, memory, and the imagination yield ideas and symbols that foster a sense of belonging and attachment to more than one nation-state. The Concurso de Popularidad and especially the Gran Festival are examples of transnational traditions that constituted both a lived social practice *and* a symbolic reconnection to the homeland.[7]

That *La Prensa* seemed aware of the transnational loyalties of its readers is not entirely surprising given that it served a predominantly immigrant population. Founded by Spanish migrant José Compubrí in 1918 to meet the needs of the rapidly growing *colonia hispana*, the newspaper provided its readers with coverage of local events relevant to the immigrant community and news of major events in Spain and throughout Latin America and the Caribbean. Hispanic literary scholar and noted publisher Nicolás Kanellos used sociologist Robert E. Park's 1922 study of the immigrant press to define the characteristics of the Hispanic immigrant press: "predominant use of the language of the homeland; the serving of a population united by that language, irrespective of national origin; the need to interpret events from their own particular racial or nationalist point of view, as well as the furthering of nationalism."[8] From this functionalist perspective, contest organizers might have modified the rule to specify that the contest was open to any Hispanic artist "regardless of nationality" in part to demonstrate an agenda of pan-ethnic inclusiveness.

Organizers modified the contest in other ways in the 1940s and 1950s. In many ways, the categories listed on the ballots were somewhat messy representations of rules shaped by gender, dance styles, and format. Some performers received a substantial number of votes in more than one category, for example. In 1941 and 1942, ballots offered readers the chance to vote for their favorite artists in three categories: *Damas* (Ladies), *Caballeros* (Men), and *Orquestas o Conjuntos Musicales*. In 1943, the contest added a category for *Parejas de Baile* (Dance Pairs) that was subdivided in 1945 into *Parejas de Baile Español* (Spanish Dance Pairs) and *Parejas de Baile Hispanoamericano* (Hispanic American Dance Pairs). In 1944, the contest began offering separate categories for *Orquestas* and *Conjuntos Musicales*. By 1945, readers could vote for their favorite artists in up to six different categories.

This study focuses on the Cuban men who were key participants in the musical popularity contests and fund-raising festivals. This focus is not to deny or silence the participation of Cuban women in these events or in the realm of the popular more generally. It is not my goal to reproduce gender hierarchies; instead, I am interested in opening a discussion of masculinity and gender. It deserves mention that Graciela was the first and only Cuban woman to win or figure prominently in the *Damas* category in the musical popularity contests. In fact, she was the only major Cuban woman artist living and working in the United States in the 1940s and 1950s. (It is true, of course, that Celia Cruz performed in the United States as early as 1957, but she was still living in Havana.) As one of the lead vocalists for Machito y sus Afro-Cubans, Graciela never quite received the same attention as Machito and Mario Bauzá, even though she has since been touted as the "First Lady of Latin Jazz." Her experiences as an

Afro-Cuban performer are evidence that as a music pioneer she transcended the boundaries of both race and gender.[9]

Despite efforts to differentiate performers through increasingly rigid contest rules, Cuban artists and orchestras often received votes in more than one category in the same year. In 1948, the only year he earned enough votes to rank in the final standings, Desi Arnaz received votes in both the *Caballeros* and *Orquestas* categories, where he came in fifth and eighth, respectively. In 1957, white Cuban performer Perucho Irigoyen won the newly created *Locutores* (Radio and Television Announcers) category and also placed second in the *Caballeros* category. Some notable performers earned votes in different categories throughout the contest's nearly two-decade run. In the 1940s, Miguelito Valdés received votes in the *Caballeros* category, but in 1950, the last year in which he placed in the contest, he earned votes in the *Orquestas* category. In 1952 and 1954, voters placed Arsenio Rodríguez in the *Conjuntos Musicales* category, while in 1956 he figured in the *Orquestas* category. Marcelino Guerra earned recognition as a *Caballero* in 1944, but the following year he began showing in the *Orquestas* category, which he finally won in 1954. While this inconsistency in voting practices reflects the versatility of some of these performers, it also demonstrates that contest voters might have been confused or did not care about category definitions.

As noted, the contest rules expanded again in 1957 to include a seventh category for *Locutores*. Organizers reasoned that the *Damas* and *Caballeros* categories did not sufficiently allow for voters to distinguish radio or television performers and announcers from singers or theatrical performers. To assist readers and voters in understanding this change and to familiarize them with potential nominees, *La Prensa* published two lists of radio and television personalities that included radio talent from *El Programa Latino* (WHOM) and *La Voz Hispana del Aire* (WWRL) and television entertainers from *Canal 13* (WATV). Most prominent among them was Irigoyen, host of WATV's *The Perucho Show*, a variety show that had become one of the most popular programs on Spanish-language television.[10]

For decades, radio had been a resource for newcomers in the United States looking for local news, entertainment, and information about their native countries, often in their own language. In the years following the end of World War II, however, television viewing became more common, developing into a daily and routine experience for families across the United States. From 1948 to 1955, television allowed spectator amusements to move from "the public space of the movie theater to the private space of the home," and many historians and cultural studies scholars have debated both the oppressive and the liberating potential of this new cultural medium. Most scholars have settled on a dialectical model that rejects a dichotomous understanding of popular culture as exclusively a propaganda tool for the mass culture industries, on the one hand, or an oppositional tool for those in subordinate or marginal positions, on the other. More than a reflection of the popularity of television in the *colonia hispana*, the addition of the *Locutores* category demonstrates this dialectical model in practice. Radio and television made it less necessary for Latino/as to come together in theaters, nightclubs, and cabarets to attend live performances by their favorite solo artists and orchestras. As we saw in chapter 2, however, Cuban social clubs often used radio listening and television viewing as a means of socializing in private among themselves. The existence of local Spanish-language radio and television programming also demonstrates that Latino/as had found ways to participate in the mass culture industries as both individual and collective producers and consumers.[11]

The newspaper explained that the addition of the *Locutores* category reflected a "mode of cultural and artistic expression that in the past few years has been gaining considerable and justified popularity."[12] As early as the spring of 1951, brief on-the-street testimonials conducted by *Diario de Nueva York* indicated that television was indeed growing as an industry that was perceived to be capable of providing both quality entertainment and opportunities for Hispanic artists throughout the United States and Latin America. One of the respondents to the newspaper's question about television's potential, Luis Mesa, a married Cuban draftsman, reasoned that television would succeed for economic reasons, namely "for the simple reason that advertisers will realize, as they do here, that advertising through that medium is good business. There is such a huge base to exploit in Spanish-speaking America that I have not the slightest doubt that it will triumph." Another respondent, Puerto Rican composer Ramón Fontan, noted that he welcomed an increase in television programming: "In the last few years, artists have not had very many stages on which to perform so opening up a new front is always welcome."[13]

COUNTING VOTES, SELLING TICKETS, AND HAILING AN AUDIENCE

Just as contest rules and categories evolved, so too did the value of each ballot submitted by contest voters. Each week during the contest voting period, the newspaper presented readers with the current vote standings in each category. From 1941 to 1943, each ballot that was cast counted for five votes. Organizers inflated the value of each ballot to count for ten votes starting in 1944. In 1959, the last year of the contest, one ballot counted for fifteen votes, perhaps in an attempt to make the totals seem more impressive to readers and entertainment industry observers. To say that the newspaper published the vote standings exclusively to increase revenues from newspaper sales would be unfair; organizers allowed readers to submit handwritten copies of ballots, eliminating the need for them to purchase additional copies of the newspaper. In fact, the newspaper seemed especially concerned about attempts to "stuff the ballots," explaining to readers that the Comisión de Escrutinio would not count any ballots that had been reproduced through mechanical means, a rule violation that was most likely committed by artist managers and record companies. As evidence of their concern, the newspaper printed a special notice in 1945 urging voters to pay close attention to the rule that mandated that each person could vote just once each day and that ballots from multiple voters received in the same envelope would not be counted.[14]

Yet even if the "number of ballots a voter could cast in *La Prensa*'s poll was limited only by the number of copies of *La Prensa* he could get his hands on," as *Time* reported in 1943, "ballot-box stuffing was general for all contestants." Nevertheless, *Time* confirmed the legitimacy of the contest results, contending that the musical popularity contests revealed just "how Latin Americans themselves estimate the rumba and conga artists now performing in the U.S." The report left little doubt that "the poll did represent a rude cross section of New York City's Latin American opinion." *Time* curiously noted that many of the contest winners were largely unknown to the U.S. public and that North American favorites Xavier Cugat and Carmen Miranda finished eighth and twentieth in their respective categories. The following year, *Time* once again assessed the newspaper's musical popularity contest in a brief review of the Cuban rumba-dancing duo Raúl and Eva Reyes, winners of the *Parejas de Baile* category. Raúl and Eva "finished far ahead of such popular [North American] favorites as Carmen Amaya, Carmen Miranda and Rosario & Antonio," the writer noted, but "nobody questioned the justice of the verdict." In that same report, *Time* described victory in the contest as "the most coveted prize in U.S. Latin American entertainment," an indication that the contest had become rapidly assimilated by the entertainment industry and, to one degree or another, the voting public as well.[15] That artist managers, nightclub owners, and record executives might engage in shady practices such as "stuffing the ballots" confirms that the contest results both reflected and helped determine the preferences of fans in the *colonia hispana*. An implicit understanding that the contest results could lead to commercial rewards through record sales and ticket purchases to upcoming live events and concerts certainly suggests that the newspaper played a key role in shaping the relationship developing between the entertainment industries and the *colonia hispana*.

The Comisión de Escrutinio, a committee made up of the presidents or designated appointees of five Hispanic societies of New York City, was solely responsible for determining the eligibility of the performers who participated in the contest. This committee also organized the fund-raising festival that followed the announcement of the contest winners each year, a responsibility that included selling tickets, creating the schedule of performances, decorating the ballroom, and ensuring that the event flowed in an orderly manner for the comfort of both the performers and the thousands of guests who attended.[16] Representatives from some of "the colonia's most prestigious" social clubs, societies, and organizations participated in the Comisión de Escrutinio, including the Asociación de Empleados Puertorriqueños, the Pan American Exporters Club, the Junta Patriótica Mexicana de Nueva York, the Hispano Tennis Club, the Asociación de Comerciantes Hispanos, Club Centro Americano de Nueva York, Centro Español/La Nacional, the Junta Patriótica Puertorriqueña, the Sociedad de Periodistas y Escritores Puertorriqueños, and the Ateneo Cubano (but not El Club Cubano).[17] The cooperation of these groups proved integral to the success of the contest; likewise, the success of the contest became so central to the liveliness of the community that most of these groups reported that they avoided scheduling their own festivals and activities on the date of this annual event. Even leaders of social clubs outside New York City recognized the importance of supporting the event, particularly in terms of establishing relationships with popular musicians and entertainers. Fernando Luis, a Cuban promoter in New York City and the owner-operator of the theater at the Centro Asturiano de Tampa, was one of the hosts for the 1945 Gran Festival; he delayed his return to Florida in the hope of securing talent for his club's events.[18]

Tickets to the fund-raising gala were sold at "various hispanic commercial establishments in various parts of the city" at sites that were chosen "for the convenience of our readers." The newspaper set up ticket sale locations throughout the 1940s and 1950s to accommodate the needs of potential attendees. Based on the requests of many of the residents living in Central Harlem, for example, the newspaper started selling tickets to the Gran Festival at La Moderna, a bakery that also operated as a "popular rumba joint." The owner of the bakery, Cuban Simón Jou, sold records in his store and was known to be a friend of many of the musicians in the area. He was also "famous for the crafting of handmade tumbadoras [conga drums]." By 1957, tickets to the event were sold at businesses, restaurants, and shops scattered across Manhattan, the Bronx, Brooklyn, and Queens.[19] The locations where tickets were sold suggest that event organizers wanted to reach an audience for the festival that was mostly local and Latino/a. But the newspaper also established ticket sale locations outside zones with high concentrations of Latino/as, revealing two underreported phenomena: first, some Latino/as lived and worked beyond the confines of Spanish Harlem and the South Bronx; and, second, *La Prensa* actively courted a non-Latino/a audience to attend its fund-raising festivals.[20]

The Gran Festival attracted residents of the *colonia hispana* in New York City and Spanish-speaking migrants from neighboring cities, towns, and states. As early as 1943, the newspaper noted that entire families from Newark, New Jersey, traveled into midtown Manhattan to attend the showcase. In 1945, the newspaper declared that the event had become "traditional among the Spanish-speaking residents of the eastern United States," and in 1946, it reported receiving telephone calls from residents outside New York City asking where they could purchase tickets. Special excursions arrived from other parts of New York, New Jersey, and Connecticut and even from as far away as Ohio and central Pennsylvania; for example, the members of a Mexican association based in Bethlehem, Pennsylvania, traveled to the Gran Festival by chartered bus in 1950.[21] Not only did Latino/as outside New York City attend the fund-raising gala, but they also sought to participate in the voting process. The newspaper reported that it had received votes from across the United States and from Spanish-speaking U.S. soldiers stationed abroad during World War II.[22] That *La Prensa* used the musical popularity contests and fund-raising festivals to extend its readership to include a broader Spanish-language audience is not unexpected, considering the fact that the newspaper also relaxed the contest rules to allow Hispanic artists who lived outside the city to participate.

The diversity of musical genres presented at the fund-raising galas likely helped attract a broad audience, much to the delight of the newspaper, entertainment industry, and performers. In fact, at the height of the Latin craze in the United States, the Concurso de Popularidad and Gran Festival also attracted audiences beyond the Spanish-speaking world, which makes sense given that a variety of English-language periodicals, from *Time* to local newspapers across the nation, covered the events. In 1950,

La Prensa reported that a delegation of North Americans from Plainville, Connecticut, would be attending the fund-raising gala, just as they had done in previous years. In 1953, the newspaper linked the contest to the enormous popularity of Latin bands across the United States, even going so far as to compare its awards ceremony to the Oscars of the dance music world.[23] Three years later, the newspaper boasted that "hundreds of men, women, and children, as many English-speaking as those from our hispanic community[,]" filled the Manhattan Center for the annual fund-raising gala.[24]

With just two exceptions, each year the newspaper selected the Manhattan Center, located at 311 West 34th Street between Eighth and Ninth Avenues, as the site of its Gran Festival. Each year, the auditorium formerly known as the Manhattan Opera House opened its doors to thousands of members of the *colonia hispana*.[25] Many factors likely influenced *La Prensa*'s choice of venue, not the least of which were rental fees and logistical concerns such as the maximum capacity of the ballroom. But place matters, and by choosing a venue in midtown Manhattan, the newspaper sent what can be viewed as mixed signals to readers, potential attendees, performers, and those outside the *colonia hispana*. An acclaimed venue for hosting community events, charitable dinners, and stage performances, the Manhattan Center offered attendees, especially Anglo attendees, a safe, reputable place to experience the "exotic" rhythms of Latin music and mingle side by side, albeit temporarily, with migrants from Puerto Rico, Cuba, Spain, and other parts of Latin America and the Caribbean. Accessibility for whites, however, may have also served to exclude dark-skinned members of the *colonia hispana* from the event, particularly in the 1940s and early 1950s, when racialized boundaries restricted the movements of African Americans and Latino/as to certain parts of the city, limiting opportunities for housing, employment, and recreation. It is also possible that Latino/as of color may have been denied entry to the event, as happened when dark-skinned Cubans, Puerto Ricans, and African Americans attempted to gain admittance to events organized by certain Cuban and Hispanic social clubs in the city. At the same time, the fund-raising gala gave lesser-known singers and performers an opportunity to perform in a grand ballroom at a venue that might otherwise have denied them entry based on their race and ethnicity. The decision to hold the Gran Festival in midtown close to other famous and well-known nightclubs, cabarets, and theaters allowed organizers to claim a space for Latino/a performers and audiences that extended well beyond the confines of Spanish Harlem, the Bronx, and other areas where Latino/as were highly concentrated. The organizers' preference for a symbolically prestigious place also seems to have reflected their own notions of how the *colonia hispana*, its leadership, and its cultural productions should be represented to wider audiences.[26]

As the size and magnitude of the fund-raising gala increased, so did the logistics of executing such a grand affair. Organizers designated seating on a first-come, first-served basis, and many ticket holders lined up outside the Manhattan Center several hours before the doors opened to secure the best seats near the stage. Maintaining order and decorum was a primary concern for the newspaper and Comisión de Escrutinio. The newspaper worried about the potential for disorder and the negative publicity that would follow such disruptions so much that each year organizers reminded readers and attendees that local police, both uniformed and undercover officers, would be present inside and outside of the ballroom. Concerns about potential disruptions were not totally unfounded, since fights and scuffles were known to break out at dance venues that featured Latin bands, including at places such as the Hunts Point Palace and the Palladium. One of the major concerns of the organizing committee was crowding in the hallways, on the sidewalks outside of the ballroom, and near the entryways and box office. At times, the crowds overwhelmed organizers. In 1945, organizers had to turn away nearly 2,000 hopeful attendees when the box office sold out of tickets and the ballroom nearly exceeded its capacity. Year after year, organizers beseeched attendees not to arrive at the event before the doors were set to open, suggesting perhaps that the midtown location required that the majority Latino/a audience be confined indoors and thus be less visible to potentially offended passers-by and residents of the area.[27]

Despite the large crowds and the length of the program, the newspaper never reported any disturbances or incidents at the Gran Festival. In fact, it deemed the police presence "unnecessary precautions" and praised the thousands who attended for their "perfect order," cooperation, and good behavior. Reports characterized the atmosphere inside the ballroom as "admirable, sincere, of contagious cordiality, of innocent and rejuvenating joy."[28] Whatever the initial concerns about possible disruptions or disorder, the newspaper's narration of a "cordial" and "orderly" event suggests that perhaps these were not characteristics and behaviors commonly used to describe events organized by the *colonia hispana*. The newspaper assured the reading public that it had, in fact, organized a "civilized" event, which also seems to reflect the organizers' own expression of self. In other words, "cordial," "orderly," and "civilized" are coded words that signify the newspaper's racial and class biases, a process other ethnic institutions used during this period.

CELEBRITY, CHARITY, AND POLITICS
AT THE GRAN FESTIVAL

Weeks of submitting ballots and counting votes culminated in a Gran Festival that was designed to raise money for the newspaper's Charity Fund and, in some years, an additional donation to the American Red Cross. Year after year, the contest and festival met the "dual goals" of promoting celebrity and charity, which included offering winners and runners-up congratulatory trophies and recognition; providing attendees with over eight hours of theatrics, music, and dancing; and giving financial support to various Hispanic organizations in the city that helped members of the community most in need. The contest and festival became annual traditions, and the newspaper boasted that "the public is already familiar with this outstanding artistic-charity event."[29] The newspaper provided readers with its most explicit and direct rationale for sponsoring the Gran Festival in 1957: "The festival has three fundamental goals: 1) to increase the resources with which the Charity Fund helps our charitable organizations and, by extension, those in need in our community; 2) to highlight the magnificent work of popularizing the folkloric and artistic work that our artists and musicians realize throughout the year; and 3) to offer the hispanic family each year the opportunity to attend a grand reunion that is both intimate and social."[30] By the late 1950s, however, repeated mention of the charitable goals of the contest and festival seemed to be an attempt to forestall what appeared to be waning interest and support for the "annual tradition."

The newspaper relied on the Sociedad Auxiliadora de San Vicente de Paul, the Corte de Honor de Lourdes, or "another institution of absolute guarantee" to determine which "hispanos in need" would benefit from the money collected from the sales of tickets to the Gran Festival. Ticket prices were set at $1.20 for adults and $.55 for children under the age of twelve until 1948, when prices increased to $1.50 for adults and $.60 for children under the age of twelve. The newspaper published detailed reports of money raised from the fund-raising gala from 1943 to 1945. In 1943, adult ticket sales brought in a total of $3,140 and sales of children's tickets yielded a total of $61.75. Proceeds from the following year's festival allowed the newspaper to allocate $1,288.35 to its Charity Fund and make a $1,000 donation to the American Red Cross. The separate donation to the Red Cross, an act of Pan-Americanism, signified the *colonia hispana*'s patriotic support of the United States during World War II and an appreciation of the services the Red Cross provided to U.S. soldiers, including those of Latino/a descent. In 1945, the Gran Festival yielded a total of $3,605.05.[31] Unfortunately, *La Prensa* did not publish exact budgets and profit details after 1945. Nonetheless, with yearly festival attendance holding steady between four and five thousand people, proceeds likely ranged between $3,000 and $4,000 until 1956. In 1957, ticket prices rose to $1.80 for adults and $.80 for children, though it remains unclear if such large crowds gathered for the final three festivals.[32]

Not to be left out of the goodwill fostered by charitable giving, the various Hispanic nightclubs, cabarets, and theaters of New York City contributed to the appeal and success of the festival by allowing their contracted solo and group acts to perform segments of their entire revues at the festival at no cost to the newspaper. Of course, for owners and managers this apparent selflessness brought with it some noticeable perks, namely free advertising in *La Prensa* for their venues and shows and the opportunity to establish and build rapport with potential clientele at the festival. The nightclubs, cabarets, and theaters of the *colonia hispana* competed for patrons, and the owners and managers who collaborated with organizers of the Gran Festival likely hoped that this cooperation would increase the popularity of their venue. Though most performers volunteered to participate in the musical showcase of their own accord, in the days leading up to the event, *La Prensa* published articles and advertisements announcing which nightclubs, cabarets, and theaters had promised to lend their performers to the showcase. Numerous venues collaborated with the newspaper, including the Havana-Madrid, El Chico, the Cuban Casino, La Conga, and the Teatro Puerto Rico, located at 490 East 138th Street in the Bronx.

The altruistic goals of raising funds for charity certainly did their part to attract an audience. Brief on-the-street testimonials solicited from readers demonstrate that the dual campaign for celebrity and charity that contest and festival organizers pursued succeeded in maintaining the support of the *colonia hispana*. When asked what he liked most about attending the fund-raising gala, Luis E. Boada responded that he attended the event "for its artists and good organization, and because the Charity Fund is for hispanos." Mercedes Matellanes explained that since she had arrived in New York City five years earlier she had not missed a Gran Festival, favoring the event held in 1954 for its "great variety of acts." Pedro G. Lanza stated, "I attend the Festival not just for the artists but also because they are held to help hispanos in need by way of very well-known and responsible institutions." Frank Flores and other respondents reported that the event also elevated their opinion of the newspaper: "*La Prensa* is the only newspaper that gets involved in charitable causes without regards to race. I have attended all the festivals and liked them all." Frank Torres echoed these remarks, commenting that "*La Prensa* is the only newspaper that's interested in all of the hispanos of New York."[33] Specific references to *La Prensa*'s commitment to "all of the hispanos of New York," "without regards to race," seem to indicate that the newspaper had successfully presented public ideologies and practices of Hispanidad that were racially and ethnically inclusive.

These responses also reveal that the Gran Festival helped *La Prensa* construct an image of itself as an institution of unparalleled selflessness, one that valued duty and commitment to the community. This marketing strategy yielded long-term results in the form of a loyal readership who continued to support the event year after year. Though some have argued that *La Prensa* specifically targeted members of the "bourgeois Latino community" through certain sections of the newspaper such as "Notas de la Colonia," the case can certainly be made that an event such as the Gran Festival aimed to include a much broader audience. While participation in the fund-raising festival required time for leisure activities and money to spend on popular entertainment, an entrance fee of $1.50 was not entirely out of reach for many of the working-class members of the *colonia hispana*. During the 1940s and 1950s, social clubs such as El Club Cubano charged between $1 and $2 for public entry into dance events, as did various nightclubs such as the Havana-Madrid and the Cuban Casino. It cost $2 to get into the Palladium on Wednesday, Friday, and Saturday nights, though Sundays were considerably cheaper ($.50 before six in the evening and $1 after that). Whatever relationship *La Prensa* tried to cultivate with the "bourgeois Latino community" through its editorial content, the price of a ticket to the Gran Festival did not present a barrier to working-class Latino/as.[34]

The publicity the Gran Festival provided appealed to all those involved, from nightclub, cabaret, and theater owners to the performers on stage and even the newspaper itself. It also caught the attention of aspiring politicians and government officials. Judging by some of the notable local political figures in attendance, entertainment, charity, and increased profits were, in some ways, only minor incentives for participating in this annual event. Local politics and popular culture merged at the fund-raising gala, and the candidates and officials who attended often used the event to gain access to or address potential supporters. The presence of local politicians

also suggests a shift toward a mutual or reciprocal interest in matters related to living and settling in New York City. The outlook seemed to be
shifting from one of temporary displacement to permanent settlement. In
1948, as he had in previous years, Assistant District Attorney Louis Pag-
nucco attended the Gran Festival with his wife and daughter. Making his
way through the crowd gathered in the entryway, he reportedly exclaimed,
"They certainly make a big fuss over this affair!"[35] New York City mayor
Vincent R. Impellitteri attended the Gran Festival in 1953. In his address
to the audience, he established his shared immigrant past with the audience, describing "his situation as an immigrant from Sicily, almost forty-
nine years ago, when his father, a shoemaker who spoke no English, brought
him, a year old, and his mother and siblings to live in this country." He
concluded his speech by praising *La Prensa*'s many years of "civic and
patriotic" service. Impellitteri's remarks were not entirely out of character, given the statements he had made just two years earlier declaring
his friendship and affection toward Cuba and the Cuban people (see
chapter 3).[36]

Those who attended the Gran Festival witnessed what amounted to a
spectacle of political offerings. No two politicians put this opportunity to
better use than did Franklin D. Roosevelt Jr. and Municipal Court Justice Benjamin Shalleck, opposing candidates for the vacant seat in the 20th
Congressional District of New York, which during this period included
much of Manhattan's Upper West Side. Both candidates attended the Gran
Festival in May 1949 just a few weeks after Roosevelt split from the Democratic Party to run against Shalleck as a candidate for the Liberal and Four
Freedoms Party. Roosevelt's candidacy renewed interest in the race, and
in the days leading up to the musical showcase it became clear that the
election had "reached the intensive fighting stage." At this critical moment
in their campaigns, both candidates attended the fund-raising festival in
the hope of securing voter support. This suggests that the Gran Festival
could, on occasion, serve an explicitly political function. Thanks to event
organizers, political candidates such as Roosevelt and Shalleck could present their platforms and make appeals to an already assembled audience:
in this case, a mostly migrant Spanish-speaking audience perhaps elevated
in significance by such targeted interest. Before presenting Doris Scoto-
liff with her trophy for winning the *Damas* category, Roosevelt "gave a few
brief and emotional words describing his political campaign and affirming his admiration for the Spanish-speaking people of North America." According to reports, the audience applauded him "wildly." Shalleck presented
a winner's trophy to Perucho Irigoyen, though the newspaper left no re-

cord of whatever remarks he may have made to the audience about his candidacy for office.[37]

NUESTRA RAZA, NUESTRA MÚSICA

Throughout the 1940s and 1950s, *La Prensa* referred to its general readership and those who were interested and involved in the contests and festivals in numerous and specific ways, including the *colonia*, the *colonia hispana*, *nuestra colonia* (our *colonia*), the *colonia de habla española* (the Spanish-speaking *colonia*), the *colonia de habla española de Nueva York y sus alrededores* (the Spanish-speaking *colonia* of New York and its surrounding areas), the *colonia de habla hispana de Nueva York y ciudades y pueblos limítrofes* (the Spanish-speaking *colonia* of New York and neighboring cities and towns), and the *colonia hispanoablante* (the Spanish-speaking *colonia*). The newspaper also used plural forms such as the *colonias hispanas* and *nuestras colonias en esta ciudad* (our *colonias* in this city), suggesting early on that a variety of ethnic groups came together to form a collectivity bound by a common language and shared experiences. In her study of Puerto Rican community development before World War II, historian Virginia Sánchez Korrol defined *colonias* as migrant neighborhoods, "geographic urban centers marked by dense settlement; they provided outlets for Puerto Rican interests, creating institutions which affirmed social identity and fostered internal activities." These neighborhoods became "area[s] where the language, customs, attitudes, interests and traditions were similar to those he or she had left in Puerto Rico." Though Sánchez Korrol's interest lies primarily in the development of the Puerto Rican *colonia*, the newspaper used the concept of the term mostly in a pan-ethnic effort "to build unity among Spanish-speaking New Yorkers." This terminology, according to historian Liz Ševčenko, referred to "a group of people who shared a common regional, class, or political background but was not defined by any geographical area in the city."[38] *La Prensa* hailed an imagined community of pan-ethnic Spanish-speaking New Yorkers, a strategy that is in line with the decision of organizers to modify one of the contest rules to specify that eligibility was open to "any hispanic artist, or artist of hispanic origin, regardless of nationality."

The dominance of the term *colonia* gave way in the 1950s to more varied descriptors such as the *comunidad de habla española* (the Spanish-speaking community), the *público de habla española de Nueva York y sus contornos* (the Spanish-speaking public of New York and its outlying areas), the *población de habla española* (the Spanish-speaking population), *nuestra comunidad* (our community), and *nuestra comunidad hispana* (our Hispanic community). The striking point here is not the less frequent use of the term *colonia hispana* to represent the Spanish-speaking population of New York City that was interested in the contest and festival but the increased use of these others terms to purposefully encompass a broader Spanish-speaking community that was not bound by geographic borders or ethnic divisions.

Early on, in 1941 and 1943, the newspaper explicitly indicated that the performers and audiences who participated in the Gran Festival were bound by a shared racial past. The newspaper reported that the fundraising gala enjoyed the "participation of the most distinguished artists of *nuestra raza.*" But the more telling comments came when the newspaper described the audience in attendance: "We noticed dozens and dozens of people from other races and nationalities that eager to get to know our artists as well as our music were some of the most animated, applauding with as much fervor as los nuestros." Obvious distinctions were made between those who belonged to *nuestra raza* and outsiders, though it is not clear what markers these observers used to arrive at their conclusions. One could speculate, however, that language use, phenotype, and other visual cues helped these observers conclude that some of those who attended were not of *nuestra raza.* Defining details about *nuestra raza* were scarce beyond what might be suggested by descriptions of the kind of music—termed *nuestra música*—performed at the Gran Festival. Reports declared that "Hispanoamerican, Afro-Cuban, and Spanish music provided the setting for the festival" and that "the applause was as warm for flamenco dances, gypsy dances and folk songs as it was for the melodies and dances of South America, the songs of Mexico, native rhythms and songs, everyone mixing together happily and harmoniously." Described variously as "the sensual harmony of gypsy and Afro-Cuban music," a "symbol of Hispano-American unity with the Spanish motherland," and "Spanish and Hispanoamerican folklores," *nuestra música* revealed the existence of an African, Spanish, and Hispanic past among the members of the *colonia* and suggested that racial and ethnic mixture fit within the parameters of what *La Prensa* had deemed *los nuestros,* at least in the realm of popular culture.[39]

From this perspective, it would seem as though the newspaper used *nuestra raza* as a pan-ethnic term synonymous with Hispanidad to signify a "composite race that encompasses an assortment of diverse national origins, various cultural heritages, and disparate phenotypes," a politically expedient mode of identification proposed by Latino/a Studies scholar

Silvio Torres-Saillant. Though the concept of *nuestra raza* can be seen as a rejection of the U.S. binary racial system and a mode of racialization that lies somewhere between whiteness and blackness, in this case it also functions in much the same way as the problematic concepts of "Hispanic" and "Latino/a." Latino/a Studies scholar Alberto Sandoval-Sánchez has argued that the terms "Hispanic" and "Latino/a" "constitute an act of racism when functioning as a fictitious homogenization of all Latin American countries into one language and one race." I argue that this can also be said of *nuestra raza*. Torres-Saillant also warns that these collective forms of identification are often used in ways that grant Latino/as symbolic inclusion in the realm of culture but do not signify inclusion and equality in the political sphere.[40] There is no evidence to suggest that *La Prensa* excluded dark-skinned members of the *colonia hispana* or other blacks at the Gran Festival, an event that celebrated and featured performances by numerous Afro-Cubans and other musicians of color. In fact, despite its use of the term Hispano/a rather than Latino/a, the newspaper did not shy away from openly discussing the meanings and inclusiveness of both terms; it did so in a series of debates published in its editorial section in the fall of 1944. Still, the newspaper's use of the concept of *nuestra raza* seems to have limited the possibility for dual and simultaneous expressions of blackness and Hispanidad.[41]

Though the newspaper and many of the performers emphasized the pan-ethnic, multinational Hispanic identity of the contest, festival, and *colonia hispana*, Cuban national identity was disproportionately at the core of the performances and the meanings inferred upon them, as demonstrated in particular through descriptions of *nuestra música*. The process was not entirely unique to *La Prensa* or even to the contests and festivals. *América en Marcha*, a New York-based Spanish-language periodical, declared that white Cuban bandleader José Curbelo, who won the contest in 1944, was one of the most distinguished of "nuestros músicos" ("our musicians"). More broadly, the report concluded that "throughout the years, nuestra música, and consequently nuestros músicos, have placed themselves on par with North American music," reflecting distinctions made within the music industry and the broader culture between North American and Latin American rhythms.[42] It should be noted, of course, that Cuban musicians of color also figured prominently among the long lists of contest winners and fund-raising gala participants. In many ways, the concept of *nuestra raza* (and, by extension, Hispanidad) is less interesting in terms of whether it was a term of "resistance" or "racism" than because it helps reveal a process by which Afro-Cuban music (and musicians) and Latin music (and musicians) were treated as synonyms in certain contexts without diminishing the simultaneous conversations in Cuba and within its diaspora about the relationship of music to race and national identity.

CUBAN NATIONAL IDENTITY IN THE
CONTESTS AND FESTIVALS

The emerging relationship between local politics and the *colonia hispana* at the fund-raising festivals followed years of support from Latin American and Caribbean consulate officials in New York City.[43] Consuls from Cuba, Mexico, the Dominican Republic, Peru, and Colombia attended the festivals to present their countrymen with their trophies, a celebratory act that effectively served to (re)claim those performers for their homelands.[44] The early participation of Cuban consulate officials suggests an active Cuban national presence in the city and demonstrates just one of the many manifestations of the "ties of singular intimacy" that had been developing between the United States and Cuba since the mid-nineteenth century. In 1943, Miguelito Valdés received his trophy from Cuban consul Roberto Hernández; he reportedly planned to dedicate his win to Cuban president Fulgencio Batista on behalf of the *colonia*. That same year, Machito received his trophy from Cuban consul-general Cayetano de Quesada in an act that left him "genuinely and visibly emotional."[45] In 1944, Consul Hernández presented trophies to several Cuban performers: Raúl y Eva, winners of the *Parejas de Baile* category, and José Curbelo and Luis Varona, first and second place finishers, respectively, in the *Orquestas* category.[46] Consul-general de Quesada returned in 1945 to present Xavier Cugat and José Curbelo with their first- and second-place trophies, respectively, in the *Orquestas* category.[47] These presentations provided unique opportunities for Cuban performers to receive national recognition, particularly given the likely gap in class and racial status between most of the performers and the consuls. For performers of Afro-Cuban music, whether it was considered to be authentic or watered down, their success in these contests and the subsequent recognition of the consuls at the festivals was part of the process by which Afro-Cubanness became synonymous with Cubanness and Latinness. The participation of diplomats from the Cuban consulate also demonstrates the effort the Cuban government made to organize and appeal to its overseas population in the *colonia hispana*. As we saw in chapter 3, this participation is an example of state-led, long-distance nationalism in practice, though it seems that Cuban consulate officials played a less direct role in organizing community life than did the Mexican consulate in Los Angeles in the 1920s, for example.[48]

Nineteen forty-three proved to be a big year for Cuban singers and orchestras. Thanks to his "meteoric career and instantaneous popularity," Miguelito Valdés finished first in the *Caballeros* category, easily defeating runners-up Bobby Capó and Jerónimo Villarino. Shortly after the release of the contest results, Valdés announced that he would postpone an already scheduled trip to Havana in order to perform at the Gran Festival, explaining to a reporter, "But I have to be there, I feel a tremendous desire to be there to express my gratitude to a public that has so generously given me first place." Described as "the singer of 'Babalú' that no other singer has since equaled," he appeared to be a man of the people "whose love for his own kind and customs and criollo artistry is one of his main characteristics." Valdés said that the Gran Festival would allow him to be reunited with "thousands of hispanos whose applause, laughter, and handshakes would have an incalculable, stimulating moral effect." Though "anxious to return to his homeland," he maintained that "there is a special place in his heart for New York, a place where he has made and spent a lot of money," an interesting reference that suggests that Valdés saw New York City as a place of economic prosperity but not as a place of permanent residence. News of his victory had already reached an "overjoyed" Cuban public and generated interest on the island for the fund-raising gala. Various news agencies in Cuba solicited film of the event and requested special interviews with the singer, according to reports in *La Prensa*. Such a response provides evidence of the Gran Festival's broad transnational appeal and its significance to Cubans in particular.[49]

That same year, Machito y sus Afro-Cubans won the *Orquestas* category, beating out the orchestras of Esteban Roig, José Curbelo, Noro Morales, Juanito Sanabria, and, most notably, Xavier Cugat. Made up of Cuban, Puerto Rican, and African American musicians, Machito's band had an "unmistakable criollo rhythm," and several of their dance compositions "delighted lovers of the Afro-Cuban rhythm" and "cemented the affection of the colonia." A lengthy follow-up article in *La Prensa* provided readers and voters with an inside look at Machito as both an ordinary migrant and a rising star in the world of entertainment. The newspaper performed a sort of unveiling of Machito, the celebrity and professional musician, and presented him as Frank Grillo, the man who had left his "beloved Cuba" never thinking that he would soon lead one of the most popular and successful orchestras in the *colonia hispana*. He explained that he "noticed that there was a growing interest around here for ritmos criollos," a realization supported by the sale of nearly 25,000 copies of his record "Sopa de Pichón," which "for a few months was the obligatory dance piece from Brooklyn to Harlem." The newspaper described the bandleader as having "a spectacular image dressed in his short suit 'zoot suit' with maracas or batuta [a stick used by conductors], singing and dancing in front of his band."[50]

The successes of Valdés and Machito could certainly be framed as shocking upsets of the internationally renowned Xavier Cugat. The three performers crossed paths repeatedly throughout the 1940s. Both Machito and Valdés started their professional careers in the United States as singers in Cugat's band, and all three entertainers performed together at La Conga in midtown Manhattan. In fact, the day after the publication of the contest results, Machito and Cugat performed on the same stage, headlining the Latin American Fiesta at the Hunts Point Palace in the Bronx.[51] But for the most part, Cugat's professional engagements during this period took him to venues and locations that were not typically frequented by the *colonia hispana*. The Waldorf-Astoria had just booked him for his eleventh season, the Paramount Theater had contracted him for various other engagements, and he had a national best-selling record, "Brazil," and a featured role in the Hollywood film *You Were Never Lovelier*, which starred Rita Hayworth and Fred Astaire. Neither Machito nor Valdés could really compete with Cugat, whose commercial act produced Latin music for mainstream, English-speaking North American audiences. It might have shocked some, then, that in 1943 "the most coveted prize in U.S. Latin American entertainment," as *Time* called it, was awarded not to world-famous Cugat but to Machito.

Shortly after *La Prensa* revealed the 1943 contest results, Machito commented on his victory to *Time*, stating plainly, "I was no [*sic*] surprised. Cugat, he is . . . commercial." Authentic music, or *música típica*, was correctly played by and for Latino/as *en clave* (in a two-bar rhythmic pattern), while the commercial variation was "visually hyped up" and "rhythmically watered down" music that appealed mostly to non-Latino/a audiences.[52] Yet the contest results suggest a messier, more complicated interpretation. To say that the *colonia hispana* rejected Cugat or deemed his role in the popularization of Latin music in the United States as insignificant would be to ignore the fact that he had already won the *Orquestas* category in 1941 and would return victorious again in 1945 and 1946.[53] Voters in the Concurso de Popularidad and, by extension, the *colonia hispana* did not consistently prefer "authentic" performers over "commercial" entertainers or vice versa. Such rigid positioning reduces what is really a continuum or matrix of never-ending negotiations, shaped by race and politics, between individual performers, multiple and overlapping audiences, and the entertainment industry. Machito's framing of his defeat of Cugat as a victory for "authenticity" over "commercialism" demonstrates that the newspaper's contest and festival generated public discourse on the various functions of music, particularly in relation to its reception as cultural expression, national symbol, and commercial product. It also reminds us of the familiar narrative commonly presented by musicians of color who claimed that they were innovators and authentic musicians rather than musicians responsible for the popularization and commercialization of Afro-Cuban music.

It makes sense that Cugat won the support of the *colonia hispana* in 1945 and 1946 given that numerous Latino musicians were drafted into the U.S. Army during World War II. Excluded from military service because of his age, Cugat remained in New York City as one of the few established Latino/a celebrities who was still selling records and able to perform regularly at nightclubs. Wartime conditions forced many local orchestras to find replacements for their musicians and prompted singers to limit their recording and performance schedules. For example, Machito's band hired his sister, Graciela (who was living in Cuba at the time), and Polito Galíndez to take over for him on vocals while he served a stint in the U.S. Army. Cugat's celebrity status allowed him to continue performing with the best of the musicians who were left in the city. Additionally, some of his songs, such as his 1941 hit "Viva Roosevelt!," demonstrated support for U.S. involvement in international affairs. As we saw in chapter 1, this popular song delivered energetic support for the United States as a hemispheric and global power, specifically in the context of World War II and more generally in terms of policies toward Latin America and the Caribbean. Interestingly, one reviewer for *Billboard* noted that because record buyers might not "harbor a conga beat with their patriotic fervor," the record would be most appealing "at the spots attracting a south-of-the-border patronage." The availability and essentialist patriotism of a performer played an important role in determining success in the early contests, more so than audience concerns or perceptions about a performer as authentic or commercial. Much like the participation of the foreign consuls in the festivals, Cugat's repeated victories in the 1940s suggest that the Latino/a public in New York City was very much aware of the rising demands for "good neighborliness."[54]

Representations of Cubanness through the dominating presence of Cuban performers in the contests and festivals peaked again in 1952. That year the Gran Festival was held on 20 May, a special day for Cubans everywhere; it was the fiftieth anniversary of Cuba's independence. The fundraising gala that year opened with patriotic remarks from Cuban journalist and host Babby Quintero and poetry readings by Cuban poet Eulogio Peraza. The festival followed days of reporting that highlighted the Cuban artists who were slated to perform at the event: Cuba, "the homeland of sugarcane, coffee, tobacco and good humor," could count on representation from Machito, Graciela, Mario Bauzá, Facundo Rivero y Conjunto, Juan Bruno Tarraza, Felo Bergaza, Perucho Irigoyen, and Willie Chevalier. Perhaps it was testimony to the relationship between performers, audiences, and national identity or perhaps it was simply coincidence, but the year that the newspaper held the contest on such a key date in Cuban national consciousness was also the year that Machito won the *Orquestas* category and Graciela won the *Damas* category. Cuban performers and Cuban national identity once again took center stage at this pan-ethnic, multinational event that sought to represent the entire *colonia hispana* and the broader Spanish-speaking Americas.[55]

CROSSING BORDERS, CREATING COMUNIDAD

While migrants who attended the Gran Festival in New York City reconnected with their homelands in symbolic and material ways, audiences back home were transported via electronic mass media to New York City. The Office of the Coordinator of Inter-American Affairs (OCIAA) transmitted portions of the Gran Festival throughout Latin America and the Caribbean via short wave radio in the early 1940s. The significance of this international broadcast was not lost on *La Prensa*. It reported that "millions of Hispanoamericanos will have the opportunity to listen, simultaneously with the public of New York City, to the famous artists that are going to sing and dance at this event." In the context of wartime calls for hemispheric solidarity, the newspaper noted in 1943 that the OCIAA "has been cooperating with anything involving Hispanic character being realized in the United States."[56]

Noting that the contest had crossed national borders for many years thanks to support from the U.S. government and other international news agencies, *La Prensa* proudly reported that it routinely received votes and inquiries from Canada, Mexico, Cuba, Puerto Rico, and Colombia.[57] Fausto, the longtime writer of the column "La Gran Vía Blanca" ("The Great White Way"), declared in 1944 that this artistic event had acquired "international proportions" that had numerous praiseworthy secondary effects: "While [the contest] honors our artists, it also serves to highlight the value of folkloric inspiration as a means of bringing together the people of the Western Hemisphere. Panamericanism owes a debt of gratitude to these artists, who, singing with their souls, with the language of the soul, through feelings, unite in unbreakable bonds people of different languages and cultures!"[58] Participation in the fund-raising gala thus served to support, from *within* the *colonia hispana*, a U.S. foreign policy of "neighborliness" toward the peoples and cultures of Latin America and the Caribbean. The contests and galas demonstrate the appropriation of Pan-Americanism as a cultural ideology of hemispheric solidarity that was developing from within the Latino/a migrant communities of New York City. In these instances, the newspaper acted as a pseudo-activist organization that sought to protect and promote the interests of the *colonia hispana* while also falling in line with the inter-American rhetoric that characterized the period.[59]

Before any presentations or performances could take place, each Gran Festival began with the singing of the "Star-Spangled Banner," a performance that reflected, in many ways, the reality that many of those in attendance faced daily pressures to shift their allegiance and adapt to their new lives in this country. This was not the only patriotic gesture executed at the fund-raising gala. Reaching back toward the homelands they had recently left, organizers went to great lengths to offer a program with (inter) nationalist overtones. In 1946, organizers reported that the festival would include "a great quantity of regional costumes" that represented various countries. The efforts apparently paid off, leading to reports that the Manhattan Center appeared "exotic" and "transported the spectators to their respective homelands across the Hispano-American world."[60] Organizers noted that performers served as symbols of their native lands, and they often grouped performers and the schedule of performances based on nationality. In 1948, for example, a miscellaneous selection of performers followed two separate groupings, one Mexican, the other Spanish. The newspaper also remarked that "Puerto Rico, Argentina, Cuba, the Dominican Republic, and other nationalities will be represented by distinguished artists that are currently in New York," evidence of the newspaper's awareness of the transnational loyalties of its public.[61] In fact, few artists were listed as participants in the Gran Festival without specific mention of their national or ethnic identities. Organizers recognized that readers and attendees maintained close ties with and affection for their homelands. This realization likely encouraged organizers to associate performers with their country of origin, a move that suggests that developing notions of Hispanidad and Latinidad did not prohibit loyalties to national origin.

Brief on-the-street testimonials solicited by *La Prensa* in 1956 reveal that tensions and conflicts sometimes developed in the *colonia hispana* as a result of these loyalties to the homeland and feelings of ethnic superiority. José García stated that in order to bring harmony to the community, "the first thing that we need to do is forget about patriotism . . . and stop saying that our homeland is better than the other and that the other is not worth anything." George García declared that Hispano/as "should leave patriotism for the homeland behind and remember that they are all in another country and think about how they can live better where they are." José R. Arroyo attributed the disunity to a lack of leadership in the community, specifically blaming the problem on the proliferation of so many different Hispanic organizations. He reasoned that "it would be better if there were less social clubs and less patriotism, particularly since here in the colonia the homeland doesn't matter much and what does matter is language." Lolita Gisbert offered the following explanation for the frictions: "Despite having a common language we are from different countries and we think in different ways, even to the point of thinking that one is better than the others. This is why there is disunity within la raza." Despite the fact that members of the *colonia hispana* shared a common language and migration experiences, nationalism sometimes led to division and disagreements. Just as clearly, though, this tension did not diminish claims of belonging to *nuestra raza* or deny that such a thing existed in the first place.[62]

As early as 1943, the newspaper suggested that tensions had developed in the *colonia hispana* as a result of political differences. A review of the Gran Festival published in *New York al Día* (and reprinted in *La Prensa*) declared the event "miraculous," emphasizing its ability each year to perform the "miracle of the spiritual UNION of the colonia, a UNION acknowledged by everyone as real utopia or beautiful impossibility." Popular culture played a role in unifying the community each year, according to the report: "Art is also very powerful, almost divine, and because of its heavenly and irresistible power, the hispanic residents of New York forget, if just for a few hours, the political hatreds that divide and confront them, and they come together, rather than lose themselves, in the shared enthusiasm prevailing in these magnificent festivals."[63] Just as the newspaper hoped to increase its daily readership, artist managers, record companies, and performers also aimed to secure the largest paying audiences possible. A cultural event such as the Gran Festival that could bring together a broad and sometimes divisive Spanish-language audience not only made for positive public relations but also increased the odds of bringing in larger profits for both the newspaper and the entertainment industries.

Nevertheless, national representation continued throughout the 1950s, when the increasing popularity of merengue from the Dominican Republic began to chip away at the dominance of other Latin rhythms such as the rumba, mambo, and cha-cha-chá. Organizers promised that those attending the 1955 Gran Festival would delight in a "genuine Dominican representation" in addition to the other rhythms of "our tropical countries." Competition and rivalry among national and ethnic groups through musical genres developed elsewhere on the cultural landscape of New York City. *La Prensa* declared that in the United States a "great battle" was taking place between the Cuban mambo and the Dominican merengue. Musical styles stood in for national representation, and "authenticity" seemed to matter. Nothing captured this concern better than Mario Bauzá's initial refusal to allow Machito y sus Afro-Cubans to perform merengue for dances at the Palladium. He relented only when he found "a genuine Dominican musician with authority to 'supervise' the rhythms and melodies of the merengue."[64]

Not only had merengue infiltrated the programming of the Gran Festival but, by 1957, so had the rhythms of calypso and rock 'n' roll, introduced by groups such as Polly y Jimmy Rogers y su Conjunto de Merengue, Cha-Cha-Chá y Rock & Roll and Minin de la Cruz y sus Merengues.[65] Brief on-the-street interviews conducted by *La Prensa* in the midst of the contest voting process revealed that rock 'n' roll had definitely attracted the attention of the young women of the *colonia hispana*. Zoe Cordero appreciated rock 'n' roll because it represented modernity: "It is a dance that responds to the present moment, not to a tradition, like the majority of the ones that we know." Clemencia Castro approached the question from a historical perspective: "The thing is that it is a different type of music. I don't think it causes any bad effects in teenagers. Just like the Charleston and Fox Trot were once popular. We are seeing that with Calypso which was once popular." Joséfa Villalba noted the crossover appeal of rock 'n' roll: "In my opinion, it is a dance wanted by the North American just as much as the hispano for its animated and emotional rhythm." Only one respondent, Sally Cordero, indicated a less favorable position; she felt that "we should insist on more 'jazz' and on a softer and melodic music."[66] These shifts in cultural preferences, characterized in large part by the surging popularity of rock 'n' roll and television in the mid- to late 1950s, render it less surprising that the popularity of the contests and fund-raising festivals would soon be in decline. In just a few short years, the Latin music industry would fall into a decade-long slump that it would not emerge from until music producer Jerry Masucci and his label Fania Records repackaged it as *salsa* and crowned Afro-Cuban singer Celia Cruz its queen in the early 1970s.[67]

By 1958, after nearly two decades of sponsoring the popularity contests and fund-raising galas, *La Prensa*'s commitment to and public interest in such events faded. No longer did category winners draw between 40,000 and 80,000 votes, as they had in the 1940s. By the late 1950s, category winners received only between 10,000 and 40,000 votes, a striking decline in voter interest considering the ballot inflation that took place throughout the years. But these were not the only or even most significant changes that affected the contests and festivals of 1958 and 1959. In May 1958, the newspaper announced that the contest and fund-raising gala would not take place in the spring, as it had for the past sixteen years, but would instead be moved to the fall. What had been an annual tradition of the *colonia hispana* for nearly two decades was indifferently bumped from its position of cultural importance for the Reina de *La Prensa* beauty pageant, which also sought to raise money for the newspaper's Charity Fund. The newspaper argued that the decision to move the musical popularity contest to the fall would prove beneficial for two main reasons: more agreeable weather and better entertainment, since the nightclubs and theaters in the city would be offering more quality shows.[68]

If the new date did not sufficiently confuse and alienate loyal voters and readers, then the new categories listed on the ballots confirmed that the contest and festival were forever changed. In 1958, readers could vote for their favorite artists in seven non-gender-based categories: *Actores* (Actors), *Bailarines* (Dancers), *Locutores*, *Cantantes* (Singers), *Solistas* (Soloists), *Orquestas*, and *Conjuntos Musicales*. The 1959 contest listed just six non-gender-based categories, offering combined categories for *Bailarines o Conjuntos de Baile* and *Orquestas o Conjuntos Musicales* and specifying that the *Cantantes* category included solo artists, duos, and trios. Most of the winners and runners-up in each category had never figured prominently in the final standings of previous contests, and artists that had won their categories in the past now received far fewer votes than usual. Perucho Irigoyen, for example, won or finished second in the *Caballeros* and *Locutores* categories each year from 1950 to 1957, but in 1958 and 1959 he barely finished sixth and fourth, respectively, in the *Actores* category. The *Orquestas* and *Orquestas o Conjuntos Musicales* categories listed contest newcomer Ricardo "El Rey del Merengue" Rico as the winner in both

1958 and 1959, and the only other familiar orchestras and *conjuntos* to place in the final standings were Oriental Cubana, Chapuseaux y Damirón, and Vicentico Valdés. In addition, the orchestras that were hired to perform at the fund-raising galas, Ricardo Rico and "the great band" Tropical Knights in 1958 and Ricardo Rico and Ramiro Medina in 1959, had never before participated in the events.[69] All this is to say that the familiar favorites of past contests and festivals no longer appeared relevant, though it is not clear if the tastes and preferences of voters changed independently from the interests of the newspaper and entertainment industry.

The role of the Comisión de Escrutinio also changed in 1958. That year, the presidents of three social clubs and organizations formed the committee: Diego Díaz of the Ateneo Cubano, Francisco Arévalo of Centro Español/La Nacional, and Victor López of the Asociación de Comerciantes Hispanos del Bronx and the Desfile Puertorriqueño. Each Saturday, the committee gathered at an event hosted by one of the social clubs of the city to count the votes received that week and announce the current standings. For example, Club Social Salinas welcomed the Comisión de Escrutinio to a dance it was hosting at the Palladium that featured Tito Puente and Caco y su Combo. Club España hosted another vote count at the Hotel Diplomat, where it was holding a dance that featured Esteban Roig. The committee revealed the final standings at the weekly dance sponsored by the Ateneo Cubano, which promised to feature many of the artists jostling for position in the contest. Organizers reasoned that "the traditional happiness that fills the dances of the Ateneo Cubano will contribute immensely to increasing the enthusiasm for the final phase of the Concurso."[70] In some ways, the more direct and active involvement of the leaders and general memberships of the *colonia*'s social clubs confirms a relationship of mutual interest and support between the newspaper and the community. But it also hints at desperation, a more confrontational means of cajoling participation and support for the contest and festival.

Despite changes in the contest dates, categories, and organizing committee, the newspaper maintained that this was still the same contest and festival that readers had anticipated and enjoyed throughout the 1940s and 1950s. And in some ways, it was the same. The newspaper reported that telephone calls and unannounced visits to its office from voters interested in the contest overwhelmed its employees so much so that some worried that there would not be enough copies of the newspaper available for those that wanted to participate. As it had in previous years, the newspaper received hundreds of letters related to the contest and festival. It saw these acts as "demonstration of the power that the contest has among the His-panoamerican public and the interest in helping its favorite artists place among the six categories presented in this Concurso de Popularidad."[71] Featuring artists from Argentina, Colombia, Ecuador, Cuba, Mexico, Puerto Rico, Spain, Brazil, the Dominican Republic, and the United States, the Gran Festival, according to the newspaper, would again have "an international character." The contest and festival allowed the newspaper to keep in touch with its readers as both a news source and as a constructive element in the *colonia hispana*, including through its continued support via the Charity Fund. The quality of the program was attributable to "the most distinguished artists of our theatrical and cultural scene [who] offer, like always, their most unselfish cooperation." Indeed, the newspaper insisted that "readers and all community members, fans of this type of show and those desirous of helping to raise money for the charity fund" continued to enthusiastically appreciate the efforts.[72]

■ The gradual changes in the contests and festivals of the mid-1950s had by 1958 and 1959 evolved into an affair that was struggling with an identity that once had proclaimed itself to be representative of the traditional and folkloric elements of New York City's *colonia hispana*, a mixture of Spanish, African, and Hispanoamerican cultures. For almost two decades, *La Prensa* played a central role in constructing Hispano/a and Latino/a identity and community through the musical popularity contests and fund-raising festivals it sponsored. That Afro-Cuban music played a major part in this process is no more surprising than the fact that black and white Cuban musicians and bandleaders took much of the credit for generating interest among audiences from within and beyond the Spanish-speaking Americas, directly as winners and participants and indirectly through the discourses produced about the contests and festivals. In 1960, there was no Concurso de Popularidad or Gran Festival, and the prominent role that Latino/a musicians and performers had struggled to achieve within the cultural landscape of New York City now faced a much less certain and stable future.

5

REAL AND IMAGINED

REPRESENTATIONS OF (AFRO-)CUBANNESS

AND LATINNESS

No Cuban entertainer was more well known among North American audiences in the 1950s than Ricky Ricardo, the fictionalized bandleader portrayed by Desi Arnaz on the hit television comedy *I Love Lucy*. Over 40 million people tuned in to CBS on Monday evenings from 1951 to 1957 to watch the half-hour sitcom that chronicled the daily lives and misadventures of Ricky and Lucy Ricardo and their neighbor-pals, Fred and Ethel Mertz. Drawing distinctions between the real-life Arnaz and the semiautobiographical character he played on television is not always an easy task. Both Ricky and Desi worked at nightclubs in Manhattan, both aspired to become film and television stars, both possessed savvy business skills, and both could credit their good looks and charismatic personalities for driving their careers in the entertainment industry. Desi was married to actress and comedienne Lucille Ball. Ricky was married to a parody of the same woman, Ball's character on the show, Lucy Ricardo. Given the show's enormous popularity and the apparent blurriness between fiction and reality in it, the actual differences between Desi's life (and the lives of other Cuban musicians) and the image of Ricky as a Cuban entertainer in the public imagination are extremely telling. The stories Desi Arnaz, Machito, Miguelito Valdés, and Perucho Irigoyen told about their lived experiences, juxtaposed with the imaginative realities presented in the fictionalized world of Ricky Ricardo on *I Love Lucy*, serve as a window into the development of a Cuban American cultural landscape that took root not only in the nightclubs and dance halls of New York City but also on television and on the Hollywood big screen.[1]

Instead of offering a complete and detailed biography of these four bandleaders and performers, this chapter examines their autobiographical writings and oral history interviews and the perspectives they expressed in interviews and reports published in Spanish- and English-language newspapers and trade magazines. In particular, I draw from the autobiography of Desi Arnaz. Literary studies and cultural studies scholar Gustavo Pérez-Firmat treats *A Book: The Outspoken Memoirs of "Ricky Ricardo"—The Man Who Loved Lucy* as both immigrant autobiography and erotic memoir, arguing that it should be understood as Arnaz's "farewell performance," one that is "far from being an innocent act of self-disclosure." While *A Book* is useful for the biographical information and anecdotal evidence it offers, it is, indeed, more interesting when examined as a cultural text that provides a unique look at how Arnaz constructed and remembered his life story.[2] Using Arnaz's career and that of his most famous character Ricky Ricardo as the main points of comparison, we can see key similarities and vital differences in the migration and work experiences of these entertainers, both real and imagined, specifically in terms of their early participation in the entertainment industry, their understanding of themselves as laborers and celebrities, the locations and settings of their musical performances, and their responses to self-representations and stereotypes that cast them variously as "Cuban," "Afro-Cuban," and "Latin."

Much of this chapter focuses on the narratives that Cuban and Latino/a musicians and audiences in New York City created about their reality in relation to the incredible visibility of the fictionalized experience on *I Love Lucy* and other Hollywood productions. Classic accounts of the history of television in the United States often consider *I Love Lucy* principally in terms of its innovations in the genre of situation comedy and its themes of subverting gender roles and the difficulties of interethnic marriage. But it is also a cultural text about show business and the tensions between claims of (Afro-)Cubanness and Latinness.[3] Ricky Ricardo lived in a comfortable apartment at 623 East 68th Street (a made-up location that would have had him in the middle of the East River) and spent his evenings headlining at the Tropicana Club, a 75-table nightclub with a visibly reserved and light-skinned audience. For the many Cuban musicians who performed at both downtown and uptown nightclubs in New York City, a career in the entertainment industry was not so neatly packaged. Most entertainers had to piece together a living by accepting bookings at multiple nightclubs and performing for private gatherings such as birthdays, weddings, and events sponsored by ethnic social clubs and cultural organizations. Nightclubs and dance halls in New York City—from the Hunts Point Palace and the Tropicana Club in the Bronx to La Conga and the Palladium in midtown Manhattan—provided musicians and audiences with opportunities for socialization and cultural expression that at times were much different and at other times were strikingly similar to the one presented on *I Love Lucy*. Race, ethnicity, and local community relationships shaped these experiences, as did the way performers responded to the demands and constraints of the commercial entertainment industry.

Cuban entertainers played key roles in the construction of discourses of Hispano/a and Latino/a identity and community, which, as we saw in the last chapter, was often referred to as belonging to *los nuestros*. This chapter reflects on performances that depicted Cubanness for spectacularly large white North American audiences. Despite its immense popularity among these audiences, the kind of Cubanness and Cuban Americanness presented on *I Love Lucy* and in other Hollywood productions operated almost entirely on its own terms, refashioning particular "authentic" performances for non-Spanish-speaking audiences. But Cuban entertainers also performed for Hispano/a and Latino/a audiences, and the content of Cubanness and discourses of authenticity they expressed, especially in the context of nightclubs and dance halls in the Bronx and on Broadway, reflect a particular mode of fashioning Cuban and Cuban American identity that was very much in dialogue with and rooted in New York City's *colonia hispana*. Examining and understanding both modes of performance reveals how particular Cuban, Afro-Cuban, and Latin representations and material experiences worked to mark entertainers as cultural insiders and musical innovators, as examples of "authentic" cultural expression, or as purveyors of a "watered-down" commercial sound and image.

A REVOLUTION CLOSE TO HOME

Desi Arnaz arrived in Key West, Florida, in 1934 neither in pursuit of a career as a professional musician nor to escape the racial prejudices and class biases that had prompted many other black and white Cuban musicians to leave the island for the United States. Instead, he left Cuba because of an immediate political and social crisis.[4] In 1933, led by the ABC Revolutionary Society, the Directorio Estudiantil Universitario, and other opposition groups, young, mostly middle- and working-class Cubans, intellectuals, professionals, sugar workers, and students took to the streets to protest the political corruption, economic depression, and violent repression that had become characteristic of life on the island under the regime of Cuban president Gerardo Machado, who had been elected to the presidency in 1925. Machado initially resisted the strikes against him but finally left his post and the island after the Cuban Army opposed him to avoid direct U.S. military intervention.[5]

As the only son of the mayor of Santiago, Arnaz had lived a life of wealth, power, and privilege. He attended private school and enjoyed the luxuries of a large estate complete with cars, speedboats, fishing vessels, horses, personal servants, and a chauffeur. Many of those luxuries came as the result of the corruption associated with the Machado regime; that, at least, was the charge levied by Octavio Siegle, secretary-general of the Liga Patriótica Cubana, in an editorial published in *Gráfico* in 1930. Siegle called the majority of the mayors of Cuba "scoundrels" and accused them of lacking principles. He singled out Desi Arnaz Sr., complaining that he had not paid municipal employees in over six months. His greatest indictment centered on the money and property that Arnaz Sr. had amassed as mayor. Although "he came to power in poverty," Siegle wrote, in 1930 he owned three farms and three brand-new buildings and had accumulated enough land to accommodate a municipal truck repair shop. The plot of land was so large that Arnaz Sr. and a business partner approached Pan American Airways about using it as a landing strip for a fee of $100,000. Siegle expressed outrage: "The municipality is bankrupt, but this Machadista hasn't lost a dime."[6]

Much of that easy living changed for the Arnaz family after the Revolution of 1933. Word quickly spread across the island that Machado had left the country, and anyone associated with his regime risked retribution or arrest. Arnaz recalled receiving a frantic phone call from his uncle, urging him and his mother to leave the house immediately because an angry mob was on its way, ready for violence. His father was in Havana (he was by that point a representative in the Cuban government), and it was up to him and one of the house servants, Bombalé, to get his mother to safety. According to Arnaz, Bombalé, whom he described as a "big wonderful black man," could not believe that the mob would be coming for them because "there are blacks in that mob." Arnaz was also surprised, reasoning that "blacks had been Dad's greatest supporters" and that "without them he would never have been elected mayor three times." Noting that one of his father's biggest projects as mayor was a plan to pave all the streets in Santiago, "particularly where the blacks and poor people lived," he insisted that he "never knew what racial prejudice was until I got to Florida. Instead of being prejudiced, we were proud of our black population."[7] White Cubans, especially those of the middle and upper classes, as we have seen, routinely expressed an image of Cuban society as racially integrated and harmonious, particularly in contrast to racial practices in the United States, despite the very real existence of racism and racial inequality on the island.

However, Arnaz's account of black political support for his father is more than white misconception or exaggeration. Just a few days after Machado's ousting and Arnaz Sr.'s subsequent arrest in Havana, African American historian and member of President Franklin D. Roosevelt's Federal Council of Negro Affairs Rayford Logan wrote in a special piece for the *Baltimore Afro-American* "that Oriente has solved the race problem with more fairness than any other region of which I know except possibly Brazil." As evidence of the lack of discrimination in Oriente, the island's easternmost province that had long been known for having the largest (and sometimes rebellious) population of Cubans of color on the island, he noted the existence of men of color in high posts in the government and as officers in the army and the many teachers and professors of color in the public schools. Logan's piece also included the rather peculiar mention of the passage of the Morúa Law of 1911, which prohibited political parties from organizing along racial lines. Though the law was intended to limit the rights of Afro-Cubans and dissolve the Partido Independiente de Color, in professing that the Cuban nation was free of racial division, the law inadvertently allowed Cubans of color to demand access to education and other rights. Logan's exact position on the law remains unclear: on the one hand, he does not indicate whether he believed Cuba had achieved racial equality, thereby making race-based organizing unnecessary; but on the other hand, he does not suggest that Afro-Cubans had used the law to make gains in certain areas of government and society. Given his overall view of race relations on the island, the former seems most likely. In any case, before advising readers to stop in Oriente rather than Havana on their next visit to Cuba, he concluded that "the situation in Oriente disproves, moreover, the current conviction that the greater the proportion of Negros in the population, the greater the discrimination. The exact opposite seems to be the case in Oriente."[8]

According to census records, almost half of the population in Oriente at the time was "black" so it seems plausible that Arnaz Sr. had relied on this constituency for political support. Other white politicians, most notably Machado, also reportedly relied on black support to secure their positions in government. In many ways, cross-racial alliances were typical of the Machado era: Machado declared 7 December, the date of Antonio

Maceo's death, a national holiday; he barred the Ku Klux Klan from establishing a chapter in Camagüey; and several Afro-Cuban candidates were elected to positions in the national government. In 1928, Afro-Cuban societies, whose memberships consisted mostly of black politicians and the black middle class, organized "a massive public homage" in honor of Machado to demonstrate their appreciation for and support of his government.[9] Also during this period, *son* emerged from its position as music of the black lower classes to achieve national acceptance by white middle- and upper-class Cubans, thanks in part to support from the Machado government. The Machado regime helped popularize *son* in numerous ways, including inviting musicians to perform at *encerrona* gatherings (extravagant private parties with dance bands where guests would be "locked in" by the host), issuing a public request from the president that the Sonora Matancera perform at his birthday party, and giving official permission to hotels and other establishments to promote *son* music and dance.[10] By the late 1920s and early 1930s, Machado had earned a reputation as a "pro-black president," but, as historian Alejandro de la Fuente cautions, that image had mostly been constructed by his opponents for their own political gain. After the fall of Machado in 1933, he argues, "it was necessary for antiblack forces to represent the anti-Machado revolution as a 'white' accomplishment in order to minimize Afro-Cubans' gains in the new Cuba."[11]

While Arnaz, his mother, and Bombalé found refuge in Santiago, rioters ransacked and destroyed most of the family's estate, leaving little more than Desi's guitar untouched. His father, meanwhile, had turned himself in to authorities at La Cabaña in Havana. Arnaz and his mother eventually made their way to the capital, and six months later his father was released from prison on a writ of *habeas corpus*. During that time, another revolt took place, this one led by sergeants and soldiers in the Cuban Army who had gathered at Camp Columbia in Havana to discuss a list of grievances they hoped to present to army officers. Officers refused to acknowledge the troops, and antigovernment civilian protestors, including the Directorio Estudiantil Universitario, gathered in support of the soldiers, who were now effectively in revolt against the presidency of Carlos Manuel de Céspedes y Quesada. The uprising, which was known as the "sergeants' revolt," left Fulgencio Batista, the coup's chief organizer, in control of the Cuban government, not officially as president but by virtue of his command of the army. He personally advised Arnaz Sr. to leave for Miami until the situation on the island stabilized.[12]

Arnaz soon joined his father in Miami, later recalling that his migration "might not have been a giant step for mankind, but it was a big one for me." Arnaz Sr. met him at the dock in Key West, and the two men rode a bus to a boardinghouse in the southwest part of Miami, where they shared a small room for $5 a week. His father claimed that he had no money, that he had been able to borrow only a few hundred dollars before his departure from Cuba. Soon, however, his father partnered with the former governors of Santa Clara and Camagüey, who were also living in Miami, to start a company that imported roof, bathroom, and kitchen tiles. Arnaz worked as the errand boy for the new company, but the tile business was slow. The men decided to live at the company's warehouse to save money on rent, and eventually they began importing bananas to increase profits. Other things were keeping Arnaz busy at the time. In the mornings, the nineteen-year-old worked as a canary cage cleaner and in the afternoons he attended St. Patrick's High School in Miami Beach, where he was a member of the swim team.[13]

Arnaz complained that the small number of Cubans in Miami in the mid-1930s made adjusting to life in the United States especially difficult. He insisted that the only Cubans in Miami during this period were former members of the Machado regime. It was, nonetheless, a member of this small but significant cohort of Cuban exiles who gave him his start in show business, a connection between power, politics, and the commercial entertainment industry that seemed lost on Arnaz. Alberto Barreras, former president of the Cuban Senate, thought immediately of Arnaz when the bandleader of the Siboney Septet, the relief band at the Roney Plaza in Miami Beach, came to him looking for a Cuban who could play the guitar and sing. Barreras reportedly told the bandleader that he had someone in mind, "but he didn't know if the boy's father would let him do it, still thinking of that old family pride. In those days, a musician came through the kitchen." That musicians "came through the kitchen," avoiding the public visibility of a front-door entrance, suggests that their chosen mode of employment was not generally well respected or held in high esteem. It also reveals that musicians were often considered no different than cooks, busboys, or janitors. When Arnaz's father heard the news, he protested, as did the parents and families of Arturo "Chico" O'Farrill, Machito, and other black and white Cubans who were interested in careers in popular music. It seems as though rejecting the idea of a career in popular music could cut across race and class. He exclaimed, "No, my son is not going to be a goddamn musician." Arnaz Sr. wanted his son to study at a university to be a doctor or a lawyer. To this race- and class-based opposition, Arnaz offered his father a practical response: "This is the United States of America, and besides, it can't be worse than cleaning birdcages." Finally, with his father's permission, he joined the band in the winter of 1936, earning $39 a week.[14]

Local theater owner Carlos Montalbán foreshadowed what would be Arnaz's trademark: the bandleader's appeal was not his musical talent but his personality and good looks. Of those early days at the Roney Plaza, Montalbán noted, "He was always off-beat, but he's an awfully nice guy, a clean-cut Latin." It was likely Arnaz's image as "clean-cut Latin" that drew the attention of Xavier Cugat, who invited him to audition for his band in New York City as soon as he graduated from high school. Arnaz recalled that from his days performing with Cugat's band at the Waldorf-Astoria, he "learned not only about how the music should be played, how it should be presented, what the American people like to dance to, but also how to handle the band, the rehearsals, the salaries, and all the angles of the band business."[15] Of course, despite what he learned, Arnaz never reached the level of musical success achieved by Cugat, who recorded extensively and whose music enjoyed the support of the mainstream dancing crowd.

After six months in New York City with Cugat, Arnaz decided to return to Miami to start his own band, which he claimed was "the only typical Cuban band in Miami Beach." With Cugat's permission and for a fee of $25 per week, he advertised his new band as "Desi Arnaz and his Xavier Cugat Orchestra direct from the Waldorf-Astoria in New York City." Cugat sent him four "lousy" musicians, an Italian bass player, a Spanish drummer, a Jewish pianist, and an Italian violinist, none of whom had any experience playing Latin rhythms. Arnaz claimed that it was during the second set of the band's first lackluster performance at Bobby Kelly's Park Plaza the week of New Year's 1937–1938 that he introduced American audiences to the 1-2-3 kick of the conga line. As music historian John Storm Roberts explains, however, the conga as a music and dance form had arrived in the United States much earlier, courtesy of Cuban composer Eliseo Grenet's "Havana Is Calling Me," which he had previously released in Cuba under the title "La Conga."[16]

Desperate to avoid being fired, Arnaz reportedly drew on musical influences from his childhood in Cuba: "And my mind did a flashback to the yearly carnivals in Santiago, when thousands of people in the streets form a conga line . . . to the beat of African conga drums."[17] Carnival celebrations had come under attack in both Havana and Santiago throughout the late nineteenth and early twentieth centuries as a result of racial ideologies and beliefs that condemned African drumming and Afro-Cubans as savage, immoral, and backward. In 1925, Arnaz Sr., then mayor of Santiago, published an edict banning congas, which he described as "that loud conjunto of drums, frying pans, and shouting," from carnival celebrations in favor of "uniform and decent" *comparsas* that "offer the community the pleasant impression of positive and honest fun." As a young boy in Santiago, Arnaz had witnessed and participated in these celebrations, and despite local, national, and familial prohibitions or possibly because of them (in 1925, his father organized what was likely a "decent" *comparsa* named Los Hijos de Arnaz), he found excitement in them.[18]

Shortly after his debut in Miami, Arnaz moved back to New York City, where he shared a room in an apartment in Brooklyn with his bass player. He brought with him the conga line he had first made popular in Miami. His band got hired at La Conga, whose name signals that the music and the dance predated Arnaz's arrival and had already achieved at least a modicum of popularity in the United States. Syndicated newspaper columnist Dorothy Kilgallen described La Conga as "the first nightclub that brought the Eastside of New York to the Westside."[19] Kilgallen seemed to credit La Conga for bringing the popular audiences and the immigrant, ethnic, and working-class popular representations that generally characterized the East Side of lower and midtown Manhattan to the West Side of the city, which was perceived to be more upscale and sophisticated, particularly in terms of arts and culture. Arnaz's conga line, she seemed to argue, allowed La Conga to emerge as a sort of middle ground, bringing together elements of the city that had previously been (mostly) separate because of differences in race, ethnicity, and class.

La Conga had a "mostly Latin" clientele, according to a reviewer who attended a show in 1946 that featured Miguelito Valdés and Machito y sus Afro-Cubans. Advertisements for the nightclub and its featured acts ran in *La Prensa*, *Diario de Nueva York*, and the *New York Times*. This marketing strategy suggests that the nightclub's "mostly Latin" customers were probably not people of color but rather middle- and upper-class white and light-skinned Spanish and Latin American and Caribbean migrants and visitors, especially from Cuba and Puerto Rico, who were interested in experiencing the conga craze and other Latin rhythms in what was described as an "unforgettable, authentic atmosphere." Advertising in the *New York Times* also shows that club owners Jack and Nat Harris were interested in attracting white North American audiences. This speculation is supported by their decision late in 1944 to dump Machito y sus Afro-Cubans

Desi Arnaz (right) at the La Conga nightclub in New York City, 5 August 1939,
with Hollywood actor Errol Flynn (left) and model Patricia Byrnes (center).
Copyright Bettmann/Corbis/AP Images. Courtesy of AP Images.

in order to "[switch] somewhat into more American channels" and "[go] in more heavily for U.S. stuff."[20]

The nightly spectacle of Arnaz's conga line drew the attention of director George Abbot and writers Richard Rodgers and Larry Hart, who cast Arnaz as Manuelito Lynch, a football (not *fútbol*) star from Argentina, in *Too Many Girls*, a musical comedy that opened on Broadway in October 1939. Six months before the release of the film version of the Broadway production, at least one reviewer noted another reason for the conga's rise as a national and international dance craze. Columbia Records had just released a four-disc set of congas performed by Arnaz's band called *Dance La Conga*, which featured "an accompanying set of instructions by Arthur Murray [that] is intended to show purchasers how to conga almost as well as Señor Arnaz."[21] In the Hollywood version of *Too Many Girls*, Manuelito leads a conga line during the film's finale in, perhaps, the strangest of contexts: at a bonfire after a football game on the campus of a college in New Mexico with an almost 10:1 female-to-male ratio. Still dressed in his football uniform, Manuelito bangs on a conga drum adorned in Indian motifs, while his classmates, including Pepe (Ann Miller), a Mexican tap dancer, perform the simplified steps in perfect sequence. The conga emerged as a popular dance form, according to Pérez-Firmat, thanks to the ease with which a diverse crowd, such as the one in *Too Many Girls*, could effortlessly and energetically follow along, "stepping to the beat of the same conga drummer." The film's release in 1940 paved the way for the inclusion of the conga in subsequent Hollywood musicals precisely because "it was a group dance, it was simple to do, and it had the requisite foreign, festive air to it."[22]

It was while filming *Too Many Girls* in Hollywood that Arnaz met Lucille Ball. Shortly after production was complete, on 30 November 1940, the two married in Connecticut in an impromptu ceremony that forced Arnaz to miss his band's scheduled performance at the Roxy Theater in New York City.[23] Arnaz went on to make other films during this first stint in Hollywood, including *Four Jacks and a Jill* and *Father Takes a Wife*. But he refused to stay out west just to be near his new bride, and with few roles coming his way, he decided to return again to New York City to perform with his band at the Rumba Casino.

Music was his main focus. One review in the *New York Times* explained: "Mr. Arnaz is a specialist in rhythm and when he leaps to the front of the line like the Pied Piper (in this case equipped with drums) one just automatically joins in. He's a very persuasive man, that one." Noting that "the drums never stop beating," another review described Arnaz as "that handsome young witch doctor who is presently causing a good deal of fluttering among the females." Though the reference to him as a "witch doctor" might suggest an awareness of his appropriation of Afro-Cuban religious rituals, his version of the practice was apparently safe enough for young, white North American women. In fact, as early as 1931, members of the American Society of Teachers of Dancing worked to replace "the short steps and stamping of the Cuban rumba" with what they called "a 'dance of decorum.'" They objected, in particular, to the "'closeness'" and "'hugging'" associated with dances such as the rumba and foxtrot. Instructors had not yet given the new dance a name, though it did, they explained, have a "'distinctly Spanish flavor because of the four-four time.'"[24] That, it seems, was also an appealing characteristic of the conga: still of "Spanish flavor," it was an easy-to-learn group dance that tempered the potentially sexual and erotic moves of partner dances such as the rumba.

DESI DIPLOMACY HITS HOLLYWOOD

Arnaz's stay in New York City was cut short in 1941, however, when officials at the U.S. State Department invited him to travel to Mexico as part of an envoy of musicians, entertainers, and actors being sent there to "kick off" President Roosevelt's Good Neighbor Policy. Acts such as this Hollywood Victory Caravan illustrate the various manifestations of hemispheric solidarity and inter-Americanism that characterized this period. When he returned, U.S. officials asked him, the only person of Latin American descent who had participated in this goodwill mission, about the Mexican reaction to the policy. His response suggests his understanding of himself as both a Latin American who was subject to the very policy he was instructed to sell *and* as an agent of the United States. He reportedly told officials, "They are suspicious. . . . 'What do they want? Take the rest of Mexico? They already have taken a big chunk. What is it they want now?' . . . We turn it on too strongly and too suddenly. They do not understand our foreign policy." He articulated a Mexican point of view that was likely more intelligible to him than to most of the non-Spanish-speaking musicians and celebrities on the Victory Caravan but still maintained his belonging to the United States through the use of the "we" and "our" pronouns. Arnaz later traveled abroad and throughout the United States entertaining troops with the USO, stopping first in Guantanamo Bay, Cuba (not Santiago) and other parts of the Caribbean "where there were many Cubans, Puerto Ricans, and other Latin boys with our American troops," a statement that again confirms his sense of inclusion but allows for the possibility that "other Latin boys" might not be so fortunate.[25]

Despite his early successes on stage and on screen, Arnaz later claimed that his accent and ethnic background limited the roles that were available to him in Hollywood in the early 1940s.[26] He described the few kinds of roles open to "Latin types," noting that "the only ones who were known then were the romantic Valentino types and the George Raft types, or the other extreme, the Chrispin Martin lazy Mexican character or the Leo Carillos." Arnaz blamed whatever problems he encountered in the entertainment industry as a result of his Cubanness not on racism or ethnic stereotypes but on his language skills and the whims of Hollywood producers. He recalled a conversation he had with MGM's Louis B. Mayer, who hoped to capitalize on the conga craze. Mayer believed that something special happened at the moment when Arnaz hung the conga drum around his shoulder, arguing that "up to that point you're just another Mexican." Though Arnaz retorted, "Not Mexican, sir, Cuban," Mayer replied, "Well, one of those Latin fellows."[27] That Mayer seemed to care little about the distinction illustrates Hollywood's general indifference to Latin American national specificity. Pérez-Firmat has argued that Arnaz refused to portray himself "as a victim of prejudice and exploitation," preferring instead to see his life as "an old-fashioned, rags-to-riches Cuban American success story."[28] Such a perspective not only reproduces notions of Cuban American exceptionalism but also fails to examine how Arnaz's whiteness privileged his experiences in the entertainment industry. Given his light skin and handsome, clean-cut appearance, it was likely his accent and last name that marked him as racially Latin. This was both an opportunity and a limitation: it created the initial interest in using him to fill Latin parts on Broadway and in Hollywood, but it also meant that other parts were closed to him and that he could be passed over when new Latin talent came along.

Arnaz seemed well aware of ethnic stereotypes, and though he appeared to have no problem reproducing them on stage and on screen, in his personal life he seemed determined to confront the possibility of negative images. With few roles open to him after Hollywood had moved on to Ricardo Montalbán, Arnaz decided to return again to the band business in New York City. Throughout the mid- to late 1940s, Arnaz performed at downtown theaters and nightclubs in New York City, such as the Roxy, Copacabana, Paramount, and Strand, and toured throughout the United States. He refused to stay in Hollywood to be kept by his wife, believing that doing so "would really have completed the image most Americans had of us Latins, especially in those days."[29] In many ways, Arnaz's personal life and professional career reflected ambivalence toward ethnic stereotypes, quietly accepting and, to a certain degree, exaggerating them in the public contexts of politics and entertainment but forcefully rejecting them in his private, domestic relationships.

Arnaz's career took another brief pause when he entered the U.S. Army in 1943. He enlisted shortly after his debut in the role of Private Félix Ramírez in the MGM production *Bataan*, which portrayed the U.S. stand in the Philippines during World War II. Advertisements in African American newspapers boasted to readers that "you'll be proud that America had such martyrs of all races, creeds and color ready to fight to the bitter end against the treacherous sons of Tokyo." African American actor-singer Kenneth Spencer was cast as Private Wesley Epps, and a reviewer for the *Baltimore Afro-American* noted that the film featured "the first colored soldier to reach the silver screen (in reel life) in an heroic role." The writer cautioned, however, that the fictionalized production failed to mirror the reality of racial inequality in the U.S. military, arguing that "instead of a democratic army as pictured above, colored troops are jim-crowed."[30] No mention was made in African American, mainstream, or Spanish-language newspapers in New York City about Arnaz's portrayal of a Latino soldier or about how the U.S. military actually treated Latino soldiers who were racialized as nonwhite but not formally segregated from white troops. Latino soldiers were disproportionately sent to the Pacific rather than the European theater during World War II, and this unusual distribution to what many considered the zone of least importance can be linked to the ambiguous question about their race. Ideas circulated that Latino soldiers could better handle the language and climate of the Philippines because, the argument went, like Mexico, Puerto Rico, and Cuba, it was a former colony of Spain with tropical weather and a jungle landscape. Army officials believed it was less dangerous to send Latinos to combat and kill nonwhites in the Pacific than to have them fight and defeat white Europeans in Italy and Germany; the latter might suggest equality or even superiority to whites.[31]

The casting of Arnaz in the film constructed Latino/as and African Americans as wholly separate races. The *Baltimore Afro-American* rightly emphasized that *Bataan* failed to depict Jim Crow, but the film also failed to reflect the ways that Latino/as and Afro-Latino/as, in particular, experienced formal and informal segregation in the U.S. armed forces. The inclusion of both an African American and a Latino soldier (and Private Yankee Salazar of the Philippine Scouts) marks *Bataan* as unique among World War II films. This inclusion, however, does not mean that the film avoided stereotypes or that the racial representations in the film portrayed only positive characteristics. The racial messages in the film, especially with regard to Private Ramírez, are mixed: at times, his status as "other" is less obvious, and the film presents him as (almost completely) Americanized; at other times, his status as "other" is marked in more direct ways, suggesting a sort of foreignness and difference. Private Ramírez introduces himself to Sergeant Dane (Robert Taylor) simply as a member of a tank battalion from California, making no reference to his national origin or ethnic background. In another scene, he finds a battery-powered radio and rejoices when he comes across a station broadcasting Tommy Dorsey live from Hollywood. When Sergeant Dane complains, "Don't tell me that's Jap jive!," Private Ramírez quickly counters, "No, Sarge, that's good ol' America, that's U.S.A. . . . . Oh, [Dorsey] sends me, Sarge! He makes me lace up my boots!" Perhaps as a reference to Arnaz's career as a bandleader and a wink to his fans, the scene ends with Ramírez tapping his hands on the table in a motion that simulates Arnaz's furious beating of the conga drum during a performance of "Babalú." Later in the film, as he nears death from malaria fever, Ramírez's otherness takes center stage when he mumbles aloud in Spanish *"pobre mamacita"* ("poor little mother") and imagines that he is confessing his sins to a priest in both Spanish and Latin. After Ramírez's death, Sergeant Dane instructs one of the other soldiers to remind Navy sailor Purckett, who had been tasked with making grave markers for the dead, of the correct spelling of his last name. That this Spanish surname required repeated instructions on its proper spelling, a process apparently not needed for the names of the other soldiers in the group, indicates that his national origin and ethnic background did not go unnoticed and that his Latinness did indeed mark him as foreign and "other" in the U.S. Army.

As *Bataan* premiered in theaters across the United States, Arnaz prepared to enter the U.S. military. Latino/as in New York City were quite aware of his decision to enter the U.S. armed forces rather than the Cuban Army. One reporter for *La Prensa* commented that Arnaz, "the well-known Cuban artist," despite his commission in the Cuban Army, chose to join the U.S. armed forces "thanks to the recently celebrated accords between Cuba and the United States."[32] A recurring knee injury prevented him from passing the physical for the U.S. Air Force, and he spent the bulk of the war years in the army entertaining wounded soldiers and personnel at Birmingham Hospital in California and other bases across the country. Though Arnaz's position in the U.S. Army had as much to do with his celebrity status and Hollywood connections, it also illustrates the privileged opportunities available to light-skinned Latinos such as himself and Marco Rizo. In fact, Arnaz revealed that his only encounter with ethnic otherness in the U.S. military came at his induction ceremony, when a sergeant who had trouble pronouncing his name suggested he shorten it on his citizenship certificate. Born Desiderio Alberto Arnaz y de Acha in Cuba, he was reborn as the American Desi Arnaz upon entering the U.S. Army.[33]

Latinos of color undoubtedly had fewer advantages as members of the U.S. armed forces. Machito's experiences in the U.S. Army illustrate the point. Drafted in 1943 in the midst of his band's long-term engagement at La Conga, the Afro-Cuban bandleader spent his time in the army as part of an all-black unit based in Camp Hood in Texas. Because his mobility was limited due to a childhood leg injury, he worked as a cook to avoid the more physically demanding tasks assigned to the other members of his tank destroyer battalion. While on the base, he formed a band that played "American music" at area hospitals, thanks to the stock arrangements his wife sent him from New York City. But by this time, Machito already had three children and his army paycheck failed to meet the needs of his growing family. He asked his wife to send him scissors, razors, brushes, and electric clippers so that he could make extra money as a barber, recalling that he "took the clippers to a ton of those Afros." After six months, the army released him with an honorable medical discharge, a timely release since just a few months later many of the men in his division died at Normandy.[34]

MACHITO'S TAKE ON LA CONGA

Not all Cubans joined the conga line craze of the 1940s, and Machito was one of the reluctant ones. He recalled performing at the Stork Club in midtown Manhattan in 1940 for a fund-raising event organized on behalf of Nelson Rockefeller. Between sets, one of the organizers requested that he form a conga line. Though he insisted that he "wasn't nor had he ever been a conguero," he grabbed the conga from his conga player and started a conga line, eventually turning the drum upside down so that guests could place their donations in its hollow. He reportedly collected over $20,000 during the dance, earning himself a $100 tip, which he feared he might lose during his subway ride uptown. Machito explained that despite the popularity of the conga line, he generally avoided drumming, especially early in his career in Cuba, where he performed with María Teresa Vera and Miguelito Valdés. He considered the practice too closely associated with *santería* and other Afro-Cuban religious rituals and himself too much of an amateur percussionist. He held the drumming rituals sacred and did not want to do such drumming casually: "I never considered myself to be qualified to play conga or to drum. . . . I didn't want to be embarrassed. It was very dangerous in Cuba in my days that you don't know how to play and you'd say let me play, you could get beat in the head."[35] Machito might also have been indirectly referencing and offering subtle criticism of Arnaz, who in his early musical career and in his performance as Ricky Ricardo lacked even the most basic conga drumming technique and merely banged away at the skin of the drum. He was perhaps frustrated that Arnaz and other musicians like him profited from conga drumming and association with Afro-Cuban religious rituals, more so, in many cases, than other excellent and well-respected conga players such as Valdés and Chano Pozo.

Though Machito largely resisted the commercialized performance of the conga line, he did not refuse the opportunity to perform at the basement nightclub made famous by the popular dance and spectacle. Whereas Arnaz accepted credit for bringing "the Eastside of New York to the Westside," Machito y sus Afro-Cubans saw their booking as the house band at La Conga in 1942 as a sign of racial progress and integration as they brought uptown music, *barrio* musicians, and, eventually, Latino/a audiences to

Miguelito Valdés (left) and Rolando Laserie (center) playing drums, 1957. Courtesy of Rolando Laserie Papers, Cuban Heritage Collection, University of Miami.

the stages and dance floors of downtown Manhattan. In his discussion of the geography of New York City's nightlife, José Curbelo mapped out the hotspots, recalling that "everything" took place on Broadway between the Hotel Astor on 45th Street and the Palladium and 54th Street. This was all the more reason to note the accomplishment of the Afro-Cubans as "the first band, black, to come from El Barrio . . . to play on Broadway," he explained. Machito's band arrived at La Conga as a replacement for the Anselmo Sacasas Orchestra; the band's booking had as much to do with their musical ability and widespread appeal as it did with the progressive vision of one of the club's owners, Jack Harris. In fact, according to Curbelo, Harris "didn't believe in color, [he believed] in music."[36]

But compromise also mattered, and one of the first moves Harris and the other owners of La Conga made was to change to the band's name to Machito y sus Afro-Cubans. The band had been performing uptown as the Siboney Orchestra, a name that emphasized their Cubanness rather than their Afro-Cubanness, perhaps in an attempt to differentiate themselves, racially and musically, from African American bands and performers in that part of the city. Harris reportedly rejected the name Siboney as much for its unfamiliar reference to indigenous peoples as for its commonness, since other bands had performed under that name in both Cuba and the United States, including, for example, the one Arnaz had joined in Miami. Machito recalled his openness to finding an original name for the band: "There was nothing that specified the type of music that we were making. So, then, [the new name] saved me because it was a name that was given to the band that was new."[37]

The bandleader, who was born Frank Grillo, explained that as the first boy born in a family with four girls, his nickname since birth had been Macho. Club owners, however, argued that "'Macho' sounded too rough" and that they preferred the diminutive "Machito." The gendered implications of this change cannot go unmentioned. The diminutive ending "ito" in Spanish serves to indicate that something is smaller in size and generally renders words less harsh in intent. In this case, owners rejected "Macho," meaning man or a person who is overtly masculine, in favor of "Machito," meaning "little man." But the "ito" ending can also signify affection, shifting the meaning in this case to signify "our little man." Intended here most likely as a term of endearment rather than as an insult, the preference for the name "Machito" over "Macho" also worked to develop familiarity and rapport between audiences and the performer.[38]

Though Mario Bauzá insisted that the band was called "Afro-Cuban" at his urging, Machito recalled that he had some concerns when club owners decided that the band would be billed as Machito y sus Afro-Cubans. He believed in a more collaborative approach and thought it best to consult with the other members of the band before settling on a name: "This band is cooperative, and I have to ask all peoples . . . and Afro was too black for the Latins, you know. So, I knew I was going to have troubles with the band." Whatever role an awareness of African roots and black consciousness played in Bauzá's preference for the "Afro-Cuban" modifier, for the other members of the band, especially those less interested in publicly acknowledging blackness as a collective identity, money and job security garnered their approval. "Money changes attitudes," Machito explained, and upon learning that they would be earning $140 a week, "they said, there is no difference on the subject of the name of the band."[39] This is not entirely surprising, especially from a marketing perspective, because of the increasing familiarity with and use of the "Afro-Cuban" modifier in musical and cultural contexts. By using this modifier in the band's name, club owners likely hoped to draw audiences looking for authentic, genuine purveyors of the popular Latin rhythms of the period without having to cross the 96th Street color line that divided New York City during this period.[40]

Machito noted this racial divide early into his stay in New York City. When he arrived in the city in 1937, his sister, who was married to Bauzá, greeted him at the dock, and the pair rode into Harlem where all three shared an apartment on 142nd Street and Seventh Avenue, near the Savoy Ballroom. On that first drive through the streets of Harlem, Machito recalled that he "had never seen so many blacks together in a long time," arguing that "Cuba was more integrated in terms of housing." "The deeper we got into Harlem the blacker it got," he explained, believing he had arrived "in paradise because I am in a country of my people." "Paradise," however, had its borders, and during this period that meant that a man with "a toasted complexion," as Machito described himself, could not be seen below 96th Street with a white woman without arousing police suspicion. As we saw in chapter 1, Bauzá recalled similar, albeit informal, restrictions against black men associating with white women in Cuba. On his first date with his light-skinned Puerto Rican girlfriend, whom he eventually married, Machito decided to take her to the Apollo Theater, which he noted was located in "my section," to avoid any problems. Interestingly, not only had she never been to the Apollo but she had also never even been to Harlem, suggesting, again, the existence of racism and racial tensions in the *colonia hispana*. But more than this, Machito's reasoning reveals his sense of belonging and inclusion in Harlem among both African Americans and dark-skinned Cubans and Puerto Ricans as well as the strategy he used to negotiate the social and legal constraints placed on interracial and interethnic relationships during this period. In the next chapter, however, we will see that Machito's sense of racial identity and his response to the biracial color divide remained inconsistent and was contingent on specific social and geographic contexts.[41]

MUSICAL LABOR AND THE LATINO/A MARKET

Machito left Cuba to establish himself as a professional musician. He reported that after he came to the United States, he generally "found work easily," booking gigs alongside Alberto Iznaga, Noro Morales, Augusto Coen, and Xavier Cugat. He admitted, however, that "it was difficult to make a living just by performing because the Latin colony was still small and we had to play small clubs and private dances." Performing at social events sponsored by Cuban, Puerto Rican, and other ethnic social clubs and organizations was a key source of income, though by the mid- to late 1950s the relationship was likely as much about maintaining and strengthening cultural ties as it was about financial necessity. In any case, Machito, who had managed to save a bit of money before leaving Cuba, explained that he had little interest in supplementing his income with odd jobs or manual wage labor. Though that is what many musicians had to do, he insisted that he "wasn't going to any factory forced."[42]

Securing a livelihood as a professional entertainer was not always so easy, and remarks Machito, Arnaz, and other black and white Cuban musicians made demonstrate that a career in the entertainment industry was mostly hard work. Arnaz's mother complained that he "worked too hard," and while he admitted that he was doing the "conga bit" up to five times a day, he reasoned that audiences "want to see me sweat, Mama, and I don't mind." Marco Rizo described Arnaz's schedule in the early 1940s as "very strenuous" and noted that "he didn't have much time to sleep," especially on the weekends, when he performed in *Too Many Girls* on stage and then went off to La Conga for shows starting at nine, eleven-thirty, and two in the morning. A reviewer for *Billboard* indicated that this rigorous pace continued into the mid-1940s: "Realizing that customers like to see boys work for their coin, Arnaz makes sure that ringsiders get their money's worth. He knocks himself out in hopping down from the bandstand to the dance floor and puts on a one-man show with conga drum and a dance to match."[43]

To develop a profitable career in the entertainment industry, a musician not only had to develop management skills, book nightly performances, and schedule regional and national tours but also had to have a keen awareness of the needs and preferences of those in the audience. Arnaz aimed to reach mainstream, white, middle-class North American audiences even if that meant displeasing critics. He insisted that "I've always got the guy in Omaha in mind."[44] Whether because of his early crossover success or his inability to compete technically and stylistically with other Cuban musicians, Arnaz had a relatively lukewarm following among Cuban and Latino/a audiences and maintained a limited physical presence in New York City in the late 1940s and 1950s.

Cubans and Latino/as, nonetheless, noted his early accomplishments. A reporter for *La Prensa* commented on Arnaz's rising popularity in the United States, a place "where so many thousands of men from all parts of the world look for a little bit of glory but where so few find it." According to this reporter, however, for Arnaz, "his arrival has been easy, without ordeal, without deception, as if a fairy godmother had taken him by the hand down the handsome road to success." A reporter for the Havana-based newspaper *Diario de la Marina* also remarked on Arnaz's rise to fame, describing him as an example of a Latin American artist who "has been able, through [his] own merits, to stand out."[45]

Despite his limited physical presence, critics and audiences in the *colonia hispana* managed to locate the origins of his professional career in New York City, all while emphasizing his Cubanness. One report in *La Prensa* noted that it was common for actors to leave the theaters of New York City for the Hollywood big screen, citing Carmen Miranda, Carmen Amaya, and Arnaz as recent examples.[46] When *Too Many Girls* was released in New York City, for example, representatives from the Spanish-language press and Cuban consul-general Cayetano de Quesada attended a private screening of the film and reviewers made sure to remind readers that the "Cuban actor" had gotten his start on the stage in New York City.[47] By 1946, many in the *colonia hispana* recognized Arnaz as a bandleader and stage and film actor. At that year's Gran Festival, *La Prensa* announced that the program would feature "the most decorated elements of the artistic nucleus of the colonia," including what was described as a "surprise" presentation by Arnaz, who was in the city to perform with his band at the Copacabana. Arnaz attended the fund-raising showcase and participated in the event by offering "excellent poetry" as he presented Cugat with his winner's trophy in the *Orquestas* category.[48] Framing his appearance as a surprise suggests that Arnaz mattered in the *colonia hispana* not as a frequent participant in community events but as a symbolic figure whose growing prominence in the entertainment industry on a national level reflected well on his origins in the city.

From a commercial and financial standpoint, it makes sense that some in the *colonia hispana*, especially white and light-skinned middle- and upper-class elements, would want to claim Arnaz as one of their own, just as it seems reasonable that the Cuban bandleader would choose to appeal mostly to white North American audiences in pursuit of bigger crowds and even bigger paychecks. Arnaz revealed that he hoped his band would benefit from the showmanship and gimmicks that had made Cugat so famous. He was not alone in adopting this strategy. José Curbelo famously dressed his band in leopard-print jackets and plaid uniforms. As a result of the "colorful" outfits, one reporter described those in the band as "real hepcats," and another noted that the fashion choice was "causing no end of comment around town." Curbelo even admitted to one reporter that "shaking a pair of maracas and beating a rhythm on the bongos . . . and the accompanying shouting in Cuban double-talk is just a part of the act that is mighty effective in selling a band to the American public as a Cuban band."[49]

Another white Cuban bandleader, Pupi Campo, used maracas to add flare and excitement to his performance. At least one music historian has claimed that the maracas were empty, that Campo, who was an excellent entertainer, used the shakers as a prop because he lacked the musical expertise to keep rhythm alongside trained musicians.[50]

When Arnaz returned to music in 1946, he explained that his band would be nothing like the Afro-Cuban/Latin jazz bands that were becoming increasingly popular in New York City. His remarks to a record producer in California demonstrate his distance from the Latin music scene in New York City and, by extension, his distance from the tastes and preferences of the *colonia hispana* and *colonia cubana*: "Latin American music in this country has had a basic fault. When a band like Machito in New York plays Latin music, the rhythm is great but the sound is not melodically good enough—it's tinny. . . . My idea is to combine the Latin rhythms of Machito with the lushness of [André] Kostelanetz." This remark seems to indicate an interest in merging influences drawn from both popular and classical music, a move that also suggests that Arnaz did not aim to impress critics or other Cuban and Latino/a musicians but wanted to appeal to as broad an audience as possible. At least one reviewer seemed to think he succeeded, describing "the musical dynamite from Cuba" as "the Toscanini of swing rhythms, the poor man's Stokowski."[51]

Arnaz's musical preferences and marketing strategies reflected his belief that both Broadway and Hollywood offered fewer opportunities to "authentic" Latin musicians and performers. In some respects, he was not alone in his implicit critique of the disadvantages of commercial markets for Latin music. Machito felt the same way, explaining that "the market had its limitations. It still has it. And it's not the fault of the Americans. It's our fault because we cater to the Spanish people, the Spanish market." Though he recognized that the "Spanish market" remained "big and productive," Machito blamed low record sales on the fact that his band performed and recorded songs exclusively in Spanish. He explained that it was not until the band recorded the *Afro-Cuban Jazz Suite* in 1950 with Norman Granz, Arturo "Chico" O'Farrill, Charlie Parker, Flip Phillips, and Buddy Rich and other instrumentals with Stan Kenton and Dizzy Gillespie that they achieved what he described as "artistic and economic success." He believed that "it was after that, that we were able to jump another hurdle in the market or in the American community that would permit us to sing in Spanish."[52] In other words, Machito argued that language, not race or ethnic representation, determined whether or not a band or performer could appeal to audiences beyond the *colonia hispana*. His reasoning is not entirely unfounded; other Cuban performers such as Cugat and Arnaz relied on instrumentals, a repertoire of English-language favorites, and "latunes" to attract as wide a public as possible. Pérez-Firmat has argued that "latunes," or rumbas with English lyrics such as Arnaz's "Cuban Pete," exemplified biculturation: "The rhythm is Cuban, the lyric is American, but the whole is Cuban American." However, this mode of thinking ignores the possibility that these other performers might have succeeded not just because some of their songs contained English lyrics but also because they were white Cubans and light-skinned Latino/as performing a watered-down, commercialized form of Afro-Cuban music that made listening and dancing easier for white North Americans.[53]

In identifying the recording of the *Afro-Cuban Jazz Suite* as a turning point for the band, at least in terms of more widespread appeal, Machito points to the significance of collaboration with well-known jazz musicians and producers. Beginning in the late 1940s, many leaders of the bebop movement, including Dizzy Gillespie, Charlie Parker, and Bud Powell, came to embrace Afro-Cuban music, and that connection helped Machito and other Afro-Cuban bands reach broader audiences. The legendary collaboration between Gillespie and Afro-Cuban drummer Chano Pozo, for example, culminated in the 1947 fusion hit "Manteca" and led to a "new, danceable music that was christened 'Cubop.'" These new partnerships revolutionized the music scene and opened up opportunities for Machito y sus Afro-Cubans to play at the Royal Roost, Birdland, and other jazz clubs, suggesting that it may have been more than language that introduced the band to the "American community."[54] Interestingly, Machito did not cite his partnerships with Miguelito Valdés as a source of his appeal to broader audiences. Music historian and journalist Max Salazar has argued, however, that the "mass exposure" the band received after appearing alongside Valdés in the film *Night in the Tropics* led to increased record sales and touring dates across the United States. From this perspective, it appears as though Hollywood was not exactly closed, just less open to "authentic" Latin performers.[55]

Machito was not alone in drawing distinctions between North American and "Spanish" markets. A sort of dialogue took place in the pages of the Spanish-language newspapers of New York City that conceded that there were differences in cultural production but contested the perceived inferiority of Latino/a performers. One reporter noted that the North American theater and the Latino/a theater in New York City were "as different as the temperaments of both races. Instead of Spanish and French sentimental plays we find here an abundance of light comedies, whose only purpose is to entertain without delving too deeply into the problems of the soul." A few years earlier, Fausto, the Broadway columnist for *La Prensa*, responded to criticisms made by American entertainment writer Ed Sullivan. Sullivan charged that with the exception of Desi Arnaz, Carlos Ramírez, Diosa Costello, and Carmen Miranda, artists from Latin America "have very little to offer" and are inferior to those from the United States, England, and France. Fausto responded that Sullivan knew very little about the "tastes and habits of the people of New York." He reasoned that New York nightclub and cabaret owners "exploit the Latin American artistic 'atmosphere' . . . because the public is who determines these things . . . because the public, obviously bored with the monotony of these atmospheres, the British, and the French, wants a change!" American record producer Ralph Peer revealed to *Diario de Nueva York* that Latin American rhythms such as rumba and samba and songs such as "Babalú" and "Brazil" were far more popular than the sounds of Tin Pan Alley because "it is primarily happy and it seems to be the preference of many people that desire to see themselves suddenly free of reality." Though Arnaz made his remarks about the function of his mode of entertainment specifically in reference to the production of *I Love Lucy*, they confirm a growing preference for light-heartedness and simplicity. He argued, "Some people call it superficial, with no literary or intellectual values—only escapism. Okay, but I see nothing wrong with a show that is just that."[56]

PERFORMING "BABALÚ"

Both La Conga as a physical place and the conga line as an expression of culture illustrate the possibilities of racial integration unaccompanied by a perception of any loss of musical and cultural authenticity, on the one hand, and the reality of racial and cultural borrowing that manifests itself in a more watered-down commercial form, on the other. Perhaps nothing illustrates this better than a comparison of performances of "Babalú" by Miguelito Valdés and Desi Arnaz/Ricky Ricardo. It deserves mention, of course, that Margarita Lecuona, cousin of well-known Cuban composer Ernesto Lecuona, wrote and composed "Babalú" during a period in the mid-1930s when the popularity of white Cuban artists "increased within Cuba and internationally," according to ethnomusicologist Robin Moore, "as a result of writing Afrocuban-inspired popular song."[57] What I provide here is not a thorough textual or musical analysis of the similarities and differences in how Valdés and Arnaz/Ricardo performed "Babalú," but rather a critical examination of how musicians and music critics, North

American audiences, and especially those within the *colonia hispana* and *colonia cubana* responded to each variation of this cultural performance with obvious Afro-Cuban themes.

Valdés's professional career in the United States is marked by his ability to navigate both the mainstream commercial entertainment industry and the local interests of the black and white residents of the *colonia hispana* and *colonia cubana*. His ability to move between the black and white worlds of entertainment highlights the perceived and, at times, purposeful and advantageous instability of his racial identity. Born in Havana to a Cuban-Spanish father and a Mayan-Indian mother, Valdés signified "whiteness" to many, though his mixed racial ancestry and, quite importantly, his upbringing among and association with blacks in Cuba signified nonwhiteness and "blackness" to others. This racial instability, which was contingent on time and place, points to the ways social actors make and unmake racial boundaries. It also reveals that race played a role in determining whether a musician would be credited for innovation or popularization or, in rare instances, a little bit of both.

More than most Cuban musicians of the era, Valdés's professional career seems to have been a balanced combination of musical authenticity and innovation, on the one hand, and commercial crossover and gimmick, on the other. As a young man in Havana, he worked for a time as a boxer while also singing in various nightclubs, including at the Havana-Riverside Casino. He left Cuba for Panama in the mid-1930s to perform as the lead vocalist with the Lucho Azcarraga orchestra. He returned to Cuba in 1936 to perform with Los Hermanos Castro but left the band in 1937 to organize his own ensemble, Orquesta Casino de la Playa, which most Cubans perceived as a "white band."[58] It was with Casino de la Playa that he first recorded his version of "Babalú" in 1939. Soon thereafter, in April 1940, he left Cuba for New York City, where he joined Cugat's band at the Waldorf-Astoria and on tour throughout the United States. In 1942, a reviewer in *Billboard* declared that "Valdés finds himself a strong attraction on the radio, in theaters, hotels and on the many Victor and Columbia records which he has made." And the source of that "strong attraction" was "Babalú," as the reviewer explained: "This lusty Latin performer . . . has carved out a unique niche for himself with his sock renditions of native Afro-Cuban songs, made more wild and rhythmic by his savage pounding on a conga drum." So intense, according to another reviewer, was his "energetic, vital, and primitive personality" that after performing "Babalú" and "Rumba Rhapsody," he "finally staggered off soaking wet and beat to the socks to bellows and shrieks that must have been heard in the streets."[59]

Valdés left Cugat's band just two years into his five-year contract, a split that was likely motivated by differences in musical style, mutual professional jealously, and disputes over money. The relationship became strained when top billing started going to Valdés instead of Cugat, and Valdés was cut out of a scene in the film *You Were Never Lovelier* in which he sang alongside Cugat. More to the heart of the matter, a clause in Valdés's contract that required him to give a percentage of his outside earnings to Cugat created tension in the relationship. According to Alberto Socarrás, Valdés reportedly disparaged Cugat, saying that "he cannot conduct," but he reasoned that "as long as he pay [*sic*] me all the money he's paying me, I take it." Cuban bandleader Nilo Curbelo said that Valdés told him that he "suffered" during his time with Cugat's band because he had to listen to and perform what he described as "such horrible music." His break with Cugat did little to stunt his professional career, and he went on to headline at nightclubs and theaters across the United States. His "barrel-chested chanting of Afro-Cuban songs," as one reporter described it, became the signature of his nightclub performances. Audiences anticipated this performative element so much that even after almost eight years of closing his shows with "Babalú" one reviewer noted that "it was the high spot of the evening. His energy and enthusiasm for it did not appear at all worn out."[60]

Most reporters and reviewers positioned "Babalú" as belonging to Valdés; eventually they referred to him simply as "Mr. Babalú." One of Valdés's earliest performances of "Babalú" was in 1943 at a dance hosted by Unificación Hispana, a civic organization in New York City. Valdés had considered backing out of the performance because of a sore throat. But according to a report in *Pueblos Hispanos*, "the great Cuban singer . . . idol of the colonia" kept his word, and "before the enthusiastic multitude, this artist of the people delivered and delighted those in attendance with his extraordinary Babalú." Two years later, RKO released *Panamericana*, which featured Valdés performing "Babalú" in a medium that allowed him to reach audiences beyond Havana and New York City. A reviewer from *Diario de Nueva York* described the film as "a musical revue of pure hispanic flavor with well-known artists from nuestra colonia," an unremarkable assessment given Hollywood's "good neighborly" gestures toward Latin America during this period.[61]

Reviewers soon recognized Valdés as a performer synonymous with "Babalú"; in fact, they insisted that he was responsible both for the song's creation and its popularity across the United States. After a performance at La Conga in 1944, one reviewer cited "the Cuban singer [who offers] picturesque Afro-Cuban interpretations" as the "creator of Babalú" and noted that he performed to a "packed house" his first evening back at the nightclub on Broadway.[62] Advertisements and announcements in Spanish-language newspapers in New York City billed Valdés not only as the "creator of Babalú," the "Great Babalú," the "inimitable Babalú," and "Mr. Babalú" but also credited him with popularizing "extensively throughout the United States the Afro-Cuban folkloric feeling." Much of this was due to his performances at hotels, nightclubs, and other venues all across the city, including downtown and midtown spots such as La Conga, the Havana-Madrid, the Hotel Diplomat, and the Manhattan Center; uptown venues such as the Hunts Point Palace, the Audubon Ballroom, and the Embassy Ballroom; and in New Jersey at the Rustic Cabin in Englewood Cliffs and the Casino in Palisades Park.[63]

Part of Valdés's success was also attributable to his awareness of the need to go beyond racialized audience expectations. He explained to Salazar, "I was always dressed in a tuxedo when I presented Afro-Cuban music to society. I tried to present it in the best light." Of course, by "society" Valdés seems to mean "white society." His crossover success with white North American audiences generated commentary, particularly in terms of his racial ambivalence and marketing strategies. Machito argued that "the people don't know Miguelito Valdés, because he created a personality. When he got here, he was inspired by Cab Calloway. He had loose hair, you understand, he was so talented that he created a personality. He made an outstanding thing of babaloo [sic], it was just another song, but his personality, his power, his know-how to play conga, he was a tremendous conga player, bongo player, timbales, forget it." Machito believed that it was a combination of Valdés's musical talent, showmanship, and European physical features that contributed to his success: "Because Miguelito was a showman. Miguelito was a nice-looking guy, you know in Havana women like men with good hair, you understand?"[64]

Musicians and music critics agreed that the singer's "good looks" and "loose" and "good" hair increased his popularity among women and contributed to his success in the entertainment industries in Havana, New York City, and Hollywood. The texture of his hair, which lacked the coarseness often associated with "bad" hair (and blackness), signified whiteness and helped facilitate his acceptance among white audiences. One reviewer in La Prensa described how Valdés would allow his "straight hair" "to fall in disarray over his temples when he is 'possessed' by any one of his songs." Afro-Cuban percussionist Armando Sánchez attributed the success of Arsenio Rodríguez's mambo to the fact that he found in Valdés an "interpreter" that appealed to wider and whiter audiences: "He was very lucky because he found in a mulatto that looked like a white man but was black inside and born from a black woman, the name was Miguelito Valdés, 'Mr. Babalú' and he was the best interpreter he could find." Sánchez explained, "And Miguelito being a light-skinned black, he had the feeling of the African music and he could express it. . . . He looked like white . . . but he never hid that he was black, that's one thing I know, he never hid it. He was accepted because, you know, by the way he looked." Many Afro-Cuban musicians cast Valdés as authentic (a mulatto) and a real musician, while also marking him less as an innovator and more as a product created by Arsenio Rodríguez and recognizing his appeal to North American audiences as whiteness of a sort. Like Sánchez, Graciela emphasized that Valdés never claimed whiteness or denied his blackness or Indianness. Lighter skin, "good hair," and other European physical features facilitated Valdés's inclusion in an entertainment industry that sometimes denied the spotlight to performers of color. As we have seen in the preceding chapters, while it was Cugat's nonwhiteness that lent him authenticity as he performed Afro-Cuban music for white North American audiences, it was Valdés's blackness that authorized and validated his performances of Afro-Cuban music among Afro-Cuban musicians and journalists.[65]

Most musicians and news reporters recognized that Valdés drew from Afro-Cuban religious and musical traditions and from his various interactions with African American musicians in New York City. Sánchez confirmed Valdés's familiarity with "practically all the religious culture that were existing in Cuba," due in part to his residence in the Jesús María *barrio* of Havana. Valdés insisted that "I believe in Santería, and I know what I am singing about when I open my mouth. Whoever sings about Santería or Ñañigo should know about these religions." A reviewer for the *Atlanta Daily World*, commenting on Valdés's performances at "swank night clubs" in Acapulco, Mexico, noted that "Mexico seems to enjoy Afro-Cuban or African entertainment. . . . 'Mister Babalú' is a singer whose style makes you think of Cab Calloway. It seems as if he is chanting the tribal war song of ancient African warriors."[66] In his performances of "Babalú," Valdés often broke from the white Afro-Cubanist representation of *santería* into actual *santero* (an initiated priest of *santería*) moves, a purposeful shift with dual significance: this was both the most commercialized moment, when he was performing the primitive, and the most authenticating moment for black musicians because he showed himself to be a cultural insider.

Though his performance of "Babalú" was widely acclaimed in the *colonia hispana* and throughout the United States, it was criticized by at least one venue owner. The owner of the Cal-Nevada Lodge in Lake Tahoe insisted that the song be cut from the set list because "I don't want no Mexicans yelling in my joint!" What was likely intended as a generic insult was not entirely inaccurate, given that Valdés was *mestizo*, the son of a Mexican-Indian mother and a white Cuban father. His mixed parentage, however, received no mention in the Spanish- or English-language press; most referred to him simply as the "Cuban warbler," the "Cuban singing favorite," the "most notable singer from Cuba," the "spectacular Cuban singer," the "great Afro-Cuban singer," the "most Cuban," and the "boy Latin singer."[67]

Two years after Valdés had popularized the routine in his nightclub and theater acts, Arnaz first performed "Babalú" at Ciro's in Los Angeles in 1945 as part of his final conga number. Marco Rizo is the only other musician who has claimed that Arnaz introduced "Babalú" in the United States before Valdés, a misstatement that was likely influenced by the pianist-composer's long-standing admiration and respect for his childhood friend.[68] In 1946, one reviewer in *Billboard* noted that the song had become Arnaz's "standard" closing number, while another concluded that he had made the number "his own, to a great extent, giving it a lot of oomph."[69] Making the song his own seemed to require playful exaggeration in the form of a huge conga drum, which one reviewer deemed "stage savvy, with his spirited ballading and gimmicks." Joe Conzo, a Latin music insider and a longtime business associate and biographer of Tito Puente, claimed that Arnaz relied on "gimmicks" when he performed "Babalú." He also revealed that Valdés and Arnaz knew that they were both performing different versions of the same song. When they attended one another's performances, both reportedly took part in stirring up a sometimes friendly, sometimes hostile rivalry, cursing each other with choruses of "*maricón*."[70]

The derogatory term *maricón*, whose literal meaning is "queer" or "fag" and has historically suggested a passive role in sexual encounters, has also held a variety of figurative meanings among Cubans. Political scientist Ian Lumsden explains that among Cuban heterosexuals the term "on occasion may be used with underlying affection," like terms such as *gordito* (to indicate chubbiness) or *negrito* (to indicate blackness). Lumsden argues that more commonly, however, the term means coward, a particularly negative association "in a country that has had to fight hard and long for its national liberation."[71] Whether uttered to signify its literal or one of its mostly negative figurative meanings, the use of the term *maricón* by Arnaz and Valdés, two men whose professional success rested as much on their handsome good looks and sexual appeal among young women as it did on their musical talents, reveals their understanding of the links between perceptions of masculinity and musical authenticity. By calling one another *maricón*, both Arnaz and Valdés made an indirect assertion about their own masculinity and manly prowess, which in the Cuban context is inextricably tied to nationhood and national pride. Each likely aimed to undermine the other's artistic value and authenticity.[72]

Though he was popular throughout the 1940s, it was not until Arnaz performed "Babalú" as Ricky Ricardo on *I Love Lucy* that millions of Americans across the United States came to recognize the act as belonging to Cuban, though not explicitly Afro-Cuban, traditions. On the show, newspaper columnists, trade magazine writers, publicity agents, teenagers, policemen, furniture salesmen, locksmiths, English tutors, old ladies, old men, housewives, bikini models, even made-up royalty such as the "Maharincess of Franistan," and real celebrities such as Harpo Marx all came to identify the Cuban Ricky Ricardo with "Babalú."[73] Even though most of the show's viewers likely knew very little about *santería* rituals or *orishas*, Ricky Ricardo introduced this Afro-Cuban religious practice and cultural expression to white North American audiences, albeit in a more watered-down and commercialized form.

Audiences saw Ricky Ricardo take the stage at the Tropicana Club to perform "Babalú" early in the first season of *I Love Lucy*. The white Cuban, dressed in a black tuxedo and backed by an orchestra of white musicians in festive rumba sleeves, loosened his tie, gazed upward as if looking toward the gods in the sky, and repeatedly chanted *"arriba con la conga"* ("let's go with the conga") as he worked himself into a sweaty, out-of-breath mess. By mid-season, Ricky's association with "Babalú" is confirmed on the television program when he enters the living room of his and Lucy's apartment with a review from the evening newspaper. Excited to share the news with Lucy and Ethel, he reads from the newspaper, "The undisputed star of a great evening of entertainment, the genius of the conga drum who as usual topped the show with his rendition of 'Babalú,' Ricky Ricardo." Although the review suggests that this is just one of many versions of "Babalú" circulating in the nightclub circuit of New York City, this does little to temper Ricky's excitement or limit the extent to which the performance or references to the performance figure throughout the series. "Babalú" becomes so synonymous with Ricky Ricardo that during the show's final season Ricky is still performing the song on stage, and after becoming part owner of the Tropicana he renames it Club Babalú. For Ricky, "Babalú" meant steady income, the possibility of reduced financial strain, and his signature achievement within and beyond the professional entertainment industry. Ricky even looked into buying a periwinkle blue Cadillac with a custom horn that played "Babalú." Later in the show's final season, stressed by the burden of homeownership, Ricky complains to Lucy, "You realize how many times I'm going to have to sing 'Babalú' to pay for that house!"[74] Perhaps the same anxieties led Arnaz to express similar concerns. After signing a deal with Orson Welles to produce *The Fountain of Youth* in 1958, he warned the director, who had a reputation for going over budget without much to show for it, "This is my 'Babalú' money, so don't you fuck around with it."[75]

During the final season of *I Love Lucy*, the Ricardos make their first trip to Havana, a trip that is organized as part family reunion, part show business engagement. As the show's only episode set in Cuba (though it was filmed in Hollywood), the plane carrying the family touches land as the Cuban national anthem plays in the background. Ricky's Cubanness and his status as a return migrant are major themes in the episode. At his fictional appearance at the Casino Parisienne at the Hotel Nacional, the nightclub's master of ceremonies narrates Ricky's migration story, explaining, "Some years ago a young boy left Cuba and went to America. The only thing he took with him was a drum full of rhythm and a heart full of hope. He's back home tonight." Interestingly, Arnaz took his guitar, not a drum, with him from Cuba to the United States. The fact that it was a drum on the television program was a creative switch that signals, as Mario Bauzá argued, the association of authentic performances of Cubanness with rhythm rather than with melody. Ricky follows these opening remarks by singing "Wherever I Am, I'm Home," a song that describes the luck he has enjoyed in both New York and Havana. The next scene points to the significance of "Babalú" as an act that, even for Ricky, signified Cuban patriotism just as much as it led to his insertion into national and international commercial entertainment markets. Ricky invites his son, Little Ricky, to join him on stage for the finale. He tells the audience that "even though Little Ricky was born in America, I want to prove to you that there's a lot of Cuba in his heart."[76] From the perspective of the North American public, Little Ricky could convey his cultural connection to the island with no other song than "Babalú."

THE PALLADIUM BALLROOM

The Cuban musicians and bands of the 1940s and 1950s worked in an industry that required creativity, openness, and an awareness of audience preferences, at least if the performer wanted to make money and sell records. The popularity of the Palladium in midtown Manhattan during this period illustrates some of the ways that Cuban and Puerto Rican promoters and musicians developed followings beyond the *colonia hispana*. It also shows how mobility in the nightclub and dance hall circuit of New York City happened alongside processes of racial negotiation, musical innovation, and creative marketing that were at times divisive and at other times harmonious.

In 1948, Tommy Morton, owner of the Palladium, hired Machito y sus Afro-Cubans to perform as the exclusive house band not just because of the band's popularity, especially among Jewish audiences, but also because of financial pragmatism. The band's ability to play Afro-Cuban music, foxtrots, waltzes, boleros, jitterbugs, and polkas eliminated the need to hire a second band. The move proved fortuitous. A report in *Diario de Nueva York* noted early on that "everything indicates [Machito y sus Afro-Cubans] will continue there for a long time." By 1950, the Palladium had become the premier destination for Afro-Cuban music and "for the first time, the Latin orchestras were acting like stars, not as the uncomfortable fill-in that they had been reduced to by the American promoters of the time." In fact, Machito credited the Palladium, at least in part, for the band's success beyond the "Spanish market." He noted that before they landed the gig at the midtown dance hall, they played mostly in nightclubs and in El Barrio and "were not known in American ballrooms and our music less."[77]

But some fans, including Jewish dancers from the Catskills, were slow to follow the band to the Palladium, as were Cuban, Puerto Rican, and African American crowds who rarely went to nightclubs or dance halls below 110th Street. Bauzá solicited the help of Puerto Rican promoter Federico Pagani, and the two set out to advertise a Sunday matinee dance that featured six bands, including Machito y sus Afro-Cubans, Noro Morales, and José Curbelo. To promote this first event, Bauzá and Pagani distributed leaflets and posted cardboard signs in neighborhoods across the city. Later, they expanded their marketing strategy by placing advertisements in both Spanish- and English-language newspapers and magazines. Bauzá recalled that "all the Latinos, the blacks, the whites, and the mulattos from Harlem and Brooklyn" traveled downtown for the dance. He believed that never before had so many Latino/as been in midtown Manhattan and reported that Morton "made more money on that one Sunday than he had done for the months since he had opened up." Pagani recalled that the racial makeup of the crowd shocked and upset the club owner, who complained that "this is Broadway and you are going to ruin my business." Morton eventually accepted Pagani's marketing strategy, giving in to the promoter's reasoning that "if you want the green, you must have the black!"[78]

An alternative version exists of Morton's awareness and response to the black crowds at the Palladium. Bauzá claimed that even before he partnered with Pagani to promote the Palladium's new image as a Latin dance hall, he warned the club owner that the crowds would be mostly black. Asked how he felt about black people, Morton reportedly replied, "Look, I'm only interested in the color green."[79] Whether it was Pagani or Bauzá who acted primarily as the agent of racial integration at the club matters less than the fact that what led the club owner to acquiesce to the new marketing strategy was not a principled commitment to racial integration but a willingness to risk the disapproval of neighbors if integration meant healthy profits.

The Palladium could host between 750 and 1,000 dancers, especially during the more "heavy" Friday and Saturday night dances, and the venue averaged between 2,300 and 2,500 dancers a week. Sociologist Vernon Boggs has argued that the audience at the Palladium "was never exclusively Latin." Wednesday nights featured mambo dance lessons and exhibitions by "Killer Joe" Piro and a decidedly Jewish, Italian, and celebrity crowd. The dance hall hosted a mostly Puerto Rican crowd on Friday nights, "Hispanics of all origins" on Saturday nights, and "American blacks" on Sundays.[80] Afro-Cuban percussionist Armando Peraza recalled that before the era of the Palladium, "New York was no integrated. . . . The Latin dancing was exclusive for Latinos." He explained, "[T]hat time was very strict to the black Americans to coming, to dance in the Latin dances. . . . After they created that Sunday, then we all integrated. . . . All these black guys from Harlem was comin' to dancing." Ray Santos similarly recalled that on Sundays "the black dancing public . . . really good dancers" from Harlem, Brooklyn, and the Bronx would come down to the Palladium. Musicians and scholars alike have described the Palladium as an "egalitarian" and "integrated" dance hall of "intercultural compatibility," though this perspective is somewhat peculiar given that different racial and ethnic groups seemed to prefer to patronize the club on different days of the week.[81]

Even though the Palladium became the premier venue for dancing and listening to mambo and other Latin rhythms in the 1950s, it remained a place where Cuban and Latino/a social clubs and civic organizations hosted events and activities. Known as "The Birthplace of Mambo," the Palladium hosted celebrations commemorating Cuban independence, sponsored cultural events such as Una Noche en Habana (A Night in Havana), and boasted regular performances by Machito y sus Afro-Cubans, Miguelito Valdés, Marcelino Guerra, Arsenio Rodríguez, Tito Puente, and Tito Rodríguez.[82] It became a fixture in the Cuban American and broader Latino/a cultural landscape that developed in New York City during this period, avoiding misappropriation or cooptation by mainstream North American audiences that might have led to formal practices of exclusion or discrimination and a watering down of musical performances.

REAL HUSTLERS AND SHOW BUSINESS ON TV

Pagani and other promoters found creative ways to attract bigger crowds to the Palladium from within and beyond the *colonia hispana*. Santos described Pagani as a "real street hustler," "the original promoter up in Harlem," and recalled that he would distribute leaflets and posters for display in barbershops and grocery stores in exchange for a few free tickets to the dance. At the Palladium, Pagani once organized a Sunday matinee dance featuring Arsenio Rodríguez and Tito Rodríguez that culminated in a television set give-away. Other promotions included a Beer and Cracker-Eating Contest and the Miss Palladium Most Beautiful Legs Contest, at which Pagani led chants of "higher, higher!" and reportedly "lift[ed] the skirt up to show more leg." These marketing gimmicks did not go unnoticed in the *colonia hispana*. One columnist for *La Prensa* suggested that these types of promotions indicated desperation: Pagani and other promoters, the writer declared, "are performing acrobatic stunts to keep their roles in the department of promotion and publicity at the Palladium Ballroom, as they are closely watched by their boss."[83]

But advertising and creative promotions were just one of the many requirements for success in the entertainment industry. A generous amount of exaggeration also worked. Arnaz noted that during the early portion of his career as a bandleader, his press agents "decided to keep building me up as a playboy and a ladies' man, which they considered would be good for business."[84] If such a reputation could increase the chances of him being cast as a "Latin lover," then it proved a smart strategy, his press agents reasoned. A similar scenario made its way into the first season of *I Love Lucy*. Ethel appears in the Ricardo's kitchen, telling Lucy that a story in the *Daily Mirror* suggests that Ricky might be a "two-time Cuban heel." Ethel reads aloud, "What Cuban bandleader with the initials R. R. is making cat's eyes at his dancing mouse? . . . There's more going on during that floor show than the script calls for." Ricky responds that his publicity agent planted the story in the newspaper to keep his name in the public and reminds Lucy that such stories will continue to appear in the press as long as he works in show business.[85]

Examples of this sort of appeal to the public and Ricky's concerns that he remain in the spotlight are numerous throughout the show's six seasons. Viewers are given a unique view into just one of the many less flashy aspects of a career in the professional entertainment industry. Ricky often complains about working in show business, and not simply because Lucy is always pestering him to be included in one of his acts down at the club, though he notes that "she is like everybody else who only sees the glamour and fame." He insists that "every day is a tough day. Everyone wants more money, better billings." This theme of despair continues in another episode when Lucy explains that Ricky is in a "Cuban snit" because "things went wrong down at the club, cleaner forgot his tux, one of the acts didn't show up, in the big number the lights went out in the whole neighborhood so everyone left and went to the nightclub across the street."[86]

A TALE OF TWO TROPICANAS

At the downtown Tropicana, Ricky attracted mostly white North American audiences looking for an evening of entertainment that included jugglers and dancers, American musical standards and tropical rhythms, and the bandleader's rendition of "Babalú." What viewers of *I Love Lucy* saw of the setting and atmosphere in a nightclub that featured a white Cuban bandleader and orchestra differed in significant ways from what Cuban, Puerto Rican, African American, and ethnic white audiences experienced at nightclubs and dance halls such as the Palladium and the Tropicana in the Bronx in late 1940s and 1950s. The Tropicana in the Bronx, located on the corner of 153rd Street and Westchester Avenue, opened in the early summer of 1946 under the ownership and management of Pepe Sánchez and Manolo and Tony Alfaro. The white Cuban Alfaro brothers reportedly worked as *boliteros* (bookmakers), a seemingly not-so-secret side project; news columnist Babby Quintero described the partners as "potentates" and the Tropicana as their "bulwark."[87] Writers Roberta L. Singer and Elena Martínez have argued that "inspired by the glitzy Tropicana Cabaret in Havana, [the Tropicana in the Bronx] was the mecca for Latinos seeking floor shows with a chorus line, first-rate dance bands, and first-class Cuban cuisine."[88] Advertisements in *La Prensa* and *Diario de Nueva York* promoted the club as a "luxurious cabaret" and promised that it would host "famous orchestras" and "acclaimed artists." The promises mostly came true. The club offered regular entertainment on Friday, Saturday, and Sunday nights that featured popular bands and performers, including Machito y sus Afro-Cubans, Marcelino Guerra, Vicente Sigler, José Luis Monero, Conjunto Puerto Rico, and Tony Novo y Su Orquesta Española.[89]

Much like the Palladium, the Tropicana also hosted cultural celebrations and community events such as a dance organized in 1950 in honor of Cuban independence that featured music by the Lecuona Cuban Boys. At times, the various venues that catered to the *colonia cubana* and *colonia hispana* joined together to promote events and dances. Managers and promoters of the Tropicana, the Palladium, and the Park Plaza and organizers at *Diario de Nueva York* worked together to generate interest for and host the Carnaval de Oro (Carnival of Gold), a dance competition that featured professional and amateur mambo dancers.[90] Sánchez and the Alfaro brothers also collaborated with members of El Club Cubano to host a dance at the nightclub to raise funds for the social club's baseball team. Club records do not indicate whether the two parties negotiated a rental fee or split the profits from cover charges, but the arrangement must have pleased both sides; in the 1950s, El Club Cubano hosted additional events to raise funds for the baseball team and to purchase a new radio at the nightclub. As two of the major venues for Cuban and Latino/a cultural expression in the Bronx, it is not entirely surprising that the owners of the Tropicana and leaders of El Club Cubano would have established at least an informal partnership.[91]

Advertisements billed the nightclub as "a tropical paradise in New York" and "a cabaret from Broadway in the Bronx." Cuban dancer Horacio Riambau believed that the latter slogan sought to attract a wider and whiter audience from downtown to the nightclub in the Bronx: "There was a lot of publicity to attract the white people to go there so they can make a living." This strategy certainly makes sense given the financial imperatives of nightclub ownership, but perhaps there is another explanation for the slogan. It also indicated to potential audiences in the *colonia hispana* that the Tropicana was no different from the nightclubs and dance halls located on Broadway in Manhattan and that there was no need to make the trip downtown (or to Miami or Havana) to visit venues that likely did not welcome people of color for a night of quality entertainment. In the context of the rising popularity of the Palladium on Broadway, a venue that by all accounts "was one of the few places [in Manhattan] where people of all colors, nationalities, and classes came together and were accepted," the slogan likely functioned as a last-ditch effort to persuade audiences that they would not miss out on any excitement by staying in the neighborhood.[92]

Whatever the intentions of the club's marketing strategy, according to Riambau, the Tropicana attracted a mostly Puerto Rican audience alongside some Cubans and "a lot of Americans," though it is not clear if he meant white or black Americans. He described the atmosphere as "rough" but insisted "that it was safe to go there, it was no problem there, you go there and nothing happen to you. Because I went many times, even at four o'clock in the morning you take the subway, no problem." Ray Santos recalled that at venues such as the Hunts Point Palace and the Tropicana "there was never any friction at all there, you know, between the Latinos and blacks" and that "the priority was good dancing." He admitted, however, that the Hunts Point Palace, in particular, became "pretty famous for its fights," and dances would sometimes end because a fight would result in "chairs flying down from the balcony onto the dance floor." Though "some rowdy elements" may have caused fights that cut the dances short, he insisted that they were not motivated by tensions "between the blacks or the Latinos or between the Latinos themselves."[93] In discussions of this "golden era" of Latin dance halls, Latino/a, African American, Jewish, and ethnic white musicians and dancers often reproduce a myth of racial harmony. Such harmony may have been a reality at times, but the myth is also clearly part of a particular reconstruction of the past.

Marketing ploys and promotional contests also targeted potential clientele from within the *colonia hispana*. In September 1950, for example, the management of the Tropicana sponsored the Premio de Verano (Summer Prize), which offered the winner a round-trip, week-long, all-expenses-paid vacation to Puerto Rico or Cuba. The winner of the raffle, a young Puerto Rican woman who lived on Tenth Street between First Avenue and Avenue A in Manhattan (an indication, perhaps, of both the Tropicana's citywide popularity and the mobility of the *colonia hispana*) chose to use the prize to "realize her dream trip" of visiting her aunt in Havana. For the managers of the club, who, according to one report, "always want to offer valuable attractions to their patrons," the raffle proved "once more that at the 'Tropicana' promises are delivered."[94]

I LOVE WHO?

While Desi Arnaz portrayed Ricky Ricardo as an entertainer and master of ceremonies at the fictional downtown Tropicana, Perucho Irigoyen, a white Cuban actor and comedian, became a fixture at the actual Tropicana in the Bronx where he worked as host and master of ceremonies throughout the late 1940s and 1950s. Irigoyen had come to New York City in 1945 from Havana, where he had starred in *teatro bufo* (Cuban comic theater) as the *negrito* (the little black man).[95] In New York City, Irigoyen performed in "virtually every hispanic theater," on radio's *La Voz Hispana del Aire* (WWRL), and on television's *Canal 13* (WATV). He was also a writer. From his office on 101 West 104th Street, he began publishing a satirical magazine, which he titled *Perucherías*, in 1954. Though he came to New York City already under contract with the Teatro Hispano, he insisted that he arrived "without anyone here knowing his name in advance . . . and [that] it was precisely here that he was 'discovered.'" Everyone came to know Irigoyen, and by 1957, he had earned himself the nickname "Mr. Television."[96]

Like Irigoyen, many of the black and white Cuban entertainers working in New York City during the 1940s and 1950s navigated careers in the entertainment industry that were not as neatly packaged as the one Ricky Ricardo enjoyed on *I Love Lucy*. For Ricky (as for Desi), much of his success as a bandleader and international star rested not on the development of a strong relationship with Cuban and Latino/a audiences but on his production of cultural representations of Cubanness and Latinness that emphasized nonblackness and tropical escape, representations that appealed mostly to white North Americans. In contrast, Irigoyen developed a professional career in the *colonia hispana* that relied on his close ties and affiliations with local nightclubs such as the Tropicana in the Bronx, ethnic social clubs and cultural organizations, and charitable causes. Latino/a New Yorkers loved neither Lucy nor Ricky. They loved Perucho.

Each year from 1946 to 1959, Irigoyen placed in *La Prensa*'s musical popularity contests. One reporter declared that he was "one of the most popular hispanic artists of New York City," and it surprised no one when he won the *Caballeros* category in 1950 and 1951 and the *Locutores* category in 1957. Reflecting on the recognition he had received in the contests, Irigoyen argued that he won only because "the public supported me with the kindness of their votes." The "very popular" entertainer also served as master of ceremonies for the newspaper's fund-raising festivals throughout the 1940s and 1950s. At the 1950 Gran Festival, Irigoyen reportedly "filled and stole the heart of the entire public with his voice of gold." He insisted that he would continue participating in the festivals "just as I have always cooperated and will cooperate in all the just causes that benefit los nuestros."[97] Irigoyen's reference to *los nuestros* indicates a sense of belonging to the Hispanic community that *La Prensa* hailed through its musical popularity contests and fund-raising festivals.

Members of the *colonia hispana* did more than use their votes in the popularity contests to demonstrate their affection for Irigoyen. Commercial venues and ethnic cultural clubs sponsored celebrations and tributes in honor of the popular host and comedian throughout the late 1940s and 1950s. So crucial was "the happy and funny entertainer and master of ceremonies" to the Tropicana that the Alfaro brothers organized a send-off for their showman before he left on a return visit to Cuba in 1948. Three years later, the Asociación de Artistas Hispanos, an organization Irigoyen had helped establish to serve the needs of the city's Hispanic artists, offered a tribute to the "well-known and popular" host and comedian at the Teatro Puerto Rico. In 1958, "various civic and social organizations" came together to organize an event in honor of "the entertaining artist" at the Teatro Puerto Rico, noting that he "has always been willing to offer his support to all charitable functions and for his colleagues."[98]

Irigoyen believed that his success rested on his ability to read his audience and pick up on cues that indicated when they were in the mood to laugh and when they preferred that he just introduce the next act. According to one reviewer in *La Prensa*, Irigoyen "was one of those artists and 'natural' humorists whose mere presence on the stage served to animate the event." His success came from "know[ing] this community to its core and know[ing] how to make the people laugh." During an interview that reportedly took place over a bottle of rum, Irigoyen told *Diario de Nueva York*'s Babby Quintero that he was "very grateful for the Hispanic population of New York and especially the Puerto Rican population. They have been very good to me." He explained, "New York is glory. This was the place I was looking for. My beautiful little Cuba is in my heart, but New York . . . man!" In 1952, after an almost year-long visit to Cuba, Irigoyen's affection for New York City had not wavered; the "celebrated comedian" explained to *La Prensa* that he had returned to the city "influenced by the nostalgia of being once again among the hispanic public that has treated me so well during the seven years that I have lived in this country." Perhaps some of his popularity also came from his ability to take a joke, as happened during an interview with Quintero, who playfully doubted Irigoyen's claim that he was born in Havana. He also avoided explicit political commentary. When asked his opinion of the *golpe de estado* (coup d'état) that had recently taken place in Cuba when Fulgencio Batista seized power three months before elections in 1952, Irigoyen responded that the only "golpe" ("blow") he had felt was the one on his head when he entered his dressing room a few months earlier.[99]

More than most other musicians and performers, Irigoyen learned how to navigate the technological changes that were affecting the mass culture industries. He adapted his style to succeed on stage, on the radio, and on television. Audiences who followed Ricky Ricardo's career on *I Love Lucy* saw the fictional entertainer make similar adaptations and career changes: he expanded his local nightclub duties to include work as a television host, he became a film star in Hollywood, and, later, he became a property owner after buying the Tropicana during the show's sixth season. But there was at least one major difference between the two performers: Irigoyen worked exclusively in Spanish while Ricky (and Desi) targeted an English-speaking public. Another difference existed as well. Occasionally, Irigoyen's jokes bordered on the "risqué," but he never failed to get plenty of laughs, at least according to a columnist for *Ecos de Nueva York*. For example, a photographer from the same newspaper once caught Irigoyen participating in an impromptu "beauty" contest. Backstage after a performance at the Tropicana, Irigoyen sought to beat out three young women—an exotic ballerina, a rumba dancer, and a mambo dancer—for the title of "most beautiful calves." With one pant leg of his formal suit rolled up to almost mid-thigh, he teased the camera and those present with an exaggerated flirtatious pose.[100]

COMMUNITY AND CITIZENSHIP

The two performers also had different attitudes toward participating in community affairs. Ricky generally preferred not to become involved in charitable events or the activities of social clubs. For example, he performed for fund-raisers or showcases organized by Lucy and Ethel's women's club only after the pair initiated some sort of scheme to force his cooperation. This is not to say that Ricky failed to notice that charity work often led to good publicity, but he aimed to appeal to broader, national audiences rather than local ones. In one episode, he volunteers to host the Heart Fund Benefit Show, likely because the program would air on national television. During the show's sixth season, Ricky excitedly organized a benefit show at the club that included the participation of Orson Welles, but he complains when he is forced to participate in charity events organized by Little Ricky's school and a local historical society.[101] Such distance from neighborhood and community activities is not surprising given that Arnaz—and here I note a particular instance of the merging of Arnaz/Ricardo—gave his time and talent mostly to events that had national and international significance, such as in 1942 when he joined the Hollywood Victory Caravan.[102]

In contrast, Irigoyen's connection to the *colonia hispana* that had welcomed him so warmly upon his arrival from Cuba did not dissipate as he became more and more popular. Alongside many other notable Cuban and Puerto Rican performers, Irigoyen participated in the annual fund-raising festival for poor students at Benjamin Franklin High School. In 1951, he recited poetry at the event, this time in a more formal role as president of the Asociación de Artistas Hispanos, one of the event's cosponsors.[103] He also participated in artistic events sponsored by ethnic cultural clubs such as Club Cultural Chileno and Acción Cívica Cubana. For the latter club's second anniversary, he organized Una Tarde Cubana (A Cuban Evening), a "show with local and foreign artists" held at the Hotel Whitehall.[104]

The yearly fund-raiser *Diario de Nueva York* organized at Benjamin Franklin High School and *La Prensa*'s annual fund-raising festivals stand out as acts of both social consciousness and positive public relations that involved collaboration between popular Cuban and Latino/a entertainers and print media. Other smaller-scale events took place throughout the 1940s and 1950s. Under the leadership of the 112th Street and Fifth Avenue block councils of the Urban League of Greater New York, "the little people of Harlem, housewives, mothers, small shopkeepers and mechanics, whose names never get into the society columns of the papers, put on a successful dance for the benefit of their East Harlem community at the Palladium Ballroom." Machito, Miguelito Valdés, José Curbelo, Fausto Curbelo, Noro Morales (the only Puerto Rican bandleader to participate), and "several Negro groups" performed at what was billed as a "benefit interracial dance." One report in the *New York Amsterdam News* explained that the two block councils served nearly "10,000 Puerto Rican and Negro families in the area" and stated that the performers and orchestras "donate[d] their services to promote interracial brotherhood among the people of the area."[105] The fact that the newspaper framed these interactions as "interracial" suggests that at least some African Americans did not see Puerto Ricans and Cubans as largely of African descent. It also confirms that, like Irigoyen, Machito and Valdés exhibited a sense of civic awareness and social responsibility.

This sense of duty extended beyond the confines of New York City. In the days leading up to the sixth annual fund-raising festival at Benjamin Franklin High School in 1953, Machito found time to lead a campaign to encourage individuals in the entertainment community to give blood to the Red Cross in support of soldiers fighting in Korea. The "popular musician" explained that "we all have to do our part," and all members of Machito y sus Afro-Cubans reportedly donated blood with their bandleader. A few days later, a photo appeared in *La Prensa* that showed a "nervous" Valdés preparing to give his donation while Machito stated that "all citizens" should participate in the blood drive.[106] Machito's involvement in this event seems quite similar to Arnaz's participation in the Victory Caravan and USO shows during World War II, but the major difference is that Machito's actions were aimed primarily at the Spanish-speaking residents of New York City while Arnaz targeted broader English-speaking audiences. Machito's participation in this sort of war effort makes sense; after all, he had served in the U.S. Army during World War II. In addition, Puerto Ricans and Cubans in New York City and Puerto Ricans on the island were subject to the draft and were considered, some more than others, collectively as "our boys." That he called specifically on "citizens" from the *colonias hispanas* to participate in this war effort raises important questions about his own citizenship.

Machito's date and place of birth remain a mystery. Journalists, historians, and even Machito himself have given different accounts of his date of birth (ranging from 1907 to 1912) and the location (Miami, Tampa, Havana, and Santiago). World War II Army Enlistment Records list 1912 as the year and Florida as the place of his birth.[107] One journalist reported that he had been born in 1907 in Miami, while another agreed on the year but listed Havana as the location. In one interview, Machito said that he had been born in Cuba and that he had automatically become a U.S. citizen ninety days after joining the U.S. Army in 1943. Carlos Ortiz, a Puerto Rican filmmaker who released a documentary on Machito's musical career in 1987, suggests that the bandleader was aware of the discrepancies regarding his place of birth but that he did nothing to dispel the errors, arguing that "although he has a deep loyalty for the country in which he is now residing, his heart and his roots are still in Cuba." Machito's father worked for a time in the tobacco business, and it is entirely plausible that he was born in Florida, possibly in Tampa, and migrated back to Cuba with his family when the cigar industry began to decline in the late 1910s and 1920s.[108] Machito's strategy of ambiguity about his birthplace was perhaps purposeful; if he had acknowledged birth in the United States, then he risked watering down his claim that he was an "authentic" performer of "música típica" and "ritmos criollos."

For at least one white bandleader, claiming U.S. citizenship was less problematic. José Curbelo was born in Havana, but his father was born in Florida, and one report noted that he "had hardly completed his first cry before his father took him to the American consulate and confirmed his American citizenship." This disclosure did little to dampen Curbelo's credibility as an authentic musician, at least among white North American audiences. One reviewer argued that a band like Curbelo's "watered down their offerings for the sake of socially acceptable smoothness and polite grooming" but concluded that his music still "contains a great deal of primitive muscle." Another reporter believed that given his rankings in *La Prensa*'s musical popularity contests "this native American of Cuban descent speaks with an indorsed authority on the subject." In fact, Curbelo's U.S. citizenship proved useful when he asked the American consul in Havana to issue him a passport so that he could visit the United States. When he was told he needed a Cuban passport, Curbelo reportedly protested, insisting that "'I am an American!'"[109] Perhaps, then, Machito's rejection of an American birth had less to do with musical authenticity and more with his use of Cubanness to temper racial prejudices and navigate the racialized expectations of Cuban cultural performances.

■ At most venues, whether they were uptown in El Barrio or the Bronx or downtown on Broadway, audiences enjoyed distinct though sometimes overlapping representations and performances of Cubanness and Afro-Cubanness. Nightclubs such as the Tropicana in the Bronx and dance halls such as the Palladium offered Cuban and Latino/a New Yorkers an opportunity for socialization and cultural expression in a mostly local community context. Black and white Cuban performers such as Machito, Miguelito Valdés, and Perucho Irigoyen enjoyed favorable reviews and strong followings at hot spots in the *colonia hispana* and at venues such as La Conga that catered mostly (though not exclusively) to a white North American audience. At the same time, millions of mostly white North American viewers gathered around their television sets to watch Desi Arnaz portray their favorite Cuban bandleader on *I Love Lucy*. The personal lives and professional careers of these black and white Cuban performers demonstrate that lived and imagined representations of Cubanness, Afro-Cubanness, and Latinness intersected in ways that shaped Cuban and Latino/a identity and community.

6

CUBANS IN MIAMI'S PAN-AMERICAN

PARADISE

Like many real-life Cuban musicians and performers based in New York City in the 1940s and 1950s, the fictional Ricky Ricardo and his band traveled south to Miami during the winter months to perform at one of a growing number of hotels and nightclubs that were popping up along the city's shoreline. During the sixth season of *I Love Lucy*, Ricky and his band travel to Miami for an engagement at the Eden Roc Hotel, a luxurious oceanfront resort on Collins Avenue between 45th and 46th Streets, located next door to the larger and perhaps even more grand Fontainebleau. Just a few days into the trip, Ricky announces to Lucy, Fred, and Ethel that producers have asked him to be in a film called *The Florida Story*, a documentary exploring the state's history, beginning with the early days of Spanish exploration. Ricky and his band have been cast to represent present-day Florida, and producers have decided to include their performances at the Eden Roc in the film. Later in the episode, the Ricardos and Mertzes are stranded on an island that they believe is deserted, only to learn that the entire production company is on location, filming a scene for the documentary with actor Claude Akins. In this scene, Akins has been cast as a native inhabitant; he is dressed in tribal war paint and an elaborate headdress.[1] Though viewers learn little else about the content of *The Florida Story*, this framing of Florida's history seems to suggest a narrative of progress, one that advances from a state of primitive nature populated by primitive peoples to one of modern architecture featuring modern performers, music, and guests.

The casting of a touring white Cuban bandleader like Ricky Ricardo as representative of 1950s Florida also reproduced the notion that the

Cuban and broader Latino/a presence in Miami and other parts of south Florida was seasonal and impermanent. But that was certainly not the case. Black and white Cubans, longtime residents and recent arrivals, ordinary migrants and professional entertainers, had all helped construct Cuban ethnic and Latino/a identity and community in Miami long before it became a refuge for the hundreds of thousands of Cuban exiles who fled the island after the Cuban Revolution of 1959. Race and uneven modes of racialization played a key role in this process, especially as relationships developed with African Americans and Puerto Ricans in the city. Ideologies and practices of Pan-Americanism also mattered as local officials and residents struggled to make sense of (and sometimes take advantage of) the increasing Cuban and Latin American presence in the city. All of these interrelated factors came to shape the character of Miami's pre-1959 Cuban diaspora.

The city's newly established nightclubs and hotels booked some of the most popular Cuban and Latin bands of the era as tourists from across the United States and Latin America, including thousands of Cuban visitors, crowded onto dance floors to the beats of the rumba, mambo, and cha-cha-chá. Not everyone saw Miami as a temporary destination or a vacationer's tropical paradise. Many Cubans made the city their home, joining Cuban social clubs and soliciting restaurants, bars, and nightclubs owned by Cubans and other Latino/as. The Cuban presence in Miami was highly visible on the terrain of popular culture, where different kinds of representations of (Afro-)Cubanness and Latinness came to be constructed and contested. Many of the city's commercial venues catered primarily to white North American and foreign tourists and hired mostly white and light-skinned Cuban musicians and performers, although there were some exceptions. Black and white Cuban musicians also performed at ethnic and cultural events that targeted mostly Cuban and Latino/a audiences. These entertainers participated in the many social activities, cultural events, and patriotic celebrations that took place in the *colonia cubana* and *colonia latina*, including those organized by the Círculo Cubano and Juventud Cubana, the two most prominent Cuban social clubs in the city.

The story of Cubans in Miami in the 1940s and 1950s offers a distinct context through which we can trace some of the same musicians, musical styles, and cultural performances that were simultaneously becoming key parts of the Cuban American cultural landscape of New York City. In fact, at key moments, the Cubans and Cuban social clubs of Miami and New York City collaborated to organize social events and participate in acts of social and cultural solidarity. However, the differences between the two communities were somewhat striking. In New York City, Cuban musicians and migrants lived and worked among a much larger population of Puerto Ricans and participated in downtown and uptown music scenes. New York City was also a place where Afro-Cubans forged independent institutions. It was in these contexts that both black and white Cubans discussed and negotiated questions of Cuban national identity, race and ethnicity, and musical authenticity. In Miami, a relatively smaller number of Cuban residents lived in the context of a large population of tourists, business professionals, and temporary workers who moved between the United States, Cuba, and the rest of Latin America. During this period, Miami belonged as much to the Jim Crow South as it did to the internationalist haven that tourism boosters and businessmen keen on strengthening commercial ties with their neighbors to the south promoted. A certain kind of Cubanness and certain kinds of Cuban performers were used to attract Anglo tourists to Miami for a "near Cuba" experience. The strategy seemed to work so well that in 1949 the Cuban government signed José Curbelo, a favorite on the Miami nightclub scene, to make a musical short "as part of its campaign to build up Havana as a rival winter resort to Miami."[2] Ideologies and commercial practices of Pan-Americanism also shaped relations between local officials, certain ethnic institutions and activities, and the city's Cuban social clubs. And in the late 1950s, island-based politics came to play an increasingly important role in structuring community life and identity, though even then there seemed to be at least a little time left for dancing.

THE MENDOZA FAMILY'S MIGRATIONS

The emergence of a Cuban music scene in Miami began early in the twentieth century, long before the boom in construction and expansion that took place in south Florida after World War II.[3] In the early 1930s, a white Cuban trumpet player named Enrique Mendoza and a few of his co-workers at the Summerfield Cigar Factory in Miami decided to start a band, which they named El Dulce after the cigars made at the factory. The musicians gathered in the evenings for "daily jam sessions, Latin style," and after a few weeks of rehearsals Mendoza decided that his rumba band was ready to perform in public. El Dulce took the stage at the Roney Plaza in Miami for the entire 1933 season. Their success that first season earned the band bookings at other hotels and clubs on the beach for the following year and captured the attention of aspiring young musicians. One such musician was Desi Arnaz, who went to Mendoza's house a few times to audition for

*Rhumba dancers at the Roney Plaza Hotel accompanied by El Dulce
Orchestra, 18 January 1933. Copyright Bettmann/Corbis/AP Images.
Courtesy of AP Images.*

the band, though he was eventually turned away because they already had
a guitarist. In any case, the band's run was short lived. El Dulce stopped
performing in the late 1930s, reportedly as a result of the poor economy,
but Mendoza and his band had played a significant role in introducing
Afro-Cuban popular music to the dancing publics of Miami and greater
south Florida. In 1957, a report in the *Miami Herald* credited Mendoza
as a "pioneer of sorts," describing him as the "man who introduced the
bongo-beating, hip-swinging Latin music to Miami." Despite this recognition, the former bandleader was working as a baggage clerk at Miami's
Greyhound terminal, an outsider looking in on the world of Latin entertainment he had helped introduce to the city two decades earlier.

But his is not simply a story of failed celebrity, for it offers an opportunity to explore the multiple ways Cubans became a part of south Florida's emerging tourism industry. Mendoza remained in Miami to raise a
family and felt a deep connection to the area that had welcomed earlier

generations of his family. His father, José González Mendoza, lived and worked in Key West at the end of the nineteenth century and used a percentage of his earnings from *bolita* (an illegal Cuban numbers game) to help finance and maintain a school there. His daughter, María Mendoza Kranz, lived most of her life in Miami and Hialeah. She too was a "pioneer of sorts": she was one of the first women—and, according to her recollections, the only one with a Spanish surname—hired to work on the assembly line at the Inter-Continent Aircraft Corporation during World War II. She was also the first Spanish-speaking saleswoman to work at S.H. Kress & Co., a "five and dime" department store, where she used her language skills to assist Cuban visitors. She convinced management to post a sign on the front window that read "*se habla español*" ("Spanish spoken here"). Mendoza Kranz affirmed that she and the generations of her family before her "always loved their two homelands," Cuba and the United States.[4]

The Mendoza family's multiple migrations from Cuba to Key West to Tampa to Miami mirror a pattern of movement and settlement many Cubans experienced in the late nineteenth and early twentieth centuries. The outbreak of the Ten Years' War in 1868 and U.S. trade policies that favored the importation of tobacco over cigars helped Key West emerge as the first Cuban settlement in Florida. By 1885, nearly 3,000 cigar makers, most of whom were Cuban, worked in Key West's ninety cigar factories. Soon, however, labor unrest and the increased involvement of cigar workers in the Cuban independence movement prompted factory owners to relocate their operations elsewhere in Florida. Thanks to an agreement brokered by a group of Spanish and Cuban manufacturers (including Vicente Martínez Ybor) and a group of local businessmen who agreed to subsidize the purchase of land, Key West's cigar factories (and cigar workers) began to move to Tampa in the late 1880s.[5] It was during this period of relocation that the Mendoza family made its move north, living and working in Tampa for some years before settling in Miami. Though most attempts to establish large-scale cigar factories in Miami failed before 1926, one exception was the Summerfield Cigar Factory, which relocated from Tampa to Miami in the late 1920s. Summerfield employed mostly Cuban migrants, including four members of the Mendoza family who had made the move south to work in the factory in October 1932. (Mendoza Kranz needed a special permit to work at the factory because of her young age.) The Mendozas found housing directly across the street from the cigar factory on 11th Street and N.E. Miami Avenue. The family chose the residence for financial reasons as much as for its convenience. Like so many other Cuban migrants during this period, members of the Mendoza family could not always afford the luxury of spending the five cents it cost to ride the streetcar.[6]

THE LATINIZATION OF MIAMI

Historians have long recognized Miami as a summer vacation destination and place of political refuge for Cubans, especially after the rise and fall of the Gerardo Machado regime in the 1930s. That Ricky Ricardo, a white Cuban bandleader who performed mostly Cuban popular music in a recently opened Miami hotel, was called upon as a representative of 1950s Florida signals, even in this fictional setting, an acknowledgement of the Latinization of Miami in the context of a burgeoning tourism industry. Tourism helped cast the city as "exotic," and, as historian Gary Mormino explains, it soon became "an international crossroads of travel, finance, and intrigue."[7]

A variety of changes in Miami's economy in the 1930s helped create and reproduce this reputation. Many of these transformations centered on efforts to attract tourists and investors from the Northeast and Midwest and Latin America. New industries emerged, but as historian Melanie Shell-Weiss has shown, only those "that would not tarnish the city's image as a tropical paradise were considered." These included food processing plants and factories that produced clothing, hats, shoes, pharmaceuticals, and furniture. Also key to the city's growth was the increase in air traffic: Pan American World Airways, which primarily provided air mail and passenger service between Key West and Havana, became the primary mail carrier for Latin America in 1925, and Eastern Airlines and National Airlines moved their headquarters to Miami in 1938. In 1941, a new 846-acre International Airport was completed in the city. The recruitment efforts of the Miami Chamber of Commerce and declining land prices attracted Jewish businessmen, especially hotel owners from the Catskills and the Jersey shore, to open hotels and inns in Miami and Miami Beach. By 1940, there were nearly 8,000 Jewish people in Miami, quite an increase from the fifty individuals that made up the city's Jewish community in 1915.[8]

But Jews were not the only newcomers to arrive in Miami in the late 1920s and 1930s. According to historian Louis A. Pérez, "A small Cuban community formed in Miami in the 1920s, consisting mainly of workers, musicians, and entertainers whose presence contributed to the local 'color' in the rendering of Miami as tropical." The size of that presence increased in the late 1920s and early 1930s as "political exiles, first as opponents of the Gerardo Machado government and subsequently as members of the fallen Machado government" sought refuge in Miami. Among the former public officials who were living in Miami was Desi Arnaz's father. Pérez conservatively estimates that "by the late 1930s, about six thousand Cubans lived in Miami." Records from the 1940 U.S. census indicate that 11,460 Cubans (defined as those who were born in Cuba or who had a mother or father who was born in Cuba) lived in Florida. Of those born in Cuba, nearly 7,000 were classified as "white"; only about 1,000 were designated "black."[9]

The onset of World War II brought additional changes to Miami. As trade with Europe and Asia was cut off by the war, officials in Miami looked to strengthen economic ties and commercial relationships with Latin America. Between 200,000 and 311,000 Latin Americans visited the city each year throughout war, according to the Miami Chamber of Commerce. The presence of the U.S. armed forces in south Florida led to improvements in the region's infrastructure. New roads and bridges were built and old ones were repaired, and the area's rail system, port, and airport were expanded. Local boosters worked to solidify Miami's role as the "Gateway to the Americas." Wartime economic expansion and the city's efforts at self-promotion attracted new residents. From 1940 to 1945, nearly 50,000 people moved to Dade County, and, by the end of the war, a majority of the residents of Miami had been born outside of the state. This growth in population included more than 80,000 newcomers from Georgia, 26,000 from New York, 14,300 from Pennsylvania, and 12,000 from Ohio, continuing the previous decade's trend of Northeasterners and Midwesterners moving to Miami. By 1950, Miami was the state's largest city, counting 250,000 inhabitants. That figure likely included the majority of the Cuban population in Florida, which held steady throughout the 1940s. The 1950 U.S. census found that 11,597 Cubans lived in the state; 7,230 of the Cuban-born individuals were assigned a racial classification of "white" and 495 were categorized as "black."[10]

Temporary visitors contributed in significant ways to the Cuban presence in south Florida. Beginning in the late nineteenth and continuing throughout the twentieth century, the back-and-forth movement of Cuban tourists, business professionals, transient workers, and political exiles and allies between Havana and Miami resulted in the "ties of singular intimacy" that have historically joined Cuba and the United States. Close proximity, favorable climate, air-conditioning, and the relatively low costs of transportation, shopping, and other services facilitated the ease of travel between Havana and Miami, leading to cultural familiarity and affection. Pérez has argued that "Miami entered the Cuban consciousness as a place of refuge and residence: it was readily accessible, the cost of living was reasonable, and most of all it was vaguely familiar." Round-trip travel by steamship cost less than $40, and round-trip airfare between Miami and Havana—a short 40-minute flight—cost about $30 in the 1950s. Pan American Airlines operated an average of twenty-eight flights between the two cities each day. Developers and architects designed Miami with Cuba in mind, working to reproduce Havana's Spanish colonial heritage in their city. At the height of the construction boom in the mid-1920s, builders and architects imported more than two million roof and floor tiles from Cuba. Perhaps hoping for his chance to reclaim a chunk of the fortune he had lost in the Revolution of 1933, Desi Arnaz's father entered the tile import business during his first few years in Miami in the 1930s.[11]

An average of 40,000 Cubans visited Miami each year throughout the 1940s; in the 1950s, the annual average increased to 50,000. Thousands of Cuban couples honeymooned in the city, including the young Fidel Castro and his bride Mirta Díaz Balart, whom he married in 1948. In fact, Castro came to Miami frequently during this period (as did many other former and hopeful Cuban politicians). He made repeated visits to the Mary Elizabeth, a black-owned hotel in Overtown, formerly called Colored Town, on the corner of N.W. Seventh Street and N.W. Second Avenue. On the hotel's first floor was a Cuban-run barbershop that attracted Cuban patrons. Historian Nathan Connolly explains that "discussing every topic between baseball and The Revolution, young Cuban men would converse in the Mary Elizabeth's barber-chairs by day and grace the hotel's dance floors by night." In fact, many of the period's most famous entertainers, both black and white, came to Miami to perform at the Mary Elizabeth and at many of the other black-owned hotspots that provided entertainment along Second Avenue between Sixth and Tenth Streets. As jazz musicians and celebrities such as Tommy Dorsey, Jimmy Dorsey, Billy Holliday, Cab Calloway, Lena Horne, and Joe Louis managed to convince white audiences to cross into Overtown, the area earned the nickname "Miami's Little Broadway."[12]

Some of the Cubans who traveled to Miami on tourist visas overstayed the conditions of their travel permits. In his memoir *Before Night Falls*, Cuban writer and poet Reinaldo Arenas tells the story of his uncle and mother who left for the United States: "In those days of extreme poverty, the dream of all who were down-and-out in Cuba was to go 'north' to work," even if that meant traveling as a tourist without permission to work. Though they may have spent just a few days, weeks, or months in Miami before returning to the island, Cuban tourists and temporary residents made symbolic and material contributions to the development of the city's *colonia cubana* and *colonia latina*.[13]

U.S. census records indicate that by 1960 the Cuban population in Florida had quadrupled, rising to just over 48,000. It would be easy to suspect that the dramatic increase in the number of Cubans living in Florida occurred mostly in the late 1950s, directly as a result of the Cuban Revolution, but even conservative estimates admit that nearly 20,000 Cubans lived in Miami before 1959. Shell-Weiss has found that local officials reported to the *Miami Herald* that 46,000 Cubans were living in Miami-Dade County by the mid-1950s, alongside an estimated 30,000 Puerto Ricans, 3,500 Colombians, 2,000 Venezuelans, 1,200 Ecuadorians, 800 Mexicans, and 2,000 individuals from other parts of Central America. All of this is to say that a stable Cuban and broader Latino/a presence in Miami began to transform the city's racial and cultural landscape in far greater numbers and much earlier in the twentieth century than has previously been acknowledged.[14]

The growing Cuban presence in the city and the influx of large numbers of tourists from Latin America complicated Miami's white-over-black racial hierarchy. Miami was, after all, still a city in the Jim Crow South and that meant the segregation of blacks and whites in public places, including in schools, restaurants, hotels, and transportation. Historians have shown that even though government and police officials in Miami worked to maintain the color line through intimidation, violence, and economic and legal means, some exceptions were made for Spanish-speaking tourists and residents, including those with dark skin. Instances of Cubans and other Latino/as of color receiving better treatment than African Americans, who remained second-class citizens, however, did not mean treatment equal with whites or that a systematic method of racial classification was in place. Connolly, for example, has argued that as tourists from the Spanish-speaking world flooded into south Florida, whiteness took on "a decidedly more diverse face." Interestingly, the 1960 U.S. census classified all of the 29,000 foreign-born Cubans in Florida as "white." What these numbers mean in the context of Jim Crow and the spread of Pan-Americanism is not entirely clear, though there are at least three possible explanations, all of which may have been in operation to one degree or another. The first possibility is that mostly white, middle- and upper-class Cubans left the island during the economic uncertainty and political turmoil that characterized Cuban society throughout the 1950s. The second explanation is that the harshness of the Jim Crow South during this period might have prompted Cubans of color not to settle permanently in south Florida. Finally, it is possible that a process of racialization was taking place within a biracial system that often classified Spanish-speaking Cubans, even those with darker skin, as different from and, in some cases, more welcome than English-speaking African Americans.[15]

LOCATING A *COLONIA CUBANA* AND A *COLONIA LATINA*

Mormino has argued that "already in 1950, Miami was the Cuban city of the future, even though no identifiable Cuban neighborhood or colony yet had taken hold."[16] As was the case with Cubans in New York City, however, claims based solely on population size or housing patterns too easily dismiss the more symbolic and cultural uses of the concepts of the *colonia cubana* or *colonia latina*. Brief on-the-street testimonials solicited by a reporter from *Diario las Américas* in 1954 reveal that Cubans and other Latino/as lived in all parts of the city, though most preferred the southwestern and northwestern sections. A *bodeguero* (owner of a *bodega*) named Miguel Mendez explained that he lived in the northwest part of Miami because he "had very good neighbors and I am very happy for that. I understand that the neighborhood doesn't make the people, but exactly the opposite, the people make the neighborhood." Another respondent, Herminia Eslos Escolas, reported that she preferred living in the southwest section of Miami because she "considers it the best situated part of the city and the one that has the best future." In 1956, a news report revealed that of the 609 students enrolled at Buena Vista Elementary School, located at 3001 N.W. Second Avenue, 239 spoke more Spanish than English. Most of the students had come to Miami from Cuba, Puerto Rico, and other Central and South American countries, and the report noted that the school "is rapidly converting itself into the first bilingual school in the county, forced by these circumstances."[17]

Miami's Spanish-language newspapers played a key role in hailing and defining the city's *colonia cubana* and *colonia latina*. The *Miami Latin News (Noticiero Latino)* and *Diario las Américas* targeted both the city's Latin American visitors and established residents, and in the pages of these newspapers Pan-Americanism circulated as public discourse. The *Miami Latin News*, which was published every Sunday, described itself as "a newspaper published in the interest of Greater Miami's Spanish-speaking population and our visitors from Latin America." The larger daily, *Diario las Américas*, which was founded in 1953, had a slogan that confirmed the city's near-obsession with Pan-Americanism: it stood "for liberty, culture, and hemispheric solidarity." It is not clear whether either of these newspapers received direct support or financial backing from tourism boosters or city officials, though it is likely that the Miami Chamber of Commerce had at least a casual interest in both publications and in attracting Cubans and other working-class Latino/as to Miami.[18]

Countless reports and advertisements published in the *Miami Latin News* and *Diario las Américas* directly and indirectly hailed a public referred to as the *colonia latina*, the *colonia latinoamericana*, the *colonia Hispanoamericana*, and the *colonia cubana* throughout the 1940s and 1950s. One of the clearest indications of a stable and identifiable Cuban and Latino/a presence in Miami can be seen in the proliferation of retail shops, hotels, and restaurants that welcomed and, in many cases, catered explicitly to consumers in the *colonia cubana* and *colonia latina*. As early as 1946, El Restaurante Habana, located at 214 N.E. Second Avenue, billed itself as "The Preferred Place of the Latinos"; its menu offered *bistec a lo cubano* (thinly sliced steak with onions) and *arroz con pollo* (yellow rice with chicken). That same year, across town at 1101 North Miami Avenue, La Concha restaurant celebrated "15 years of service in the colonia latina." María Mendoza Kranz recalled that many Cubans, including her brothers, spent time hanging out at the Spanish-owned restaurant.[19] Other restaurants, retail shops, and food stores opened their doors throughout the late 1940s and 1950s, such as El Toreador, Panadería y Dulcería El Siboney, Alva Upholsterers, Restaurante Florida, Cuqui Peluquería Cubana, Dixon Barber Shop, and Quinta Avenida and La Cubanita (both of which were described as "latino" butcher shops and markets).[20]

Many of these businesses published advertisements that emphasized Cuban, Puerto Rican, and Latino/a ownership and management. Those who announced their ties to Cuba, Latin America, and other Latino/a communities in the United States most directly included La Casa Caribe, a retail and wholesale import shop recently opened by Mario Pérez at 513 North Miami Avenue; La Giralda Churrería-Restaurant, which was owned by the Rodríguez family, who had previously managed a restaurant in New York; and La Sin Rival de José Álvarez, a shop that specialized in knife-sharpening "by the most famous scissor-sharpener in Havana." Advertisements for Hilda's Beauty Salon and the Feliz Barber Shop announced that their stylists had received training and had arrived directly from the "best salons" in New York and Havana. An advertisement for Carlo's restaurant promised "the best arroz con pollo in the city" and noted that its owners were "from the internationally renowned Sorrento Restaurant in Havana, Cuba." The two Cuban owners of Las Brisas Cubanas invited diners to enjoy their "traditional foods" and "feel as if they were in Cuba."[21] In

Marketing Cuba!

1956, a reporter for *Diario las Américas* argued that "with each day that passes, Miami becomes more and more hispanic," to the extent that "we do not know with scientific precision the exact number of 'peluquerías' [hair salons], 'barberías' [barber shops], 'colmados' [grocery stores], 'bodegas,' 'almacenes' [warehouses], 'tiendas' [shops] (they are known by all of these and other names) at which nuestra colonia acquires 'hispanic' provisions."[22]

MIAMI'S NIGHTCLUB SCENE

During World War II, the many hotels, inns, and restaurants dotting Miami's landscape took on a different purpose. As wartime rationing made travel and discretionary spending difficult, many of the city's tourist attractions were converted to military housing and training sites. This temporary dip in growth in the tourism sector improved as economic investment in the tourism industry, particularly in hotel and nightclub development, intensified in Miami immediately after the end of the war. But that growth came about a bit faster than the number of "war-profit-laden tourists" making their way to Miami for the winter season. In 1946, Miami's nightclubs could seat as many as 20,000 guests, an expansion in capacity that was both a blessing and a curse. One report in *Billboard* estimated that this "would put the area in a class with New York, the largest night club center in the world (all year round) and leave Miami in a most unfavorable position vis-à-vis profits." Established nightclubs such as the Colonial Inn, the Copa, the Beachcomber, the Mocambo, and the Brook Club; recently opened hot spots such as the Burgundy Club, the Blackamoor, and the Park Avenue; and numerous local hotels competed not only for patrons but also for quality entertainers.[23] Competition among the many hotels, nightclubs, and entertainment promoters in the city continued throughout the late 1940s and 1950s, but what may have been troubling to club owners and promoters proved beneficial to entertainers and audiences. In this climate, Xavier Cugat commanded a $15,000 contract for a one-week booking at the Americana. In 1956, Miami's nightclub scene boasted a veritable "who's who among stars from television, screen, night club and stage for appearances in the hotel-cafes around which nocturnal activities will center." In fact, a reporter for the *New York Times* put a positive spin on the "conflict between rival hotel groups here in booking dazzling attractions," arguing that "the whole thing looks very good for customers who enjoy famous performers, particularly as it seems to involve cut rates for these patrons."[24]

Well-known Cuban musicians and entertainers performed in Miami during the 1940s and 1950s. Cugat was at the Beachcomber and the Americana, Desi Arnaz performed at the Roney Plaza and the Brook Club, Miguelito Valdés took top billing at the Mocambo and the Hotel Saxony, and Cuban dance team Raúl y Eva Reyes delighted at the Colonial Inn.[25] José Curbelo had an extensive run in Miami and Miami Beach, where he booked engagements at Sunny Isles, the Sans Souci, the Mocambo, the Beachcomber, the Rumba Casino, and the Clover Club.[26] Hotels and night-clubs such as the Hotel Caribbean, the Hotel Cadillac, Club Chalet en la Playa at the Hotel Lucerne, Salon Pompey at the Eden Roc Hotel, and the Cha Cha Lounge also featured performances by less well-known entertainers such as Tony Meléndez, Bobby Escoto, Fernando "Caney" Storch, Arturo Santirzo, Fausto Curbelo, and Los Tres Galanes.[27] Cuban dancer Olga Chaviano came to Miami in 1954 to perform at the Teatro Olympia after having performed in musical revues and film productions in Venezuela and Mexico and at the Sans Souci and the Tropicana in Havana. Chaviano told a reporter for *Diario las Américas* that "the public in Miami is the most friendly I have seen, it knows how to understand my dances and admires with much enthusiasm the efforts we have made to present to them this type of revue."[28]

Some nightclubs and bars in Miami specifically targeted the city's *colonia cubana* and *colonia latina*. A "devoted" public could do more than listen to "music from our native countries" on local radio stations. They could also come together in commercial and cultural spaces to enjoy live performances by their favorite musical acts. A reporter for *Diario las Américas* exclaimed, "And with what delight and nostalgia we attend evening gatherings, concerts, or recitals at which some local or imported hispanic group delights us with happy or romantic and even dancing notes of the music of nuestra raza!" Music and entertainment became central components of a Latino/a identity that was defined by a shared racial past. This reporter seemed to treat "hispanic" and "nuestra raza" as synonyms, although he distinguished between "local" or "imported" musicians. Perhaps the remark suggests that audiences in Miami, including Cuban and Latino/a audiences, took more notice of (and cared more about) these differences, which makes sense given the city's dependence on tourism and travel. In any case, throughout the 1940s and 1950s, the many hotels and nightclubs in Miami and Miami Beach not only promoted Cuban, Puerto Rican, and other Latino/a musicians and performers but also promised audiences evenings full of "genuine Latin American atmosphere." These promises, which appeared in the pages of the city's Spanish-language news-

Miami music appeals to both tourists & latin Community

papers, indicate that these events and venues welcomed and actively solicited the participation of the growing Cuban and Latino/a resident community in addition to domestic and foreign tourists. In 1956, the "sumptuous" Club Chalet at the "exclusive" Hotel Lucerne advertised its Fiesta del Cha-Cha-Chá, noting that the event would be "livened up by the most popular orchestra of maestro Luis Varona," a Cuban pianist who had previously been a member of Machito y sus Afro-Cubans. The management of the hotel reportedly "had special interest in inviting the members of Miami's colonia Hispanoamericana to enjoy the [event]," as evidenced by the announcement that guests would not be charged a cover fee and that "popular prices" would be extended to all in attendance.[29] Of course, eliminating cover charges gave a venue an edge over the competition, including over clubs that may not have been able or willing to lower their pricing scales or be less selective in their admittance policies.

One nightclub took the lead in reaching out to local and visiting Cuban and Latino/a crowds. Not to be overshadowed by Havana or New York City, Miami had a Tropicana Club of its own in the 1950s, located at 420 S.W. Eighth Avenue in the space formerly occupied by the Círculo Cubano. One of its earliest events was a 1956 New Year's Eve dance that featured continuous music by two large bands from eight in the evening to five in the morning, all at "popular prices." The Tropicana quickly developed a reputation as "the most excellent public center for dancing in Miami." It hosted a variety of events, including dance competitions, raffles, and other contests, and performers such as the Conjunto Palladium from New York, the Orquesta Casino de Miami, Conjunto Caney, Juanito Sanabria, Vitín Avilés, and Noro Morales. Owner Joe Colón, who was Puerto Rican, and manager José Montoro created a "modern and welcoming" space that "had definitely earned the support of young people of all ages." According to one reporter, Colón "spared no expense in offering Miami's colonia Hispanoamericana a welcoming, beautifully decorated place with the best music." The reporter predicted that because of these efforts the Tropicana would "be patronized more and more by Miami's vast colonia Hispanoamericana."[30]

On Saturday and Sunday nights, the "popular inter-American club" drew onto its dance floor what one reporter described as "excellent young people." In framing the Tropicana as "inter-American," advertisements suggest not only the diversity of Miami's *colonia latina* but also the diffusion of Pan-American ideology on the terrain of popular culture. It seems that the Tropicana's owner purposefully worked to attract a large and diverse crowd to the nightclub. Colón waived the cover charge for hundreds of his guests several times in 1957, a gesture that likely went a long way toward

Integration in Miami Club Scene

attracting loyal patrons. In fact, the nightclub "saw a steady increase in its clientele"; one report noted that "both a North American and Hispanic American public is attending the Tropicana on the weekends." Colón also partnered with Club Damas Panamericanas to host dances at the Tropicana, which reportedly "resulted in a complete success, as much for the quantity as for the quality of the people that come to the club every weekend."[31]

The weekend dances at the Tropicana regularly featured local bands such as Conjunto Caney and Orquesta de Miami and more famous performers such as Juanito Sanabria and Noro Morales. The club succeeded in attracting a steady stream of quality local performers and internationally recognized Cuban singers. Benny Moré, for example, performed at the Tropicana. Celia Cruz also debuted at the club, a booking that caused "all of Miami, especially members of the amusing colonia Hispanoamericana [to fill] with liveliness." For unknown reasons, however, the Tropicana ended 1957 under new management, which promised that it would offer "popular American music" in addition to "Latin American music."[32]

Just a few steps down from the Tropicana, another bar and nightclub seemed to target the *colonia cubana* of Miami more directly. An advertisement for Barra Guys and Dolls, which was located at 442 S.W. Eighth Street, announced, "Cuban friends, if you want to have a good time in distinctly criollo atmosphere, visit Barra 'Guys and Dolls,' where you can dance and have as much fun as you desire."[33] If the bar's owner, Octavio Tacón, drew any inspiration from the wildly successful 1950 Broadway musical and 1955 Hollywood film when he named his business, then an evening at Barra Guys and Dolls might have included a little more than dancing and drinking. *Guys and Dolls* portrayed Havana as home to casinos and exotic nightlife, as a place to let loose, dance, and drink delicious Bacardí rum. In the film, Sky Masterson (Marlon Brando) is a bold gambler who takes on a seemingly impossible $1,000 bet: he must convince Sarah Brown (Jean Simmons), an uptight sergeant in the Save-a-Soul Mission, to go to dinner with him in Havana, a difficult proposition since Sarah and the mission are vehemently opposed to gambling. She agrees to the date only because Sky pretends to be interested in reform and promises to bring a dozen sinners to the mission.

The couple goes to a nightclub in Havana, where they appear to be the only Anglo tourists. Sarah is transformed by her exposure to Afro-Cuban music, hip-pulsating dancers, a rum drink served in a coconut shell, and sexual jealousy. When an alluring, dark-haired, red-lipped, brown-skinned Cuban woman tries to seduce Sky, her response is almost immediate: she finds herself a Cuban partner and joins in the dancing, shaking her hips and shimmying her shoulders. She also confronts her Cuban competition with a quick punch to the face. This scene provides a snapshot of the image of Cuban tourism that was being captured by local entrepreneurs in Miami, who hoped to keep tourists from making the easy hop from Miami (or New York City) to Havana for exotic revelry by offering a near-Cuba experience in their city. In hailing the image of *Guys and Dolls*, Tacón's message was clear: his bar in Miami could provide just as much excitement and tropical escape as any bar in Havana. Instead of rejecting what some would rightly perceive as a negative or exaggerated stereotype, this bar owner used familiar cultural (mis)representations of Havana's nightlife as a means of drawing Cuban patrons to what he deemed a "distinctly criollo atmosphere." Whether Cuban residents or tourists responded positively to the advertisement is not known, but that Tacón would want to attract Cubans to his club makes sense if he also hoped to convince U.S. and foreign tourists that they could find a genuine *Guys and Dolls*–type experience in his club.

CUBAN SOCIAL CLUBS AND PATRIOTIC CELEBRATIONS

For Cubans, Puerto Ricans, and other Latino/as in Miami, dancing and socializing happened in other venues besides hotels, nightclubs, and bars. As the Cuban population in Miami increased throughout the 1950s, so did the number and variety of social events, cultural activities, and patriotic celebrations hosted by two of the city's Cuban social clubs, the Círculo Cubano and Juventud Cubana. The Círculo Cubano opened its doors at 420 S.W. Eighth Avenue on 20 May 1952, a historic date that marked the fiftieth anniversary of Cuba's formal independence from the United States. The club was at this address until 1956, when it moved to 90 N.W. 27th Avenue between Flagler and First Avenue. While club members prepared this "new and modern" space in a "magnificent and special building" for its grand opening, the banquet hall at the headquarters of the Miami Police Benevolent Association, located at 2300 N.W. 14th Street, served as the temporary venue for club functions. When the preparations were completed, on 8 December 1956, the Círculo Cubano invited "all of the Latinos in the city of Miami" to celebrate the opening of its new social space with a dance that featured the music of Hilda Salazar y sus Guaracheras.[34]

The Círculo Cubano hosted countless social events that offered Miami's *colonia cubana* and *colonia latina* an opportunity to enjoy musical performances by a variety of Cuban singers and orchestras. The "enthusiastic and friendly society" hosted afternoon and evening dances throughout the year that included nearly five hours of continuous music from performers such as Arturo Santirzo, Hilda Salazar y sus Guaracheras, Arturo Benson y su Orquesta Cubanacán, Luis Varona, Cheche de la Cruz y sus Ases del Ritmo, Heriberto Curbelo, and Conjunto Casino de Miami.[35] Many club activities centered on Cuban themes, such as the club's Carnaval Habanero in 1957. Advertisements for club events invited members of the *colonia cubana*, and most noted that events were also open to all members of the *colonia latina*. The club celebrated its two-year anniversary in 1954 with "a traditional Cuban event" that featured "a parade of highly sought-after jewels in nuestra colonia" and was open to "all our compatriots as well as anyone else who wants to attend these festivities." In October 1956, the club organized a matinee dance that featured Rogelio Dárias, a former member of Cugat's band in New York City. One report noted that the event generated anticipation "among Cubans as well as the rest of the city's very important colonia Hispanoamericana." Other events the club hosted included musical battles that pitted the cha-cha-chá rhythms of Hilda Salazar against the music of The Five-Spades, an American rock 'n' roll band.[36]

Like the Cuban organizations of New York City, social clubs in Miami hosted celebrations in honor of Cuban national holidays, and many of these honored national hero José Martí. In January 1957, the Círculo Cubano marked Martí's birthday with a celebration at its clubhouse that featured music and performances by Hilda Salazar. More than 500 people attended the event, including Eduardo Hernández, the consul-general of Cuba; municipal and county public officials; and "other personalities of Miami public life." As in New York City, Cuban consular officials in Miami participating in events organized by Cuban social clubs helped shape the presence of the homeland in the diaspora. Of this specific event, German Negroni, a reporter for *Diario las Américas*, boasted that "few times has there been celebrated in the city of Miami an act that displayed such sparkle and signaled such importance as the one hosted by the Círculo Cubano de Miami."[37]

Often, events to honor Martí's birth also included an announcement of the winner of the *canastilla martiana*. At the 1957 celebration, the basket went to Puerto Rican Ramón Rivera González and his Colombian wife María Garzón, who gave birth to a baby boy whom they aptly named José Martí Rivera. Negroni described this naming act as one of the "most sublime demonstrations of panamericanism that he, also a jíbaro borinqueño [Puerto Rican peasant], had had the opportunity to witness in a long time."

This remark demonstrates that Pan-Americanism, as an institutional and everyday act of inter-American cooperation, could also be an expression of pan-Latino/a unity (rather than an exclusive Anglo-Latin American relationship), particularly drawing on the history of joint Cuban and Puerto Rican nationalist movements.[38]

A few days after this event, club president Antonio Larrondo emphasized that the Círculo Cubano welcomed not only Cubans but all members of the city's *colonia latina* to its civic and social events. Larrondo explained that he and club members aimed "to unite the club, which honors and represents Cuba, in the interamerican cause, of which José Martí, the great American, was an eternal champion." More than ever, Larrondo promised, the club would "warmly welcome . . . the residents of Miami that belong to other Latin American extractions." Negroni concluded that the 1957 celebration of Martí's birthday had solidified the Círculo Cubano's position of leadership in the *colonia latina*, especially in terms of organizing local activities of a civic, social, and political nature. In "battling against the apathy of many," the club drew on the leadership of both men and women and the cooperation of "various artists and notable personalities in Miami." As a result, Negroni concluded that the club had "definitely established its role as an entity that honors the community in which we live as an indisputable factor of progress and cultural dissemination."[39]

Juventud Cubana entered the scene in 1956, four years after the founding of the Círculo Cubano. It hosted social and musical events in rented spaces and venues scattered across the city, including at the P.B.A. on 2300 N.W. 14th Street and the Hungarian Club on 3901 N.W. Second Avenue. Within the year, on the eve of 1957, the "friendly and dynamic society" inaugurated its new clubhouse, located at 768–770 S.W. Eighth Street, with a "monumental dance" that featured performances by "the well-known orchestra" of Arturo Santirzo. Juventud Cubana opened its own social hall shortly before celebrating its first anniversary in early January 1957. One advertisement indicated that the anniversary festivities would be transmitted live on Miami's WMIE, an act that would broadcast the club's rising prominence in the *colonia cubana* and *colonia latina* and reach audiences not able to afford the event's strikingly pricey entrance fees of $5 and $3 for men and women club members and $6 and $4 for men and women nonmembers.[40]

Many of the social and cultural events that Juventud Cubana organized featured musical performances by some of the same singers and orchestras that were hired to perform at events sponsored by the Círculo Cubano, including Luis Herrero, Hilda Salazar, Conjunto Caney, Arturo Santirzo,

is Everywhere in Miami!

Orquesta Casino de Miami, and Cheche de la Cruz.[41] In addition to weekly matinee and evening dances, some of which were held at commercial venues in the city such as the Tropicana, Juventud Cubana also hosted events to celebrate Cuban national holidays such as El Grito de Yara and U.S. holidays such as Halloween and Thanksgiving. Advertisements commonly invited "all of the colonia Hispanoamericana and people in general" to events, and festivities drew audiences from within and beyond the *colonia cubana* and *colonia latina*, including "distinguished personalities from local society."[42]

Sometimes the Círculo Cubano and Juventud Cubana cooperated to organize social events and extend publicity beyond Miami. The 1957 Miss Caribe contest offers a good example. The beauty pageant was sponsored and organized by German Negroni; Mario Pérez, the main distributor in Florida of Café Caribe, a popular brand of coffee; and Ramón Gutierrez, the director of the radio program *Hora Caribe*. Contest organizers counted the final mailed-in votes at a dance hosted by the Círculo Cubano, and Juventud Cubana hosted the official coronation of Miss Caribe, a young woman who would be chosen "for her friendliness and popularity within Miami's colonia hispanoamericana." Rosita González, a young Puerto Rican woman, won that year's contest and Hilda Serrano, of Cuba, claimed second place. Many in the *colonia latina* were reportedly engaged in the buildup to the contest results. The managers of the Tropicana were also watching closely. Shortly after the end of the contest, they announced that they would host a dance "dedicated to the colonia puertorriqueña in Miami" and promised that Miss Caribe would attend as the guest of honor. Spanish-language newspapers in New York City, including both *La Prensa* and *Diario de Nueva York*, also featured stories on the Miss Caribe contest and later reported on González and Serrano's celebratory visit to New York City. "The most beautiful young woman in the hispanic community established in Miami, Florida," one report explained, attended receptions and dances organized by the city's many Hispanic organizations, including the Centro Mexicano, the Ateneo Cubano, the Spanish Baseball League, and the Círculo de Escritores y Poetas Iberoamericanos. González also did interviews with various radio and television programs, including the very popular *The Perucho Show*.[43]

Perhaps inspired by the success of the Miss Caribe contest, the Círculo Cubano announced later in 1957 that one of the first moves of the club's new board of directors would be to sponsor a pageant to select the club's first Miss Círculo Cubano. The club's new president, Mario Pérez, had helped organize the Miss Caribe contest, and his experience likely motivated club leaders and members to mount their own contest. The pageant offered the winner a free trip to Spain and promised to find the "most attractive" young woman in greater Miami.[44]

Other social events organized during this period demonstrate collaboration between Miami's Cuban social clubs and the broader Latino/a communities of both Miami and New York City. In 1957, Juventud Cubana, Casa Caribe (the company producing Café Caribe), and Mario and Elio Pérez offered a reception and matinee dance to honor the Reina del Desfile Hispano de Nueva York (Queen of the Hispanic Parade of New York). Though not explicitly stated, this event must have also drawn the participation of members of the Círculo Cubano, given that Mario Pérez was president of the club during this period. Later that year, Hugo Jiménez organized what was billed as a "sensational dance festival" that featured two orchestras, free beer, and thousands of dollars in prizes at Bayfront Park Auditorium on Biscayne Boulevard and N.E. Third Street. Neither the Círculo Cubano nor Juventud Cubana were official sponsors of the event, but advertisements stated that members of these clubs would receive reduced admission prices. This marketing strategy likely encouraged members of both clubs to attend in greater numbers, suggesting that event organizers believed that their presence would motivate others in the *colonia latina* to attend.[45]

Organizational records for the Círculo Cubano and Juventud Cubana are missing, and information on the memberships and missions of the clubs is limited to what can be gleaned from newspaper clippings in *Diario las Américas*. These reports indicate that the social clubs operated independently of one another. Though it is possible that some individuals belonged to both clubs simultaneously, it seems much more likely that members of the *colonia cubana* and *colonia latina* joined one or the other. The actions and perspectives of Cuban businessman Augusto Piloto in response to the Círculo Cubano's officer elections in 1956 support this analysis. Piloto, the losing candidate for president, wrote an open letter to Jesús Solis, the newly elected president of the club, reminding him that the close vote indicated that members wanted "a general meeting every month, at least one free dance a month exclusively for members and their families, and an improvement to all the services that the club offers its associates and that are very deficient." The latter portion of Piloto's message pointed to the club's larger role as an extension of the homeland in the diaspora. He asked the club's new leadership to "keep fighting for and defending the Círculo Cubano de Miami, a piece of our beloved Cuba that today more than ever needs the affection of its children."[46]

Piloto appears to have left the Círculo Cubano soon after losing the election. One of the first moves the "businessman and dynamic entrepreneur of nuestra colonia hispanoamericana" made after his departure was to join Juventud Cubana. He wasted no time making his presence felt in the club, donating a Cuban flag to be used as a prize for an upcoming raffle. But just as he had been critical of the leadership of the Círculo Cubano, Piloto continued to issue protests as a member of Juventud Cubana. In 1957, for example, he complained that the club's leaders had decided to commemorate El Grito de Yara with a dance and show without first seeking the approval of club members. He encouraged members not to attend the festivities, arguing that "this is a sad day for our beloved Cuba until she is once again free." Piloto's remarks signaled that he was closely following the political violence that was taking place in Cuba, and he urged Cubans, on and off the island, to work together for a truly independent homeland. He also had very specific ideas about what the "thousands of naturalized North Americans, descendants of Cubans" could do to "make visible our sympathies with the Cuban people." These included writing letters to U.S. senator George A. Smathers and pinning a piece of black cloth to shirt sleeves to demonstrate mourning for Cuba until freedom was realized.[47] Here we see Cubans in the diaspora making claims on the U.S. government as a means of prompting change in the homeland, a pattern of transnational thinking and organizing that was familiar by the 1950s.

CUBAN PATRIOTISM BEYOND THE CLUBHOUSE

During the 1940s and 1950s, a variety of Cuban cultural celebrations took place in Miami that were separate from the events and activities organized by the Círculo Cubano and Juventud Cubana. Every September, Cubans celebrated the feast of the Virgen de la Caridad del Cobre. In 1956, individual families opened up their homes for public commemorations of Cuba's patron saint. Miami, one reporter noted, had become a city that was "unable to escape the miraculous influence" of its thousands of Cuban residents. So widespread was the devotion to the Virgen de la Caridad that another reporter estimated that "the patron Saint was celebrated and venerated by thousands of Cuban residents in Miami as well as those that found themselves as tourists in the welcoming city." Some of these Cuban residents, such as Esther Llanos of 861 S.W. 12th Court and José Manuel and Odalina de Armas of 1720 N.W. 4th Street, erected small altars in their homes in honor of the saint. Hilda Negretti, the Cuban wife of Miami lawyer Gino P. Negretti, donated an image of the patron saint to Saint

Michael the Archangel Catholic Church, located on Flagler and N.W. 29th Avenue. The following year an advertisement in *Diario las Américas* asked the city's Cuban residents to send donations to a project that sought to bring an image of the Virgen de la Caridad to Corpus Christi Catholic Church at 3222 N.W. Seventh Avenue. A *botánica* named La Caridad del Cobre opened at 726 North Miami Avenue in 1957. The shop sold herbs, oils, religious beads and cords, candles, holy water, and images of Catholic saints, among other things, that were used in *santería* and other African-derived spiritual practices. What is perhaps more significant is that the shop's owner had recently moved to Miami not from Havana or anywhere else on the island but from the Bronx, where he had owned a *botánica* known as El Rastro Cubano for more than ten years.[48]

Other celebrations in honor of Cuban national holidays took place in Miami throughout the 1950s. In 1954, for example, Dr. Julio Salabarria, president of the Club de las Américas, commemorated Martí's birthday by delivering remarks "on behalf of the city's hispanic civic association" a few steps from a statue of the Cuban revolutionary. In 1957, Natalio Galán, "the well-known Cuban bandleader, who has toured all of the Americas, taking Cuban rhythms even to the most far-away corners of the continent," played an important role in organizing festivals to honor El Grito de Yara. The Cuban pianist and composer had left Cuba to study music in New York City in 1947. He composed mostly chamber music and operas, but he also composed a few pieces for smaller orchestras. One reporter concluded that because of Galán's participation the events "are sure to be grand."[49] That this event featured the musical talents of a more "serious" musician like Galán suggests that more well-known popular musicians may have been unavailable at the time as well as the possibility that the tastes of audiences in the *colonia cubana* and *colonia latina* in Miami varied from those in New York City.

PAN-AMERICANISM AND PAN-LATINO/A CAMARADERIE

Miami's near-obsession with Pan-Americanism infiltrated the city's Cuban social clubs. Both the Círculo Cubano and Juventud Cubana celebrated dates of significance that were not explicitly marked as Cuban national holidays. In 1957, the Círculo Cubano placed an advertisement in *Diario las Américas* extending "a cordial and respectful greeting to the authorities and governments of the Americas on the 67th anniversary of Panamerican Day." Juventud Cubana also celebrated Pan-American Day in 1957 with a matinee dance. Its advertisement for the event sent "a respectful greeting to the authorities and governments of the twenty-one nations of the Americas, fervently in favor of the democratic unity among their noble peoples." The message of democratic unity is somewhat curious given that military dictators—Batista in Cuba and Rafael Trujillo in the Dominican Republic, as just two examples—had taken power away from the "noble peoples" of the Americas. Later that year, the Círculo Cubano and Juventud Cubana also organized dances to celebrate Día de la Raza.[50]

Many of the events the Círculo Cubano hosted in the 1950s indicate the club's commitment to inter-American ideals and its interest in having the entire *colonia latina* attend its events. Some news reports suggest that the club maintained a reputation for inclusion and openness beyond the *colonia cubana*. For example, in 1954, the Círculo Cubano celebrated a Carnaval Latino Americano that featured the Cuban dance team Raúl y Eva, who reportedly had established residence in Miami some time earlier, and musical performances by the Orquesta de Luis Herrero. The event also featured a competition to decide the best *comparsa* from among "an entertaining group of 'mexicanos,' 'gitanos' [gypsies], 'apaches,' and others, all ready to come out winners." The event earned the club praise for the success of the dance and for "its tenacious work toward the cultural rapprochement of the resident hispanoamericano entities in the city of Miami."[51]

Despite these numerous examples of the club's commitment to Pan-Americanism and Latinidad, evidence also exists to suggest that events and activities the Círculo Cubano sponsored sometimes excluded or aimed to exclude some members of the city's *colonia latina*. At the very least, some members of the *colonia latina* in Miami felt less than welcome at club activities, as evidenced by a letter to the editor a former member of the club sent to German Negroni at *Diario las Américas* late in 1957. The letter charged that the Círculo Cubano discriminated specifically against Puerto Ricans and more broadly against other members and organizations within the *colonia latina*. In response, the club's president, Mario Pérez, and its secretary, Heriberto Borroto, insisted that the Círculo Cubano had "never rejected nor censored anyone because of nationality, especially given that all decent people are welcomed in our organization." The letter explained that "[our] doors have always been and will always be open to all and especially to those who, without being Cuban, join us to strengthen the ties that should unite all latinos in general." Pérez and Borroto cited the participation of many individuals of "distinct nationalities" in club activities and in positions of leadership as evidence of the Círculo Cubano's openness and argued that for these reasons they could not accept such "unjust declarations." Whether these specific accusations came from a club member who was interested in generating bad press for the club or a member who had directly witnessed or been subject to racial or ethnic discrimination in formal and informal gatherings is not entirely clear. What matters more, for our purposes, is that the public discourse generated as a result of these accusations reveals an example of the coded language that the Círculo Cubano (and presumably other social clubs in Miami) used to exclude unwanted persons from their activities. It also suggests tensions within the *colonia latina*, particularly between Cubans and Puerto Ricans, the two largest migrant groups from Latin America in Miami during this period. The statement that all "decent people" are welcomed at club activities and as club members leaves open the possibility of exclusion based on unstated variables. It is likely that race, ethnicity, class, and political affiliation shaped how some club associates used this discretionary language in their social practices.[52]

Other more subtle attempts at exclusion can be found in the club's many advertisements in *Diario las Américas*. Many of these stated that the club "reserves the right to refuse admission," a clause that suggests that club members minding the door could deny entry to individuals or groups at their discretion. As we saw with the Ateneo Cubano and other Cuban social clubs in New York City, this policy often served to exclude persons of color from events and activities. Juventud Cubana adopted a similar admissions policy; its advertisements outlined a strict dress code that required a "jacket and tie" and noted that "the commission reserved the right of entrance."[53]

Still, positive encounters and interactions seemed to be more the norm. Interethnic marriage was one means of bringing together Cubans and Puerto Ricans on a broader, more public stage. The marriage of Cuban José and Puerto Rican Alice Ricardo serves as a case in point. The couple had settled in Miami in 1955 and owned the "well-known" Centro de Televisión, located at 3933 N.W. Seventh Avenue. In 1957, they purchased the rights to *Hora Latina*. One report declared that they had "earned a seat of honor of special popularity within nuestra colonia hispanoamericana." The Miami Ricardos, who were not entirely different from the Ricardos of *I Love Lucy* in terms of their interethnic and charismatic appeal, represented "the two most populous colonias hispanas" as "the soul and dynamism" of one of the city's main venues of pan-Latino/a popular cultural expression.[54]

Cubans and Puerto Ricans living in Miami in the 1950s also collaborated on a political level, perhaps in symbolic demonstration that Cuba and Puerto Rico are "of one bird the two wings," as many believed.[55] A group of Cubans and Puerto Ricans, including two lawyers, one pharmacist, one professor of public instruction, and one former chief of police, came together in 1956 to protest statements Charles Snowden, a municipal court judge, and Thomas O'Connell, an assistant district attorney, had made in the *Miami Daily News*. Judge Snowden had stated that Cubans and Puerto Ricans committed the majority of the store robberies in Miami. The group took their rebuttals to the editorial staff at *Diario las Américas*, explaining that remarks such as these "stomp [on] . . . the efforts invested by fair and impartial public officials, eager to improve relations with Hispanoamérica." Importantly, here we see resident Latino/as using Pan-Americanism to defend themselves against unfair accusations based on their race and ethnicity. One member of this group, Ricardo Morales, a lawyer, insisted that "as a Cuban, resident in the country for more than fifty years, I protest that now that we are known as more than tourists in the city, we, hispanos, are insulted in this way."[56] This act by Cuban and Puerto Rican residents of Miami demonstrates an early, albeit seemingly ad hoc, instance of pan-Latino/a unity in the struggle for social justice in south Florida. Of course, the use of the term "hispanos" in this case might also have functioned to distance the group from associations with blackness.

It also suggests that as Cubans and Puerto Ricans came to be seen more and more as residents rather than tourists, it became harder for them to achieve and maintain the privileges of white racial membership. Increasingly during the 1950s, Shell-Weiss explains, many of the city's Cubans and Puerto Ricans came to Miami from the Northeast, especially from Spanish Harlem, rather than from the islands to work in the city's hotels and other industries. For some whites, Harlem evoked images of "dark and volatile people," and some city officials issued false reports about Latino/as. For example, Miami's police chief Walter Headley stated that crime was on the rise and that "working-class Latinos . . . were the root of the problem." For some members of the *colonia latina*, however, white racial membership may not have been the only or the preferred category of identification. It seems that at least some migrants found ways to come together as *hispanos* to represent pan-ethnic community interests and reject stereotypes and negative perceptions.[57] The less-than-positive remarks of police officials are also striking, given that Cuban social clubs such as the Círculo Cubano and Juventud Cubana rented space from the Police Benevolent Association to host social functions. Perhaps the police association rented this space to members of the *colonia latina* strictly out of economic interest or because they perceived the individuals they were doing business with to be white and of higher economic standing. Whatever the motivations for the arrangement, at least in some instances, Cuban migrants managed to stay in the good graces of Miami's police department.

RADICALIZED PAN-AMERICANISM

In Miami, the ideology of Pan-Americanism often referred to close relations between Cuba and the United States. It manifested itself quite clearly in annual celebrations of Día de Cuba. Records from meetings of the board of directors of the Miami Chamber of Commerce indicate that as early as 1941 members of what was called the Miami-Cuba Committee sought to "arrange for a Cuba day in Miami . . . with a view to trade development between the two points."[58] At least one report in *Diario de la Marina* suggested that Cubans on the island took notice of patriotic celebrations held in Miami. In January 1946, Cubans in Cuba and Miami participated in a simultaneous commemoration of the Cuban flag with coordinated ceremonies taking place at Bayfront Park and at the provincial palace in Havana. In Miami, "a large group of beautiful Cuban and American girls as well as another of officials from the United States army and navy" attended the event, which reportedly reached "extraordinary proportions." The event signaled inter-American cooperation and was seen as "one more confirmation of the sincere and profound friendship that unites the great nation of the North to our homeland."[59]

In 1948, "numerous" Cubans, including "more than 20 civil and government officials," celebrated Día de Cuba with the aim of "strengthening Pan-American friendship." The festivities that year included banquets, popular music concerts, rumba contests, and an evening baseball game between athletic clubs based in Miami Beach and Havana. In 1951, the Primera Conferencia Interamericana de Música organized celebrations of Día de Cuba. The main event, which was held at the Dade County Auditorium in Miami, featured a dance recital by Cuban ballerina Alicia Alonso and musical performances by the Philharmonic Orchestra of Havana under the direction of Gonzalo Roig, who along with Ernesto Lecuona and Cesar Pérez Sentenat had founded the National Symphony Orchestra in 1922.[60] Whether the motive for choosing these performers was principally to increase tourism, to appease white government officials and residents of the city, or to appeal to Cuban residents in Miami who preferred this genre of music, the choice of classical music over more popular Afro-Cuban rhythms served in some ways to whiten and make less exotic the representations of Cubanness. This choice of performers is even more interesting in light of the fact that many North American tourists, including thousands of

Miamians, traveled to Cuba precisely to experience the island's exotic allure and dance to the popular rhythms of the rumba, mambo, and cha-cha-chá supplied by Afro-Cuban performers at nightclubs and hotels in Havana. Connolly has argued that funding musical performances in the European classical tradition for Pan-American events represented "an obvious departure from the 'African' culture of black Miami and certain Caribbean locales (i.e. Haiti and Jamaica [and Cuba])." It seems that at least when they were on the northern side of the Florida Straits, Miamians, Cubans and Anglos alike, sometimes preferred performances and representations of Cubanness that they perceived as elite and "synonymous with a kind of whiteness."[61] In certain contexts, a sort of generic, tamed Latinness stood in for Cubanness.

For an upcoming celebration of Columbus Day in 1949, members of the city's Pan American Committee decided on a "new approach to Latin American entertainment for this area." The committee planned to subsidize ticket prices to the event by selling placards and posters, making clear that the event was "aimed at reaching the masses rather than the select few who have been able to attend dinners and similar balls in the past." Miami Chamber of Commerce records indicate that local officials consistently sought to expand the reach of the city's Pan-American agenda to "all Latin residents of Greater Miami and visiting Latins."[62] The status of Miami's "Latin residents" was fundamentally shaped by their—real and imagined—relations with "visiting Latins." Given the city's goals of increasing tourism and trade with other Latin American nations, it stands to reason that the Miami Chamber of Commerce and other booster groups wanted to encourage, or at least appear to encourage, positive encounters with residents and visitors from those countries. Cubans and Puerto Ricans living in Miami in the 1940s and 1950s were decidedly working class; most found employment in the tourism industry and, to a lesser extent, in manufacturing, construction, and agriculture. The majority of tourists from Latin America, however, were of the middle and upper classes, and higher economic status afforded these visitors, even those with darker skin, the privilege of racial tolerance if not always inclusion. It probably helped, too, that the number of dark-skinned Latin American visitors was "fewer than a hundred per year." During this period, the number of Cuban-born individuals who were racially classified as "black" decreased from almost 1,000 in 1940 to less than 500 in 1950 to zero in 1960. Though it may have been that the migration of darker-skinned Cubans to Florida dissipated because of the harshness of Jim Crow, the finding might also be an unexpected consequence of Pan-Americanism. In relation to Latin Americans and the

Pan-Americanism encourages
inclusion of Brown + Black

prospects of economic growth, Pan-Americanism contributed t
of racialization in which whiteness became a more flexible cate;
which brown and even black Cubans might find themselves inc

Throughout the mid-twentieth century, business elites and
ficials worked to cast Miami as a global city, a welcoming de;
tourists and investors from Latin America. Pan-Americanism functioned
as a sort of racialized hemispheric neighborliness that penetrated all aspects of life in Miami, from housing and schooling to public transportation and entertainment. It was, however, largely light-skinned and fair-
haired Latin Americans who benefited from the hold Pan-Americanism
had on the city. In 1949, the Miami City Commission granted Havana
mayor Nicolás Castellanos permission to erect a monument of Martí in
Bayfront Park. Connolly argues that the gesture signaled "the cultural and
commercial ties between the so-called 'sister cities'" and takes notice of
the fact that Antonio Maceo, "a black national hero equal to Martí in his
importance to Cuban independence, received no such honor from the City
of Miami." He attributes this purposeful oversight to a racialized Pan-
Americanism that white government officials and tourism boosters im-
plemented in Miami. Of course, it was not uncommon for the white Martí
to be elevated over the black Maceo, at least in public contexts. The choices
local government officials made in Miami reflect that in Havana, Miami,
and New York City, Martí had become the national symbol of Cuba even
though another hero was available. In the late 1940s and early 1950s, Cubans of color in New York City and working-class Cubans in Miami tried
to promote combined celebrations of the two heroes. But, as we saw happen in New York City in El Club Cubano's failure to erect a Monumento
Martí-Maceo, a privileging of nationalized whiteness over blackness existed in the *colonias cubanas* of both cities that operated on its own, though
it was surely influenced by ideologies of Pan-Americanism.[64]

[Margin note, right side:] Not be included w/U.S. in Pan-Americanism, both Miami, NY neglected Black Cubans Here

Events to honor Maceo did take place in Miami, but they generally occurred in explicitly politicized and working-class contexts. "An extraordinary amount" of "exiled and migrant Cubans," mostly women, gathered
in December 1957 to commemorate Maceo's death under the auspices of
the Auténtico Party. The event was led by former Cuban president Carlos
Prío Socarrás, who was living in exile in Miami. In 1957, the city's 26 of
July Movement invited "all members of the colonia cubana" to tune in to
WAHR to listen to its broadcast commemorating Maceo. Also that year,
nearly 100 Cuban workers from the Arnold Company and other factories
in Miami came together to commemorate the anniversary of Maceo's death.
One of the Cuban workers at the event told *Diario las Américas* that "Cuba

_aces the most difficult stage of its republican life" and called for unity among Cuban workers in the United States.[65] The mobilization of the Cuban working class is not surprising. As was the case among Cuban cigar workers in Tampa during the late nineteenth-century struggles for independence from Spain, Cuban laborers, especially those of color and those with a sense of racial consciousness, had a history of organizing for the cause of national liberation.

MACHITO IN MIAMI

The capacity of Pan-Americanism to facilitate racial inclusion and equality for dark-skinned Latin Americans was tested in 1946 when Machito y sus Afro-Cubans traveled to Miami to perform at the whites-only Mocambo nightclub for the winter season. In fact, music is one of the most important sites for examining the potential and limits of the ideology as it became social practice. While orchestral music and ballet were part of official Pan-American programming, the nightlife that was so crucial to attracting tourists to Miami depended on a form of Latin music that was explicitly constructed by participants as Afro-Cuban. And in many instances, black Cubans were the most popular performers of this music.

African American newspapers noted the significance of the band's booking at the "exclusive" Mocambo nightclub, explaining that "Miami Beach, that part of Southern Florida, which is the rendezvous of the rich and ultra-fashionable members of the upper strata of society, has for the first time in its history accepted an orchestra composed partly of colored musicians." "But," as one reporter quickly pointed out, "these colored men are not Negroes; they are 'Afro-Cubans.' The leader of the orchestra is Machito, a Cuban, [and] their contract calls for Cuban music only."[66] Here we see "Cuban" and "Afro-Cuban" presented as synonymous, and Afro-Cubans are perceived as distinct from African Americans despite similarities in skin color. Throughout their stay in Miami, Machito and his band mates found themselves in a Jim Crow city that was protective of its black-white model of racial classification but inconsistent in its treatmeant and categorization of Cubans and Latino/as of color.

Afro-Cubans and other dark-skinned Latino/as sometimes managed to negotiate a place for themselves in segregated Miami between the poles of white inclusion and black exclusion. Machito booked a room at the whites-only Miami Hotel, while other members of the band, including Mario Bauzá and Graciela, chose to board in Overtown at the Dorsey Hotel, the first black-owned hotel in Miami. Enoc Waters, a reporter for the *Chi-*

Afro-Cubans play to a white Miami

cago Defender, noticed that Machito had booked the room ev[
the Miami Hotel was "a white establishment from which Ne[
American variety at least) are barred from bedding down by u
Jim Crow laws."[67] Bauzá recalled that he had reluctantly agree[
form at the Mocambo because of past negative experiences in M
claimed that he had told the promoter who booked the engagement for the
band that "nobody colored play Miami Beach. . . . No, don't put me through
that, I don't wanna go through that. I been to Miami too many times with
the colored bands." But he agreed to go with the band anyway and concluded that their performances at the Mocambo that winter "opened the
door for colored performers."[68]

   Historians have noted that it became more difficult, though not impossible, for whites to maintain the color line that divided the Jim Crow South
in the late 1940s and 1950s because of a practice known as racial "Trojan
horsing" by which an individual pretended to speak or spoke a foreign language so as not to be perceived as a U.S. black.[69] The strategy was familiar to Machito and his band, which included some African Americans with
no Cuban background. But language alone did not deter exclusion. Rather,
as some band members found, it was the use of Spanish plus claims to Cubanness that allowed them to escape the hardened racial codes that confined the movement of U.S. blacks in the South. According to Graciela, one
time as the band gathered in the lobby of the Miami Hotel, a white patron
complained to the manager about the presence of U.S. blacks. The white
patron charged that none of them were speaking Spanish. Machito immediately insisted that there were no U.S. blacks among the group, only
Cubans. Graciela recalled that Machito pointed to his various band mates,
identifying everyone as a Cuban "even though right there were the Americans . . . like four or five of them." This explanation was enough to please
the manager, who moments later responded to the white patron, "How can
you tell me that there are blacks here? They are Cuban." Graciela questioned this distinction when she told the story to oral history interview-
ers: "We were lucky because we were Hispanic. You know how they didn't
think that Hispanics were black, only black Americans. They were so stu-
pid!"[70] The incident might have played out a little differently elsewhere in
the United States. Waters of the *Chicago Defender* explained that the "un-
authentic Afro-Cubans" had gone undetected in New York City. "Of course,"
he reasoned, "no one cared very much in New York City, but Miami is quite
different," pointing to Miami's more rigid racial code.[71]

   Racial "Trojan horsing" did not always work. When it did, it may have
been celebrity status that made racial inclusion possible rather than the

Handwritten margin note (right side): Bauzá as a Pioneer

Handwritten margin note (right side, vertical): Only Cloaked as "Cubans" allowed Blacks to Navigate Segregated Miami!

ability to speak Spanish or make claims of Cubanness. It could be that Machito's popularity as a Latin musician during this period made it possible for him to stay at a whites-only hotel. But even celebrity had its limits, and Machito was reportedly unable to convince the managers at the Miami Hotel to allow his brown-skinned Puerto Rican wife to stay with him during her visit to Miami. Instead, she rented a room at the Dorsey where Machito visited her, and the pair dined at several "Negro restaurants in definance [sic] of the state separation laws if he is white as implied by his residing at the Miami Hotel." Waters reported that Machito asked the black press "not to discuss the matter in their columns," apparently aware of "the confusion in the minds of the darker elements of the local population." The episode was not lost on contemporary observers, who raised an important and controversial question: "Is an admitted Afro-Cuban a Negro?"[72]

For Afro-Cuban percussionist Armando Sánchez, the process of negotiating a place between the poles of white inclusion and black exclusion materialized both as metaphor and reality. On his way from Key West to New York City in June 1945, Sánchez took a seat on the bus "in between the front and the back," even though he knew that "at that time blacks had to sit in the back." At a stop in Jacksonville, a white man asked him to move to the back of the bus so that he could offer the seat to his wife. Sánchez refused, telling the man, in English, that he had paid his fare and would not move. Confusion followed. The couple saw that he was "dark" but presumably because of his accent, they realized that he was probably not a U.S. black. When asked where he was from, Sánchez responded that he was from Cuba. That declaration seemed to further confuse both the couple and the bus driver, who concluded that "he wasn't gonna mess with that." Sánchez rode all the way to New York City in that seat. Whether he saw himself as distinct from U.S. blacks and, therefore, not subject to southern Jim Crow laws is not clear. Though this story of racialization is on its own a meaningful example of racial protest, what is perhaps more interesting is that Sánchez linked his sense of a struggle for racial equality not to his own experiences with racism in Cuba, Florida, or Harlem but to the nineteenth-century rebellions for Cuban independence from Spain. Explaining that his grandfather had been a member of Antonio Maceo's staff in the Cuban independence army, he charged, "I was a rebel since I was born. I come from a warrior family."[73]

By the mid- to late 1950s, the political unrest and revolutionary spirit that had come to characterize life in Cuba infiltrated and, in many ways, benefited symbolically and materially from the presence of Cubans in Miami. In particular, Castro's 26 of July Movement targeted Cubans in Miami, and its members worked to draw more of their countrymen to the cause of overthrowing Batista's increasingly unpopular regime. Almost every day throughout 1957, the 26 of July Movement placed advertisements in *Diario las Américas* that urged the *colonia cubana* to attend rallies and informational events at the Edificio de las Logias, located at 215 N.W. Fourth Street on the corner of Second Avenue, with a message of "Cuban! Fidel calls you! Now or Never! The End of the Monster Is Near!" Many of the advertisements featured a pair of images, one a formal headshot of Castro, the other an almost floating caricatured disembodied head of the bearded leader. Each image seemed to serve a distinct purpose: the first portrayed Castro as a serious, respected leader, confirming the legitimacy of the revolutionary cause; the second conveyed a sense of whimsy and romance.[74] These were not unfamiliar representations. Images in other newspapers consistently presented a short-bearded Castro wearing a military uniform and cap and holding a rifle surrounded by trees, leaves, and other jungle matter; his eyes appeared to be contemplative and his gaze fixed in the distance. Herbert L. Matthews of the *New York Times* declared that the Cuban people "worshipped" Castro and reported that the young revolutionary had "become the leader and symbol of the struggle against the dictatorship of General Batista."[75] On a more practical level, the advertisements also listed the bus routes that interested participants could take to get to the political events. That advertisements and coverage of transnational grassroots organizing took up an increasingly larger presence in the pages of *Diario las Américas* suggests that what might have been first devised as a vehicle of hemispheric solidarity and tourism propaganda had evolved into a pseudo-activist local newspaper of the *colonia cubana* and *colonia latina*. The newspaper seems to have played an integral role in developing and disseminating island and exile politics, and there is little evidence to suggest that it served only the interests of tourism boosters, Latin American governments (and consulate officials), or other proponents of Pan-American ideology.

By 1957, political mobilization on behalf of the Revolution was in full swing. Clandestine student groups such as the Directorio Revolucionario, members of the ousted Auténtico Party in Cuba and in exile in Miami, Castro and his 26 of July Movement, and peasants and squatters in Oriente all came together as rural and urban insurgent forces opposed to Batista's U.S-supported dictatorship. In April 1957, Miami's 26 of July Movement honored those who had died the year before in the Auténtico-led failed attack on the Goicuría garrison, the military headquarters in Matanzas, by laying floral wreaths at the foot of a statue of Martí in Bayfront Park. A few weeks later, the 26 of July Movement and the Directorio Revolucionario again used the site of the statue of Martí in Bayfront Park to rally supporters and honor the memories of the university students who had participated in an unsuccessful attack on the presidential palace in Havana.[76] News reports indicated that Prío Socarrás and two of Castro's sisters, Emma and Lydia, attended these events, which were organized by "political Cubans" and "produc[ed] commentary from the entire colonia cubana in the city." These remarks and those that distinguished between "exiled and migrant Cubans" suggest that the *colonia cubana* was far from monolithic. While there may have been "political" or "exiled" Cubans in Miami who were interested and engaged in revolutionary activities, other Cubans in the city touted the official representation of the consulate and were supportive of the Batista government. Still, others were not interested in politics and focused more on work and their private lives. Cubans on the island, for their part, took notice of acts of solidarity; one report declared that "without exaggeration, we can say that Cubans, from the neighboring island, have their eyes fixed on what happens in Miami."[77]

Advertisements for the 26 of July Movement used the growing celebrity of the Castro sisters and references to dates of national significance to help raise funds for the movement. One advertisement announced to "Cuban residents in Miami" that "just as our apostle José Martí did yesterday, Fidel Castro knocks on your door and your heart to ask for a contribution." It also listed the address where the Castro sisters would be "waiting for greetings from all the Cuban residents of Miami." By framing Castro as the Martí of today, the advertisement reclaimed the nineteenth-century independence movement led by Martí (no mention was made of Maceo) and served as a point of symbolic motivation to join the current revolutionary cause.[78] Historian Lillian Guerra argues that in the early twentieth century, "the 'myth' that Cubans constructed of José Martí as a signifier of social unity was a fictional narrative, based on their desire for a harmonious, even utopic future as well as the need to shape and recollect the past in such terms." Cubans, she explains, invoked the myth of Martí "to connote the common essence or root of Cubans' nationality in the repeated narrative of self-sacrifice, collective struggle, and commitment to a 'nation for all' that emerged during the War of 1895." As we have seen, the myth was still powerful and useful among black and white Cubans in both New York City and Miami in the 1940s and 1950s. Martí remained a unifying symbol, but different groups of Cubans invoked that symbol to support their own visions of Cuban identity and the future of the nation on the verge of yet another revolution.[79]

While the presence of the Castro sisters in Miami and elsewhere in the United States, including New York City, Chicago, and Washington, D.C., helped raise money, boost morale, and attract additional supporters to the revolutionary cause, it also served to create tensions and highlight dissension in the ranks of Miami's 26 of July Movement. One controversy stemmed from remarks the sisters made to an unnamed newspaper in Miami. They stated that the only organization in Miami founded as an official affiliate of the 26 of July Movement was formed by Fidel Castro during a visit to the city and that he himself had designated Juan Cheda as its president. In an open letter published in *Diario las Américas*, Jacinto Vázquez countered that Juan Orta had been named president and charged that the sisters "hold no position of leadership or responsibility in the revolutionary organization" and "have no authority of any kind to alter the course of the struggle." To this, Juan Orta responded with his own public letter, affirming the statements made by the Castro sisters and charging that Vázquez had never held any position of leadership and was not even a member of the organization. Whatever the details of this disagreement, the point is that the *colonia cubana*, at least its political elements, appeared somewhat fragmented and disorganized. In an open letter "to all Cubans," Rafael Izquierdo resigned his position as treasurer of the Miami chapter, lamenting that "division signifies [personal] ambition."[80]

Awareness of the political situation in Cuba manifested itself in other ways. Luis Cabaleiro and Roberto and Amparo Pérez Antelo, owners of Un Restaurante Latino, which was located at East First Avenue between North Second and Third Streets, "decorated" an entire window of their restaurant with clippings from newspapers and magazines that "allud[ed] to the insurrectional crisis in Cuba." Some political demonstrations were less subtle. In June 1957, police intervened as a group of Cubans holding Cuban flags and placards protesting Batista marched from the Cuban embassy to the statue of Martí in Bayfront Park. Police arrested thirty people after they reportedly tried to disperse the group. Several witnesses explained, however, that the scuffle started when an officer tried to take a Cuban flag from one of the marchers.[81] What we see in Miami by the mid- to late 1950s is the beginning of the mass politicization of the Cuban migrant community in the United States well before Castro's march into Havana in 1959.

■ In what was likely a savvy publicity stunt orchestrated by local officials and television producers, in November 1956 Desi Arnaz made a journey to the city that had first welcomed him when he left Cuba in 1933. When Arnaz and Lucille Ball arrived in south Florida, they were greeted by thousands of fans at Miami International Airport. The ostensible purpose of the visit was to spend a few days with Desi's parents, who lived in Coral Gables. While in Miami, the couple invited the city's reporters to a reception at the Eden Roc and participated in a benefit show at Bayfront Park Auditorium. But their trip was more than a family vacation or charitable arrangement. During this four-day visit, Cuban consul Eduardo Hernández presented the couple with the La Orden Nacional de Mérito Carlos Manuel de Céspedes. The award reportedly served "as testimony of the admiration and respect his homeland had for the artist and his wife" and realized the call Marco Rizo had made three years earlier that the Cuban government recognize Arnaz's artistic and diplomatic achievements.[82]

Though the couple was described as "stars of the North American artistic world," it was recognition by the Cuban government that brought Desi and Lucy to Miami from Hollywood. Noting that the pair had not visited Miami for quite some time, German Negroni explained that Arnaz, "whose hispanic origin we know well (he was born in Cuba), treated us with unlimited courtesy and spoke Spanish to us the entire time, with a light North American accent." To the newspaper's thousands of readers, Arnaz declared: "I could see among those gathered many Cubans and latinos that called me by name, talking to me in Spanish. I felt very happy seeing those friendly demonstrations and I answered them in Spanish as well. You can tell the readers of *Diario las Américas* that I as a Cuban and both of us as artists, my wife Lucy and I, send them a warm embrace and we are sure that we will see each other again in the future."[83] Just as Ricky Ricardo and his brand of Latin entertainment had been tagged to represent contemporary Florida in the fictional *The Florida Story* (in an episode that aired the very same week of the trip), Desi Arnaz came to symbolize the idealized Cuban American, particularly in the context of Miami's racialized Pan-Americanism. Not only did the award demonstrate friendly and cordial relations between the Cuban government and local officials in Miami, it also signaled a preferred performance of Cubanness: white, handsome, and "with a light North American accent."

a Cuban entertainer, more so than NY!

Pan-American Cubanness marked by its white features; but tourism + immigration made it a hospitable place

)reu is Giving Agency
e Cuban Musicians &
uunity; Not Just
e pop Culture" Tastes!

CONCLUSION

. . . . .gan working on this project, I decided to start by calling a library in Miami. I explained my research ideas to the archivist on the other end of the telephone line and expected her to supply me with an endless list of potential collections, newspapers, and other resources for consultation. Instead, the archivist asserted unequivocally, *"Ay, niña, pero aquí no habian Cubanos en esos tiempos*!" ("Oh, hon, but there weren't any Cubans here during those years!") I had been naïve to think that the very assertion of the presence and significance of Cuban migrants in New York City and Miami in the 1940s and 1950s would not only disrupt but also directly question what many of the Cuban exiles of the postrevolutionary period had come to believe about their migration and their identity and community development in the United States. By challenging the long-held belief that Cuban American identity and a Cuban American cultural landscape originated with the massive post-1959 waves of exiles, this book takes aim at feelings of Cuban exceptionalism and finds that Cuban migration experiences had much more in common with the Puerto Rican and Mexican migrations of the 1940s and 1950s than scholars have previously acknowledged. Though this project identifies some of these similarities and interethnic interactions, it leaves to future scholars the crucial work of examining these comparative moments at greater depth.

That there were few collections dedicated to my particular research topic did not mean that I abandoned the questions that had first triggered my interest in this topic. Instead, these initial difficulties encouraged me to situate questions of "Cuban" and "Afro-Cuban" identity not only within broader ideologies and discourses of Hispanidad and Latinidad but also in social and cultural contexts more commonly associated with the experiences of Puerto Ricans and African Americans in New York City and

Miami. This expanded mode of inquiry allowed me to reconstruct the perspectives and experiences of the Cuban musicians and migrants of the 1940s and 1950s from a variety of oral history interviews, press clippings, archival sources, and cultural texts. The result, I hope, is a rich and multilayered narrative that demonstrates the ways that Cubans in this period debated ideas and shaped practices related to musical and cultural authenticity and commercialism, racial and ethnic identity, and political consciousness, all while circulating in multiple and overlapping—real and imagined—local and transnational contexts.

WHAT HAPPENED NEXT?

One of the major consequences of the massive exodus of Cubans to the United States since Fidel Castro's rise to power is that the flourishing of Cuban and Cuban American culture in earlier periods has become overshadowed by and deeply connected to the Cuban Revolution of 1959. Yet without the nearly 90,000 black and white Cuban migrants in New York City and Miami in the 1940s and 1950s, the great boom in transnational Cuban and Cuban American cultural production that characterized this and later periods would have been quite impossible. It was in nightclubs and dance halls, at social club meetings and citywide cultural events, and within the pages of Spanish-language newspapers in New York City and Miami that Cuban migrants and the popular culture they produced played key roles in constructing a national and ethnic identity that was not always distinct from the prevailing discourses and experiences of Hispano/a and Latino/a identity and community. Within this cohort of black and white Cuban musicians, entertainers, and migrants, the Cubans who arrived in the United States in the postrevolutionary period could find traces of the racial (and racist) ideologies and practices, musical traditions and innovations, and nationalist sensibilities that marked prerevolutionary Cuba. However, the relative openness and inclusiveness of the 1940s and 1950s was not always or even commonly extended to Cubans and Latino/as of color. By the 1970s and 1980s, the Cuban ethnic community had closed in on itself as the majority of Cubans in the United States, especially those in Miami and south Florida, came together as a "moral community" that was focused on ousting Castro from power.[1]

The popular culture landscape also began to change in the early 1960s. Cuban and Latino/a audiences seemed to prefer rock music and the Rolling Stones instead of mambo and Machito. As a result, few of the musicians examined in this book maintained the same level of popularity or achieved the same success as they had at the peak of their professional careers in the 1940s and 1950s. Still, they continued to perform throughout the latter half of the twentieth century. After production of new episodes of *I Love Lucy* ended in 1957, Desi Arnaz continued to work in television throughout the 1960s and 1970s, most notably as producer for the television series *The Untouchables*. He made occasional guest appearances on television, including his famed spot as celebrity host in the first season of *Saturday Night Live*. Machito y sus Afro-Cubans held on to their ten-week summer engagements at the Concord Hotel in the Catskills throughout the late 1960s, and the band, including Mario Bauzá, continued recording and touring across the United States and abroad well into the 1980s. Machito died in London in 1984, and Bauzá died in New York City in 1993, but not before enjoying a guest appearance on *The Cosby Show*. In 1966, Xavier Cugat married his fourth wife, Charo, a Spanish comedienne who fronted his band until the mid-1970s. After the couple divorced, the bandleader eventually returned to Spain after five decades of immense commercial success in the world of Latin music entertainment. Marco Rizo pursued a solo career throughout the 1960s and 1970s, recording mostly piano and orchestral compositions, especially his own arrangements of the music of Ernesto Lecuona. Arsenio Rodríguez continued performing for dances and social events organized by El Club Cubano until about the mid-1960s, when the club turned to newer and hipper bands, like those of Johnny Pacheco and Ray Barretto, that could attract younger audiences. Rodríguez left New York City for Los Angeles in 1969 and died the following year after suffering a stroke.[2] Miguelito Valdés entered semi-retirement in the late 1950s, though he returned to the world of entertainment in 1963 to record with Machito y sus Afro-Cubans. He also hosted his own television show from 1966 to 1976. He died two years later when he suffered a heart attack on stage in Colombia. José Curbelo is an interesting exception to this pattern of fading celebrity. In 1959, he swapped his role at the front of the band for one behind the scenes, when he founded the booking agency Alpha Artists. He emerged as an influential manager and savvy promoter and earned a reputation as a tough and uncompromising negotiator for his clients, including Tito Puente and Machito. He died in Miami in 2012.[3]

Changes also came to the social clubs, ethnic organizations, and nightclubs and dance halls of New York City and Miami. Some of the venues and organizations that hosted social and cultural events during the 1940s and 1950s, such as the Hunts Point Palace, remained open until the mid-1980s, while others, such as the Tropicana and the Palladium, closed in the early and mid-1960s.[4] El Club Cubano maintained its clubhouse until

1996, but former members and friends of the organization continue to gather formally once a year for the Baile del Mamoncillo (Dance of the Spanish Limes). In Miami, Cuban social clubs, including the Círculo Cubano and Juventud Cubana, eventually became overshadowed by the rapid proliferation of exile organizations that emerged in the city in the early 1960s. It seems possible that these two social clubs, given the political activism of leaders such as Augusto Piloto, gave way without much resistance to the anti-Castro missions of these new groups.[5]

MARCO RUBIO: ACT ONE

In the fall of 2011, the privileging of the Cuban exiles of the post-1959 era—in historiography, popular memory, and politics—made national news. Through the lens of this episode, we see how the stories told in this book might help us better understand present-day Cuban racial and ethnic identity, especially in relation to broader Latino/a identity and community. That October, a reporter for the *Washington Post* accused Florida senator Marco Rubio of misrepresenting the story of his parents' migration from Cuba to the United States. Rubio, a rising star in the Republican Party and rumored nominee for vice president, had throughout his career presented himself as the son of Cuban exiles who fled Castro's regime and came to the United States in the early 1960s. In truth, Rubio's parents left Cuba in 1956 and were admitted as permanent residents shortly thereafter. They spent most of their time in Miami and south Florida. His mother worked as a hotel maid and stocked shelves at K-Mart. His father worked as a bartender and a school crossing guard. In 1958, his father reportedly worked at the Roney Plaza, the same hotel that almost two decades earlier had introduced the Cuban music of El Dulce and Desi Arnaz to audiences in Miami Beach. His parents did visit the island a few times after Castro took power in 1959, but their return trips were brief; only one stay lasted longer than a few weeks.[6]

Rubio's response to the accusation that he consistently misrepresented and exaggerated his family's history is quite telling, for it illustrates the significance of two of the main areas of intervention this project is engaged in: methodology and periodization. First, Rubio blamed oral history for the false reports. To the *New York Times*, he explained, "The dates I have given regarding my family's history have always been based on my parents' recollections of events that occurred over 55 years ago and which were relayed to me by them more than two decades after they happened." Similarly, he told the *Miami Herald*, "I didn't lie about the date. I wasn't aware of it." The *Washington Post* reported a now-familiar rebuttal from the young senator: "I'm going off the oral history of my family. All of these documents and passports are not things that I carried around with me."[7] In effect, Rubio charged that his error was not purposeful, that it was carelessness in storytelling and the absence of written records that caused the accidental misinformation. This explanation is not entirely convincing, given the ways that 1959 is memorialized among Cuban families and within the Cuban exile community. It does, however, leave open the question of whether Rubio independently changed his family's origin story or whether it was his parents who had misremembered their dates of migration in their storytelling.

Second, he dismissed the relevance of the discrepancy. He argued that "the date doesn't really add anything. It doesn't embellish anything. The date is less relevant than the experience, the experience of people who came here to make a better life and who could never go back." In a column released on Politico.com, Rubio argued that "people didn't vote for me because they thought my parents came in 1961, or 1956, or any other year. Among other things, they voted for me because, as the son of immigrants, I know how special America really is."[8] But dates and identity have come to matter, particularly within the context of Cubanidad, and Rubio's not-so-accurate biographical narrative reveals some of the political reasons behind his attempts to distinguish himself from the Cuban migration that took place in the decades that preceded the Cuban Revolution of 1959. As historian María Cristina García has argued, Cubans who left the island in the 1960s called themselves exiles, not immigrants: "*Immigrant* implies a choice, and most Cuban émigrés believed that they had no choice; they had been pushed out of their country by the social, economic, and political chaos of the Castro regime. . . . It was a powerful political statement."[9] By insisting that his parents had come to the United States in the 1960s because of Castro, Rubio claimed an exile rather than an immigrant identity for himself, and that positioning, especially in Florida, has a cachet that is not available to prerevolutionary Cuban migrants.[10] His claim to an exile identity not only brought him favor among conservative Cubans in Florida but also rendered his experiences entirely different from (and, by extension, more acceptable than) those of other Latino/a migrants, whose presence in the United States, whether documented or undocumented, remains controversial and, for some, unwanted.

What the very public Rubio drama reveals is that historians, political scientists, and other scholars have not been alone in constructing a narrative that locates the origins of a Cuban American identity within the first cohort of Cubans who came to the United States in the wake of the Revolution of 1959. The migrations of Cubans, especially Cubans of color, who lived, worked, and performed in the United States in the two decades that preceded the Revolution have been rendered irrelevant at best and non-existent at worst. In focusing on the stories of the nearly 90,000 black and white Cubans who came to New York City and Miami in the 1940s and 1950s, my goal has been to draw connections between the late nineteenth- and early twentieth-century Cubans who came to the United States fleeing the independence wars and looking for work in the cigar industry and the post-1959 Cubans who left the island to escape communism and Castro. This challenge to the idea of a radical discontinuity in the migration of Cubans to the United States draws the necessary links between these earlier and later periods of migration and points to a historical moment when Cuban American experiences are most similar to those of other Latino/a migrants. It is no surprise, then, that it was at this moment when Cuban migrants and musicians played such a central role in constructing broader Hispano/a and Latino/a identity.

MARCO RUBIO: ACT TWO

Two more recent Rubio controversies offer additional connections to this project. Even Rubio's (perhaps unexpected) musical preferences managed to garner the attention of the news media. In November 2012, Rubio told a reporter for *GQ* that he cared little for the "party songs" released by Pitbull, the Cuban American rapper and Miami native who is famous for megahits such as "I Know You Want Me" and "Hotel Room Service." Rubio quipped, "There's no message for him, compared to like Eminem.... There's always been a party person, but he's a young guy.... I mean, he's not Tupac. He's not gonna be writing poetry." Instead, the avid fan of West Coast rap listed "Straight Outta Compton" by N.W.A., "Killuminati" by Tupac Shakur, and "Lose Yourself" by Eminem as his three favorite rap songs.[11] Worried that he had "thrown shade at a native son of Florida," whose popularity outmeasured his own by at least seven million Twitter followers, Rubio went on the defensive, posting the following tweet: "Story about me not liking @Pitbull music flat wrong. Have much respect 4 & proud he comes from #305. Read chapter 1 of my book #AnAmericanSon." Rubio later posted and subsequently deleted a second tweet, explaining that "@Pitbull makes party music not message music. Always been place for that in #HipHop. As he gets older he will have more 2 say about life."[12] A few months later, "message music" made its way onto the floor of the

U.S. Senate as Rubio quoted Wiz Khalifa's "Work Hard Play Hard" and Jay-Z's "A Week Ago" during a filibuster led by Republican senator Rand Paul.[13]

As much as Rubio worked to distance himself from the "party" elements of Pitbull's music in favor of the "messages" of Jay-Z, his preference for the latter soon came into question. When Jay-Z and Beyoncé visited Cuba in April 2013, Rubio blasted the couple for making the trip. Appearing on ABC's "This Week," he insisted that "Jay-Z needs to get informed. One of his heroes is Che Guevara. Che Guevara was a racist. Che Guevara was a racist that wrote extensively about the superiority of white Europeans over people of African descent, so he should inform himself on the guy that he's propping up." He also criticized the rapper for not meeting with those who are oppressed in Cuba and specifically mentioned a hip-hop artist on the island who was in the midst of a hunger strike to protest government censorship of his political lyrics. Jay-Z responded to critics with "Open Letter," a song in which he relates that he "got White House clearance" for his trip to the island.[14] A few days later, Pitbull entered the fray with a message of his own, one that had very little to do with partying and much more to do with documenting his own history as the son of Cuban exiles living in Miami. The song defends Jay-Z and Beyoncé for visiting Cuba and raises an important but controversial question: "Politicians love to hate you / But then they run away when it's time to debate you. Question of the night / Would they have messed with Mr. Carter if he was white?" Perhaps a jab aimed directly at Rubio, whose brother-in-law did nearly fifteen years in prison for various drug crimes in the late 1980s, Pitbull also slips in the following line: "Let's not act like half our families ain't flipped bricks."[15]

Rubio and Pitbull both used race to either condemn or defend Jay-Z in his visit to Cuba. Rubio questioned Jay-Z's admiration of Che Guevara and was outraged that a black man could prop up the legacy of a revolutionary who once held racist views and used racist language to describe blacks. Pitbull wondered aloud whether a similar trip to Cuba by a white rapper or performer would have caused such a stir in public opinion. Both perspectives demonstrate the role musicians, music, and performance play in shaping debates and experiences of race, ethnicity, and national identity and community. As we have seen, in New York City and Miami in the 1940s and 1950s, Cuban musicians and entertainers played key roles in shaping Cuban ethnic identity and experiences for other Cubans and for multiple and overlapping audiences of Puerto Ricans, African Americans, Latin American tourists, and white North Americans. Black and white Cuban bandleaders, singers, percussionists, and comedians participated in the construction of popular representations of Cubanness, Afro-Cubanness, and Latinness for these different publics. In the process, the content and meaning of these representations changed, revealing the ways that different social contexts in Cuba and the United States informed how Cuban migrants and musicians (and their audiences) thought about and experienced race, ethnicity, and culture. These performers and their audiences demonstrated ties to their new local neighborhoods and to a broader diasporic community of (Afro-)Cubans and (Afro-)Latino/as. Indeed, the controversy surrounding Rubio, Jay-Z, and Pitbull suggests that the local and transnational dimensions of identity making and community building that once took place in the mambo dance halls of Spanish Harlem and nightclubs of Miami continue to persist and circulate today in the form of rap songs and tweets.

Notes

INTRODUCTION

1. Cruz and Reymundo, *Celia*, 131.

2. *Orishas* are deities or spirits in *santería*, a widespread syncretic religious practice that blends West African and Roman Catholic elements.

3. La Fountain-Stokes, "Translating Latina/o Studies."

4. In English, *azúcar* means sugar, but scholars and journalists have interpreted Cruz's use of the term in the contexts of Spanish colonialism and the legacies of slavery and racial inequality, *santería*, and the Cuban exile experience. See Cruz and Reymundo, *Celia*; Aparicio, "The Blackness of Sugar"; John Lannert, "The Latin Music Hall of Fame Welcomes Celia and Cachao," *Billboard*, 21 May 1994, LM-6; Mirta Ojito, "America's Queen of Salsa: Singer's Popularity Rides Waves of Immigration," *New York*

Times, 27 June 1998, B1; Leila Cobo, "The *Billboard* Interview: Celia Cruz," *Billboard,* 28 October 2000, 50.

5. I use the phrase "of color" in this book to refer to Cubans who self-identified and were identified by others as black or mulatto, the latter term suggesting African and Spanish racial mixture. The experiences of Cuban musicians of color, in the United States as in Cuba, were not at all consistent or reflective of unchanging and uncontested systems of racial classification. What this somewhat problematic phrase makes clear, however, is that these Cubans were seen (and usually saw themselves) as nonwhite and subject to informal and formal practices of racial exclusion. See Ferrer, *Insurgent Cuba,* 10–12.

6. Laó-Montes, "Mambo Montage," 4, 8, 17, 21.

7. Latino/a American literary, visual, and cultural studies scholar Claire F. Fox draws from historian Eric Zolov to distinguish between elite and popular Pan-Americanism: the term "Panamericanism" signifies "official governmental or institutional initiatives to link the countries of the hemisphere" whereas the "lower-case 'panamericanism' is used [by scholars] to describe vernacular or everyday forms of interaction across the Americas." Such a neat distinction is not always easy to make, given the way hemispheric relations oftentimes materialized and the diffusion of the ideology among, in this case, Cubans and other Latino/as in New York City and Miami. *Making Art Panamerican,* 213, 314.

8. For more on the various debates on the role of popular culture in American society, see also Adorno, "Culture Industry Revisited"; Hall, "Notes on Deconstructing 'the Popular'"; Lipsitz, *Time Passages*; Ohmann, *Selling Culture*; Kammen, *American Culture, American Tastes*; Cook, "The Return of the Culture Industry"; Moore, *Nationalizing Blackness.*

9. The literature on Latin musical styles and genres is rich and vast. For some notable examples, see Roberts, *The Latin Tinge*; Leymarie, *Cuban Fire*; Boggs, *Salsiology*; Fernández, "The Course of U.S. Cuban Music"; Fernández, *Afro-Cuban Rhythms*; Manuel, "Latin Music in the United States"; Manuel, *Creolizing Contradance.*

10. Mirabal, "'Ser De Aquí.'" For studies that focus specifically on nineteenth- and early twentieth-century migration and settlement, see Greenbaum, *More Than Black*; Mormino and Pozzeta, *The Immigrant World of Ybor City*; Poyo, "With All, and for the Good of All"; Haslip-Viera, "The Evolution of the Latino Community in New York City"; Weisman, *Soldiers and Patriots.* For studies that focus on the migration and settlement of the post-1959 exiles, see García, *Havana USA*; Portes and Stepick, *City on the Edge*; Masud-Piloto, *From Welcomed Exiles to Illegal Immigrants*; Pedraza, "Cuba's Refugees"; Eckstein, "The Transformation of the Diaspora"; Torres, *In the Land of Mirrors*; Capó, "Queering Mariel."

11. Greenbaum, *More Than Black,* 12, 155, 260–261, 266.

12. Guridy, *Forging Diaspora*; Ortíz, *Cultural Erotics in Cuban America*; López, *Unbecoming Blackness.*

13. Pérez, *On Becoming Cuban,* 5, 7, 10.

14. Guridy, *Forging Diaspora,* 6; López, *Unbecoming Blackness,* 7.

15. Ferrer, *Insurgent Cuba,* 191–192, 197. See also Pérez, *Cuba: Between Reform and Revolution*; Helg, *Our Rightful Share*; Pérez, *The War of 1898.*

16. De la Fuente, *A Nation for All*, 10–11.

17. Burgos, *Playing America's Game*; Gómez, *Manifest Destinies*; Fernández, *Brown in the Windy City*.

18. Borrowing from President William McKinley, historian Louis A. Pérez uses the phrase "ties of singular intimacy" to describe the historical links between the United States and Cuba, specifically U.S. involvement in all aspects of Cuban life—politics, society, trade and economics, and culture. Pérez, *Cuba and the United States*; Pérez, *On Becoming Cuban*.

19. Sandoval-Sánchez, *José, Can You See?*, 14; Pérez, *On Becoming Cuban*, 214.

20. Thomas, *Puerto Rican Citizen*, 53; Dmitri Ivanovitch, "Latinoamericanos o Hispanoamericanos?," *La Prensa*, 18 October 1944, 4; Dmitri Ivanovitch, "Latinoamericanos o Hispanoamericanos?," *La Prensa*, 21 October 1944, 4; Julio Garzon, "Del Gentilicio 'Hispanoamericano,'" *La Prensa*, 24 October 1944, 4; Julio Garzon, "Del Gentilicio 'Hispanoamericano,'" *La Prensa*, 25 October 1944, 4; Rafael Belaunde, "Propósito eliminatorio del calificativo 'Latino,'" *La Prensa*, 28 October 1944, 4; Rafael Belaunde, "Respondiendo a Cinco Preguntas Concretas," *La Prensa*, 2 November 1944, 4.

21. Laó-Montes, "Mambo Montage," 15; Oboler, *Ethnic Labels, Latino Lives*, 2–3; Sandoval-Sánchez, *José, Can You See?*, 12; Flores, *From Bomba to Hip Hop*, 7–8; Haslip-Viera, "The Evolution of the Latino Community in New York City," 23. For a more detailed historiographical survey of these debates, see also Padilla, *Latino Ethnic Consciousness*; Anzaldúa, *Borderlands/La Frontera*; Torres-Saillant, "Inventing the Race"; Dávila, *Latino Spin*.

22. Jiménez Román and Flores, "Introduction," 2, 11.

23. Moore, *Nationalizing Blackness*.

24. Cook and Glickman, "Twelve Propositions," 49–50.

CHAPTER 1

1. This chapter draws heavily from oral history interviews conducted by historian Ruth Glasser and radio programmer, producer, music journalist, and librarian David Carp in the late 1980s and early 1990s (exceptions are listed in the corresponding note and in the bibliography). I transcribed Glasser's interviews with Mario Bauzá, but audio recordings of the interviews Carp conducted were unavailable at the time of my visit to the archive in June 2010. However, I had access to thousands of pages of interview transcripts. Direct quotes from the interviews preserve the exact spelling, grammar, and punctuation presented in the transcriptions. For more on the history of the David Carp Collection of Latin Jazz, see Heather Haddon, "Bronx Jazz Scene Back in Swing at Historical Society," *Norwood News*, Bronx, New York, 14 December 2010.

2. Fernández, *Afro-Cuban Rhythms*, 53.

3. "Music: Personality," *Time*, 26 July 1946; Joseph J. Ryan, "Good-Will Set to Music," *New York Times*, 20 July 1941, X8; Fausto, "La Gran Vía Blanca," *La Prensa*, 8 June 1943, 5; "En Broadway," *La Prensa*, 24 May 1951, 6; "Nice People Suddenly Get the Urge to Become Vulgar," *Baltimore Afro-American*, 14 June 1941, 1; "Music: Eet Ees Deesgosting!," *Time*, 28 December 1942. For more on Cugat, see Roberts, *The Latin Tinge*, 86–87; Orovio, *Cuban Music*.

4. "Music: Personality," *Time*, 26 July 1946; *Billboard*, 19 April 1947, 42; *Billboard*, 22 November 1947, 40; *Billboard*, 15 March 1947, 32.

5. "Music: Eet Ees Deesgosting!," *Time*, 28 December 1942; Hazel Lamarre, "All the World's a Stage," *Los Angeles Sentinel*, 24 June 1952, B2; *Billboard*, 14 October 1944, 19; Paul Denis, "Night Club Review," *Billboard*, 25 July 1942, 14; *Billboard*, 22 April 1942, 13; *Billboard*, 3 October 1942, 22.

6. *Billboard*, 17 June 1944, 65. See also Jones, *The Songs that Fought the War*, 147; Capó, "Cuban Culture in New York City."

7. Boggs, "Salsa Music," 355; Fernández, *Afro-Cuban Rhythms*, 43.

8. Burgos, *Playing America's Game*, 4, 85–87, 96, 242. See also Jacobson, *Whiteness of a Different Color*; Guglielmo, *White on Arrival*.

9. Moore, *Nationalizing Blackness*.

10. "Xavier Cugat Praises Duke Ellington, Lena Horne and Others at Press Party," *Chicago Defender*, 14 June 1947, 19; "Nice People Suddenly Get the Urge to Become Vulgar," *Baltimore Afro-American*, 14 June 1941, 1.

11. "En Broadway," *La Prensa*, 24 May 1951, 6; Jerry Lesser, "Radio Talent New York," *Billboard*, 12 December 1942, 6; "Music: Personality," *Time*, 26 July 1946; Joseph J. Ryan, "Good-Will Set to Music," *New York Times*, 20 July 1941, X8; "Music: Eet Ees Deesgosting!," *Time*, 28 December 1942. The various newspapers and magazines to which I refer include *La Prensa*, *Ecos de Nueva York*, *New York Times*, *Time*, and *Billboard*.

12. "Xavier Cugat el domingo en el Manhattan Center," *La Prensa*, 17 April 1957, 5; "Xavier Cugat y su Orquesta tocará el día 21 en el Manhattan Center," *La Prensa*, 8 April 1957, 4; "En Manhattan Center Cugat tocará mañana," *La Prensa*, 20 April 1957, 5; Francisco V. Portela, "Recordando con Xavier Cugat," *La Prensa*, 23 March 1958, 5.

13. Jesús Colón, "Lo Que el Pueblo Me Dice," *Pueblos Hispanos*, 20 March 1943, 3.

14. Thomas, *Puerto Rican Citizen*.

15. Nilo Curbelo, interview with David Carp, 3 October 1993, David Carp Collection of Latin Jazz, Bronx County Historical Society, Bronx, New York (hereafter DCC); Boggs, "Al Santiago"; Arnaz, *A Book*, 50–51.

16. Mario Bauzá, interview with David Carp, 18 April 1991, DCC; "Cugat y Machito en el Hunts P. Palace el próximo domingo," *La Prensa*, 19 March 1943, 5.

17. Mario Bauzá, interview with Ruth Glasser, 19 April 1989, Ruth Glasser/Puerto Rican Musicians Collection, Centro de Estudios Puertorriqueños, Hunter College, City University of New York, New York, New York (hereafter RG/PRM); Fernández, *Afro-Cuban Rhythms*, 16, 42.

18. Gottlieb, "What Makes Rhumba?," 25; Alberto Socarrás, interview with Max Salazar, 16 January 1983, DCC; "En Broadway," *La Prensa*, 24 May 1951, 6.

19. *Billboard*, 24 December 1949, 36; *Billboard*, 27 May 1950, 47; *Billboard*, 8 July 1950, 40.

20. Ray Santos, interview with David Carp, 5 August 1991, DCC; Boggs, "Founding Fathers," 99; Fernández, *Afro-Cuban Rhythms*, 61.

21. Arturo "Chico" O'Farrill, interview with David Carp, 31 July 1991, DCC.

22. My research has uncovered conflicting dates for Marco Rizo's birth. In an oral history interview with David Carp on 22 July 1993, Rizo stated that he was born on

30 November 1920, and various materials distributed by his South American Music Project (SAMPI) also list 1920 as the year he was born. However, his World War II honorable discharge certificate indicates that he was born on 30 March 1915, while other U.S. government documents list 15 November 1915 and 15 November 1916 as his date of birth.

23. Marco Rizo, interview with David Carp, 22 July 1993, DCC; Luis Miranda, interview with David Carp, 16 April 1994, DCC; Armando Peraza, interview with David Carp, 21 May 1993, DCC.

24. De la Fuente, *A Nation for All*, 12–13; Pérez, "Peasants, Politics, and People of Color," 510, 516, 531, 536; Helg, *Our Rightful Share*, 2–3, 16–19; See also Ferrer, *Insurgent Cuba*; Bronfman, *Measures of Equality*.

25. Peraza, interview with David Carp, 21 May 1993; Miranda, interview with David Carp, 16 April 1994; De la Fuente, *A Nation for All*, 14–16.

26. Honorable discharge certificate, Box 1, Folder 10, Marco Rizo Papers, New York Public Library for the Performing Arts, New York, New York (hereafter MRP); Rizo, interview with David Carp, 22 July 1993; Program for Marco Rizo's memorial service, Private Collection of Vilma Rizo, New York, New York (hereafter PCVR).

27. Rizo, interview with David Carp, 22 July 1993; Vilma Rizo, interview with author, 28 September 2009.

28. Jaime Taronji, "José Curbelo, en el Cabaret 'La Conga,'" *Nueva York al Día*, 28 August 1943, 1, José Curbelo Papers, Cuban Heritage Collection, Otto Richter Library, University of Miami, Coral Gables, Florida (hereafter JCP); "Chick Madison Introduces You to America's Top Rhumba Man," *Musical Express*, 19 August 1949, JCP; Virginia Forbes, "Café Life in New York," *New York Sun*, 19 June 1945, JCP; *Tele-Pics*, 5 December 1948, JCP; Orovio, *Cuban Music*, 63; José Curbelo, interview with David Carp, 3 October 1993, DCC; Jaime Taronji, "Desde Nueva York: José Curbelo y su Orquesta, ganadores de la Copa 1944," *Radio Cuba*, March 1945, 41, 97, JCP; Paul M. Bruun, "Father Curbelo Plays Bass in Orchestra of Famous Son," *Miami Beach Sun Tropics*, 28 December 1944, 20, JCP.

29. O'Farrill, interview with David Carp, 31 July 1991.

30. Gender also played a role in shaping Cuban perceptions of popular musicians and performers. See, for example, Vazquez, *Listening in Detail*; Boggs, *Salsiology*; Aparicio, "'Así Son'"; Aparicio, "The Blackness of Sugar"; Aparicio, "La Lupe, La India, and Celia"; Abreu, "Celebrity, 'Crossover,' and Cubanidad"; Castro, *Queens of Havana*.

31. Isabelle Ortiz, "Machito A Living Legend," *Canales*, January 1979, Box 7, Folder 8, Carlos Ortiz Collection, Centro de Estudios Puertorriqueños, Hunter College, City University of New York, New York, New York (hereafter COC); Machito interview, WKCI, 1980s, Box 7, Folder 9, COC.

32. Rizo, interview with David Carp, 22 July 1993; Marco Rizo, interview with David Carp, 6 August 1993, DCC; Miranda, interview with David Carp, 16 April 1994; "Music Notes," *New York Times*, 27 September 1940, 31; Honorable discharge certificate, Box 1, Folder 10, MRP.

33. Rizo, interviews with David Carp, 22 July 1993 and 6 August 1993; A. R. Rodríguez, "Otro Músico Cubano Que se Abre Camino," Box 2, Folder 9, MRP; Marco Rizo, "The Desi I Knew: The Music Man behind the Desi Arnaz Legend for over

50 Years," as told to C. David Younger, 1991, Box 5, Folder 6, MRP. "The Desi I Knew" is Rizo's unpublished biography of Desi Arnaz.

34. Rizo, interview with David Carp, 22 July 1993; *Billboard*, 29 March 1947; A. R. Rodríguez, "Otro Músico Cubano Que se Abre Camino," Box 2, Folder 9, MRP; Rizo, "The Desi I Knew"; Rizo, interview with David Carp, 6 August 1993.

35. A. R. Rodríguez, "Otro Músico Cubano Que se Abre Camino," Box 2, Folder 9, MRP.

36. *Billboard*, 29 March 1947; Rizo, interview with David Carp, 22 July 1993; Program for Marco Rizo's memorial service, PCVR; Rizo, interview with David Carp, 6 August 1993.

37. Rizo, interview with David Carp, 6 August 1993.

38. Horacio Riambau, interview with David Carp, 1 December 1995, DCC; Miller, *Voices of the Leopard*; Powell, *Tito Puente*.

39. Riambau, interview with David Carp, 1 December 1995; De la Fuente, *A Nation for All*, 11–17.

40. Rizo, interviews with David Carp, 22 July 1993 and 6 August 1993; Rizo, "The Desi I Knew."

41. "Entrevista Relámpago," *Prensa Libre*, 3 December 1953, Box 2, Folder 9, MRP; Rizo, "The Desi I Knew"; Bettelheim, Bridges, and Yonker, "Festivals in Cuba, Haiti, and New Orleans."

42. Rita Conde, "Hollywood de Día y de Noche," Box 2, Folder 9, MRP; Rizo, interview with David Carp, 22 July 1993.

43. "Club Cubano Inter-Americano, Inc.," *La Prensa*, 23 November 1959, 17; Letter signed by Gilberto Villa and Melba Alvarado, Box 5, Folder 13, Club Cubano Inter-Americano Papers, Schomburg Center for Research in Black Culture, New York Public Library, New York, New York (hereafter CCI); Manuel Laverde, "Más Artistas de nota se suman a nuestro Festival," *La Prensa*, 16 November 1958, 5; Flyer for Festival Antillano, Box 1, Folder 14, MRP.

44. "Marco Rizo, Pianist, Offers Own Works," *New York Times*, 7 April 1958, 26; "Marco Rizo in Recital," *New York Times*, 9 March 1959, 35.

45. Rizo, interview with David Carp, 22 July 1993; *Billboard*, 19 May 1958, 23; *Billboard*, 14 April 1958.

46. Rizo, interviews with David Carp, 22 July 1993 and 6 August 1993; Henry Cowell, "Serious Composers of Cuba," *New York Times*, 29 April 1945, X4; Fernández, *Afro-Cuban Rhythms*, 46.

47. Rizo, interview with author, 28 September 2009; Fernández, *Afro-Cuban Rhythms*, 61.

48. Moreno, "Bauzá-Gillespie-Latin/Jazz," 84; Mario Bauzá, interviews with David Carp, 8 February 1989 and 18 April 1991, DCC; Bauzá, interview with Ruth Glasser, 19 April 1989.

49. Ibid.

50. Peraza, interview with David Carp, 21 May 1993.

51. Mario Bauzá, interviews with Ruth Glasser, 19 April 1989 and 2 June 1989, RG/PRM; Bauzá, interview with David Carp, 18 April 1991; Miranda, interview with David Carp, 16 April 1994.

52. Bauzá, interviews with Ruth Glasser, 19 April 1989 and 2 June 1989; Bauzá, interview with David Carp, 18 April 1991; Ferrer, *Insurgent Cuba*, 126.

53. Bauzá, interview with David Carp, 18 April 1991; Helg, *Our Rightful Share*, 16–19; For more on the relationship between race, marriage, class, and sexual values in nineteenth-century Cuba, see Stolcke, *Marriage, Class, and Color*; Kutzinski, *Sugar's Secrets*; Martínez-Echazábal, "Mestizaje"; Arrizón, *Queering Mestizaje*.

54. O'Farrill, interview with David Carp, 31 July 1991; Burgos, *Playing America's Game*, 6, 39; De la Fuente, *A Nation for All*, 11.

55. Bauzá, interview with Ruth Glasser, 19 April 1989; Hall, "Negotiating Caribbean Identities," 14; Nicolás Guillén, "El Camino de Harlem," *Diario de la Marina*, 21 April 1929, 11. See also López, *Unbecoming Blackness*, 18–20.

56. Moreno, "Bauzá-Gillespie-Latin/Jazz," 87; See also Miller, "Mario Bauzá."

57. Bauzá, interview with David Carp, 8 February 1989; Bauzá, interview with Ruth Glasser, 19 April 1989; Fletcher, *All Hopped Up and Ready to Go*; Fernández, *Afro-Cuban Rhythms*, 61.

58. Bauzá, interview with Ruth Glasser, 19 April 1989; Armando Sánchez, interview with David Carp, 19 September 1995, DCC; Fernández, *Afro-Cuban Rhythms*, 43–44.

59. "Mellizas del Campo en el Festival de Mayo," *La Prensa*, 28 April 1957, 1; Miranda, interview with David Carp, 16 April 1994.

60. Bauzá, interviews with Ruth Glasser, 19 April 1989 and 2 June 1989. Bauzá reported that in the early 1930s he lived on 129th Street between Lenox and Fifth Avenue and later on 166th Street and Seventh Avenue. He returned to Cuba in 1936 to marry his wife, Elena, one of Machito's sisters. The couple moved to 144th Street between Lenox and Seventh Avenue. For more on the geographic and demographic distinctions between Harlem and El Barrio, see Salazar, *Mambo Kingdom*, 1; Haslip-Viera, "The Evolution of the Latino Community in New York City," 7; Glasser, *My Music Is My Flag*, 95–96.

61. Salazar, *Mambo Kingdom*, 1.

62. Armando Sánchez, interviews with David Carp, 19 September 1995 and 2 September 1992, DCC; Salazar, *Mambo Kingdom*, 1.

63. Socarrás, interview with Max Salazar, 16 January 1983; Peraza, interview with David Carp, 21 May 1993.

64. Watkins-Owens, *Blood Relations*; James, *Holding Aloft the Banner of Ethiopia*; Biondi, *To Stand and Fight*, 17; Fernández, *Afro-Cuban Rhythms*, 43; Burgos, *Playing America's Game*.

65. Bauzá, interview with Ruth Glasser, 2 June 1989.

66. Salazar, *Mambo Kingdom*, 5, 55–56; Mary Lynn Conejo, interview with author, 9 April 2010.

67. Bauzá, interviews with David Carp, 18 April 1991 and 8 February 1989.

68. Bauzá, interview with David Carp, 18 April 1991; Boggs, "Salsa Music," 355; Glasser, *My Music Is My Flag*, 9, 73, 199.

69. Bauzá, interviews with David Carp, 18 April 1991 and 8 February 1989; Loza, *Tito Puente*, 222; Ray Santos, interview with David Carp, 8 August 1995, DCC.

70. Fernández, *Afro-Cuban Rhythms*, 36, 87; José Curbelo, interview with David Carp, 3 October 1993.

71. Burgos, *Playing America's Game*, 112.

72. Salazar, *Mambo Kingdom*, 5–8.

73. Bauzá, interviews with Ruth Glasser, 19 April 1989 and 2 June 1989; Bauzá, interview with David Carp, 8 February 1989.

74. Ibid; Glasser, *My Music Is My Flag*, 78.

75. *Billboard*, 22 November 1947, 26; *Billboard*, 8 January 1949, 35.

76. "Escuelas y organizaciones cívicas celebran el 'Día de las Américas,'" *La Prensa*, 12 April 1951, 6; "Arsenio Rodríguez dará a conocer el capetillo y el son montuno aquí," *La Prensa*, 13 April 1951, 5; "En Broadway," *La Prensa*, 16 April 1951, 5; "El Festival Artístico pro Fondo de Caridad fue un éxito extraordinario," *La Prensa*, 22 May 1951, 1; "Amenizarán el baile del Festival de 'La Prensa' la Orq. de Machito," *La Prensa*, 4 May 1952, 3.

77. Bauzá, interview with Ruth Glasser, 19 April 1989; Fernández, *Afro-Cuban Rhythms*, 43; Glasser, *My Music Is My Flag*, 9, 162–163.

78. Bauzá, interviews with David Carp, 8 February 1989 and 18 April 1991; Bauzá, interview with Ruth Glasser, 19 April 1989; Fernández, *Afro-Cuban Rhythms*, 46.

79. Fernández, *Afro-Cuban Rhythms*, 54; Rizo, interviews with David Carp, 22 July 1993 and 6 August 1993.

CHAPTER 2

1. "Mixed Group Refused Admittance to Public Dance at Hall near Harlem," *Amsterdam Star-News*, 13 September 1941, 20.

2. Pérez, *On Becoming Cuban*, 411. For more on migration from Latin America and the Caribbean in the context of U.S. imperialism, see LaFeber, *Inevitable Revolutions*; Paterson, *Contesting Castro*; Pérez, *The War of 1898*; Kvisto, "Theorizing Transnational Immigration"; González and Fernández, "Empire and the Origins of Twentieth-Century Migration from Mexico to the United States"; Pérez, *Cuba and the United States*; Love, *Race over Empire*; García, *Seeking Refuge*; Hoffnung-Garskof, *A Tale of Two Cities*; González, *Harvest of Empire*.

3. According to the U.S. census, between 1900 and 1920 the number of Cubans (defined as individuals born in Cuba or individuals who had a mother or father who was born in Cuba) living in the state of New York hovered between five and six thousand. In 1930, the Cuban population in New York more than doubled to just over 13,000. See Integrated Public Use Microdata Series (hereafter IPUMS) samples for 1900, 1910, 1920, and 1930. See also introduction, note 10.

4. See the IPUMS sample for 1940; Hoffnung-Garskof, "The Migrations of Arturo Schomburg"; Jacobson, *Whiteness of a Different Color*; Rodríguez, *Puerto Ricans*.

5. See the IPUMS samples for 1950 and 1960; Clark, "The Exodus from Revolutionary Cuba," 75–78. For more on major political events, economic changes, and social happenings in Cuba between 1930 and 1959, see Thomas, *Cuba or The Pursuit of Freedom*; Morley, "The U.S. Imperial State in Cuba"; Pérez, *Cuba: Between Reform and*

Revolution; Pérez, *On Becoming Cuban*; Pérez-Stable, *The Cuban Revolution*; De la Fuente, *A Nation for All*; Argote-Freyre, *Fulgencio Batista*.

6. Mary Lynn Conejo, interview with author, 9 April 2010; Guillermo Álvarez Guedes, interview with Julio Estorino, 28 January 2012, Luis J. Botifoll Oral History Project, Cuban Heritage Collection, University of Miami, Coral Gables, Florida; Mirabal, "Scripting Race, Finding Place."

7. Armando Sánchez, interview with David Carp, 19 September 1995, DCC; "Cuba establece regulaciones para conceder pasaporte a los artistas," *La Prensa*, 27 October 1953, 5. On the U.S. side of the migration process, some artists also experienced difficulty. Most notable is the case of Celia Cruz, who reportedly had problems entering the United States because she had been a singer with a radio station in Havana that was branded communist. To be granted access into the country, Celia had to prove to U.S. authorities, specifically the U.S. consul in Havana, that she had never been a member of the Communist Party. "Disco de Oro a Celia Cruz en N. York," *La Prensa*, 9 April 1957, 3; "Celia Cruz y Conjunto Cortijo en el festival del Sábado 20 en S. Nicholas," *La Prensa*, 12 April 1957, 5.

8. García, "Contesting that Damned Mambo," 191; Molina, Burgos, Ramírez, and Mitchell, "Where Is the Latino Past in the Future?"

9. "Las minorías latinoamericanas en EE. UU.," *La Prensa*, 10 June 1943, 4; "Las minorías latinoamericanas en EE. UU.," *La Prensa*, 11 June 1943, 4.

10. Greenbaum, *More Than Black*, 236–238; Mirabal, "Melba Alvarado," 121–122; García, "Contesting that Damned Mambo," 193.

11. Greenbaum, *More Than Black*, 236–238; Mirabal, "Melba Alvarado," 121–122; Graciela, "¡Eso era Tremendo!," 150–151. For more on Eusebia Cosme, see López, *Unbecoming Blackness*.

12. Barbershop operator Generoso Pedroso served as the first president of El Club Cubano in 1945 and 1946. Narciso Saavedra was club president in 1950 and 1951, followed by José J. León in 1952. Other club presidents from the 1940s and 1950s include Marcos Llerena (1947, 1962), Pablo Soublet (1948), Pedro Millet (1949, 1965), Joaquin Maldonado (1953), Francisco Cardenal (1954, 1955), Aurelio O'Reilly (1956), Melba Alvarado (1957, 1958), and Pedro Guibert (1959). Loose-leaf page, Box 1, CCI; Greenbaum, *More Than Black*, 237.

13. Article 1, Reglamento, Box 1, Folder 1, CCI; Article 3, Reglamento, Box 1, Folder 1, CCI; Ferrer, *Insurgent Cuba*, 38–39, 121–127.

14. Article 1, Reglamento, Box 1, Folder 1, CCI; Article 3, Reglamento, Box 1, Folder 1, CCI. For more on the founding of El Club Cubano and the scope of its social activities, see Greenbaum, *More Than Black*, 237–238; Singer and Martínez, "A South Bronx Latin Music Tale," 198; Mirabal, "Melba Alvarado," 120–126; García, "Contesting that Damned Mambo," 193. Fuller treatment of El Club Cubano and its development as a political organization is forthcoming in historian Nancy Raquel Mirabal's manuscript "Hemispheric Notions: Diaspora, Masculinity, and the Racial Politics of Cubanidad, 1823–1945."

15. Relación de Socios Fundadores, 22 February 1946, Box 1, Folder 8, CCI. This list also provided addresses for each founding member, including Generoso Montesino

(764 Tinton Avenue, Bronx), Alberto Socarrás (250 West 47th Street), and Marcelino Guerra (1786 Madison Avenue).

16. Board of Directors Meeting Minutes (hereafter BDMM), 31 March 1949, Box 1, Folder 11, CCI. See also BDMM, 5 March 1951, Box 1, Folder 11, CCI; BDMM, 12 April 1951, Box 1, Folder 11, CCI.

17. "Dos espléndidas orquestas para el baile final," *La Prensa*, 28 March 1941, 3; "Montesino es un verdadero maestro cubano 'del ritmo,'" *La Prensa*, 11 April 1942, 3; "Baile del Club 21 Repúblicas Americanas," *La Prensa*, 1 October 1941, 8; "Baile del Comité Latino Americano el Sábado Próximo," *La Prensa*, 29 March 1945, 8.

18. Souvenir Journal, 12 October 1946, Box 5, Folder 1, CCI; "Circular, Acuerdos y Noticias," 23 July 1945, Box 5, Folder 12, CCI; Julio Garzon, "Del gentilicio 'Hispano-americano,'" *La Prensa*, 24 October 1944, 6. See also BDMM, 12 April 1951, Box 1, Folder 11, CCI; BDMM, 14 May 1951, Box 1, Folder 11, CCI; *Boletín Oficial*, May 1947, Box 15, Folder 11, Jesús Colón Collection, Centro de Estudios Puertorriqueños, Hunter College, City University of New York, New York, New York (hereafter JCC); "Día de la Raza," *Ecos de Nueva York*, 23 October 1955, 47.

19. Federico Pagani interview, 1980s, Box 4, Folder 22, COC; Machito interview at home, ca. 1985, Box 4, Folder 14, COC; Ray Santos, interview with David Carp, 3 August 1992, DCC; "Dará Gran Festival El Habana Social Club el Sábado 16," *La Prensa*, 3 March 1940, 8; "El Habana Social Club da su Baile de Temporada Hoy," *La Prensa*, 16 March 1940, 8.

20. "Dos espléndidas orquestas para el baile final," *La Prensa*, 28 March 1941, 3; "Montesino es un verdadero maestro Cubano 'del ritmo,'" *La Prensa*, 11 April 1942, 3.

21. Castro, *Queens of Havana*.

22. Alberto Socarrás, interview with Max Salazar, 16 January 1983, DCC; Burgos, *Playing America's Game*, 204.

23. Socarrás, interview with Max Salazar, 16 January 1983; Narration of *Machito: A Latin Jazz Legacy*, English, ca. 1985, Box 4, Folder 18, COC; Graciela Pérez, interview with Raúl A. Fernández and René López, 19 September 1998, Latino History Oral History Project, National Museum of American History.

24. BDMM, 14 February 1952, Box 1, Folder 11, CCI; BDMM, 31 March 1952, Box 1, Folder 11, CCI; "España y la América Hispana estarán representadas en el festival," *La Prensa*, 27 April 1952, 3.

25. "Gran desfile de artistas en el Festival Pro Estudiantes el 5," *Diario de Nueva York*, 28 March 1950, 1; "Gavilán y Robinson en festival de la B.F.H.S., mañana domingo," *La Prensa*, 26 April 1952, 2; "Extraordinario programa artístico el domingo en la Benjamin Franklin," *La Prensa*, 11 March 1953, 5.

26. According to music scholar John Storm Roberts, Robbins Music brought Guerra to the United States in 1945 to work as an arranger. *The Latin Tinge*, 123.

27. BDMM, 6 June 1949, Box 1, Folder 11, CCI; BDMM, 14 March 1949, Box 1, Folder 11, CCI; Sánchez, interview with David Carp, 19 September 1995; BDMM, 13 July 1950, Box 1, Folder 11, CCI; BDMM, 5 March 1951, Box 1, Folder 11, CCI; BDMM, 25 November 1958, Box 1, Folder 7, CCI.

28. Graciela Pérez, interview with Max Salazar, 10 May 1985, DCC; Ray Santos, interview with David Carp, 2 August 1993, DCC; "Dos Grandes Bailes en el Manhat-

tan Center," *La Prensa*, 15 March 1950, 5; "Dos Próximos Bailes en el Manhattan Center," *La Prensa*, 23 March 1950, 5; *Diario de Nueva York*, 25 March 1950, 5; "En Broadway," *Diario de Nueva York*, 31 March 1950, 5; "Baile hoy en el Manhattan Center con las orquestas de Machito y M. Guerra," *La Prensa*, 1 April 1950, 3.

29. See "El Club Social San Moritz celebra un baile hoy," *La Prensa*, 21 August 1948, 8; "El Club Social San Moritz prepara un baile," *La Prensa*, 15 September 1948, 8; *Diario de Nueva York*, 18 September 1948, 5; *Diario de Nueva York*, 23 April 1949, 5.

30. Santos, interview with David Carp, 2 August 1993.

31. "La Juventud Panamericana celebra 'Día Panamericano,'" *La Prensa*, 12 April 1947, 3. Pan-American Day commemorates the First International Conference of American States. The conference, which ended on 14 April 1890, resulted in the creation of the International Union of American Republics, a precursor to the Organization of American States.

32. *Diario de Nueva York*, 25 February 1950, 3.

33. "Contratada la Orquesta de Marcelino Guerra para el Baile del Festival," *La Prensa*, 24 April 1954, 1; "Otro memorable acontecimiento fue el Festival de La Prensa de 1954," *La Prensa*, 4 May 1954, 1; "Las Hermanas Márquez y la orquesta de Marcelino Guerra en el festival," *La Prensa*, 23 April 1955, 1; "Mercedes y Albano en el Festival pro Caridad de La Prensa el domingo," *La Prensa*, 29 April 1955, 1; Roberts, *The Latin Tinge*, 123; Salazar, *Mambo Kingdom*, 67–68.

34. *Palo monte* is an Afro-Cuban belief system with roots in the Congo region of Africa. Practitioners believe in the powers of spirits and natural or earthly objects.

35. García, *Arsenio Rodríguez*, 14–18, 35, 68.

36. BDMM, 14 May 1957, Box 1, Folder 7, CCI; BDMM, 25 January 1951, Box 1, Folder 11, CCI; BDMM, 30 August 1951, Box 1, Folder 11, CCI; "Cóctel del Club Cubano Inter-Americano," *La Prensa*, 4 April 1953, 6; "Club Cubano Inter-Amer.," *La Prensa*, 13 March 1954, 6; "Club Cubano Inter-Amer.," *La Prensa*, 19 March 1954, 5; "Baile del Club Cubano," *La Prensa*, 5 November 1955, 4; "En el Club Cubano Inter-Americano," *La Prensa*, 30 March 1957, 4. See also García, "Contesting that Damned Mambo," 193–194.

37. Postcard, 11 August 1951, Box 1, Folder 2, CCI; BDMM, 29 July 1951, Box 1, Folder 11, CCI; *Boletín Oficial*, July 1959, Box 5, Folder 11, CCI; *Boletín Oficial*, September 1959, Box 5, Folder 11, CCI. See also Harold L. Keith, "Data about Discs," *Pittsburgh Courier*, 5 October 1957, A24.

38. García, *Arsenio Rodríguez*, 5.

39. Fuentes, *Los Rostros de la Salsa*, 41.

40. García, *Arsenio Rodríguez*, 20, 28, 57–60, 66–67, 75–77, 85–86, 112.

41. BDMM, 15 March 1950, Box 1, Folder 11, CCI; BDMM, 29 June 1950, Box 1, Folder 11, CCI.

42. BDMM, 5 March 1951, Box 1, Folder 11, CCI.

43. BDMM, 13 September 1951, Box 1, Folder 11, CCI; BDMM, 14 March 1952, Box 1, Folder 11, CCI; BDMM, 31 March 1952, Box 1, Folder 11, CCI; BDMM, 30 June 1952, Box 1, Folder 11, CCI.

44. General Meeting Minutes, 1 July 1953, Box 1, Folder 11, CCI.

45. Ray Santos, interview with David Carp, 8 August 1995, DCC. In fact, *Billboard* reported that the "coarse-textured Cuban group's appeal here is limited to Latin neighborhood." *Billboard*, 19 February 1949, 110. See also *La Prensa*, 23 February 1950, 5; *Diario de Nueva York*, 25 February 1950, 5; *Billboard*, 25 March 1950, 50; "Baile de Pascua, mañana, en el Manhattan Center," *La Prensa*, 8 April 1950, 3; "Baile del club San Moritz con Orq. de Noro Morales," *La Prensa*, 3 March 1951, 5; *Diario de Nueva York*, 3 March 1951, 6; García, *Arsenio Rodríguez*; García, "Contesting that Damned Mambo."

46. "Homenaje Artístico del Ateneo de N.Y.," *La Prensa*, 7 March 1954, 5.

47. "En Broadway," *La Prensa*, 4 April 1956, 5; "Actos del Ateneo Cubano," *La Prensa*, 19 April 1956, 5; García, *Arsenio Rodríguez*, 75, 84; Moore, *Nationalizing Blackness*.

48. *Ecos de Nueva York*, 23 May 1954, 21; "Banquete-baile," *La Prensa*, 16 May 1958, 5.

49. Boggs, "The Palladium Ballroom and Other Venues," 129; Boggs, "Ernie Ensley," 147.

50. *Diario de Nueva York*, 1 April 1950, 5; "En Broadway," *La Prensa*, 28 March 1952, 5; "En Broadway," *La Prensa*, 11 April 1952, 5; "El Palladium regalará el domingo un 'set' de televisión," *La Prensa*, 12 April 1952, 5; "Gran Programas de variedades el domingo 27," *La Prensa*, 12 April 1952, 5; "Pupi Campo En El Palladium Este Sábado," *La Prensa*, 22 September 1955, 5; "Llega el carnaval a Broadway en gran fiesta el domingo 4 en el Palladium," *La Prensa*, 2 March 1956, 5.

51. "Arsenio Rodríguez dará a conocer el capetillo y el son montuno aquí," *La Prensa*, 13 April 1951, 5; "Resultó muy lucido el festival de la Benjamin Franklin High School," *La Prensa*, 18 April 1951, 3.

52. "En Broadway," *La Prensa*, 16 April 1951, 5.

53. Ibid.; Socarrás, interview with Max Salazar, 16 January 1983; Armando Sánchez, interviews with David Carp, 2 September 1992 and 19 September 1995, DCC; Pérez, interview with Max Salazar, 10 May 1985.

54. Helio Orovio, "El mambo nació en La Habana," *Tropicana Internacional*, 17–19; "D. Pérez Prado," *Radio Magazine*, November and December 1945, in "El mambo nació en La Habana," *Tropicana Internacional*, 17; "Dámaso Pérez Prado Triunfó en Nueva York," *Radio Magazine*, August 1946, in *Apuntes para la Historia*, 110–113.

55. Related to this confusion about musical origins, it should also be noted that the word "mambo" has had different meanings at different times. For example, when recordings used the word mambo in the mid-1940s, they were likely referring to a section within the dance portion of a song that often featured improvisation. It was not until the late 1940s and early 1950s that mambo came to refer to the commercial dance and music style associated with Pérez Prado. See García, *Arsenio Rodríguez*; Fernández, *Afro-Cuban Rhythms*.

56. Sublette, *Cuba and Its Music*, 534–535.

57. *Diario de Nueva York*, 16 January 1952, 7; *Diario de Nueva York*, 24 January 1952, 15; *Diario de Nueva York*, 25 January 1952, 7; *New York Amsterdam News*, 19 January 1952, 12. For more on comparisons between Arsenio Rodríguez and Pérez Prado and debates over "empirical distinctions between an 'inauthentic' and 'authen-

tic' mambo style," see García, "Contesting that Damned Mambo," 187–198; García, *Arsenio Rodríguez*, 75–92.

58. García, *Arsenio Rodríguez*, 94, 112, 114–115.

59. Santos, interview with David Carp, 8 August 1995; "Arsenio Rodríguez será festejado aquí," *La Prensa*, 10 July 1947, 4; *La Prensa*, 12 July 1947, 5; "Un baile-homenaje hoy a Arsenio Rodríguez," *La Prensa*, 12 July 1947, 8. See also *Diario de Nueva York*, 8 March 1950, 5; *Diario de Nueva York*, 11 March 1950, 5.

60. Antonio Riva, "Torre de Babel," *La Prensa*, 8 September 1957, 4. Federico Pagani became a club member in December 1950; BDMM, 12 December 1950, Box 1, Folder 11, CCI.

61. My argument here is informed by Benedict Anderson's definition of nation as "an imagined political community—and imagined as both inherently limited and sovereign. It is *imagined* because the members of even the smallest nation will never know most of their fellow-members, meet them, or even hear them, yet in the minds of each lives the image of their communion." *Imagined Communities*, 6.

62. BDMM, 26 July 1957, Box 1, Folder 7, CCI; BDMM, 7 November 1949, Box 1, Folder 11, CCI; BDMM, 13 September 1951, Box 1, Folder 11, CCI.

63. BDMM, 23 April 1958, Box 1, Folder 7, CCI; BDMM, 27 March 1957, Box 1, Folder 7, CCI.

64. *Diario de Nueva York*, 15 September 1950, 7.

65. BDMM, 12 December 1950, Box 1, Folder 11, CCI; BDMM, 13 December 1951, Box 1, Folder 11, CCI; BDMM, 14 April 1952, Box 1, Folder 11, CCI.

66. BDMM, 16 June 1949, Box 1, Folder 11, CCI. See also BDMM, 30 September 1952, Box 1, Folder 11, CCI; BDMM, 11 April 1949, Box 1, Folder 11, CCI; BDMM, 25 April 1949, Box 1, Folder 11, CCI; "Homenaje del Club Cubano Interamericano," *La Prensa*, 9 May 1949, 5.

67. For more on the role of radio and television in American society, see Cohen, "Encountering Mass Culture at the Grassroots"; Douglas, *Listening In*; Marling, *As Seen on TV*; Baughman, *Same Time, Same Station*; Burns, *Invasion of the Mind Snatchers*. See also the sources cited in the introduction, note 8.

68. *Boletín Oficial*, February and March 1950, Box 5, Folder 11, CCI; BDMM, 26 March 1950, Box 1, Folder 11, CCI; BDMM, 30 March 1950, Box 1, Folder 11, CCI; BDMM, 13 July 1950, Box 1, Folder 11, CCI. Casa Siegel was a well-known record and electronics store on 1393–95 Fifth Avenue near 115th Street.

69. BDMM, 16 June 1958, Box 1, Folder 7, CCI; BDMM, 11 November 1958, Box 1, CCI; BDMM, 18 December 1958, Box 1, CCI. Competition between radio and television intensified in the early 1950s, and performers had to be careful not to ally themselves with one medium over another. In 1951, radio stations boycotted Xavier Cugat after he made negative comments about radio while appearing on a television show. "Proscriben los discos de Cugat en una emisora local," *Diario de Nueva York*, 7 June 1951, 3.

70. "Adviertan a los periódicos sobre la competencia que ofrece la televisión," *La Prensa*, 22 April 1954, 1.

71. BDMM, 28 August 1952, Box 1, Folder 11, CCI; BDMM, 30 September 1952, Box 1, Folder 11, CCI.

1. Greenbaum, *More Than Black*, 236–238; Mirabal, "Melba Alvarado," 121–122; Graciela, "¡Eso era Tremendo!," 150–151.

2. The case can easily be made that Cuban New Yorkers created rich and vibrant social and cultural lives for themselves in the 1940s and 1950s. A few examples of events hosted by the lesser-known clubs make the point clear. El Círculo Cubano and El Habana Social Club sponsored dances and other social events like the dance at the Broadway Casino the latter hosted that featured "música criolla." Logia Isla de Cuba No. 173 de la I.O.O.F., which was founded in 1945 and shared its club space with Club Social Cuba, organized dances, theatrical events, and other activities that reportedly generated "a great deal of enthusiasm within the colonia cubana." For many of its dances and other social events, including a picnic held on the grounds of the International Park in the Bronx, the club hired Cuban-led bands, such as Orquesta de Montecarlo, Orquesta Renovación, José Budet, Sonora Antilla, and Orquesta Tropical Knights. Logia Rebekah Isla de Cuba also hosted dances and musical events throughout the 1950s, such as an event held at the Hotel Empire that featured music by Tropical Knights. "Círculo Cubano de N.Y. tiene baile mañana," *La Prensa*, 13 January 1940, 8; "Círculo Cubano celebra un baile mañana," *La Prensa*, 20 January 1940, 8; "Círculo Cubano en N. York," *La Prensa*, 3 February 1940, 8; *La Prensa*, 16 November 1940, 8; "Circulan las invitaciones del Club Social Cuba," *La Prensa*, 8 March 1946, 6; "Logia Isla de Cuba," *La Prensa*, 9 March 1946, 8; "Baile en la Logia Isla de Cuba 173," *La Prensa*, 22 April 1946, 6; "Baile del Comité de la Logia Isla de Cuba," *La Prensa*, 27 April 1946, 8; "Club Social Cuba," *La Prensa*, 1 April 1948, 5; "Club Isla de Cuba," *La Prensa*, 21 April 1948, 5; "La Logia Isla de Cuba da Baile Hoy," *La Prensa*, 25 April 1953, 4; "La Logia Isla de Cuba 173 da baile aniversario," *La Prensa*, 2 March 1955, 6; "El baile aniversario de la Logia Isla de Cuba," *La Prensa*, 9 March 1955, 6; "La Logia Isla de Cuba da picnic el domingo," *La Prensa*, 1 June 1955, 6; "La Logia Rebekah Isla de Cuba da un baile," *La Prensa*, 20 May 1954, 6. See also Singer and Martínez, "A South Bronx Latin Music Tale."

3. "El Ateneo Cubano Conmemorará el 'Grito de Baire' y Celebró un Acto Patriótico," *La Prensa*, 1 February 1945, 3; "Souvenir del Comité Gestor del Club Cubano Inter-Americano en el Aniversario del Natalicio del Apostol José Martí," Box 5, Folder 1, CCI; "Velada Conmemorativa Esta Noche en el Ateneo Cubano," *Diario de Nueva York*, 28 January 1949, 7; "El Club Cubano Interamericano Conmemora el Natalicio de Martí," *Diario de Nueva York*, 28 January 1949, 7; "Elecciones del Club Cubano Interamericano," *La Prensa*, 12 January 1956, 5. For more on Martí's role in the construction of Cuban national identity, see Pérez, *Cuba: Between Reform and Revolution*; Belnap, Fernández, and Pease, *José Martí's "Our America"*; Rodríguez-Luis, *Re-Reading José Martí*; De la Fuente, *A Nation for All*; Guerra, *The Myth of José Martí*; Font and Quiroz, *The Cuban Republic and José Martí*; López, *José Martí and the Future of Cuban Nationalisms*; Lomas, *Translating Empire*.

4. BDMM, 5 January 1950, Box 1, Folder 11, CCI; BDMM, 25 January 1951, Box 1, Folder 11, CCI; BDMM, 28 August 1952, Box 1, Folder 11, CCI. For more on Martí's poetry, see Rodríguez-Luis, *Re-Reading José Martí*. An English translation of this short

poem reads: "I have a white rose to tend / In July as in January; / I give it to the true friend / Who offers his frank hand to me. / And to the cruel one whose blows / Break the heart by which I live, / Thistle nor thorn do I give: / For him, too, I have a white rose." See Martí, *Versos sencillos/Simple Verses*.

5. Ferrer, *Insurgent Cuba*, 15. For more on the Ten Years' War, see Robert, "Slavery and Freedom in the Ten Years' War"; Pérez, *Cuba: Between Reform and Revolution*, 121, 125.

6. Invitation to celebrate the anniversary of the Grito de Yara, 9 October 1946, Box 5, Folder 1, CCI.

7. "Soirée bailable del Club Cubano Interamericano," *Diario de Nueva York*, 7 October 1948, 7; "Continúan los preparativos para la soirée del Club Cubano," *Diario de Nueva York*, 1 October 1948, 5; "Fiesta Social del Club C. Interamericano," *Diario de Nueva York*, 9 October 1948, 7.

8. "Celebró el 'Grito de Yara' el Club Social Cubano," *Diario de Nueva York*, 12 October 1948, 8.

9. "Celebró Bien Baile el Ateneo Cubano," *Diario de Nueva York*, 12 October 1948, 8; "Celebrarán el Grito de Yara," *Diario de Nueva York*, 1 October 1948, 5; "Baile Patriótico del Ateneo Cubano," *Diario de Nueva York*, 9 October 1948, 7; "Entre Nosotros," *Diario de Nueva York*, 9 October 1948, 7.

10. "El Ateneo Cubano da un baile esta noche," *La Prensa*, 24 February, 1945, 8; "Lucida Velada Bailable Celebró el Ateneo Cubano," *Diario de Nueva York*, 14 February 1949, 5; "Ecos de Sociedad," *Ecos de Nueva York*, 16 March 1952, 26; "Baile del Ateneo Cubano," *La Prensa*, 25 February 1956, 6; "Club Cubano Inter-Amer.," *La Prensa*, 25 February 1956, 6. See also Ferrer, *Insurgent Cuba*, 141; Pérez, *Cuba: Between Reform and Revolution*; Helg, *Our Rightful Share*.

11. "El Círculo Cubano Celebra su Fiesta Patriótica Hoy," *La Prensa*, 24 February 1940, 8. See also Greenbaum, *More Than Black*, 238.

12. "'El Grito de Baire' esta noche en el Grand Plaza," *La Prensa*, 24 February 1945, 8. My research uncovered mention of the Cuban society Maceo y Martí only a handful of times throughout 1945. Newspapers and existing historical scholarship on Cuban social clubs (which do not mention La Sociedad Maceo y Martí) provide no connection between this club and La Union Martí-Maceo in Tampa or El Club Cubano Inter-Americano in the Bronx.

13. "Velada del Club Cubano Interamericano el día 24," *La Prensa*, 17 February 1947, 4.

14. BDMM, 9 February 1950, Box 1, Folder 11, CCI; BDMM, 15 February 1951, Box 1, Folder 11, CCI; "Velada del Club Cubano Interamericano," *La Prensa*, 23 February 1950, 5; "Club Cubano Interamericano," *Diario de Nueva York*, 26 February 1950, 5.

15. "Ateneo Cubano," *Diario de Nueva York*, 27 February 1950, 5; "Club Social Cuba," *Diario de Nueva York*, 27 February 1950, 5.

16. Pérez, *Cuba: Between Reform and Revolution*, 192. For more on the War of Independence and U.S. intervention in Cuba in the late nineteenth and early twentieth centuries, see also Pérez, *The War of 1898*; Ferrer, *Insurgent Cuba*; Pérez, *On Becoming Cuban*.

17. A few highlights of the Ateneo Cubano's Cuban Independence Day celebrations include a 1948 dance that featured Orquesta Renovación at the Hotel Taft and an

artistic conference on the life of Cuban patriot Marta Abreu at its clubhouse; a 1956 evening gathering with Dr. Emilio Nuñez Portuondo, Cuban ambassador to the United States; and a 1958 event that featured Francisco Jorge Cardona, director of *La Prensa*. "En el Ateneo Cubano," *La Prensa*, 15 May 1948, 3; "Actividades de la Colonia," *Mundo Latino*, 15 May 1948, 5; "Velada y baile del Ateneo Cubano," *La Prensa*, 16 May 1951; "Ateneo Cubano," *Diario de Nueva York*, 22 May 1951; "En el Ateneo Cubano," *La Prensa*, 17 May 1956, 6; "Celebra Ateneo Cubano fecha histórica," *La Prensa*, 17 May 1958, 5. See also "Hernández Travieso Dio Conferencia en el Ateneo Cubano," *La Prensa*, 2 May 1944, 8; "El 20 de Mayo en el Ateneo Cubano," *Pueblos Hispanos*, 20 May 1944, 3; "Ateneo Cubano," *Diario de Nueva York*, 16 May 1950, 6; "Baile del Ateneo Cubano," *La Prensa*, 10 May 1952, 4; "Fiesta conmemorativa en el Ateneo Cubano," *La Prensa*, 19 May 1954, 6; "Actos del Ateneo Cubano," *La Prensa*, 13 May 1955, 5; "En Broadway," *La Prensa*, 12 May 1955, 5; "En el Ateneo Cubano," *La Prensa*, 21 May 1955, 5.

18. "El Ateneo Cubano Festeja el Aniv. de la República de Cuba," *La Prensa*, 20 May 1943, 6; "El Ateneo Cubano celebra elegante baile social hoy," *La Prensa*, 22 May 1943, 8; "El Ateneo Cubano celebró una espléndida velada," *La Prensa*, 21 May 1946, 8; "El Ateneo Cubano dará un baile el día 18 de mayo," *La Prensa*, 18 April 1946, 8; "Mirándolos Pasar," *Semanario Hispano*, 25 May 1946, 10; "El Ateneo Cubano tiene un baile de gala hoy," *La Prensa*, 17 May 1947, 3; "Festivales patrióticos del Ateneo Cubano," *La Prensa*, 19 May 1947, 3.

19. For more on the theoretical concept and social practice of appropriation, see Chartier, "Texts, Printing, Readings"; Hall, "What Is This 'Black' in Black Popular Culture?"; Lott, *Love and Theft*; Moore, *Nationalizing Blackness*; Lipsitz, *Time Passages*; Rivero, *Tuning Out Blackness*; Cook, "The Return of the Culture Industry."

20. "Velada del Club Cubano Interamericano del Bronx," *La Prensa*, 18 May 1946, 8; "Mirándolos Pasar," *Semanario Hispano*, 25 May 1946, 10. See also "Baile del Club Cubano Inter-Americano," *La Prensa*, 22 May 1954, 6; "Club Cubano Inter-Amer.," *La Prensa*, 21 May 1955, 5; "En Broadway," *La Prensa*, 12 May 1955, 5.

21. "Velada del Club Cubano Interamericano el día 20," *La Prensa*, 16 May 1947, 3; "Cuba celebra aniversario de su Independencia," *La Prensa*, 20 May 1947, 1; "Velada del Club Cubano Inter-Americano," *La Prensa*, 24 May 1947, 8; *Boletín Oficial*, February and March 1950, Box 5, Folder 11, CCI; BDMM, 9 February 1950, Box 1, Folder 11, CCI; BDMM, 20 March 1950, Box 1, Folder 11, CCI; "Velada del Club Cubano Interamericano," *La Prensa*, 13 May 1950, 3.

22. Club Cubano Inter-Americano Journal, August 1958, Box 5, Folder 13, CCI; García, *Arsenio Rodríguez*, 27–28.

23. Club Cubano Inter-Americano Journal, August 1958, Box 5, Folder 13, CCI; "Celebración de independencia," *La Prensa*, 20 May 1958, 5; "Club Cubano Interamericano," *La Prensa*, 22 May 1958, 2.

24. "Baile para celebrar la Independencia de Cuba," *La Prensa*, 14 May 1945.

25. "Proyectarse formar una nueva Sociedad Cubana," *La Prensa*, 13 May 1946, 6; "Grupo de Cubanos festejó con cena la fecha patria," *La Prensa*, 25 May 1946, 8; "Mirándolos Pasar," *Semanario Hispano*, 25 May 1946, 10.

26. "La Sociedad Maceo y Martí prepara un baile," *La Prensa*, 6 April 1945, 3; "Da un baile la Sociedad Maceo y Martí," *La Prensa*, 8 May 1945, 8; "La independencia cubana, celebrada en 'La Conga,'" *La Prensa*, 20 May 1946, 6; "Mirándolos Pasar," *Semanario Hispano*, 25 May 1946, 10.

27. "Baile dedicado a Cuba en el Palladium Ballroom," *La Prensa*, 19 May 1951, 6; "Fiesta en honor a Cuba en el 'Palladium-Ballroom,'" *Diario de Nueva York*, 19 May 1951, 5; "Fiesta Cubana en el Palladium," *La Prensa*, 17 May 1952, 6; "En Broadway," *La Prensa*, 12 May 1955, 5.

28. Letter to President Ramón Grau San Martín, 11 March 1946, Box 5, Folder 1, CCI. The letter indicated that each of the presidents signed the letter in his/her name on behalf of club members: Blas González Martín, Centro Artesanos Cubano (241 East 121st Street, Apartment 14); Tomás López, Club Social Cuba (2018 Amsterdam Avenue); Francisco Soler, Logia Isla de Cuba (2018 Amsterdam Avenue); and Señora Eulalia Parodi, Club Habana (850 East 161st Street, Apt. 2D, Bronx). For more on Ramón Grau San Martín's presidency, see Pérez, *Cuba: Between Reform and Revolution*, 283–288; Ameringer, *The Cuban Democratic Experience*. For more on Afro-Cuban interactions with African Americans and other migrants of color from the Caribbean, see James, *Holding Aloft the Banner of Ethiopia*; Brock and Castañeda Fuertes, *Between Race and Empire*; Guridy, "From Solidarity to Cross-Fertilization"; Burgos, *Playing America's Game*; Jiménez Román and Flores, *The Afro-Latin@ Reader*; Guridy, *Forging Diaspora*.

29. "Elegante Baile Social se Celebrará el Sábado," *La Prensa*, 6 November 1944, 3; "Comité de Ayuda a Cuba Activa su Baile del Sábado," *La Prensa*, 26 December 1944, 8; "Hay Gran Animación Para el Beneficio Cubano del Sábado," *La Prensa*, 28 December 1944, 8. Historian Frank Guridy has argued that "a small Cuban community" existed in Washington, D.C., in the 1940s. The Comité Cubano de Washington counted on Evelio and Sergio "Henry" Grillo as members and organized social and cultural events for Afro-Cuban *excursionistas* as well as cultural exchanges between Afro-Cubans and African Americans. *Forging Diaspora*, 190–192.

30. Fox, *Making Art Panamerican*, 314.

31. "La Bandera de Cuba será izada otra vez en el Ayuntamiento," *Diario de Nueva York*, 10 May 1950, 1; "Dramatizaron hoy en La Habana por radio la gesta del Gral. Narciso López," *La Prensa*, 19 May 1950, 4. O'Dwyer was New York City's mayor from 1946 to 1950 and seemed to have a relatively favorable relationship with the *colonia hispana*. For more on New York City politics, especially in relation to Spanish-speaking migrants, see Sánchez Korrol, *From Colonia to Community*; LaGumina, *New York at Mid-Century*; McNickle, *To Be Mayor of New York*; Biondi, *To Stand and Fight*; Hoffnung-Garskof, *A Tale of Two Cities*; Thomas, *Puerto Rican Citizen*.

32. "La Bandera de Cuba será izada otra vez en el Ayuntamiento," *Diario de Nueva York*, 10 May 1950, 1; "Nueva York rinde tributo a la bandera de Cuba izándola publicamante," *Diario de Nueva York*, 20 May 1950, 3.

33. *La Prensa*, 20 May 1952, 3; *La Prensa*, 20 May 1953, 3.

34. "Embajador de Cuba impone medalla al Alcalde de N. York," *Diario de Nueva York*, 19 May 1951, 1.

35. *Boletín Oficial*, August 1947, Box 5, Folder 11, CCI; *Boletín Oficial*, September 1959, Box 5, Folder 11, CCI; BDMM, 30 June 1952, Box 1, Folder 11, CCI; *Boletín Oficial*, August 1947, Box 5, Folder 11, CCI; BDMM, 6 June 1949, Box 1, Folder 11, CCI; Invitation to Club Cubano Inter-Americano events, 1951, Box 5, Folder 2, CCI.

36. Guridy, *Forging Diaspora*, 190–192.

37. "Cuban Goodwill Group Visits the United States," *Atlanta Daily World*, 29 August 1950, 3.

38. *Boletín Oficial*, August 1947, Box 5, Folder 11, CCI; *Boletín Oficial*, September 1959, Box 5, Folder 11, CCI; BDMM, 30 June 1952, Box 1, Folder 11, CCI; BDMM, 6 June 1949, Box 1, Folder 11, CCI; Invitation to Club Cubano Inter-Americano events, 1951, Box 5, Folder 2, CCI.

39. BDMM, 30 June 1951, Box 1, Folder 11, CCI; BDMM, 12 July 1951, Box 1, Folder 11, CCI; BDMM, 29 July 1951, Box 1, Folder 11, CCI; "Club Cubano Inter-Americano," *La Prensa*, 19 May 1951, 6; "Excursión Patriótica del Club Cubano," *Diario de Nueva York*, 22 May 1951, 5.

40. "Circular, Acuerdos y Noticias," 30 May 1946, Box 5, Folder 12, CCI.

41. "La Bandera de Cuba será izada otra vez en el Ayuntamiento," *Diario de Nueva York*, 10 May 1950, 1; "Rinden emocionado tributo a la bandera de la República de Cuba," *Diario de Nueva York*, 16 May 1950, 1.

42. BDMM, 14 April 1952, Box 1, Folder 11, CCI; BDMM, 15 May 1952, Box 1, Folder 11, CCI; "Actos del cincuentenario de la República de Cuba," *La Prensa*, 15 May 1952, 5; Mirabal, "Melba Alvarado," 124–125.

43. "Entrevistas Brevísimas," *Diario de Nueva York*, 2 June 1951, 4.

44. "Una edición especial publicará 'La Prensa,'" *La Prensa*, 12 April 1943, 1; "Desfile de las naciones unidas, punto culminante en la temporada del Circo," *La Prensa*, 12 April 1943, 5; "Edición especial de La Prensa mañana," *La Prensa*, 13 April 1943, 1.

45. "Actos de Semana Panamericana darán comienzo en Nueva York el 8 de abril," *Diario de Nueva York*, 11 March 1950, 3; "Baile de gala en el Manhattan Center," *Diario de Nueva York*, 29 March 1950, 7; "Cadetes cubanos en desfile del 15," *Diario de Nueva York*, 29 March 1950, 1; "Gran Baile Panamericano de Gala hoy Sábado," *La Prensa*, 8 April 1950, 3; "Cadetes cubanos participarán en el desfile Panamericano de N. York," *La Prensa*, 11 April 1950, 2; "Actividades del Ateneo Cubano," *La Prensa*, 11 April 1950, 3. El Club Cubano was not mentioned specifically as one of the Hispanic organizations that supported "this grand panamerican social event."

46. "Desfile Panamericano," *La Prensa*, 4 April 1951, 3; "Reunión en el Ateneo Cubano," *Diario de Nueva York*, 5 April 1951, 7; "El Ateneo Cubano da baile este Sábado," *La Prensa*, 11 April 1951, 3; "Baile del Ateneo Cubano," *Diario de Nueva York*, 12 April 1951, 5; "Ateneo Cubano," *Diario de Nueva York*, 14 April 1951, 5.

47. BDMM, 29 March 1951, Box 1, Folder 11, CCI; Mirabal, "Melba Alvarado."

48. BDMM, 29 March 1951, Box 1, Folder 11, CCI; BDMM, 12 April 1951, Box 1, Folder 11, CCI; BDMM, 15 May 1952, Box 1, Folder 11, CCI.

49. BDMM, 30 September 1952, Box 1, Folder 11, CCI.

50. "Club Cubano Inter-Amer.," *La Prensa*, 7 September 1957, 5.

51. For more on the history of the Virgen de la Caridad, Afro-Cuban religious practices, and Cuban national identity, see Díaz, *The Virgin, the King, and the Royal Slaves of El Cobre*; De la Fuente, *A Nation for All*; Tweed, *Our Lady of the Exile*, esp. 16–25; Portuondo Zúñiga, "The Virgin of Charity of Cobre, Cuba's Patron Saint"; Sublette, *Cuba and Its Music*; González, *Afro-Cuban Theology*; Miller, *Voices of the Leopard*.

52. BDMM, 15 September 1958, Box 1, Folder 11, CCI.

53. "En Broadway," *La Prensa*, 8 September 1955, 5.

54. Díaz, *The Virgin, the King, and the Royal Slaves of El Cobre*.

55. Mary Lynn Conejo, interview with author, 9 April 2010.

56. "El Comité Cubano celebra festival en honor de la Virgen de la Caridad," *La Prensa*, 11 September 1943, 8; "El Comité Cubano logró un éxito en el Festival en honor de la Caridad," *La Prensa*, 13 September 1943, 8. "Comité Parroquial Cubano," *Diario de Nueva York*, 7 September 1950, 5; *Diario de Nueva York*, 9 September 1950, 6; "En Broadway," *La Prensa*, 8 September 1955, 5. See also Loza, *Tito Puente*; Mirabal, "Scripting Race, Finding Place."

57. "El Ateneo Cubano dará un baile hoy," *La Prensa*, 10 September 1955, 6; "Baile del Ateneo Cubano," *La Prensa*, 8 September 1956, 6; "Baile a la Caridad en el Ateneo Cubano," *La Prensa*, 7 September 1957, 5.

58. Ferrer, *Insurgent Cuba*, 4, 126–127.

59. Ibid., 4, 84, 60. For more on Maceo's leadership and legacy, see Foner, *Antonio Maceo*; Franco, *Antonio Maceo: Apuntes para una historia de su vida*; Helg, *Our Rightful Share*; De la Fuente, *A Nation for All*; Scott, *Degrees of Freedom*; Tone, *War and Genocide in Cuba*.

60. "Dice Nuestra Comunidad," *La Prensa*, 9 April 1955, 4.

61. BDMM, 13 July 1950, Box 1, Folder 11, CCI; BDMM, 30 August 1951, Box 1, Folder 11, CCI.

62. Memorandum, 6 December 1946, Box 5, Folder 1, CCI.

63. "Velada del Club Cubano Inter-Americano," *La Prensa*, 3 July 1947, 4; "Velada pro Martí y Maceo el miércoles en esta," *La Prensa*, 7 July 1947, 6; *Boletín Oficial*, July 1947, Box 15, Folder 7, JCC.

64. BDMM, 9 February 1950, Box 1, Folder 11, CCI; BDMM, 13 September 1951, Box 1, Folder 11, CCI.

65. Reinaldo Fernández Rebull to El Club Cubano, 15 November 1947, Box 5, Folder 1, CCI. Relations with Consul-General Rebull had been warm since 1945, when club president Generoso Pedroso sent the consul a handwritten letter inviting him to a celebration in honor of Maceo at Club Obrero Español, located at 1490 Madison Avenue. This was apparently El Club Cubano's first social event. Generoso Pedroso to Reinaldo Fernández Rebull, 1 December 1945, Box 5, Folder 1, CCI.

66. BDMM, 7 March 1949, Box 1, Folder 11, CCI; BDMM, 14 March 1949, Box 1, Folder 11, CCI; BDMM, 31 March 1949, Box 1, Folder 11, CCI. Records at the time of my visit did not contain all of the letters El Club Cubano received and did not specify which Cuban politicians wrote to express support for the Martí-Maceo project.

67. Francisco Orue to Narciso Saavedra, 3 May 1951, Box 5, Folder 2, CCI.

68. "Portuondo Calá fue homenajeado por el Club Cubano Interamericano," 13 March 1948, *Liberación*, 9.

69. "Gestiones en Cuba Pro Monumento a Martí en Nueva York," *La Prensa*, 4 April 1949, 3. The Comité Pro Monumento a Martí y Maceo seems to have been a separate commission dedicated to raising funds for the monument. It appears, however, that many members of El Club Cubano formed part of its core, including Francisca Cardenal and Narciso Saavedra. For more on Francisca Cardenal and the role of women in El Club Cubano, see Mirabal, "Melba Alvarado," 124–125.

70. "Club Cubano Interamericano," *Diario de Nueva York*, 1 May 1951, 5.

71. BDMM, 30 June 1951, Box 1, Folder 11, CCI; BDMM, 31 March 1952, Box 1, Folder 11, CCI.

72. "Un homenaje Americano a José Martí," *La Prensa*, 19 May 1951, 4; "Tributo a Martí en N.Y. tuvo viso continental," *Diario de Nueva York*, 29 January 1952, 3.

73. "Fijan sitio para la estatua de Martí," *La Prensa*, 30 April 1956, 1. When sculptor Anna Hyatt Huntington finally completed the statue in 1959, it was presented without dedication or dates. According to literary scholar Antonio López, "For 'security reasons,' the statue was stored in a garage until 1965, when it was presented without ceremony (no Cubans were invited to participate) and without dedication. The Batista regime paid $100,000 for the pedestal and landscaping." See López, "Chronicling Empire." See also BDMM, 6 June 1949, Box 1, Folder 11, CCI; BDMM, 14 November 1957, Box 1, Folder 7, CCI.

74. Helg, *Our Rightful Share*; De la Fuente, *A Nation for All*; Mirabal, "Melba Alvarado."

75. "58 cubanos han ido al exilio por oponerse políticamente al Gbno.," *La Prensa*, 31 March 1954, 3.

76. For more on the Cuban Revolution and the 26 of July Movement, see Paterson, *Contesting Castro*; Pérez, *Cuba: Between Reform and Revolution*; Pérez-Stable, *The Cuban Revolution*; Sweig, *Inside the Cuban Revolution*; DePalma, *The Man Who Invented Fidel*.

77. "Mitin cubano," *La Prensa*, 9 March 1955, 5; "Movimiento 26 de Julio," *La Prensa*, 21 May 1957, 2; "Club Cubano Interamericano," *La Prensa*, 22 May 1958, 2.

78. Conejo, interview with author, 9 April 2010; "Entrevistas Brevísimas," *Diario de Nueva York*, 4 January 1952, 8.

79. BDMM, 14 November 1957, Box 1, Folder 7, CCI; BDMM, 2 April 1957, Box 1, Folder 7, CCI; BDMM, 14 May 1957, Box 1, Folder 7, CCI; BDMM, 19 June 1957, Box 1, Folder 7, CCI; "En el Club Cubano Inter-Americano," *La Prensa*, 30 March 1957, 4.

80. *La Prensa*, 10 February 1956, 2; "En Broadway," *La Prensa*, 13 September 1956, 5.

81. BDMM, 30 April 1958, Box 1, Folder 7, CCI; BDMM, 16 June 1958, Box 1, Folder 7, CCI.

82. "En Broadway," *Diario de Nueva York*, 11 September 1950, 5; "Comité Cubano-Americano Pro-Batista," *Diario de Nueva York*, 1 January 1952; "Batististas de N. York expresan su júbilo," *Diario de Nueva York*, 11 March 1952, 4. Support for Batista would soon shift. As early as 1954, two Cuban men were arrested for helping ship weapons and munitions to Cuba for the purpose of bringing down the Batista government. Police reportedly found the supplies at a storefront rented by the men at 173 West 93rd

Street. "Dice el fiscal que cubanos detenidos han hecho embarques de armas a Cuba," *La Prensa*, 7 March 1954, 1.

83. "Casa Cuba Celebra Fecha Martiana," *La Prensa*, 27 January 1959, 5; "El Ateneo Cubano se une al dolor de la patria," *La Prensa*, 2 January 1959, 2; *La Prensa*, 5 January 1959, 5.

84. "Actividades del Ateneo Cubano," *La Prensa*, 7 January 1959, 5; "Casa Cuba Celebra Fecha Martiana," *La Prensa*, 27 January 1959, 5; "Ateneo Cubano celebra con baile Independencia de Cuba," *La Prensa*, 24 May 1959, 5.

85. "Dio baile el Club Unidad Cubana de New York," *La Prensa*, 21 May 1959, 5; "Club Unidad Cubana," *La Prensa*, 20 May 1959, 5; "Fiesta patriótica cubana para el 20 de mayo," *La Prensa*, 19 May 1959, 5; "Sociedades Cubanas se reúnen," *La Prensa*, 13 December 1959, 8. For more on the politics of the Cuban American community of the postrevolutionary period, see García, *Havana USA*; Torres, *In the Land of the Mirrors*; García, "Hardliners v. 'Dialogueros'"; Pedraza, *Political Disaffection in Cuba's Revolution and Exodus*.

86. "Será Pro Fondo de Caridad de 'La Prensa,'" *La Prensa*, 2 May 1958, 5.

87. "Baile de Coronación, la nota mas brillante de la temporada," *La Prensa*, 24 April 1959, 5. El Club Cubano held a separate event at its clubhouse in 1959 in honor of its representative in the contest, Nydia I. "Actividades del Club Cubano Inter-Americano," *La Prensa*, 31 March 1959, 5. During this visit to the United States, Castro came without an invitation from the U.S. government; he was a guest of the American Society of Newspaper Editors. Much of the historiography on U.S.-Cuba relations cites President Dwight D. Eisenhower's refusal to meet with Castro during this visit as setting off tense relations between the two nations. See Pérez, "Fear and Loathing of Fidel Castro"; Schoultz, *That Infernal Little Cuban Republic*.

88. "Fidel Castro Sigue Leyendo 'La Prensa,'" *La Prensa*, 20 May 1959, 8.

CHAPTER 4

1. "La Gran Función y Baile Pro Fondo de Caridad, en El Royal Windsor Mañana," *La Prensa*, 29 March 1941, 1; "Carmen Amaya bailará en el Festival pro Caridad," *La Prensa*, 26 March 1941, 1; "Consuelo Moreno, Don Arres, y Xavier Cugat, vencedores en el Certamen de Artistas," *La Prensa*, 28 February 1941, 1; "Más Que un Festival," *La Prensa*, 8 May 1948, 3; "Otro memorable acontecimiento fue el Festival de La Prensa de 1954," *La Prensa*, 4 May 1954, 1. In 1933, the contest winners were Consuelo Moreno in the *Damas* category, Ortiz Tirado in the *Caballeros* category, and the orchestra of Don Alberto in the *Orquesta o Conjunto Musical* category. Both the newspaper and the Charity Fund were founded by José Comprubí, and the first festival was held at the Manhattan Casino on 155th Street and Eighth Avenue. In 1944, *La Prensa* changed the official name of the contest to Concurso de Popularidad de Artistas, Orquestas, Grupos Musicales y Parejas de Bailes Hispanos de Nueva York to reflect the addition of new categories to the ballot.

2. "La brillantez del Festival de Caridad 'La Prensa' sobrepasó a todo calor," *La Prensa*, 1 April 1941, 3; "Espléndido balance artístico del 'Festival' de 'La Prensa,'" *La Prensa*, 10 May 1949, 1.

3. "Certamen de Popularidad de Artistas Hispanos de Nueva York," *La Prensa*, 6 March 1942, 2; "Votos a favor de M. Valdés, Carlos Ramírez, C. Amaya," *La Prensa*, 1 March 1941, 3.

4. "Reglas del Certamen de 'La Prensa,'" *La Prensa*, 14 March 1949, 2; "Reglas del Certamen de 'La Prensa,'" *La Prensa*, 1 April 1950, 2.

5. Haslip-Viera, "The Evolution of the Latino Community in New York City," 12–16.

6. Glick Schiller and Fouron, *Georges Woke Up Laughing*, 4.

7. For more on transnationalism and international migration, see Appadurai, "Global Ethnoscapes"; Glick Schiller, Basch, and Blanc, "From Immigrant to Transmigrant"; Hondagneu-Sotelo and Avila, "'I'm Here, but I'm There'"; Jacobson, *Whiteness of a Different Color*; Smith and Guarnizo, *Transnationalism from Below*; Duany, "Reconstructing Racial Identity"; Portes, Guarnizo, and Landolt, "Transnational Communities"; Gabaccia, "Is Everywhere Nowhere?"; Kvisto, "Theorizing Transnational Immigration"; Duany, *The Puerto Rican Nation on the Move*; Torres-Saillant, "Inventing the Race"; Ngai, *Impossible Subjects*; García, *Seeking Refuge*; Guglielmo, "Fighting for Caucasian Rights"; Hoffnung-Garskof, *A Tale of Two Cities*; Briggs, McCormick, and Way, "Transnationalism."

8. Kanellos, "Cronistas and Satire in Early Twentieth Century Hispanic Newspapers," 3; Thomas, *Puerto Rican Citizen*, 26. For more on *La Prensa* and José Comprubí, see Sánchez Korrol, *From Colonia to Community*, 71, 152, 158; Ševčenko, "Making Loisaida"; Johnson, *Ernest Gruening and the American Dissenting Tradition*. More research is needed on the Spanish-language press in New York City. Models for this work include Meyer, *Speaking for Themselves*; Meléndez, *Spanish-Language Newspapers in New Mexico, 1834–1958*; Tovares, "*La Opinión*."

9. Examination of the winners and runners-up in the *Damas, Parejas de Baile Español*, and *Parejas de Baile Hispanoamericano* categories is beyond the scope of this project, though it should be noted that solo male artists and orchestras catered to a dancing public and often worked in nightclubs alongside professional dancers, many of whom were Cuban. See also chapter 1, note 30.

10. "Manifiéstase gran interés en los locutores de radio y televisión," *La Prensa*, 22 March 1957, 1; "Brillantes locutores deleitan a los televidentes hispanos de N.Y.," *La Prensa*, 23 March 1957, 1; *La Prensa*, 28 March 1958, 4.

11. Spigel, *Make Room for TV*, 1. See also introduction, note 8; chapter 2, note 67.

12. "Manifiéstase gran interés en los locutores de radio y televisión," *La Prensa*, 22 March 1957, 1.

13. "Creé que la televisión será un éxito en Hispanoamérica?," *Diario de Nueva York*, 23 April 1951, 4.

14. "Atención, votantes del Concurso de Popularidad de 'La Prensa,'" *La Prensa*, 14 March 1945, 2.

15. "Music: Leading Latins," *Time*, 23 April 1943; "Music: Raúl & Eva," *Time*, 24 April 1944. A variety of Spanish- and English-language newspapers and magazines, including a few periodicals based in Cuba, reported on the contests and fund-raising

festivals, including *Time, Billboard, Latin Talk, New York Sun, Miami Beach Sun Trop-ics, Tampa Sunday Tribune, Musical Express, Radio Cuba, New York al Día*, and *El Anunciador*.

16. "Comisiones especiales en el festival del día 28," *La Prensa*, 20 March 1943, 1; "El Comité de Escrutinio de 'La Prensa' examina el recuento de votos," *La Prensa*, 21 April 1947, 2; "Avanzan los preparativos para el festival de caridad del día 2," *La Prensa*, 21 April 1948, 2; "Verifícase hoy el festival pro Fondo de Caridad de 'La Prensa' en N. York," *La Prensa*, 20 May 1951, 1; "Mañana domingo se celebra el Gran Festival Artístico Anual de Caridad," *La Prensa*, 1 May 1954, 1.

17. "Comisiones especiales en el festival del día 28," *La Prensa*, 20 March 1943, 1; "Gran interés por el Festival del Fondo de Caridad," *La Prensa*, 5 April 1944, 2; "Avanzan los preparativos para el festival de caridad del día 2," *La Prensa*, 21 April 1948, 2; "El programa para el festival del dos de mayo adquiere grandes proporciones," *La Prensa*, 24 May 1948, 2; "Mañana se verificará el gran festival anual pro caridad," *La Prensa*, 1 May 1948, 1; "Se reúne esta noche la Comisión de Escrutinio del Concurso de Artistas," *La Prensa*, 1 May 1952, 1.

18. "El Festival Anual de Caridad," *La Prensa*, 2 May 1957, 4; "El Festival de La Prensa fue un gran éxito artístico," *La Prensa*, 1 May 1945, 1–2; Alberto Socarrás, interview with Max Salazar, 16 January 1983, DCC.

19. Jottar, "Central Park Rumba," 22. La Moderna was located at 107 Lenox between 115th and 116th Streets. Some of the other businesses and sites where readers could buy tickets include Tipografía Colombia (502 West 145th Street); Jai Alai (82 Bank Street); Nuevo Mundial (513 West 145th Street); Quincallera La Sultana (147 East 116th Street); El Mundial (222 West 116th Street); La Mercedita (386 East Thirteenth Street); Centro Español/La Nacional (239 West 14th Street); La Ideal Market (166 Eighth Avenue); La Nueva Ideal between Roosevelt and Madison Streets; Cesar González Studio (526 West 145th Street); Carlton Photo Shop (280 Flatbush Avenue, Brooklyn); Florería Moscoso (139 Court Street, Brooklyn); Colmado Las Tres T.T.T. (919 Third Avenue, Bronx); Farmacia Rita (836 Westchester Avenue, Bronx); La Giralda (866 Longwood Avenue, Bronx); Florería Moscoso (791 Westchester Avenue, Bronx); and Colmado Tommy Rivera (83–04 Baxter Avenue, Queens).

20. For more on Latino/a community development, see Haslip-Viera, "The Evolution of the Latino Community in New York City"; Pritchett, "Race and Community in Post-war Brooklyn," 445–472; Thomas, *Puerto Rican Citizen*; Sánchez Korrol, *From Colonia to Community*; Iglesias, *Memoirs of Bernardo Vega*; Glasser, *My Music Is My Flag*.

21. "Fue un gran éxito el festival de 'La Prensa,'" *La Prensa*, 29 March 1943, 1; "Miguel Ferriz y Matilde Palou en el programa del festival del 29," *La Prensa*, 18 April 1945, 1; "El 'Havana-Madrid' brinda su revista para el festival Pro Caridad del 26," *La Prensa*, 16 May 1946, 1; "Verifícase Mañana el Gran Festival Pro Caridad de 'La Prensa' en el M. Center," *La Prensa*, 10 May 1947, 1; "El famoso tenor mexicano Nestor Chayres cantará en el Festival," *La Prensa*, 26 April 1955, 1; "El Festival Anual de Caridad," *La Prensa*, 2 May 1957, 4.

22. "Nuestro Concurso de Popularidad de Artistas," *La Prensa*, 5 April 1947, 2; "Interés internacional en el Concurso de Artistas Hispanos," *La Prensa*, 1 April 1948, 2; "Mañana se verificará el gran festival anual pro caridad," *La Prensa*, 1 May 1948; "El

lunes publicaremos el último escrutinio de nuestro concurso," *La Prensa*, 5 May 1950, 1; "Se reúne esta noche la Comisión de Escrutinio del Concurso de Artistas," *La Prensa*, 1 May 1952, 1; "Vencedores del Concurso de Popularidad de 'La Prensa,'" *La Prensa*, 18 March 1943, 1, 2.

23. "Nuestro concurso demuestra la gran popularidad de orquestas hispanas," *La Prensa*, 22 March 1953, 1; "Daniel Santos hoy y mañana en el Palladium con Machito y T. Puente," *La Prensa*, 30 September 1955, 5. See also introduction, note 9.

24. "El lunes publicaremos el último escrutinio de nuestro concurso," *La Prensa*, 5 May 1950, 1; "Gran Éxito el Festival de 'La Prensa,'" *La Prensa*, 7 May 1956, 1.

25. In 1941 and 1943, *La Prensa* hosted the fund-raising gala at the Royal Windsor, located at 69 West 66th Street. The newspaper never disclosed or discussed its reasons for switching the location to the Manhattan Center.

26. For more on the relationship between race and Latino/a nightlife, see Boggs, *Salsiology*; Loza, *Tito Puente*; Singer and Martínez, "A South Bronx Latin Music Tale"; Salazar, *Mambo Kingdom*. See also chapter 1, note 64.

27. "Celebrase Mañana el Festival de 'La Prensa,'" *La Prensa*, 27 March 1943, 1; "La Argentinita en el Festival de mañana," *La Prensa*, 15 April 1944, 1; "Mañana se verificará el gran festival anual de 'La Prensa,'" *La Prensa*, 28 April 1945, 1; "El Festival de 'La Prensa' fue un gran éxito artístico," *La Prensa*, 1 May 1945, 1; "Verifícase Mañana el Gran Festival Pro Caridad de 'La Prensa' en el M. Center," *La Prensa*, 10 May 1947, 1; "Mañana se verificará el gran festival anual pro caridad," *La Prensa*, 1 May 1948, 1; "Mañana domingo se celebra el Gran Festival Artístico Anual de Caridad," *La Prensa*, 1 May 1954, 1; Ray Santos, interview with David Carp, 2 August 1993, DCC.

28. "El festival culminó en un éxito," *La Prensa*, 17 April 1944, 1; "El Festival de 'La Prensa' fue excelente en calidad artística y en concurrencia," *La Prensa*, 13 May 1947, 1; "Más que un festival," *La Prensa*, 8 May 1948, 3; "Hoy llevase a cabo el grandioso Festival y Baile pro Caridad," *La Prensa*, 21 May 1950, 1; "Puntualidad, orden y alegría fueron las características del Gran Festival," *La Prensa*, 5 May 1953, 3; "Gran Éxito del Festival de La Prensa," *La Prensa*, 3 May 1955, 1.

29. "Cantarán y bailarán pro Caridad el domingo aquí," *La Prensa*, 28 March 1941, 3; "Verifícase mañana el Gran Festival Pro Caridad de *La Prensa* en el M. Center," *La Prensa*, 10 May 1947, 1; "Más que un Festival," *La Prensa*, 8 May 1948, 3; "En Broadway," *La Prensa*, 4 April 1956, 5.

30. "El Festival Anual de Caridad," *La Prensa*, 2 May 1957, 4.

31. "Artistas y público colaboraron para el éxito del festival de 'La Prensa,'" *La Prensa*, 30 March 1943, 3; "Beneficio líquido de $2,288.35 dio el Festival de 'La Prensa' pro Caridad," *La Prensa*, 20 April 1944, 2; "El Festival Pro Ayuda Fondo Social de 'La Prensa' dio un producto de $3,605.09," *La Prensa*, 7 May 1945, 2.

32. "Triunfadores en 2o. Puesto del Certamen de 'La Prensa,'" *La Prensa*, 25 April 1949, 8; "Aristas y público colaboraron para el éxito del festival de La Prensa," *La Prensa*, 30 March 1943, 3; "Beneficio líquido de $2,288.35 dio el Festival de 'La Prensa' pro Caridad," *La Prensa*, 20 April 1944, 2; "El Festival Pro Ayuda Fondo Social de 'La Prensa' dio un producto de $3,605.09," *La Prensa*, 7 May 1945, 2. In 1941 and 1942, the newspaper set ticket prices for men at $1, for women at $.50, and for children at $.25, a gendered pricing scale that was practiced by many of the nightclubs of the city.

33. "Dice nuestra comunidad," *La Prensa*, 15 March 1957, 4.

34. Ševčenko, "Making Loisaida," 294–295. For more on ethnic marketing and ethnic entrepreneurs, see Sánchez Korrol, *From Colonia to Community*, 70–71, 152; Sánchez, *Becoming Mexican American*, 174; Glasser, *My Music Is My Flag*; Dávila, *Latinos, Inc.*; Dávila, *Latino Spin*; Cohen, "Encountering Mass Culture at the Grassroots"; Cohen, *A Consumers' Republic*, 318, 329–331.

35. "Más que un Festival," *La Prensa*, 8 May 1948, 3.

36. *La Prensa*, 2 May 1953, 1; "Éxito sin precedente en el Festival de La Prensa," *La Prensa*, 4 May 1953, 1.

37. "Democratic Split Stirs Republicans," *New York Times*, 13 April 1949, 44; James A. Hagerty, "Fight Intensified for Bloom's Seat," *New York Times*, 7 May 1949, 8; "Brillante el Festival de 'La Prensa' en Manhattan Center," *La Prensa*, 9 May 1949, 1.

38. Sánchez Korrol, *From Colonia to Community*, 4, 52–53, 69, 77, 81; Ševčenko, "Making Loisaida," 294.

39. "El festival culminó en un éxito," *La Prensa*, 17 April 1944, 1; "El público quedó muy complacido del brillante festival que dio 'La Prensa,'" *La Prensa*, 18 April 1944, 2; "Se celebró anoche con gran entusiasmo el gran festival pro fondo de caridad," *La Prensa*, 27 May 1946, 1; "Más de 4,000 personas en la fiesta de ayer," *La Prensa*, 31 March 1941, 1, 2; "Artistas y público colaboran para el éxito del festival de 'La Prensa,'" *La Prensa*, 30 March 1943, 3; "Famosos artistas colaboran en preparar programa para el festival pro caridad," *La Prensa*, 23 April 1948, 1. See also introduction, note 9.

40. Torres-Saillant, "Inventing the Race," 127, 135, 147; Sandoval-Sánchez, *José, Can You See?*, 12. For more on race and racialization, including the concept of *mestizaje*, see Vasconcelos, *The Cosmic Raza/La raza cósmica*; Anzaldúa, *Borderlands/La Frontera*; Rodríguez, *Puerto Ricans*; Omi and Winant, *Racial Formation in the United States*; Oboler, *Ethnic Labels, Latino Lives*; Martínez-Echazabal, "Mestizaje"; Jacobson, *Whiteness of a Different Color*; González, *Harvest of Empire*; Laó-Montes, "Mambo Montage"; Guglielmo, *White On Arrival*; Dávila, *Latino Spin*; Burgos, *Playing America's Game*; Macías, *Mexican American Mojo*.

41. See introduction, note 20; Jiménez Román and Flores, *The Afro-Latin@ Reader*, 13.

42. "Nuestros Artistas," *América en Marcha*, 1 April 1948, 8, JCP.

43. Much has been written about U.S. interventions in Latin America and the Caribbean as a result of the Good Neighbor Policy and the Cold War. For some key works, specifically in terms of cultural "encounters," see Fein, "Hollywood and United States-Mexico Relations"; Pérez, *On Becoming Cuban*; Hoffnung-Garskof, *A Tale of Two Cities*. Less is known about Latin American and Caribbean interventions in the United States during this period, specifically in terms of how Latin American and Caribbean governments participated in Latino/a community development and political mobilization during the 1940s and 1950s through consular offices, for example. One notable exception is Guglielmo, "Fighting for Caucasian Rights."

44. "Mañana se verificará el gran festival anual de 'La Prensa,'" *La Prensa*, 28 April 1945, 1; "El Festival de 'La Prensa' para entregar los trofeos artísticos fue insuperable,"

La Prensa, 28 May 1946, 2; "Hoy llevase a cabo el grandioso Festival y Baile pro Caridad," *La Prensa*, 21 May 1950, 1.

45. "Artistas y público colaboran para el éxito del festival de 'La Prensa,'" *La Prensa*, 30 March 1943, 3; Fausto, "La Gran Vía Blanca," *La Prensa*, 2 April 1943, 5.

46. "Dos Ganadores más en el grandioso Festival del 16," *La Prensa*, 13 April 1944, 1; Paul M. Bruun, "Farther Curbelo Plays Bass in Orchestra of Famous Son," *Miami Beach Sun Tropics*, 28 December 1944, 20, JCP; Jaime Taronji, "Desde Nueva York: José Curbelo y su orquesta, ganadores de la Copa 1944," *Radio Cuba*, March 1945, 31, 97, JCP.

47. "El Festival de 'La Prensa' fue un gran éxito artístico," *La Prensa*, 1 May 1945, 1; *El Anunciador*, 26 May 1945, 16, JCP; Virginia Forbes, "Café Life in New York," *New York Sun*, 19 June 1945, JCP.

48. See Sánchez, *Becoming Mexican American*, 108–125.

49. "Vencedores del Concurso de Popularidad de 'La Prensa,'" *La Prensa*, 18 March 1943, 1, 2; "Miguelito Valdés demora su viaje para cantar en el festival del 28," *La Prensa*, 24 March 1943, 3; "Artistas y público colaboran para el éxito del festival de 'La Prensa,'" *La Prensa*, 30 March 1943, 3.

50. "Vencedores del Concurso de Popularidad de 'La Prensa,'" *La Prensa*, 18 March 1943, 1, 2; "'Machito,' el director de orquesta que triunfa con el ritmo criollo," *La Prensa*, 27 March 1943, 2.

51. "Cugat y Machito en el Hunts P. Palace el próximo domingo," *La Prensa*, 19 March 1943, 5; *La Prensa*, 20 March 1943, 5.

52. "Music: Leading Latins," *Time*, 12 April 1943; Narration of *Machito: A Latin Jazz Legacy*, English, ca. 1985, Box 4, Folder 18, COC; Mario Bauzá, interview with David Carp, 8 February 1989, DCC. My perspective on the debate about "authentic" and "commercial" strands of Latin music agrees with the view presented by historian Raúl A. Fernández: "It is misinformed to regard 'commercialism' or 'the music industry' as unmitigated evils that affect the 'authenticity' of a genre. Much of what is regarded today as 'classic' Afro-Cuban music, the 'truly authentic,' developed in the ambiance of nightclubs and casinos patronized by U.S. tourists in Havana, a testimony to the ability of popular musicians to extract meaning out of sometimes societally demeaning situations." *Afro-Cuban Rhythms*, 19. See also Pérez, *On Becoming Cuban*, 198–216; Moore, *Nationalizing Blackness*; García, *Arsenio Rodríguez*; introduction, note 9.

53. "Orquesta de Xavier Cugat y La Pareja de Raúl y Eva Reyes en el Gran Festival," *La Prensa*, 16 April 1945, 1; "Resultado final de la votación del Concurso de Popularidad," *La Prensa*, 14 May 1946, 1; "Enorme entusiasmo por asistir mañana al Gran Festival Pro Fondo de Caridad," *La Prensa*, 25 May 1946, 1; "El Festival de 'La Prensa' para entregar los trofeos artísticos fue insuperable," *La Prensa*, 28 May 1946, 2.

54. *Billboard*, 31 January 1942, 88. Machito, Marco Rizo, Desi Arnaz, and Alberto Iznaga are just four of the more notable Cuban performers who were drafted to serve in the U.S. Army during World War II. See also Capó, "Cuban Culture in New York City"; Graciela Peréz, interview with Raúl A. Fernández and René López, 19 September 1998, Latino History Oral History Project, National Museum of American History; "New Father Draft Expected to Cut Heavily into Agency Rosters," *Billboard*, 9

October 1943, 16; *Billboard*, 9 October 1943, 65; "More AA Orks in the Making," *Billboard*, 6 November 1943, 14; John Desmond, "Making Catnip for the Hepcats," *New York Times Magazine*, 20 June 1943, SM16. For more on Latino/a labor and culture during the World War II era, see Sánchez Korrol, *From Colonia to Community*; Ruiz, *Cannery Women/Cannery Lives*; Sánchez, *Becoming Mexican American*; García, *A World of Its Own*; Escobedo, *From Coveralls to Zoot Suits*.

55. "Extraordinario resulto por todos conceptos el Festival de La Prensa," *La Prensa*, 20 May 1952, 3; "Los Cubanos en el Gran Festival," *La Prensa*, 18 May 1952, 3; "Programa," *La Prensa*, 17 May 1952, 2.

56. "Hispanoamérica escuchará el Festival de 'La Prensa,'" *La Prensa*, 4 April 1942, 1; "Celebrase Mañana el Festival de 'La Prensa,'" *La Prensa*, 27 March 1943, 1; "Fue un gran éxito el festival de 'La Prensa,'" *La Prensa*, 29 March 1943, 1. See also Fernández, *Afro-Cuban Rhythms*, 55–56; Warner, *Publics and Counterpublics*.

57. "Nuestro Concurso de Popularidad de Artistas," *La Prensa*, 5 April 1947, 2; "Interés internacional en el Concurso de Artistas Hispanos," *La Prensa*, 1 April 1948, 2; "Mañana se verificará el Gran Festival anual Pro Caridad," *La Prensa*, 1 May 1948; "El lunes publicaremos el último escrutinio de nuestro Concurso," *La Prensa*, 5 May 1950, 1; "Se reúne esta noche la Comisión de escrutinio del Concurso de Artistas," *La Prensa*, 1 May 1952, 1.

58. Fausto, "La Gran Vía Blanca," *La Prensa*, 7 April 1944, 5.

59. For more on Pan-Americanism and the Good Neighbor Policy, see Connolly, "By Eminent Domain"; Lockley, "The Meaning of Pan Americanism"; Scott, "Good Neighbor Policy"; Gerstle, *American Crucible*.

60. "Promete superar a los anteriores el Festival 'Pro Caridad' del domingo," *La Prensa*, 13 May 1946, 1; "Se celebró anoche con gran entusiasmo el gran festival Pro Fondo de Caridad," *La Prensa*, 27 May 1946, 1.

61. "Famosos Artistas Colaboran en Preparar Programa para el Festival pro Caridad," *La Prensa*, 23 April 1948, 1.

62. "Dice nuestra comunidad," *La Prensa*, 14 April 1956, 4.

63. "El Festival de 'La Prensa,'" *La Prensa*, 14 April 1943, 14.

64. "El 'Merengue' dominicano en el programa del Festival de mayo 1," *La Prensa*, 9 April 1955; "Destacados artistas actuarán en el Festival del 1ro. de mayo," *La Prensa*, 11 April 1955, 1. For more on merengue, Dominican popular culture, and Dominican migration to the United States, see Austerlitz, *Merengue*; Pacini Hernández, *Bachata*; Hoffnung-Garskof, *A Tale of Two Cities*; Manuel, *Creolizing Contradance*.

65. "Rock 'n' Roll, Calypso y Merengue," *La Prensa*, 24 April 1957, 1.

66. "Dice nuestra comunidad," *La Prensa*, 31 March 1957, 4.

67. For more on the history of the development of salsa music and the rise of ethnic identity in the 1970s, see "Enter Salsa: Some Like It Hot," *Time*, 5 May 1975, 56; Linda Bird Francke and Janet Huck, "The Hot New Sound of Salsa," *Newsweek*, 26 May 1975, 58; Boggs, *Salsiology*; Aparicio, *Listening to Salsa*; Loza, *Tito Puente*; Salazar, *Mambo Kingdom*; Haslip-Viera, "The Evolution of the Latino Community in New York City"; Flores, *From Bomba to Hip Hop*; Laó-Montes, "Mambo Montage"; Leymarie, *Cuban Fire*; Fernández, "The Course of U.S. Cuban Music: Margin and Mainstream"; Manuel, "Latin Music in the United States"; Fernández, *Afro-Cuban Rhythms*. For more

on rock 'n' roll and its influence on younger generations of Latino/as at midcentury, see Loza, *Barrio Rhythm*; García, *A World of Its Own*; Macías, *Mexican American Mojo*.

68. "Será Pro Fondo de Caridad de 'La Prensa,'" *La Prensa*, 2 May 1958, 5; "Se inician los preparativos del Festival Artístico de La Prensa," *La Prensa*, 3 October 1958, 5.

69. "Se añaden dos nuevas clasificaciones al certamen," *La Prensa*, 9 August 1958, 5; "El Escrutinio Final del Concurso de La Prensa Reveló Grandes Sorpresas," *La Prensa*, 6 October 1958, 5; "Resultado final del Concurso de Popularidad de Artistas," *La Prensa*, 23 November 1959, 22; "Crece el entusiasmo del público y de los artistas por el Festival," *La Prensa*, 13 November 1958, 5; *La Prensa*, 13 September 1959, 5; "Más artistas de nota se suman a nuestro Festival," *La Prensa*, 16 November, 1959, 5; "Programa," *La Prensa*, 16 November 1958, 1, 16; "Programa," *La Prensa*, 6 December 1959, 25.

70. "Crece el entusiasmo por el Concurso de Popularidad," *La Prensa*, 19 August 1958, 5; "Será el Sábado en el Palladium en el baile del Club Salinas," *La Prensa*, 4 September 1958, 5; "En el baile del Club España 7o. Escrutinio el Sábado," *La Prensa*, 24 September 1958, 5; "Escrutinio final en el baile del Ateneo Cubano, el Sábado," *La Prensa*, 2 October 1958, 5; "El Ateneo Cubano anunció final del escrutinio," *La Prensa*, 5 October 1958, 5.

71. "Concurso agota 'La Prensa' en los expendios," *La Prensa*, 22 August 1958, 5; "Crece el entusiasmo por el Concurso de Popularidad," *La Prensa*, 19 August 1958, 5; "El Ateneo Cubano anuncia final de Escrutinio," *La Prensa*, 5 October 1958, 5.

72. "Danzas Españolas y Ballet en Festival de La Prensa," *La Prensa*, 2 December 1959, 18; "El Festival Artístico Pro Fondo de Caridad de La Prensa," *La Prensa*, 6 December 1959, 5.

CHAPTER 5

1. Jack Gould, "Why Millions Love Lucy," *New York Times*, 1 March 1953, SM16. The show ranked number one in Nielsen ratings throughout its second, third, fourth, and sixth seasons.

2. Literary studies and cultural studies scholar Gustavo Pérez-Firmat offers the following clarification: "It's not that what he says is untrue—other sources confirm the veracity of his claims—but that all we are allowed is a partial portrait of the Cuban American artist." *Life on the Hyphen*, 71, 193.

3. Pérez-Firmat has described the show as "the great Cuban American love story. Essentially a chronicle of how a Cuban man and an American woman live together, this show is as fine an example as we have of the pleasures and perils of bicultural romance." *Life on the Hyphen*, 44, 65. For more on actor biographies and the production of *I Love Lucy*, see Arnaz, *A Book*; Harris, *Lucy & Desi*; Sanders and Gilbert, *Desilu*; Oppenheimer, *Laughs, Luck . . . and Lucy*.

4. Marco Rizo, "The Desi I Knew: The Music Man behind the Desi Arnaz Legend for over 50 Years," as told to C. David Younger, 1991, Box 5, Folder 6, MRP; Marco Rizo, interview with David Carp, 22 July 1993, DCC; "Radio: Sassafrassa, the Queen," *Time*, 26 May 1952.

5. Pérez, *Cuba: Between Reform and Revolution*, 251–275; Carr, "Mill Occupations and Soviets."

6. Rizo, "The Desi I Knew"; Rizo, interview with David Carp, 22 July 1993; "Radio: Sassafrassa, the Queen," *Time*, 26 May 1952; Octavio Siegle, "Los Alcaldes de Machado," *Gráfico*, 14 June 1930, 4, 14.

7. Arnaz, *A Book*, 13, 21–25; Pérez, *Cuba: Between Reform and Revolution*, 251–275. See also J. D. Phillips, "Soldiers Eject Officers: Enlisted Men Say Coup Was Aimed at Machado Followers in Regime," *New York Times*, 6 September 1933, 1.

8. Rayford Logan, "No Color Line Down in Cuba, Logan Finds," *Baltimore Afro-American*, 9 September 1933, 1. See also Pérez, *Cuba: Between Reform and Revolution*, 221–226; De la Fuente, *A Nation for All*, 71–91.

9. De la Fuente, *A Nation for All*, 92–93; Bronfman, *Measures of Equality*.

10. Moore, *Nationalizing Blackness*, 100, 104.

11. De la Fuente, *A Nation for All*, 93, 200–201.

12. Pérez, *Cuba: Between Reform and Revolution*, 266–275; Arnaz, *A Book*, 33; Rizo, "The Desi I Knew"; *Ecos de Nueva York*, 31 October 1954, 21; "Radio: Sassafrassa, the Queen," *Time*, 26 May 1952.

13. Arnaz, *A Book*, 32, 36, 40–41; "Radio: Sassafrassa, the Queen," *Time*, 26 May 1952.

14. Arnaz, *A Book*, 43; Rizo, "The Desi I Knew."

15. Arnaz, *A Book*, 44, 50–51, 69–74; "Radio: Sassafrassa, the Queen," *Time*, 26 May 1952.

16. Arnaz, *A Book*, 57, 59, 62–63; Roberts, *The Latin Tinge*, 78, 81–82.

17. Arnaz, *A Book*, 57, 59, 62–63.

18. Moore, *Nationalizing Blackness*, 64, 68, 72; Pérez Rodríguez, *El Carnaval Santiaguero*, 336–338, 384. Arnaz Sr.'s banning of congas is more than just ironic given that his son would soon make a name for himself popularizing his own version of the very performances he had prohibited.

19. Arnaz, *A Book*, 57, 59, 62–63.

20. *Billboard*, 5 October 1946, 37; *New York Times*, 8 July 1943, 22; "La Conga Op Turns Band Leader Again," *Billboard*, 23 December 1944, 24; Interview with Bobby Woodland and Freddie Scarett, WKCI, 1980s, Box 7, Folder 9, COC.

21. "Music: April Records," *Time*, 1 April 1940.

22. Pérez-Firmat, *Life on the Hyphen*, 53–56.

23. "Lucille Ball Married," *New York Times*, 1 December 1940, 63.

24. Theodore Strauss, "News of the Night Clubs," *New York Times*, 7 May 1939, X3; "News of the Night Clubs," *New York Times*, 7 April 1940, 124; "'Dance of Decorum' to Replace Rumba," *New York Times*, 29 August 1931, 10.

25. Arnaz, *A Book*, 135–137, 141–142; Roberts, *The Latin Tinge*, 108. See also Fein, "Everyday Forms of Collaboration."

26. Arnaz, *A Book*, 132–133; Ramírez Berg, *Latino Images in Film*, 66. See also Rodríguez, *Latin Looks*; Beltrán and Fojas, *Mixed Race Hollywood*.

27. Arnaz, *A Book*, 77, 141–142.

28. Pérez-Firmat, *Life on the Hyphen*, 72.

29. Arnaz, *A Book*, 161, 173; Rizo, "The Desi I Knew"; Rizo, interview with David Carp, 22 July 1993.

30. *Atlanta Daily World*, 21 May 1943, 3; *Baltimore Afro-American*, 22 May 1943, 10; "Uncle Sam Could Easily Do This," *Baltimore Afro-American*, 13 March 1943, 10; "Dead Film Stars in Resurrection," *Chicago Defender*, 30 January 1943, 18; "This Proves a Guy Is as Old as His Whiskers Even When a Star," *Chicago Defender*, 6 February 1943, 19.

31. For more on Latino/a participation in the U.S. armed forces during World War II, see Rivas-Rodríguez and Zamora, *Beyond the Latino World War II Hero*. For a very brief analysis of Arnaz's performance in the film, see Pérez-Firmat, *Life on the Hyphen*, 57–58.

32. *La Prensa*, 6 May 1932, 2.

33. "Desi Arnaz, Film Actor, in Army," *New York Times*, 28 April 1943, 20; "Radio: Sassafrassa, the Queen," *Time*, 26 May 1952; Arnaz, *A Book*, 10, 141, 146–147, 161.

34. Graciela Pérez, interview with Raúl A. Fernández and René López, 19 September 1998, Latino History Oral History Project, National Museum of American History; Machito, interview with Patricia Wilson Cryer, 20 January 1981, Box 7, Folder 5, COC; Graciela Pérez, interview with Max Salazar, 10 May 1985, DCC.

35. Machito, interview with Patricia Wilson Cryer, 20 January 1981; Machito interview, WKCI, 1980s, Box 7, Folder 9, COC.

36. José Curbelo, interview with David Carp, 3 October 1993, DCC; *Billboard*, 17 October 1942, 24.

37. Machito, interview with Patricia Wilson Cryer, 20 January 1981; Machito interview, WKCI, 1980s, Box 7, Folder 9, COC.

38. Ibid.

39. Machito interview, WKCI, 1980s, Box 7, Folder 9, COC; Machito, interview with Patricia Wilson Cryer, 20 January 1981.

40. See Moore, *Nationalizing Blackness*; De la Fuente, *A Nation for All*. See also chapter 1, note 68.

41. Isabelle Ortiz, "Machito A Living Legend," *Canales*, January 1979, Box 7, Folder 8, COC; Machito interview, WKCI, 1980s, Box 7, Folder 9, COC; Machito, interview with Patricia Wilson Cryer, 20 January 1981.

42. Ibid.

43. Rizo, "The Desi I Knew"; Arnaz, *A Book*, 99; *Billboard*, 2 March 1946, 24.

44. "Television: The New Tycoon," *Time*, 7 April 1958; Hazel Washington, "This Is Hollywood," *Chicago Defender*, 24 February 1958, A17; Arnaz, *A Book*, 199–200.

45. Sandra Joy, "La Semana en Hollywood," *La Prensa*, 27 November 1940, 5; "Nuevos Triunfos Conquista Desi Arnaz," *Diario de la Marina*, 2 February 1941, 22.

46. "La Guerra Ha Oscurecido la Gran Vía Blanca," *La Prensa*, 14 April 1943, 5.

47. "Exhibición privada de 'Too Many Girls' dio aquí la R.K.O.," *La Prensa*, 31 October 1940, 5; "Proyección especial en honor al actor cubano Desi Arnaz," *La Prensa*, 24 October 1940, 5.

48. "Enorme Entusiasmo por Asistir Mañana al Gran Festival Pro Fondo de Caridad," *La Prensa*, 25 May 1946, 1; *Billboard*, 25 May 1946, 53; "El Festival de 'La Prensa' para entregar los trofeos artísticos fue insuperable," *La Prensa*, 28 May 1946, 2.

49. "José Curbelo's First Job Was with Gilberto Valdés," *Latin Talk*, February 1951, JCP; Al Salerno, "Nightlife," *Brooklyn Eagle*, 27 September 1949, JCP; Dorothy Kilgallen, press clipping, 24 February 1950, JCP; John Ball, "Records for Pleasure," *New York World-Telegram*, 1 September 1948, JCP; Virginia Forbes, "Café Life in New York," *New York Sun*, 19 June 1945, JCP.

50. Raúl A. Fernández, Skype conversation with author, March 2013.

51. Arnaz, *A Book*, 161; Jack Rachman, "Desi, Band Acclaimed," Box 2, Folder 9, MRP.

52. Machito, interview with Patricia Wilson Cryer, 20 January 1981.

53. *Billboard*, 24 April 1948, 36; *Billboard*, 2 March 1946, 24; *Billboard*, 13 April 1946, 126; *Billboard*, 1 November 1947, 115; Pérez-Firmat, "Latunes: An Introduction"; Pérez-Firmat, *Life on the Hyphen*, 88.

54. Fernández, *Latin Jazz*, 52, 57.

55. Salazar, *Mambo Kingdom*, 45; Max Salazar, "Machito the Musician," *Latin Exchange*, Spring 1980, Box 7, Folder 5, COC.

56. "La Guerra Ha Oscurecido la Gran Vía Blanca," *La Prensa*, 14 April 1943, 5; Fausto, "La Gran Vía Blanca," *La Prensa*, 8 October 1940, 5; "La música latinoamericana es la más popular en el mundo," *Diario de Nueva York*, 13 March 1950, 2; Arnaz, *A Book*, 267.

57. Moore, *Nationalizing Blackness*, 137; Salazar, *Mambo Kingdom*, 42; "Margarita Lecuona en la coronación de Olga Primera," *La Prensa*, 7 May 1958, 5.

58. Armando Sánchez, interview with David Carp, 2 September 1992, DCC; Luis Miranda, interview with David Carp, 16 April 1994, DCC; Salazar, *Mambo Kingdom*.

59. "Miguelito Valdés: Sock Song Salesman of the Good Neighbor Policy," *Billboard*, 25 March 1945, 4; *Billboard*, 25 April 1942, 4; *Billboard*, 5 October 1946, 37.

60. Salazar, *Mambo Kingdom*, 43–45; "Valdés Quits Cugat as Offers Pour In," *Billboard*, 18 July 1942, 19; Alberto Socarrás, interview with Max Salazar, 16 January 1983, DCC; Nilo Curbelo, interview with David Carp, 3 October 1993, DCC; *Billboard*, 22 January 1949, 26; *Billboard*, 24 April 1948, 41.

61. "Se Comenta," *Pueblos Hispanos*, 20 March 1943, 6; "'Panamericana,' nueva película RKO de sabor hispana, en los Loews," *Nueva York al Diario*, 24 March 1945, 12; "Mirándolos Pasar," *Semanario Hispano*, 25 May 1946, 10; Miranda, interview with David Carp, 16 April 1994.

62. "Miguelito Valdés demora su viaje para cantar en el festival del 28," *La Prensa*, 24 March 1943, 3; "Unos dicen que es 'sex appeal,'" *La Prensa*, 28 October 1944, 5.

63. *La Prensa*, 30 April 1947, 4; *La Prensa*, 22 May 1947, 6; Bobby Quintero, "En Broadway," *Diario de Nueva York*, 5; "Noche Antilla hoy, en el Hunts Point Palace," *La Prensa*, 11 December 1948, 3; "Festival Antillano en el Hunts Point Palace," *Diario de Nueva York*, 11 December 1948, 7; *La Prensa*, 13 December 1948, 5; "En Broadway," *Diario de Nueva York*, 17 December 1948, 7; *La Prensa*, 5 March 1949, 5; "En Broadway," *Diario de Nueva York*, 24 March 1950, 5; "En Broadway," *Diario de Nueva York*, 13 September 1950, 6; "En Broadway," *La Prensa*, 23 April 1952, 5; *La Prensa*, 25 April 1952, 5; "En Palisades Park," *La Prensa*, 3 May 1952, 5; "Miguelito Valdés y la pareja de Raúl y Estrellita en el Festival de Mayo," *La Prensa*, 22 April 1953, 1; "En Broadway y en todas partes," *La Prensa*, 15 April 1954, 5; "En Broadway," *La Prensa*,

9 May 1955, 5; Babby Quintero, "En Broadway y en todas partes," *La Prensa*, 8 February 1956, 5; *Billboard*, 5 October 1946, 37.

64. Salazar, *Mambo Kingdom*, 39; Machito interview, WKCI, 1980s, Box 7, Folder 9, COC.

65. "Unos dicen que es 'sex appeal,'" *La Prensa*, 28 October 1944, 5; Armando Sánchez, interviews with David Carp, 19 September 1995 and 2 September 1992, DCC; Pérez, interview with Raúl A. Fernández and René López, 19 September 1998; Burgos, *Playing America's Game*, 4, 85–87, 96, 242.

66. Sánchez, interview with David Carp, 2 September 1992; Salazar, *Mambo Kingdom*, 39; "Notes from Mexico," *Atlanta Daily World*, 2 January 1955, 4.

67. *Billboard*, 24 April 1948, 20; *Billboard*, 17 January 1942, 20; "Miguelito Valdés Strand Hold-Over," *New York Amsterdam News*, 15 April 1950, 17; *La Prensa*, 1 October 1941, 5; "Vencedores del Concurso de Popularidad de 'La Prensa,'" *La Prensa*, 18 March 1943, 1–2; "Miguelito Valdés Huésped de Honor en el Baile, Hoy," *La Prensa*, 23 December 1944, 8; "Efectuarán mañana el sexto festival de la Benjamin Franklin," *La Prensa*, 14 March 1953, 6; *Billboard*, 5 October 1946, 37.

68. Arnaz, *A Book*, 164; Marco Rizo, interview with David Carp, 6 August 1993, DCC.

69. *Billboard*, 25 May 1946, 53; *Billboard*, 22 June 1946, 49.

70. *Billboard*, 29 October 1949, 52; Joe Conzo, interview with author, 20 March 2010.

71. Lumsden, *Machos, Maricones, and Gays*, 7, 30, 53, 217. See also Nesvig, "The Complicated Terrain of Latin American Homosexuality."

72. Ferrer, *Insurgent Cuba*, 126–127.

73. *I Love Lucy*, 19 November 1951, 4 February 1952, 25 February 1952, 12 May 1952, 6 October 1952, 24 November 1952, 29 December 1952, 22 June 1953, 5 October 1953, 9 May 1955, 26 November 1956.

74. *I Love Lucy*, 19 November 1951, 4 February 1952, 15 February 1954, 4 February 1957.

75. Arnaz, *A Book*, 307.

76. *I Love Lucy*, 3 December 1956.

77. Loza, *Tito Puente*, 55; Salazar, *Mambo Kingdom*, 88–89; "En Broadway," *Diario de Nueva York*, 24 December 1948, 6; Boggs, "The Palladium Ballroom and Other Venues," 127–128; Machito interview at home, ca. 1985, Box 4, Folder 14, COC.

78. Machito interview at home, ca. 1985, Box 4, Folder 14, COC; Loza, *Tito Puente*, 55–56; Federico Pagani interview, 1980s, Box 4, Folder 22, COC; Alberto Socarrás and Machito original materials, ca. 1979, Box 4, Folder 2, COC; Armando Peraza, interview with David Carp, 21 May 1993, DCC.

79. Loza, *Tito Puente*, 55–56; Salazar, *Mambo Kingdom*, 89; Pérez, interview with Raúl A. Fernández and René López, 19 September 1998.

80. *Billboard*, 19 July 1947, 27; Boggs, "The Palladium Ballroom and Other Venues," 129; Boggs, "Ernie Ensley," 147; Lenny Hambro interview, WKCI, 1980s, Box 7, Folder 9, COC; Ray Santos, interview with David Carp, 3 August 1992, DCC; *Billboard*, 27 November 1948, 42; *Billboard*, 8 January 1949, 35; Pérez-Firmat, *Life on the Hyphen*, 96.

81. Peraza, interview with David Carp, 21 May 1993; Ray Santos, interview with David Carp, 2 August 1993, DCC; Singer and Martínez, "A South Bronx Latin Music Tale," 184; Loza, *Tito Puente*, 222.

82. "Baile dedicado a Cuba en el Palladium Ballroom," *La Prensa*, 19 May 1951, 6; "En Broadway," *La Prensa*, 28 March 1952, 5; "Fiesta Cubana en el Palladium," *La Prensa*, 17 May 1952, 6; "Noche Cubana en el Palladium Ballroom," *La Prensa*, 20 May 1952, 5; "En Broadway," *La Prensa*, 12 May 1955, 5; *Pasatiempo*, 21 March 1951, 13.

83. Santos, interview with David Carp, 2 August 1993; "El Palladium regalará el domingo un 'set' de televisión," *La Prensa*, 12 April 1952, 5; "En Broadway," *La Prensa*, 30 April 1952, 5.

84. Arnaz, *A Book*, 174.

85. *I Love Lucy*, 17 December 1951.

86. Ibid., 8 December 1952, 5 October 1953, 26 April 1954.

87. Horacio Riambau, interview with David Carp, 1 December 1995, DCC; Babby Quintero, "En Broadway," *Diario de Nueva York*, 24 November 1948, 5; Babby Quintero, "En Broadway," *Diario de Nueva York*, 3 January 1949, 5; Santos, interview with David Carp, 2 August 1993. Manolo Alfaro achieved notoriety unrelated to the Tropicana in the late 1950s and early 1960s as the manager of Afro-Cuban boxer Benny "Kid" Paret. When Paret died on 3 April 1962 as the result of injuries sustained during a title bout against Emile Griffith, many news columnists and sportswriters charged that Alfaro could have done more to protect Paret both in and out of the ring. Instead, critics claimed, the restaurateur and promoter cared more about money than about the health and well-being of the young boxer he had recruited from the island. Paret met his Puerto Rican wife at the Tropicana, where she worked as a dancer in one of the floor shows. See Abreu, "The Story of Benny 'Kid' Paret."

88. Singer and Martínez, "A South Bronx Latin Music Tale," 192.

89. *La Prensa*, 31 May 1946, 5; *Diario de Nueva York*, 3 March 1950, 6; *Diario de Nueva York*, 31 March 1950, 5; *Diario de Nueva York*, 13 May 1950, 5; "En Broadway," *Diario de Nueva York*, 15 May 1950, 5; *Diario de Nueva York*, 8 September 1950, 6; *Diario de Nueva York*, 3 March 1951; *Diario de Nueva York*, 4 May 1951, 5; "En Broadway," *La Prensa*, 23 May 1951, 5.

90. *Diario de Nueva York*, 19 May 1950, 5; "Una Pareja de 'Mambo' fue la primera en inscribirse en el Palladium Ballroom," *Diario de Nueva York*, 5 September 1950, 2.

91. BDMM, 15 January 1952, Box 1, Folder 11, CCI; BDMM, 31 March 1952, Box 1, Folder 11, CCI; BDMM, 30 September 1952, Box 1, Folder 11, CCI.

92. *Diario de Nueva York*, 29 April 1949, 7; *La Prensa*, 24 May 1951, 6; Riambau, interview with David Carp, 1 December 1995; Singer and Martínez, "A South Bronx Latin Music Tale," 184.

93. Riambau, interview with David Carp, 1 December 1995; Santos, interview with David Carp, 2 August 1993.

94. "Premios en el 'Tropicana Club,'" *Diario de Nueva York*, 21 September 1950, 5.

95. In *teatro bufo*, the *negrito* played opposite the *gallego* (the Spanish immigrant from Galicia) and the *mulatta* (mixed-race woman). The *negrito* character typically reproduced racial stereotypes and played a central role as a singer and dancer in blackface performances. For more on *teatro bufo*, see Moore, *Nationalizing Blackness*, 41–61;

López, *Unbecoming Blackness*, 23–60; Kanellos, *A History of Hispanic Theatre in the United States*, 104–145.

96. "Charlando Tres Minutos con: Perucho Irigoyen," *Diario de Nueva York*, 25 May 1950, 5; "Manifiéstase gran interés en los locutores de radio y televisión," *La Prensa*, 22 March 1957, 1; "Brillantes locutores deleitan a los televidentes hispanos de N.Y.," *La Prensa*, 23 March 1957, 1; "Por los Teatros," *La Prensa*, 28 March 1947, 5; "Laurita y Rey, Perucho y Ramonita y León el domingo," *La Prensa*, 6 May 1949, 1; *Ecos de Nueva York*, 26 February 1950, 28; "Ecos de Broadway," *Ecos de Nueva York*, 22 August 1954, 23; "Ecos de Broadway," *Ecos de Nueva York*, 5 September 1954, 20; "'Botaron la pelota con el festival' opine Perucho," *La Prensa*, 23 May 1946, 2; Ángel M. Arroyo, "Magno Éxito del Festival de Caridad," *La Prensa*, 7 May 1957, 1; "Pasajes interesantes de Perucho Irigoyen," *La Prensa*, 17 November 1958, 5; "Ecos de Broadway," *Ecos de Nueva York*, 15 January 1956, 24.

97. "Perucho Irigoyen en N.Y. influido por la nostalgia," *La Prensa*, 10 April 1952, 3; "Charlando Tres Minutos con: Perucho Irigoyen," *Diario de Nueva York*, 25 May 1950, 5; "Rita Montaner, Pous, Bergaza y Perucho en el Programa Artístico del Manhattan," *La Prensa*, 27 April 1948, 1; "Celebrase ayer con todo splendor el Festival y Baile pro Caridad," *La Prensa*, 22 May 1950, 1; "Diego y Anita, y Oreste Menéndez en el Festival Artístico del domingo 18," *La Prensa*, 8 May 1952, 1.

98. Babby Quintero, "En Broadway," *Diario de Nueva York*, 24 November 1948, 5; "Homenaje a Irigoyen será un espectáculo excepcional," *Diario de Nueva York*, 21 June 1951, 5; "Homenaje a Perucho," *La Prensa*, 23 May 1958, 7; "Gran homenaje hoy en el 'Puerto Rico' a Perucho," *La Prensa*, 7 June 1958, 7.

99. "'Botaron la pelota con el festival' opine Perucho," *La Prensa*, 23 May 1946, 2; "Laurita y Rey, Perucho y Ramonita y León el domingo," *La Prensa*, 6 May 1949, 1; *La Prensa*, 27 March 1958, 4; "Charlando Tres Minutos con: Perucho Irigoyen," *Diario de Nueva York*, 25 May 1950, 5; "Perucho Irigoyen en N.Y. influido por la nostalgia," *La Prensa*, 10 April 1952, 3.

100. "Ecos de Broadway," *Ecos de Nueva York*, 5 September 1954, 20; "Concurso de 'Belleza,'" *Ecos de Nueva York*, 10 October 1954, 30.

101. *I Love Lucy*, 7 January 1952, 14 January 1952, 4 February 1952, 28 March 1955, 15 October 1956, 17 December 1956, 18 March 1957.

102. "Ilona Massey, Jon Hall Get Lead Roles in 'The Invisible Spy' at Universal," *New York Times*, 14 April 1942, 17; Thomas Brady, "Shooting Scripts by Uncle Sam," *New York Times*, 19 April 1942, X3; "Farley Described Tuberculosis Rise," *New York Times*, 19 May 1946, 44; "Actors' Temple Benefit," *New York Times*, 9 December 1949, 37; Brooks Atkinson, "Barrymore Comes to Town," *New York Times*, 11 February 1940, 127.

103. "Gran desfile de artistas en el Festival Pro Estudiantes el 5," *Diario de Nueva York*, 28 March 1950, 1; "Resultó muy lucido el festival de la Benjamin Franklin High School," *La Prensa*, 18 April 1951, 3; "Extraordinario programa artístico el domingo en la Benjamin Franklin," *La Prensa*, 11 March 1953, 5.

104. "Club Cultural Chileno," *Diario de Nueva York*, 14 March 1950, 6; "La Acción Cívica da un baile el domingo," *La Prensa*, 21 April 1954, 6.

105. "Housewives Give Dance," *Chicago Defender*, 11 June 1949, 8; "Two E. Harlem Block Councils to Hold Dance," *New York Amsterdam News*, 14 May 1949, 26.

106. *La Prensa*, 11 March 1953, 6; *La Prensa*, 14 March 1953, 6.

107. Electronic Army Serial Number Merged File, ca. 1938–1946, World War II Army Enlistment Records, National Archives and Records Administration, Washington, D.C.

108. Socarrás and Machito original materials, ca. 1979, Box 4, Folder 2, COC; Synopsis of *Machito: La Herencia del Jazz Latino*, Spanish, ca. 1985, Box 5, Folder 11, COC; Isabelle Ortiz, "Machito A Living Legend," *Canales*, January 1979, Box 7, Folder 8, COC; Machito, interview with Patricia Wilson Cryer, 20 January 1981; Pagani interview, 1980s, Box 4, Folder 22, COC; Machito interview at home, ca. 1985, Box 4, Folder 14, COC.

109. Paul M. Bruun, "Father Curbelo Plays Bass in Orchestra of Famous Son," *Miami Beach Sun Tropics*, 28 December 1944, 20, JCP; John Ball, "Records for Pleasure," *New York World-Telegram*, 1 September 1948, JCP; Virginia Forbes, "Café Life in New York," *New York Sun*, 19 June 1945, JCP.

CHAPTER 6

1. *I Love Lucy*, 26 November 1956.

2. Virginia Forbes, "Café Life in New York," *New York Sun*, 19 December 1949, JCP.

3. Mormino, *Land of Sunshine*, 25.

4. Bill Kennedy, "How the Rumba Got Started," *Miami Herald*, 28 April 1957, María Mendoza Kranz Papers, Cuban Heritage Collection, Otto Richter Library, University of Miami, Coral Gables, Florida (hereafter MMK); "Los Mendoza," *El Sol de Hialeah*, 13 April 1989, MMK; Miñuca Villaverde, "Antes del exilio, aquí ya se hablaba español," *El Nueva Herald*, 21 July 1996, 1, 2E, MMK; June Darichuk, "A Day to Remember—And How It Was," *Home News/Hialeah News/Las Noticias/Spring News*, 9 December 1982, 12, MMK.

5. Greenbaum, *More Than Black*, 58–60.

6. Miñuca Villaverde, "Antes del exilio, aquí ya se hablaba español," *El Nueva Herald*, 21 July 1996, 1, 2E, MMK; Rosendo, "Christmas Smoke."

7. Mormino, *Land of Sunshine*, 25.

8. Shell-Weiss, *Coming to Miami*, 103–105, 122. Despite the recruitment of Jews to Florida, discriminatory policies persisted well into the 1950s; one in five Miami Beach hotels barred Jews in 1953. See Mormino, *Land of Sunshine*, 96.

9. Pérez, *On Becoming Cuban*, 431–434. See the IPUMS sample for 1940.

10. Shell-Weiss, *Coming to Miami*, 124–129; Connolly, "By Eminent Domain," 9, 163–164; Mormino, *Land of Sunshine*, 25. See the IPUMS sample for 1950.

11. Pérez, *On Becoming Cuban*, 432–444. See also Mormino, *Land of Sunshine*, 282–284; Shell-Weiss, *Coming to Miami*, 104–105.

12. Pérez, *On Becoming Cuban*, 434–435; Connolly, "By Eminent Domain," 252–257; Dunn, *Black Miami*, 143–151.

13. Arenas, *Before Night Falls*, 31–32; Mary Lynn Conejo, interview with author, 9 April 2010.

14. Pérez, *On Becoming Cuban*, 501; Connolly, "By Eminent Domain," 211–212; Shell-Weiss, *Coming to Miami*, 152.

15. Connolly, "By Eminent Domain," 33, 163–164, 188, 204–205; Shell-Weiss, *Coming to Miami*, 155; Dunn, *Black Miami*. See the IPUMS sample for 1960. See also Burgos, *Playing America's Game*; Portes and Stepick, *City on the Edge*, 101; Tscheschlok, "'So Goes the Negro,'" 45; Winsberg, "Housing Segregation of a Predominantly Middle Class Population."

16. Mormino, *Land of Sunshine*, 17.

17. Paul D. Pérez, "Entrevistas Breves," *Diario las Américas*, 11 February 1954, 3; "Más Estudiantes Hispanos Hay Ahora en Dade County," *Diario las Américas*, 18 September 1956, 5. In late 1960, a map published in the *Miami Herald* showed that the largest concentrations of Latino/as could be found in the southwestern and northwestern parts of the city on both sides of the Miami River and along N.E. Second Avenue; Shell-Weiss, *Coming to Miami*, 154. See also Winsberg, "Housing Segregation of a Predominantly Middle Class Population," 408–409.

18. *Miami Latin News*, 11 August 1946, 1; *Diario las Américas*, 19 December 1953, 1; Shell-Weiss, *Coming to Miami*, 6, 132, 152–157.

19. *Miami Latin News*, 11 August 1946, 2, 7; "Mientras Miami Duerme Lo Vi . . . Y me Lo Contaron," *Miami Latin News*, 14 July 1946, 4; Miñuca Villaverde, "Antes del exilio, aquí ya se hablaba español," *El Nueva Herald*, 21 July 1996, 1, 2E, MMK.

20. *Diario las Américas*, 21 March 1954, 4; *Diario las Américas*, 29 December 1956, 4; *Diario las Américas*, 16 March 1957, 4; *Diario las Américas*, 21 April 1957, 4; *Diario las Américas*, 8 December 1957, 4; *Diario las Américas*, 10 December 1957, 6; *Diario las Américas*, 12 December 1957, 8.

21. *Diario las Américas*, 19 December 1953, 3; *Diario las Américas*, 29 December 1956, 4; *Diario las Américas*, 21 April 1957, 4; *Diario las Américas*, 6 October 1957, 8; *Diario las Américas*, 24 October 1957, 6; *Diario las Américas*, 10 December 1957, 6.

22. Manuel H. López, "Día de Reyes en Miami," *Diario las Américas*, 24 November 1956, 6. See also Pérez, *On Becoming Cuban*, 434–444, 501; Shell-Weiss, *Coming to Miami*, 153–155.

23. Connolly, "By Eminent Domain"; Mormino, *Land of Sunshine*, 308; "Miami a Showbiz Bust—So Far," *Billboard*, 12 January 1946, 33, 37.

24. Lary Solloway, "Stars over Miami," *New York Times*, 2 December 1956, XX4; C. E. Wright, "Seeing Stars," *New York Times*, 133; "New Show System at Miami Beach," *New York Times*, 2 November 1958, XX5. See also Revels, *Sunshine Paradise*, 2, 104; Mormino, *Land of Sunshine*.

25. "Xavier Cugat en festival de Westchester County el domingo próximo," *La Prensa*, 7 March 1941, 3; "En Broadway," *Diario de Nueva York*, 29 November 1948, 5; *Billboard*, 6 March 1948, 40; *Billboard*, 12 January 1946, 36; *Billboard*, 16 June 1951, 32; *Billboard*, 15 December 1951, 13; *Billboard*, 26 January 1952, 45; *Diario las Américas*, 4 February 1954, 3; Lary Solloway, "Stars Over Miami," *New York Times*, 2 December 1956, XX4; "New Show System at Miami Beach," *New York Times*, 2 November 1958, XX5.

26. *Miami Daily News*, 31 January 1948, JCP; *Miami Herald*, 30 December 1949, JCP; Paul M. Bruun, "Midnight Memos," 29 January 1950, JCP; *Miami Herald*, 3 De-

cember 1950, JCP; "José Curbelo's First Job Was with Gilberto Valdés," *Latin Talk*, February 1951, JCP; Paul M. Bruun, "Father Curbelo Plays Bass in Orchestra of Famous Son," *Miami Beach Sun Tropics*, 28 December 1944, 20, JCP; Press clipping, 16 July 1949, JCP; Jaime Taronji, "José Curbelo, en el Cabaret 'La Conga,'" *Nueva York al Día*, 28 August 1943, 1, JCP.

27. *Miami Latin News*, 7 July 1946, 5; *Miami Latin News*, 28 July 1946, 4; *Miami Latin News*, 11 August 1946, 6; *Diario las Américas*, 20 October 1956, 4; *Diario las Américas*, 26 October 1956, 6; *Diario las Américas*, 15 June 1957, 4.

28. Marcos Martínez, "Olga Chaviano La Reina del Mambo," *Diario las Américas*, 2 May 1954, 4.

29. Manuel H. López, "Día de Reyes en Miami," *Diario las Américas*, 24 November 1956, 6; *Miami Latin News*, 7 July 1946, 5; *Diario las Américas*, 5 October 1956, 4.

30. *Diario las Américas*, 29 December 1956, 4; *Diario las Américas*, 19 January 1957, 4; *Diario las Américas*, 15 February 1957, 5; *Diario las Américas*, 1 March 1957, 4; "Club Tropicana Rompe Marca de Popularidad," *Diario las Américas*, 5 March 1957, 4, 7.

31. *Diario las Américas*, 10 March 1957, 4; "Baile Mañana Sábado en el Tropicana Tiene Gran Sorpresa," *Diario las Américas*, 29 March 1957, 4; *Diario las Américas*, 13 April 1957, 4; *Diario las Américas*, 19 April 1957, 5; *Diario las Américas*, 25 May 1957, 4; "Club Tropicana," *Diario las Américas*, 27 April 1957, 4.

32. *Diario las Américas*, 25 May 1957, 4; "Tropicana Club," *Diario las Américas*, 5 June 1957, 4; *Diario las Américas*, 27 December 1957, 6.

33. *Diario las Américas*, 16 March 1957, 6.

34. "Celebrará Aniversario el Círculo Cubano de Miami," *Diario las Américas*, 9 May 1954, 7; *Diario las Américas*, 12 October 1956, 4; *Diario las Américas*, 27 October 1956, 4; *Diario las Américas*, 8 December 1956, 4.

35. "Gran entusiasmo para el baile del Círculo Cubano," *Diario las Américas*, 21 September 1956, 4; "Baile del Círculo Cubano," *Diario las Américas*, 6 October 1956, 4; *Diario las Américas*, 12 October 1956, 4; *Diario las Américas*, 15 December 1956, 4; *Diario las Américas*, 12 January 1957, 4; *Diario las Américas*, 23 March 1957, 4; *Diario las Américas*, 5 April 1957, 4; *Diario las Américas*, 19 April 1957, 5; *Diario las Américas*, 24 October 1957, 6; *Diario de las Américas*, 14 November 1957, 6; *Diario las Américas*, 14 December 1957, 6.

36. "Celebrará Aniversario el Círculo Cubano de Miami," *Diario las Américas*, 9 May 1954, 7; "Anuncia un grandioso baile el Círculo Cubano de Miami," *Diario las Américas*, 29 October 1954, 5; "Gran matinee bailable en el Círculo Cubano," *Diario las Américas*, 7 October 1956, 7; *Diario las Américas*, 7 February 1957, 4; *Diario las Américas*, 1 June 1957, 4; *Diario las Américas*, 23 March 1957, 4.

37. German Negroni, "Extraordinario homenaje a José Martí en Miami," *Diario las Américas*, 30 January 1957, 7.

38. Ibid.

39. German Negroni, "Cronica Gráfica de la Velada Martiana del Círculo Cubano," *Diario las Américas*, 3 February 1957.

40. *Diario las Américas*, 31 January 1957, 4; "Baile de fin de año en Juventud Cubana de Miami," *Diario las Américas*, 28 December 1956, 4; *Diario las Américas*, 28

December 1956, 4. Many of the club's events were free for members, though some required an entrance fee of $1 for club members, $1.50 for nonmember men, and $1 for nonmember women.

41. *Diario las Américas*, 5 October 1956, 4; *Diario las Américas*, 15 December 1956, 4; *Diario las Américas*, 7 December 1956, 4; *Diario las Américas*, 18 January 1957, 4; "Juventud Cubana de Miami," *Diario las Américas*, 4 October 1957, 4.

42. *Diario las Américas*, 27 October 1956, 4; *Diario las Américas*, 17 November 1956, 4; *Diario las Américas*, 18 November 1956, 4; *Diario las Américas*, 6 October 1957, 8; *Diario las Américas*, 9 October 1957, 4; *Diario las Américas*, 10 October 1957, 6; *Diario las Américas*, 12 October 1957, 4; *Diario las Américas*, 15 June 1957, 4.

43. "Gran Baile de Carnaval Ofrece el Sábado el Concurso Caribe," *Diario las Américas*, 26 February 1957, 4; "'Diario de Nueva York' destaca del progreso del 'Concurso Caribe,'" *Diario las Américas*, 1 March 1957, 4; "Baile de Carnaval Hoy en el Círculo Cubano de Miami," *Diario las Américas*, 2 March 1957, 4; "Proclamación de 'Miss Caribe' será mañana Sábado, Marzo 16," *Diario las Américas*, 15 March 1957, 4; "Hoy Sábado se proclamará con gran Pompa a 'Miss Caribe 1957,'" *Diario las Américas*, 16 March 1957, 4; "Baile del Tropicana de Mañana Sábado dedicado a 'Miss Caribe,'" *Diario las Américas*, 22 March 1957, 4; "Sociedades hispanas agasajan a la Reina," *La Prensa*, 5 April 1957, 3.

44. *Diario las Américas*, 12 July 1957, 4.

45. "Reina Hispana de Nueva York llega mañana a esta ciudad," *Diario las Américas*, 8 June 1957, 4; "Matinee Bailable," *Diario las Américas*, 9 June 1957, 4; *Diario las Américas*, 22 September 1957, 8.

46. "Nueva Directiva Fue Electa por Círculo Cubano de Miami," *Diario las Américas*, 6 December 1955, 4.

47. Ibid.; *Diario las Américas*, 26 November 1956, 4; *Diario las Américas*, 14 June 1957, 4; "Piloto Protesta de Acto de la Juventud Cubana," *Diario las Américas*, 10 October 1957, 4; Letter to the editor, *Diario las Américas*, 20 June 1957, 6.

48. René Viera, "La Caridad del Cobre en Miami," *Diario las Américas*, 9 September 1956, 4; *Diario las Américas*, 11 April 1957, 4; *Diario las Américas*, 10 March 1957, 4; *Diario de las Américas*, 5 May 1957, 4.

49. "Ante el busto de José Martí," *Diario las Américas*, 3 February 1954, 3; *Diario las Américas*, 9 October 1957, 4; Orovio, *Cuban Music*, 88.

50. *Diario las Américas*, 14 April 1957, 3; *Diario las Américas*, 6 October 1957, 8; *Diario las Américas*, 9 October 1957, 4; *Diario las Américas*, 10 October 1957, 6; *Diario las Américas*, 12 October 1957, 4.

51. "La Voz de Tampa," *Diario las Américas*, 23 March 1954, 7; "Carnaval Latino Americano," *Diario las Américas*, 26 March 1954, 4; Chichi Aloy, "Notas Sociales," *Diario las Américas*, 31 March 1954, 4.

52. *Diario las Américas*, 14 December 1957, 6.

53. *Diario las Américas*, 7 December 1956, 4; *Diario las Américas*, 8 December 1956, 4; *Diario las Américas*, 29 December 1956, 5; "Baile de Carnaval Hoy en el Círculo Cubano de Miami," *Diario las Américas*, 2 March 1957, 4.

54. "Como los esposos Ricardos se han ganado las simpatías de todo Miami," *Diario las Américas*, 14 July 1957, 8.

55. The phrase "of one bird the two wings" can be traced to "Cuba y Puerto Rico Son," a popular verse written by Puerto Rican poet and revolutionary Lola Rodríguez de Tío in 1893. German Negroni of *Diario las Américas* used the saying to dismiss the notion of strained relations between Cubans and Puerto Ricans.

56. German Negroni, "Expresan su Protesta a las Palabras de un Juez," *Diario las Américas*, 14 November 1956, 1.

57. Connolly, "By Eminent Domain," 210–212; Shell-Weiss, *Coming to Miami*, 149, 153–153.

58. Board of Directors Meeting Minutes, Miami Chamber of Commerce, 3 November 1941, Greater Miami Chamber of Commerce Collection, Historical Museum of Southern Florida, Miami, Florida (hereafter MCC).

59. "En Miami y La Habana se ha rendido simultáneamente un homenaje a la bandera," *Diario de la Marina*, 8 January 1946, 12.

60. "Numerosos cubanos celebran el 'Día de Cuba' en Miami," *La Prensa*, 7 September 1948, 5; *La Prensa*, 10 April 1951, 5; "Se estrechan los lazos culturales entre Miami e Iberoamérica," *Diario de Nueva York*, 22 May 1951, 3; Orovio, *Cuban Music*, 183–184.

61. Connolly, "By Eminent Domain," 198–199.

62. Board of Directors Meeting Minutes, Miami Chamber of Commerce, 19 September 1949, MCC.

63. Connolly, "By Eminent Domain," 204, 209, 212.

64. Ibid., 9, 197.

65. *Diario las Américas*, 6 December 1957, 9; "Exilados Cubanos Conmemoraron Muerte del Patriótica Gral. Maceo," *Diario las Américas*, 10 December 1957, 1, 6; *Diario las Américas*, 7 December 1957, 9; "Obreros Cubanos de la Arnold Co. conmemoraron aniversario de Maceo," *Diario las Américas*, 13 December 1957, 6.

66. "Miami Beach Boasts 'Afro-Cuban' Band," *Pittsburgh Courier*, 19 January 1946, 22.

67. Enoc P. Waters, "Dixie Hotel Rule Admits Cuban Ork Leader but Bars his Wife, Men," *Chicago Defender*, 9 February 1946, 16; Dunn, *Black Miami*, 81.

68. Mario Bauzá, interview with Ruth Glasser, 19 April 1989, RG/PRM; Mario Bauzá, interview with David Carp, 18 April 1991, DCC. Bauzá likely traveled through Miami on the "colored" circuit when he performed with Chick Webb and Cab Calloway before starting his band with Machito. See Connolly, "By Eminent Domain," 252–257; Dunn, *Black Miami*, 143–151.

69. Connolly, "By Eminent Domain," 205–206; Shell-Weiss, *Coming to Miami*, 155.

70. Graciela Pérez, interview with Raúl A. Fernández and René López, 19 September 1998, Latino History Oral History Project, National Museum of American History.

71. Enoc P. Waters, "Dixie Hotel Rule Admits Cuban Ork Leader But Bars His Wife, Men," *Chicago Defender*, 9 February 1946, 16.

72. Ibid.

73. Armando Sánchez, interview with David Carp, 19 September 1995, DCC.

74. *Diario las Américas*, 27 April 1957, 7.

75. Herbert L. Matthews, "Cuban Rebel Is Visited in Hideout," *New York Times*, 24 February 1957, 1; "Stories on Rebel Fiction, Cuba Says," *New York Times*, 28 February

1957, 13; "Cuban Navy Men Revolt," *New York Times*, 6 September 1957, 1; Herbert L. Matthews, "Castro Rebels Gain in Face of Offensive by the Cuban Army," *New York Times*, 9 June 1957, 1.

76. *Diario las Américas*, 27 April 1957, 7; *Diario las Américas*, 12 May 1957, 7.

77. Shell-Weiss, *Coming to Miami*, 153; Joseph Rosendo, interview with author, 15 May 2012; Conejo, interview with author, 9 April 2010; René Viera, "Inusitado actividad desplegaron los políticos cubanos este fin de semana," *Diario las Américas*, 21 May 1957, 1.

78. *Diario las Américas*, 23 May 1957, 7.

79. Guerra, *The Myth of José Martí*, 1–21.

80. José A. Benítez, "Buscan cooperación de los exilados cubanos," *La Prensa*, 26 March 1957, 2; "Club 26 de Julio de Miami, A la Opinión Pública," *Diario las Américas*, 28 May 1957, 7; "A la Opinión Pública," *Diario las Américas*, 31 May 1957, 9; "A Todos los Cubanos, Carta Abierta," *Diario las Américas*, 4 June 1957, 3.

81. *Diario las Américas*, 29 June 1957, 5; "Policía de Miami disolvió manifestación de Cubanos," *Diario las Américas*, 1 June 1957, 1, 7.

82. "Llegan hoy Lucy y Desi," *Diario las Américas*, 26 November 1956, 4; German Negroni, "Miami y Cuba Rinden homenaje a Desi Arnaz y Lucille Ball," *Diario las Américas*, 27 November 1956, 5; "Cuba Condecoró a los Arnaz," *Diario las Américas*, 27 November 1956, 5; German Negroni, "Cuba les Rinde Homenaje: Los Arnaz Lloran," *Diario las Americias*, 28 November 1956, 1, 5; "Top Cuban Prize to 'I Love Lucy,'" *Chicago Defender*, 28 November 1956, 14.

83. "Llegan hoy Lucy y Desi," *Diario las Américas*, 26 November 1956, 4; German Negroni, "Miami y Cuba Rinden homenaje a Desi Arnaz y Lucille Ball," *Diario las Américas*, 27 November 1956, 5.

CONCLUSION

1. Portes, "The Cuban-American Political Machine," 198–199; Portes and Stepick, *City on the Edge*, 107, 135, 142–144.

2. García, "Contesting that Damned Mambo," 196.

3. Daniel E. Slotnik, "José Curbelo, Manager Behind Latin Music Acts, Dies at 95," *New York Times*, 21 September 2012.

4. García, "Contesting that Damned Mambo," 196.

5. For more on the kinds of exile organizations that developed in Miami after 1960, see García, "Hardliners v. 'Dialogueros'"; Torres, *In the Land of Mirrors*.

6. Manuel Roig Franzia, "Marco Rubio's Compelling Family Story Embellishes Facts, Documents Show," *Washington Post*, 20 October 2011.

7. Michael D. Shear, "Rubio Denies Embellishing Family History," *New York Times*, 20 October 2011; Marc Caputo, "Marco Rubio Defends Himself Amid Family Exile Saga," *Miami Herald*, 21 October 2011; Manuel Roig Franzia, "Marco Rubio's Compelling Family Story Embellishes Facts, Documents Show," *Washington Post*, 20 October 2011.

8. Marc Caputo, "Marco Rubio Defends Himself amid Family Exile Saga," *Miami Herald*, 21 October 2011; Rubio, "Marco Rubio: My Family's Flight from Castro."

9. García, *Havana USA*, 84.

10. Manuel Roig Franzia, "Marco Rubio's Compelling Family Story Embellishes Facts, Documents Show," *Washington Post*, 20 October 2011; Fred Grimm, "Marco Rubio's Biography Didn't Need Fudging," *Miami Herald*, 24 October, 2011.

11. Michael Hainey, "All Eyez on Him," *GQ*, December 2012.

12. Adam Martin, "Marco Rubio Insists He Likes Pitbull Just Fine," *New York*, 19 November 2012.

13. "Marco Rubio Filibusters with Jay-Z, Wiz Khalifa Quotes," *New York*, 7 March 2013.

14. Bell, "Marco Rubio: Jay-Z Needs to Get Informed on Cuba."

15. "Pitbull 'Open Letter' Released."

Bibliography

ARCHIVAL COLLECTIONS

Centro de Estudios Puertorriqueños, Hunter College, City University of New York,
New York, New York
    Carlos Ortiz Collection
    Jesús Colón Collection
Cuban Heritage Collection, Otto Richter Library, University of Miami, Coral Gables,
Florida
    José Curbelo Papers
    María Mendoza Kranz Papers
Historical Museum of Southern Florida, Miami, Florida
    Greater Miami Chamber of Commerce Collection
Integrated Public Use Microdata Series
    1900, 1910, 1920, 1930, 1940, 1950, and 1960, www.ipums.umn.edu
National Archives and Records Administration, Washington, D.C.
    Electronic Army Serial Number Merged File, ca. 1938–1946
New York Public Library for the Performing Arts, New York, New York
    Marco Rizo Papers
Private Collection of Vilma Rizo, New York, New York
Schomburg Center for Research in Black Culture, New York Public Library,
New York, New York
    Club Cubano Inter-Americano Papers

INTERVIEWS

Álvarez Guedes, Guillermo. Interview by Julio Estorino. Recorded by Javier
Carrion. Video recording. 28 January 2012. Luis J. Botifoll Oral History Project.
Cuban Heritage Collection. University of Miami, Coral Gables, Florida.
Pérez, Graciela. Interview by Raúl A. Fernández and René López. Engineered by
Matt Watson. Sound recording. 19 September 1998. Latino History Oral History
Project, National Museum of American History.

The following interviews were conducted by the author. Recordings and/or notes are
currently in the author's possession.
    Conejo, Mary Lynn. Telephone interview. 23 January 2010.
    Conejo, Mary Lynn. 9 April 2010. Orlando, Florida.
    Conzo, Joe. Telephone interview. 23 September 2009.
    Conzo, Joe. 20 March 2010. Bronx, New York.
    Fernández, Raúl A. Skype conversation. March 2013.

Gantz, Sarita. 13 April 2010. West Palm Beach, Florida.
Rizo, Vilma. 28 September 2009. New York, New York.
Rosendo, Joseph. Telephone interview. 15 May 2012.

The following interviews are held in the Ruth Glasser/Puerto Rican Musicians Collection, Centro de Estudios Puertorriqueños, Hunter College, City University of New York, New York, New York.

Bauzá, Mario. Interviewed by Ruth Glasser. 19 April 1989.
Bauzá, Mario. Interviewed by Ruth Glasser. 2 June 1989.

The following interviews are held in the David Carp Collection of Latin Jazz, Bronx County Historical Society, Bronx, New York.

Bauzá, Mario. Interviewed by David Carp. 8 February 1989, 18 April 1991.
Curbelo, Fausto. Interviewed by David Carp. No date given.
Curbelo, José. Interviewed by David Carp. 3 October 1993.
Curbelo, Nilo. Interviewed by David Carp. 3 October 1993.
Grillo, Mario. Interviewed by Paul Austerlitz. 28 August 1998.
Miranda, Luis. Interviewed by David Carp. 16 April 1994.
O'Farrill, Arturo "Chico." Interviewed by David Carp. 31 July 1991.
Peraza, Armando. Interviewed by David Carp. 21 May 1993.
Pérez, Graciela. Interviewed by Max Salazar. 10 May 1985.
Riambau, Horacio. Interviewed by David Carp. 1 December 1995.
Rizo, Marco. Interviewed by David Carp. 22 July 1993, 6 August 1993.
Sánchez, Armando. Interviewed by David Carp. 2 September 1992, 19 September 1995.
Santos, Ray. Interviewed by David Carp. 5 August 1991, 3 August 1992, 2 August 1993, 8 August 1995.
Socarrás, Alberto. Interviewed by Max Salazar. 16 January 1983.
Sullivan Niles, Sugar, and Sonny Allen. Interviewed by David Carp. 14 April 1993.

NEWSPAPERS AND PERIODICALS

Amsterdam Star-News (New York)
Atlanta Daily World
Baltimore Afro-American
Billboard
Chicago Defender
Diario de la Marina (Havana)
Diario de Nueva York
Diario las Américas (Miami)
Ecos de Nueva York
GQ
Gráfico (New York)
La Prensa (New York)

Liberación (New York)

Los Angeles Sentinel

Los Angeles Times

Miami Herald

Miami Latin News

Mundo Latino (New York)

Newsweek

New York

New York Amsterdam News

New York Times

New York Times Magazine

Norwood News (Bronx, New York)

Pasatiempo (New York)

Pittsburgh Courier

Pueblos Hispanos (New York)

Semanario Hispano (New York)

Time

Tropicana Internacional (Havana)

Washington Post

OTHER PRIMARY SOURCES

Bell, Benjamin. "Marco Rubio: Jay-Z Needs to Get Informed on Cuba." ABCNews, 14 April 2013. http://abcnews.go.com/m/blogEntry?id=18951567&sid=77&cid=77. Accessed 9 June 2013.

"'Pitbull Open Letter' Released: Rapper Responds to Jay-Z, Marc Rubio." The Hollywood Gossip. 15 April 2013. http://www.thehollywoodgossip.com/2013/04/pitbull-open-letter-track-released-rapper-responds-to-jay-z-marc/. Accessed 9 June 2013.

Rosendo, Joseph. "Christmas Smoke." Joseph Rosendo's Travelscope. 20 December 2011. http://travelscope.net/blog/view_post/christmas_smoke/. Accessed 15 May 2012.

Rubio, Marco. "Marco Rubio: My Family's Flight from Castro." Politico, 21 October 2011. http://www.politico.com/news/stories/1011/66567.html. Accessed 9 June 2013.

SECONDARY SOURCES

Abreu, Christina D. "Celebrity, 'Crossover,' and Cubanidad: Celia Cruz as 'La Reina de Salsa.'" *Latin American Music Review* 28, no. 1 (2007): 94–124.

———. "The Story of Benny 'Kid' Paret: Boxing, U.S.-Cuba Relations, and U.S. Media Representations, 1959–1962." *Journal of Sport History* 38, no. 1 (2011): 401–419.

Ackerman, Holly, and Juan M. Clark. *The Cuban Balseros: Voyages of Uncertainty.* Miami: Policy Center of the Cuban American National Council, 1995.

Adorno, Theodor. "Culture Industry Revisited." *New German Critique* 6 (Autumn 1975):12–19.

Ameringer, Charles D. *The Cuban Democratic Experience: The Auténtico Years, 1944-1951*. Gainesville: University Press of Florida, 2000.

Anderson, Benedict. *Imagined Communities: Reflections on the Origin and Spread of Nationalism*. New York: Verso Press, 1991.

Anzaldúa, Gloria. *Borderlands/La Frontera: The New Mestiza*. San Francisco: Spinster/Aunt Lute Books, 1987.

Aparicio, Frances. "'Así Son': Salsa Music, Female Narratives, and Gender (De) Construction in Puerto Rico." In *Daughters of Caliban: Caribbean Women in the Twentieth Century*, ed. Consuelo López Springfield, 259-284. Bloomington: Indiana University Press, 1997.

———. "The Blackness of Sugar: Celia Cruz and the Performance of (Trans) Nationalism." *Cultural Studies* 13, no. 2 (1999): 223-236.

———. "La Lupe, La India, and Celia: Toward a Feminist Genealogy of Salsa Music." In *Disciplines on the Line: Feminist Research on Spanish, Latin American, and U.S. Latina Women*, ed. Anne J. Cruz, Rosilie Hernández-Pecoraro, and Joyce Tolliver, 37-57. Newark, Delaware: Juan de la Cuesta-Hispanic Monographs, 2003.

———. *Listening to Salsa: Gender, Latin Popular Music, and Puerto Rican Cultures*. Hanover: University of New Hampshire Press, 1998.

Appadurai, Arjun. "Global Ethnoscapes: Notes and Queries for a Transnational Anthropology." In *Recapturing Anthropology: Working in the Present*, ed. Richard G. Fox, 191-210. Santa Fe, N.M.: School of American Research Press, 1991.

Arenas, Reinaldo. *Before Night Falls: A Memoir*. New York: Penguin Books, 1993.

Argote-Freyre, Frank. *Fulgencio Batista: From Revolutionary to Strongman*. New Brunswick, N.J.: Rutgers University Press, 2006.

Arnaz, Desi. *A Book*. New York: Morrow, 1976.

Arrizón, Alicia. *Queering Mestizaje: Transculturation and Performance*. Ann Arbor: University of Michigan Press, 2006.

Arsenault, Raymond, and Gary R. Mormino. "From Dixieland to Dreamland: Demographic and Cultural Change in Florida, 1880-1980." In *Shades of the Sunbelt: Essays on Ethnicity, Race, and the Urban South*, ed. Randall M. Miller and George E. Pozzetta, 161-191. Gainesville: University Press of Florida, 1988.

Austerlitz, Paul. *Merengue: Dominican Music and Dominican Identity*. Philadelphia: Temple University Press, 1997.

Baughman, James L. *Same Time, Same Situation: Creating American Television, 1948-1961*. Baltimore, Md.: Johns Hopkins University Press, 2007.

Beer, Amy Barnes. "From Bronx to Brooklyn: Spanish-language Movie Theaters and Their Audiences in New York City, 1930-1999." PhD diss., Northwestern University, 2001.

Belnap, Jeffrey, and Raúl A. Fernández, eds. *José Martí's "Our America": From National to Hemispheric Cultural Studies*. Durham, N.C.: Duke University Press, 1998.

Beltrán, Mary C. *Latina/o Stars in U.S. Eyes: The Making and Meanings of Film TV Stardom*. Champaign: University of Illinois Press, 2009.

Beltrán, Mary C., and Camilla Fojas, eds. *Mixed Race Hollywood*. New York: New York University Press, 2008.

Betancourt, Enrique C. *Apuntes para la Historia: Radio, Televisión y Farándula de la Cuba de Ayer*. San Juan, Puerto Rico: Ediciones Universal, 1986.

Bettelheim, Judith, Barbara Bridges, and Dolores Yonker. "Festivals in Cuba, Haiti, and New Orleans." In *Caribbean Festival Arts: Each and Every Bit of Difference*, ed. John W. Nunley and Judith Bettelheim, 137–164. Seattle: University of Washington Press, 1988.

Biondi, Martha. *To Stand and Fight: The Struggle for Civil Rights in Postwar New York City*. Cambridge, Mass.: Harvard University Press, 2003.

Boggs, Vernon W. "Al Santiago: Alegre Superstar." In *Salsiology: Afro-Cuban Music and the Evolution of Salsa in New York City*, ed. Vernon W. Boggs, 201–228. New York: Greenwood Press, 1992.

——. "Ernie Ensley, Palladium Mambero." In *Salsiology: Afro-Cuban Music and the Evolution of Salsa in New York City*, ed. Vernon W. Boggs, 143–154. New York: Greenwood Press, 1992.

——. "Founding Fathers and Changes in Cuban Music called Salsa." In *Salsiology: Afro-Cuban Music and the Evolution of Salsa in New York City*, ed. Vernon W. Boggs, 95–106. New York: Greenwood Press, 1992.

——. "The Palladium Ballroom and Other Venues: Showcases for Latin Music in N.Y.C." In *Salsiology: Afro-Cuban Music and the Evolution of Salsa in New York City*, ed. Vernon W. Boggs, 125–132. New York: Greenwood Press, 1992.

——. "Salsa Music: The Latent Function of Slavery and Racialism." In *Salsiology: Afro-Cuban Music and the Evolution of Salsa in New York City*, ed. Vernon W. Boggs, 353–359. New York: Greenwood Press, 1992.

——. *Salsiology: Afro-Cuban Music and the Evolution of Salsa in New York City*. New York: Greenwood Press, 1992.

Briggs, Laura, Gladys McCormick, and J. T. Way. "Transnationalism: A Category of Analysis." *American Quarterly* 60, no. 3 (2008): 625–648.

Brock, Lisa, and Digna Castañeda Fuertes, eds. *Between Race and Empire: African Americans and Cubans before the Cuban Revolution*. Philadelphia: Temple University Press, 1998.

Bronfman, Alejandra. *Measures of Equality: Social Science, Citizenship, and Race in Cuba, 1902–1940*. Chapel Hill: University of North Carolina Press, 2002.

Burgos, Adrian, Jr. "'The Latins from Manhattan': Confronting Race and Building Community in Jim Crow Baseball, 1906–1950." In *Mambo Montage: The Latinization of New York*, ed. Agustín Laó-Montes and Arlene Dávila, 57–72. New York: Columbia University Press, 2001.

——. *Playing America's Game: Baseball, Latinos, and the Color Line*. Berkeley: University of California Press, 2007.

Burns, Eric. *Invasion of the Mind Snatchers: Television's Conquest of America in the Fifties*. Philadelphia: Temple University Press, 2010.

Bush, Gregory W. "'Playground U.S.A.': Miami and the Promotion of Spectacle." *Pacific Historical Review* 68, no 2 (1999): 153–172.

——. "'We Must Picture an Octopus': Anticommunism, Desegregation, and Local News in Miami, 1945–1960." *Tequesta* 65 (2005): 48–63.

Capó, Julio, Jr. "Cuban Culture in New York City: American Labor Unions and the Changing Face of Entertainment, 1939–1945." Paper presented at the annual meeting of the Florida Conference of Historians, Florida Gulf Coast University, Fort Myers, Florida, 27–28 February 2009.

———. "Queering Mariel: Mediating Cold War Foreign Policy and U.S. Citizenship among Cuba's Homosexual Exile Community, 1978–1994." *Journal of American Ethnic History* 29, no. 4 (2010): 78–106.

Carini, Susan M. "Love's Labors Almost Lost: Managing Crisis during the Reign of 'I Love Lucy.'" *Cinema Journal* 43, no. 1 (2003): 44–62.

Carney, James J. "Population Growth in Miami and Dade County, Florida." *Tequesta* 6 (1946): 50–55.

Carr, Barry. "Mill Occupations and Soviets: The Mobilisation of Sugar Workers in Cuba 1917–1933." *Journal of Latin American Studies* 28, no. 1 (1996): 129–158.

Castro, Alicia. *Queens of Havana: The Amazing Adventures of Anacaona, Cuba's Legendary All-Girl Dance Band.* New York: Grove Press, 2007.

Chartier, Roger. "Texts, Printing, Readings." In *The New Cultural History: Essays*, ed. Aletta Biersack and Lynn Avery Hunt, 154–175. Berkeley: University of California Press, 1989.

Clark, Juan M. "The Exodus from Revolutionary Cuba (1959–1974): A Sociological Analysis." PhD diss., University of Florida, 1975.

Cohen, Lizabeth. *A Consumers' Republic: The Politics of Mass Consumption in Postwar America.* New York: Vintage Books, 2003.

———. "Encountering Mass Culture at the Grassroots: The Experience of Chicago Workers in the 1920s." *American Quarterly* 41, no. 1 (1989): 6–33.

Conde, Yvonne M. *Operation Pedro Pan: The Untold Exodus of 14,048 Cuban Children.* New York: Routledge, 1999.

Connolly, Nathan Daniel Beau. "By Eminent Domain: Race and Capital in the Building of an American South Florida." PhD diss., University of Michigan, 2008.

Cook, James W. "The Return of the Culture Industry." In *The Cultural Turn in U.S. History: Past, Present, Future*, ed. James W. Cook, Lawrence Glickman, and Michael O'Malley, 291–318. Chicago: University of Chicago Press, 2009.

Cook, James W., and Lawrence Glickman. "Twelve Propositions for a History of U.S. Cultural History." In *The Cultural Turn in U.S. History: Past, Present, Future*, ed. James W. Cook, Lawrence Glickman, and Michael O'Malley, 3–58. Chicago: University of Chicago Press, 2009.

Croucher, Sheila L. "Ethnic Inventions: Constructing and Deconstructing Miami's Culture Clash." *Pacific Historical Review* 68, no. 2 (1999): 233–251.

Cruz, Celia, and Ana Cristina Reymundo. *Celia: My Life.* New York: HarperCollins Publishers, 2004.

Cushman, Gregory T. "¿De qué color es el oro? Race, Environment, and the History of Cuban National Music, 1898–1958." *Latin American Music Review* 26, no. 2 (2005): 164–194.

Dávila, Arlene. *Latinos, Inc. The Marketing and Making of a People.* Berkeley: University of California Press, 2001.

———. *Latino Spin: Public Image and the Whitewashing of Race.* New York: New York University Press, 2008.

De la Fuente, Alejandro. *A Nation for All: Race, Inequality, and Politics in Twentieth-Century Cuba.* Chapel Hill: University of North Carolina Press, 2000.

DePalma, Anthony. *The Man Who Invented Fidel: Castro, Cuba, and Herbert L. Matthews of the New York Times.* New York: Public Affairs, 2007.

Díaz, María Elena. *The Virgin, the King, and the Royal Slaves of El Cobre: Negotiating Freedom in Colonial Cuba, 1670–1780.* Stanford, Calif.: Stanford University Press, 2001.

Díaz Ayala, Cristóbal. *Cuando Salí de la Habana, 1898–1997: Cien Años de Música Cubana por el Mundo.* San Juan, Puerto Rico: Fundación Musicalia, 1998.

Dolan, Jay P., and Jaime R. Vidal, eds. *Puerto Rican and Cuban Catholics in the U.S., 1900–1965.* Notre Dame, Ind.: Notre Dame University Press, 1994.

Douglas, Susan. *Listening In: Radio and American Imagination.* Minneapolis: University of Minnesota Press, 1999.

Duany, Jorge. *The Puerto Rican Nation on the Move: Identities on the Island and in the United States.* Chapel Hill: University of North Carolina Press, 2002.

———. "Reconstructing Racial Identity: Ethnicity, Color, and Class among Dominicans in the United States and Puerto Rico." *Latin American Perspectives* 25, no. 3 (1998): 147–172.

Dunn, Marvin. *Black Miami in the Twentieth Century.* Gainesville: University Press of Florida, 1997.

Dzidzienyo, Anani, and Suzanne Oboler, eds. *Neither Enemies nor Friends: Latinos, Blacks, Afro-Latinos.* New York: Palgrave Macmillan, 2005.

Eckstein, Susan. *The Immigrant Divide: How Cuban Americans Changed the U.S. and Their Homeland.* New York: Routledge, 2009.

———. "The Transformation of the Diaspora and the Transformation of Cuba." In *Changes in Cuban Society since the Nineties*, ed. Joseph Tulchin, Lilia Bodea, Mayra P. Espino Prieto, and Rafael Hernández with Elizabeth Bryan, 207–230. Washington, D.C.: Woodrow Wilson Center for Scholars, 2005.

Eckstein, Susan, and Lorena Barberia. "Grounding Immigrant Generations in History: Cuban Americans and Their Transnational Ties." *International Migration Review* 46, no. 3 (2002): 799–837.

Escobedo, Elizabeth R. *From Coveralls to Zoot Suits: The Lives of Mexican American Women on the World War II Home Front.* Chapel Hill: University of North Carolina Press, 2013.

Fein, Seth. "Everyday Forms of Collaboration: U.S. Film Propaganda in Cold War Mexico." In *Close Encounters of Empire: Writing the Cultural History of U.S. Latin American Relations*, ed. Gilbert M. Joseph, Catherine LeGrand, and Ricardo D. Salvatore, 400–450. Durham, N.C.: Duke University Press, 1998.

———. "Hollywood and United States-Mexico Relations in the Golden Age of Mexican Cinema." PhD diss., University of Texas at Austin, 1996.

Fernández, Lilia. *Brown in the Windy City: Mexicans and Puerto Ricans in Postwar Chicago.* Chicago: University of Chicago Press, 2012.

Fernández, Raúl A. "The Course of U.S. Cuban Music: Margin and Mainstream."
    Cuban Studies 24 (January 1995): 105–122.

———. *From Afro-Cuban Rhythms to Latin Jazz*. Berkeley: University of California
    Press, 2006.

———. *Latin Jazz: The Perfect Combination/La Combinación Perfecta*. San
    Francisco: Chronicle Books, 2002.

Ferrer, Ada. *Insurgent Cuba: Race, Nation, and Revolution, 1868–1898*. Chapel Hill:
    University of North Carolina Press, 1999.

Figueroa, Frank M. *Machito and His Afro-Cubans*. Oldsmar, Florida: Pillar
    Publications, 2007.

Fletcher, Tony. *All Hopped Up and Ready to Go: Music from the Streets of New York
    1927–77*. New York: W.W. Norton & Company, 2009.

Flores, Juan. *From Bomba to Hip Hop: Puerto Rican Culture and Latino Identity*.
    New York: Columbia University Press, 2000.

Foner, Philip S. *Antonio Maceo: The "Bronze Titan" of Cuba's Struggle for Indepen-
    dence*. New York: Monthly Review Press, 1977.

Font, Mauricio A., and Alfonso W. Quiroz, eds. *The Cuban Republic and José Martí:
    Reception and Use of a National Symbol*. Lanham, Md.: Lexington Books, 2006.

Forman, Murray. "'One Night on TV Is Worth Weeks at the Paramount': Musicians
    and Opportunity in Early Television, 1948–1955." *Popular Music* 21, no. 3 (2002):
    249–276.

Foster, Mark D. "In the Face of 'Jim Crow': Prosperous Blacks and Vacations, Travel and
    Outdoor Leisure, 1890–1945." *Journal of Negro History* 84, no. 2 (1999): 130–149.

Fox, Claire F. *Making Art Panamerican: Cultural Policy and the Cold War*.
    Minneapolis: University of Minnesota Press, 2013.

Franco, José Luciano. *Antonio Maceo: Apuntes para una historia de su vida*.
    Havana, Cuba: Editorial de Ciencias Sociales, 1989.

Fuentes, Leonardo Padura. *Los Rostros de la Salsa*. Havana, Cuba: Ediciones Unión,
    1997.

Gabaccia, Donna R. "Is Everywhere Nowhere? Nomads, Nations, and the
    Immigrant Paradigm of United States History." *Journal of American History* 86,
    no. 3 (1999): 1115–1134.

Gallagher, John, and Ronald Robinson. "The Imperialism of Free Trade." *Economic
    History Review* 6, no. 1 (1953): 1–15.

García, David F. *Arsenio Rodríguez and the Transnational Flows of Latin Popular
    Music*. Philadelphia: Temple University Press, 2006.

———. "Contesting that Damned Mambo: Arsenio Rodríguez and the People of
    El Barrio and the Bronx in the 1950s." In *The Afro-Latin@ Reader: History and
    Culture in the United States*, ed. Miriam Jiménez Román and Juan Flores,
    187–198. Durham, N.C.: Duke University Press, 2010.

García, María Cristina. "Hardliners v. 'Dialogueros': Cuban Exile Political Groups and
    United States-Cuba Policy." *Journal of American Ethnic History* 17, no. 4 (1998):
    3–28.

———. *Havana USA: Cuban Exiles and Cuban Americans in South Florida,
    1959–1994*. Berkeley: University of California Press, 1996.

——. *Seeking Refuge: Central American Migration to Mexico, the United States, and Canada*. Berkeley: University of California Press, 2006.

García, Matt. *A World of Its Own: Race, Labor, and Citrus in the Making of Greater Los Angeles, 1900–1970*. Chapel Hill: University of North Carolina Press, 2001.

Gavin, James. *Intimate Nights: The Golden Age of New York Cabaret*. New York: Back Stage Books, 2006.

Gerard, Charley. *Music from Cuba: Mongo Santamaría, Chocolate Armenteros, and Cuban Musicians in the United States*. Westport, Conn.: Praeger, 2001.

Gerstle, Gary. *American Crucible: Race and Nation in the Twentieth Century*. Princeton, N.J.: Princeton University Press, 2001.

Gil, Vincent Edwards. "The Personal Adjustment and Acculturation of Cuban Immigrants in Los Angeles." PhD diss., University of California, Los Angeles, 1976.

Glasser, Ruth. "The Backstage View: Musicians Piece Together a Living." *Centro de Estudios Puertorriqueños Bulletin* 3, no. 2 (1991): 24–49.

——. *My Music Is My Flag: Puerto Rican Musicians and Their New York Communities, 1917–1940*. Berkeley: University of California Press, 1997.

Glick Schiller, Nina, Linda Basch, and Cristina Szanton Blanc. "From Immigrant to Transmigrant: Theorizing Transnational Migration." *Anthropological Quarterly* 68, no. 1 (1995): 48–83.

Glick Schiller, Nina and Georges Fouron. *Georges Woke Up Laughing: Long-Distance Nationalism and the Search for Home*. Durham, N.C.: Duke University Press, 2001.

Gómez, Laura E. *Manifest Destinies: The Making of the Mexican American Race*. New York: New York University Press, 2007.

González, Gilbert, and Raúl A. Fernández. "Empire and the Origins of Twentieth-Century Migration from Mexico to the United States." *Pacific Historical Review* 71, no. 1 (2002): 19–57.

González, Juan. *Harvest of Empire: A History of Latinos in America*. New York: Viking, 2000.

González, Michelle A. *Afro-Cuban Theology: Religion, Race, Culture, and Identity*. Gainesville: University Press of Florida, 2009.

Gottlieb, William. "What Makes Rhumba?" In *Salsiology: Afro-Cuban Music and the Evolution of Salsa in New York City*, ed. Vernon W. Boggs, 23–28. New York: Greenwood Press, 1992.

Graciela. "¡Eso Era Tremenedo!: An Afro-Cuban Musician Remembers." In *The Afro-Latin@ Reader: History and Culture in the United States*, ed. Miriam Jiménez Román and Juan Flores, 150–156. Durham, N.C.: Duke University Press, 2010.

Greenbaum, Susan D. *More Than Black: Afro-Cubans in Tampa*. Gainesville: University Press of Florida, 2002.

Grenier, Guillermo J., and Lisandro Pérez. *The Legacy of Exile: Cubans in the United States*. Boston: Pearson Education, 2003.

Gronbeck-Tedesco, John A. "Reading Revolution: Politics in the U.S.-Cuban Cultural Imagination, 1930–1970." PhD diss., University of Texas at Austin, 2009.

Guerra, Lillian. *The Myth of José Martí: Conflicting Nationalisms in Early Twentieth-Century Cuba*. Chapel Hill: University of North Carolina Press, 2005.

Guevara, Gema. "Racial Authority in Cuban Popular Music." *Journal of Popular Music Studies* 17, no. 3 (2005): 255–275.

Guglielmo, Thomas A. "Fighting for Caucasian Rights: Mexicans, Mexican Americans, and the Transnational Struggle for Civil Rights in World War II Texas." *Journal of American History* 92, no. 4 (2006): 1212–1237.

———. *White on Arrival: Italians, Race, Color, and Power in Chicago, 1890–1945*. New York: Oxford University Press, 2003.

Guridy, Frank. *Forging Diaspora: Afro-Cubans and African Americans in a World of Empire and Jim Crow*. Chapel Hill: University of North Carolina Press, 2010.

———. "From Solidarity to Cross-Fertilization: Afro-Cuban/Afro-American Interaction during the 1930s and 1940s." *Radical History Review* 87 (Fall 2003): 19–48.

Hall, Stuart. "Negotiating Caribbean Identities." *New Left Review* 209 (January–February 1995): 3–14.

———. "Notes on Deconstructing 'the Popular.'" In *Cultural Theory and Popular Culture: A Reader*, ed. John Storey, 508–518. London: Longman, 2009.

———. "What Is This 'Black' in Black Popular Culture?" *Social Justice* 20, no. 1–2 (1993): 104–115.

Harper, Paula. "Cuba Connections: Key West, Tampa, Miami, 1870 to 1945." *The Journal of Decorative and Propaganda Arts* 22 (1996): 279–291.

Harris, Daryl. "Generating Racial and Ethnic Conflict in Miami: Impact of American Foreign Policy and Domestic Racism." In *Blacks, Latinos, and Asians in Urban America*, ed. James Jennings, 79–94. Westport, Conn.: Praeger, 1994.

Harris, Warren G. *Lucy & Desi: The Legendary Love Story of Television's Most Famous Couple*. New York: Simon & Schuster, 1991.

Haslip-Viera, Gabriel. "The Evolution of the Latino Community in New York City: Early Nineteenth Century to the Present." In *Latinos in New York: Communities in Transition*, ed. Gabriel Haslip-Viera and Sherrie L. Baver, 3–29. Notre Dame, Ind.: University of Notre Dame Press, 1996.

Helg, Aline. "Black Men, Racial Stereotyping, and Violence in the U.S. South and Cuba at the Turn of the Century." *Comparative Studies in Society and History* 42, no. 3 (2000): 576–604.

———. *Our Rightful Share: The Afro-Cuban Struggle for Equality, 1886–1912*. Chapel Hill: University of North Carolina Press, 1995.

Hewitt, Nancy A. *Southern Discomfort: Women's Activism in Tampa, Florida, 1880s–1920s*. Champaign: University of Illinois Press, 2001.

Hoffnung-Garskof, Jesse. "The Migrations of Arturo Schomburg: On Being *Antillano*, Negro, and Puerto Rican in New York, 1891–1938." *Journal of American Ethnic History* 21, no. 1 (2001): 3–49.

———. *A Tale of Two Cities: Santo Domingo and New York after 1950*. Princeton, N.J.: Princeton University Press, 2007.

Hondagneu-Sotelo, Pierrette, and Ernestine Avila. "'I'm Here, but I'm There': The Meanings of Latina Transnational Motherhood." *Gender and Society* 11, no. 5 (1997): 548–571.

Howard, Philip A. *Changing History: Afro-Cuban Cabildos and Societies of Color in the Nineteenth Century*. Baton Rouge: Louisiana State University Press, 1998.

Iglesias, Cesar Andreu. *Memoirs of Bernardo Vega: A Contribution to the History of the Puerto Rican Community in New York*. New York: Monthly Review Press, 1984.

Jacobson, Matthew Frye. *Whiteness of a Different Color: European Immigrants and the Alchemy of Race*. Cambridge, Mass.: Harvard University Press, 1999.

James, Winston. *Holding Aloft the Banner of Ethiopia: Caribbean Radicalism in Early Twentieth-Century America*. New York: Verso, 1998.

Jenkins, Henry, Tara McPherson, and Jane Shattuc. "Defining Popular Culture." In *Hop on Pop: The Politics and Pleasures of Popular Culture*, ed. Henry Jenkins III, Tara McPherson, and Jane Shattuc, 26–42. Durham, N.C.: Duke University Press, 2002.

Jiménez Román, Miriam, and Juan Flores, eds. *The Afro-Latin@ Reader: History and Culture in the United States*. Durham, N.C.: Duke University Press, 2010.

———. "Introduction." In *The Afro-Latin@ Reader: History and Culture in the United States*, ed. Miriam Jiménez Román and Juan Flores, 1–15. Durham, N.C.: Duke University Press, 2010.

Johnson, Robert David. *Ernest Gruening and the American Dissenting Tradition*. Cambridge, Mass.: Harvard University Press, 1998.

Jones, John Bush. *The Songs that Fought the War: Popular Music and the Home Front, 1939–1945*. Lebanon, N.H.: Brandeis University Press, 2006.

Joseph, Gilbert M., Catherine LeGrand, and Ricardo D. Salvatore, eds. *Close Encounters of Empire: Writing the Cultural History of U.S.-Latin American Relations*. Durham, N.C.: Duke University Press, 1998.

Jottar, Berta. "Central Park Rumba: Nuyorican Identity and the Return to African Roots." *CENTRO Journal* 23, no. 1 (2011): 5–29.

Juffer, Jane. "In Search of the Latino Public Sphere: Everywhere and Nowhere." *Nepantla: Views from South* 4, no. 2 (2003): 263–268.

Kammen, Michael. *American Culture, American Tastes: Social Change and the Twentieth Century*. New York: Basic Books, 2000.

Kanellos, Nicolás. "Cronistas and Satire in Early Twentieth Century Hispanic Newspapers." *MELUS* 23, no. 1 (1998): 3–25.

———. *A History of Hispanic Theater in the United States: Origins to 1940*. Austin: University of Texas Press, 1990.

Kennedy, David. *Freedom from Fear: The American People in Depression and War, 1929–1945*. New York: Oxford University Press, 2001.

Kun, Josh. "Bagles, Bongos, and Yiddishe Mambos, or The Other History of Jews in America." *Shofar: An Interdisciplinary Journal of Jewish Studies* 23, no. 4 (2005): 50–68.

Kutzinski, Vera M. *Sugar's Secrets: Race and the Erotics of Cuban Nationalism.*
Charlottesville: University Press of Virginia, 1993.

Kvistos, Peter. "Theorizing Transnational Immigration: A Critical Review of
Current Efforts." *Ethnic and Racial Studies* 24, no. 4 (2004): 549–577.

LaFeber, Walter. *Inevitable Revolutions: The United States in Central America.* New
York: W.W. Norton & Company, 1993.

La Fountain-Stokes, Larry. "Translating Latina/o Studies in the Classroom with Ricky
Ricardo and Babalú Ayé." Translation at University of Michigan, 1 December 2011.
http://translation.lsa.umich.edu/2012/12/translating-latinao-studies-in-the
-classroom-with-ricky-ricardo-and-babalu-aye/. Accessed 15 May 2013.

LaGumina, Salvatore J. *New York at Mid-Century: The Impellitteri Years.* Westport,
Conn.: Greenwood Press, 1992.

Laó-Montes, Agustín. "Mambo Montage: The Latinization of New York City." In
Mambo Montage: The Latinization of New York, ed. Agustín Laó-Montes and
Arlene Dávila, 1–54. New York: Columbia University Press, 2001.

Laó-Montes, Agustín, and Arlene Dávila, eds. *Mambo Montage: The Latinization of
New York.* New York: Columbia University Press, 2001.

Levine, Barry B. "Miami: The Capital of Latin America." *Wilson Quarterly* 9, no. 5
(1985): 46–69.

Leymarie, Isabelle. *Cuban Fire: The Story of Salsa and Latin Jazz.* London and New
York: Continuum, 2002.

Lipsitz, George. *Time Passages: Collective Memory and American Popular Culture.*
Minneapolis: University of Minnesota Press, 2001.

Lockey, Joseph B. "The Meaning of Pan Americanism." *The American Journal of
International Law* 19, no. 1 (1925): 104–117.

Lomas, Laura. *Translating Empire: José Martí, Migrant Latino Subjects, and
American Modernities.* Durham, N.C.: Duke University Press, 2008.

López, Alfred J. *José Martí and the Future of Cuban Nationalisms.* Gainesville:
University Press of Florida, 2006.

López, Antonio. "Chronicling Empire: José Martí on the Avenue of the Americas."
In *The Cuban Republic and José Martí: Reception and Use of a National Symbol,*
ed. Mauricio A. Font and Alfonso W. Quiroz, 128–134. Lanham, Md.: Lexington
Books, 2006.

———. *Unbecoming Blackness: The Diaspora Cultures of Afro-Cuban America.* New
York: New York University Press, 2012.

Lott, Eric. *Love and Theft: Blackface Minstrelsy and the American Working Class.*
New York: Oxford University Press, 1995.

Love, Eric. *Race over Empire: Racism and U.S. Imperialism, 1865–1900.* Chapel
Hill: University of North Carolina Press, 2000.

Loza, Steven. *Barrio Rhythm: Mexican American Music in Los Angeles.*
Champaign: University of Illinois Press, 1993.

———. *Tito Puente and the Making of Latin Music.* Champaign: University of
Illinois Press, 1999.

Lumsden, Ian. *Machos, Maricones, and Gays: Cuba and Homosexuality.*
Philadelphia: Temple University Press, 1996.

Macías, Anthony. *Mexican American Mojo: Popular Music, Dance, and Urban Culture in Los Angeles, 1935-1968*. Durham, N.C.: Duke University Press, 2008.

Manuel, Peter. "Latin Music in the United States: Salsa and the Mass Media." *Journal of Communication* 41, no. 1 (1991): 104-116.

———. "Puerto Rican Music and Cultural Identity: Creative Appropriation of Cuban Sources from Danza to Salsa." *Ethnomusicology* 38, no. 2 (1994): 49-80.

———, ed. *Creolizing Contradance in the Caribbean*. Philadelphia: Temple University Press, 2009.

Marling, Karal Ann. *As Seen on TV: The Visual Culture of Everyday Life in the 1950s*. Cambridge, Mass.: Harvard University Press, 1994.

Martí, José. *Versos sencillos/Simple Verses*. Translated by Manuel A. Tellechea. Houston, Texas: Arte Público Press, 1997.

Martínez-Echazábal, Lourdes. "Mestizaje and the Discourse of National/Cultural Identity in Latin America, 1845-1959." *Latin American Perspectives* 25, no. 3 (1998): 21-42.

Masud-Piloto, Félix. *From Welcomed Exiles to Illegal Immigrants: Cuban Migration to the U.S., 1959-1995*. Lanham, Md.: Rowman & Littlefield, 1996.

McHugh, Kevin E., Ines M. Miyares, and Emily H. Skip. "The Magnetism of Miami: Segmented Paths in Cuban Migration." *Geographical Review* 87, no. 4 (1997): 504-519.

McNickle, Chris. *To Be Mayor of New York: Ethnic Politics in the City*. New York: Columbia University Press, 1993.

McPherson, Alan. *Yankee No!: Anti-Americanism in U.S.-Latin American Relations*. Cambridge, Mass.: Harvard University Press, 2006.

Meléndez, A. Gabriel. *Spanish-Language Newspapers in New Mexico, 1834-1958*. Tucson: University of Arizona Press, 2005.

Merrill, Dennis. *Negotiating Paradise: U.S. Tourism and Empire in Twentieth-Century Latin America*. Chapel Hill: University of North Carolina Press, 2009.

Meyer, Doris. *Speaking for Themselves: Neomexicano Cultural Identity and the Spanish-Language Press, 1880-1920*. Albuquerque: University of New Mexico Press, 1996.

Miller, Ivor. L. *Voices of the Leopard: African Secret Societies and Cuba*. Jackson: University Press of Mississippi, 2009.

Miller, Nathan Brad. "Mario Bauzá: Swing Era Novelty and Afro-Cuban Authenticity." PhD diss., University of Missouri, 2007.

Mirabal, Nancy Raquel. "Melba Alvarado, El Club Cubano Inter-Americano, and the Creation of Afro-Cubanidades." In *The Afro-Latin@ Reader: History and Culture in the United States*, ed. Miriam Jiménez Román and Juan Flores, 120-126. Durham, N.C.: Duke University Press, 2010.

———. "Scripting Race, Finding Place: African Americans, Afro-Cubans, and the Diasporic Imaginary in the United States." In *Neither Enemies nor Friends: Latinos, Blacks, Afro-Latinos*, ed. Anani Dzidzienyo and Suzanne Oboler, 189-208. New York: Palgrave Macmillan, 2005.

———. "'Ser De Aquí': Beyond the Cuban Exile Model." *Latino Studies* 1, no. 3 (2003): 366-382.

Mohl, Raymond A. "Black Immigrants in Early Twentieth-Century Miami." *Florida Historical Quarterly* 65, no. 3 (1987): 271–297.

———. "Making the Second Ghetto in Metropolitan Miami, 1940–1960." *Journal of Urban History* 21, no. 3 (1998): 3–21.

———. "Shadows in the Sunshine: Race and Ethnicity in Miami." *Tequesta* 49 (1989): 63–80.

———. "Whitening Miami: Race, Housing and Government Policy in Twentieth-Century Dade County." *Florida Historical Quarterly* 79, no. 3 (2001): 319–345.

Molina, Natalia, Adrian Burgos Jr., Daniel Ramírez, and Pablo Mitchell. "Where Is the Latino Past in the Future?: Trends in Latino/a History and Historiography." Panel presented at Latina/o Studies Silver Symposium, University of Michigan, Ann Arbor, 30 October 2009.

Moore, Robin. *Nationalizing Blackness: Afrocubanismo and Artistic Revolution in Havana, 1920–1940*. Pittsburgh: University of Pittsburgh Press, 1997.

Morales, Ed. *The Latin Beat: The Rhythms and Roots of Latin Music from Bossa Nova to Salsa and Beyond*. Cambridge, Mass.: De Capo Press, 2003.

Moreno, Jairo. "Bauzá-Gillespie-Latin/Jazz: Difference, Modernity, and the Black Caribbean." *South Atlantic Quarterly* 103, no. 1 (2004): 81–99.

Morley, Morris. "The U.S. Imperial State in Cuba, 1952–1958: Policymaking and Capitalist Interest." *Journal of Latin American Studies* 14, no. 1 (1982): 143–170.

Mormino, Gary R. *Land of Sunshine, State of Dreams: A Social History of Modern Florida*. Gainesville: University Press of Florida, 2005.

———. "Midas Returns: Miami Goes to War, 1941–1945." *Tequesta* 57 (1997): 5–51.

Mormino, Gary R. and George E. Pozzetta. *The Immigrant World of Ybor City: Italians and Their Latin Neighbors in Tampa, 1885–1985*. Gainesville: University Press of Florida, 1998.

Nelson, William Javier. "Their Loss—Our Gain: The Gift of Latin Music in the U.S." *Afro-Hispanic Review* 6, no. 2 (1987): 19–24.

Nesvig, Martin. "The Complicated Terrain of Latin American Homosexuality." *Hispanic American Historical Review* 81, no. 3–4 (2001): 689–729.

Ngai, Mae. *Impossible Subjects: Illegal Aliens and the Making of Modern America*. Princeton, N.J.: Princeton University Press, 2005.

Oboler, Suzanne. *Ethnic Labels, Latino Lives: Identity and the Politics of (Re)Presentation in the United States*. Minneapolis: University of Minnesota Press, 1995.

Ohmann, Richard. *Selling Culture: Magazines, Markets, and Class at the Turn of the Century*. New York: Verso Press, 1996.

Omi, Michael, and Howard Winant. *Racial Formation in the United States: From the 1960s to the 1990s*. New York: Routledge, 1994.

O'Neil, Brian. "The Demands of Authenticity: Addison Durland and Hollywood's Latin Images during World War II." In *Classic Hollywood, Classic Whiteness*, ed. Daniel Bernardi, 359–385. Minneapolis: University of Minnesota Press, 2001.

Oppenheimer, Jess. *Laughs, Luck . . . and Lucy: How I Came to Create the Most Popular Sitcom of All Time*. Syracuse, N.Y.: Syracuse University Press, 1999.

Orovio, Helio. *Cuban Music from A to Z*. Durham, N.C.: Duke University Press, 2004.

Ortíz, Ricardo L. *Cultural Erotics in Cuban America*. Minneapolis: University of Minnesota Press, 2007.

Pacini Hernández, Deborah. *Bachata: A Social History of a Dominican Popular Music*. Philadelphia: Temple University Press, 1995.

Padilla, Félix M. *Latino Ethnic Consciousness*. Notre Dame, Ind.: University of Notre Dame Press, 1985.

Paterson, Thomas. *Contesting Castro: The United States and the Triumph of the Cuban Revolution*. New York: Oxford University Press, 1994.

Pedraza, Silvia. "Beyond Black and White: Latinos and Social Science Research on Immigration, Race, and Ethnicity in America." *Social Science History* 24, no. 4 (2000): 697–726.

——. "Cuba's Refugees: Manifold Migrations." In *Origins and Destinies: Immigration, Race, and Ethnicity in America*, ed., Silvia Pedraza and Rubén G. Rumbaut, 263–279. Belmont, Calif.: Wadsworth Publishing, 1996.

——. *Political Disaffection in Cuba's Revolution and Exodus*. New York: Cambridge University Press, 2007.

Pérez, Louis A. *Cuba: Between Reform and Revolution*. New York: Oxford University Press, 1988.

——. *Cuba and the United States: Ties of Singular Intimacy*. Athens: University of Georgia Press, 2003.

——. *Cuba in the American Imagination: Metaphor and the Imperial Ethos*. Chapel Hill: University of North Carolina Press, 2008.

——. "Fear and Loathing of Fidel Castro: Sources of U.S. Policy toward Cuba." *Journal of Latin American Studies* 34 (May 2002): 227–254.

——. *On Becoming Cuban: Identity, Nationality, and Culture*. Chapel Hill: University of North Carolina Press, 1999.

——. "Peasants, Politics, and People of Color: The 1912 'Race War' in Cuba Reconsidered." *Hispanic American Historical Review* 66, no. 3 (1986): 509–539.

——. *The War of 1898: The United States and Cuba in History and Historiography*. Chapel Hill: University of North Carolina Press, 1998.

Pérez-Firmat, Gustavo. "Latunes: An Introduction." *Latin American Music Review* 43, no. 2 (2008): 180–203.

——. *Life on the Hyphen: The Cuban-American Way*. Austin: University of Texas Press, 1994.

Pérez Rodríguez, Nancy. *El Carnaval Santiaguero, Tomo I*. Santiago de Cuba: Editorial Oriente, 1988.

Pérez-Stable, Marifeli. *The Cuban Revolution: Origins, Course, and Legacy*. New York: Oxford University Press, 1998.

Podell-Raber, Mickey, and Charles Pignone. *The Copa: Jules Podell and the Hottest Club North of Havana*. New York: Harper, 2007.

Portes, Alejandro. "The Cuban-American Political Machine: Reflections on Its Origins and Perpetuation." In *Changes in Cuban Society since the Nineties*. ed. Joseph Tulchin, Lilian Bodea, Mayra P. Espina Prieto, and Rafael Hernández with Elizabeth Bryan, 187–206. Washington, D.C.: Woodrow Wilson International Center for Scholars, 2005.

Portes, Alejandro, and Ramón Grosfoguel. "Caribbean Diasporas: Migration and Ethnic Communities." *Annals of the American Political Science Society* 533 (May 1994): 48–69.

Portes, Alejandro, Luis Guarnizo, and Patricia Landolt. "Transnational Communities: Pitfalls and Promise of an Emergent Research Field." *Ethnic and Racial Studies* 22, no. 2 (1999): 217–237.

Portes, Alejandro, and Alex Stepick. *City on the Edge: The Transformation of Miami.* Berkeley: University of California Press, 1993.

Portuondo Zúñiga, Olga. "The Virgin of Charity of Cobre, Cuba's Patron Saint." In *The Cuba Reader: History, Culture, Politics,* ed. Aviva Chomsky, Barry Carr, and Pamela María Smorkaloff, 490–497. Durham, N.C.: Duke University Press, 2004.

Powell, Josephine. *Tito Puente: When the Drums Are Dreaming.* Baltimore, Md.: AuthorHouse, 2007.

Poyo, Gerald E. *"With All, and For the Good of All": The Emergence of Popular Nationalism in the Cuban Communities of the United States, 1848-1898.* Durham, N.C.: Duke University Press, 1989.

Prieto, Yolanda. *The Cubans of Union City: Immigrants and Exiles in a New Jersey Community.* Philadelphia: Temple University Press, 2009.

Pritchett, Wendell E. "Race and Community in Postwar Brooklyn: The Brownsville Neighborhood Council and the Politics of Urban Renewal." *Journal of Urban History* 27, no. 4 (2001): 445–471.

Pulido, Laura. *Black, Brown, Yellow, and Left: Radical Activism in Los Angeles.* Berkeley: University of California Press, 2006.

Radano, Ronaldo, and Philip V. Bohlman, eds. *Music and the Racial Imagination.* Chicago: University of Chicago Press, 2000.

Ramírez Berg, Charles. *Latino Images in Film: Stereotypes, Subversion, and Resistance.* Austin: University of Texas Press, 2002.

Ramsey, Guthrie, Jr. *Race Music: Black Cultures from Bebop to Hip-Hop.* Berkeley: University of California Press, 2003.

Revels, Tracy J. *Sunshine Paradise: A History of Florida Tourism.* Gainesville: University Press of Florida, 2011.

Reyes-Schramm, Adelaida. "The Role of Music in the Interaction of Black Americans and Hispanos in New York City's East Harlem." PhD diss., Columbia University, 1975.

Rivas-Rodríguez, Maggie, and Emilio Zamora. *Beyond the Latino World War II Hero: The Social and Political Legacy of a Generation.* Austin: University of Texas Press, 2009.

Rivero, Yeidy M. *Tuning Out Blackness: Race and Nation in the History of Puerto Rican Television.* Durham, N.C.: Duke University Press, 2005.

Robert, Karen. "Slavery and Freedom in the Ten Years' War, Cuba, 1868-1878." *Slavery & Abolition* 13 (December 1992): 181–200.

Roberts, John Storm. *Black Music of Two Worlds: African, Caribbean, Latin, and African American Traditions.* New York: Schirmer Trade Books, 1998.

———. *The Latin Tinge: The Impact of Latin American Music on the United States.* New York: Oxford University Press, 1979.

Rodríguez, Clara. *Latin Looks: Images of Latinas and Latinos in the U.S. Media.* Boulder, Colo.: Westview Press, 1997.

———. *Puerto Ricans: Born in the U.S.A.* Boulder, Colo.: Westview Press, 1991.

Rodríguez-Luis, Julio. *Re-Reading José Martí: One Hundred Years Later.* New York: State University of New York Press, 1999.

Rondón, César Miguel. *El Libro de la Salsa: Crónica de la Musica del Caribe Urbano.* Caracas, Venezuela: Editorial Arte, 1980.

Rose, Chanelle Nyree. "Neither Southern nor Northern: Miami, Florida and the Black Freedom Struggle in America's Tourist Paradise, 1896–1968." PhD diss., University of Miami, 2007.

Ruiz, Vicki. *Cannery Women/Cannery Lives: Mexican Women, Unionization and the California Food Processing Industry, 1930–1950.* Albuquerque: University of New Mexico Press, 1987.

Salazar, Max. *Mambo Kingdom: Latin Music in New York.* New York: Schirmer Trade Books, 2002.

Sánchez, George J. *Becoming Mexican American: Ethnicity, Culture, and Identity in Chicano Los Angeles, 1900–1945.* Berkeley: University of California Press, 1997.

Sánchez Korrol, Virginia E. *From Colonia to Community: The History of Puerto Ricans in New York City.* Berkeley: University of California Press, 1994.

Sanders, Coyne Steven, and Thomas W. Gilbert. *Desilu: The Story of Lucille Ball and Desi Arnaz.* New York: Morrow, 1993.

Sandoval-Sánchez, Alberto. *José, Can You See?: Latinos On and Off Broadway.* Madison: University of Wisconsin Press, 1999.

Schoultz, Lars. *Beneath the United States: A History of U.S. Policy toward Latin America.* Cambridge, Mass.: Harvard University Press, 1998.

———. *That Infernal Little Cuban Republic: The United States and the Cuban Revolution.* Chapel Hill: University of North Carolina Press, 2009.

Scott, James Brown. "Good Neighbor Policy." *The American Journal of International Law* 30, no. 2 (1936): 287–290.

Scott, Rebecca J. *Degrees of Freedom: Louisiana and Cuba after Slavery.* Cambridge, Mass.: Belknap Press, 2008.

Ševčenko, Liz. "Making Loisaida: Placing Puertorriqueñidad in Lower Manhattan." In *Mambo Montage: The Latinization of New York*, ed. Agustín Laó-Montes and Arlene Dávila, 293–318. New York: Columbia University Press, 2001.

Shell-Weiss, Melanie. *Coming to Miami: A Social History.* Gainesville: University Press of Florida, 2009.

Shirley, Paula W. "Reading Desi Arnaz in 'The Mambo Kings Play Songs of Love.'" *MELUS* 20, no. 3 (1995): 69–78.

Sicius, Francis J. "The Miami-Havana Connection: The First Seventy-Five Years." *Tequesta* 58 (1998): 5–45.

Singer, Roberta L. "My Music Is Who I Am and What I Do: Latin Popular Music and Identity in New York City." PhD diss., Indiana University, 1982.

Singer, Roberta L., and Elena Martínez. "A South Bronx Latin Music Tale." *CENTRO Journal* 16, no. 1 (2004): 177–201.

Smith, Michael, and Luis Guarnizo, eds. *Transnationalism from Below*. Piscataway, N.J.: Transaction Publishers, 1998.

Soruco, Gonzalo R. *Cubans and the Mass Media in Southern Florida*. Gainesville: University Press of Florida, 1996.

Spigel, Lynn. *Make Room for TV: Television and the Family Ideal in Postwar America*. Chicago: University of Chicago Press, 1992.

Stolcke, Verena. *Marriage, Class, and Color in Nineteenth-Century Cuba: A Study of Racial Attitudes and Social Values in a Slave Society*. New York: Cambridge University Press, 1974.

Sublette, Ned. *Cuba and Its Music: From the First Drums to the Mambo*. Chicago: Chicago Review Press, 2004.

Sweig, Julie E. *Inside the Cuban Revolution: Fidel Castro and the Urban Underground*. Cambridge, Mass.: Harvard University Press, 2004.

Thomas, Bert. "Historical Functions of Caribbean-American Benevolent/Progressive Associations." *Afro-Americans in New York Life and History* 12, no. 2 (1988): 45–51.

Thomas, Hugh. *Cuba or The Pursuit of Freedom*. New York: Da Capo Press, 1998.

Thomas, Lorrin. *Puerto Rican Citizen: History and Political Identity in Twentieth-Century New York City*. Chicago: University of Chicago Press, 2010.

Tone, John Lawrence. *War and Genocide in Cuba, 1895–1898*. Chapel Hill: University of North Carolina Press, 2008.

Torres, María de los Angeles. *In the Land of Mirrors: Cuban Exile Politics in the United States*. Ann Arbor: University of Michigan Press, 2001.

——. *The Lost Apple: Operation Pedro Pan, Cuban Children in the U.S., and the Promise of a Better Future*. Boston: Beacon Press, 2004.

Torres-Saillant, Silvio. "Inventing the Race: Latinos and the Ethnoracial Pentagon." *Latino Studies* 1, no. 1 (2003): 123–167.

Tovares, Raúl D. "*La Opinión* and Its Contribution to the Mexican Community's Adaptation to Life in the U.S." *Latino Studies* 7, no. 4 (2009): 480–499.

Triay, Victor Andres. *Operation Pedro Pan and the Cuban Children's Program*. Gainesville: University Press of Florida, 1999.

Tscheschlok, Eric. "'So Goes the Negro': Race and Labor in Miami, 1940–1963." *Florida Historical Quarterly* 76, no. 1 (1997): 42–67.

Tweed, Thomas A. *Our Lady of the Exile: Diasporic Religion at a Cuban Catholic Shrine in Miami*. New York: Oxford University Press, 2002.

Vasconcelos, José. *The Cosmic Race/La raza cósmica*. Los Angeles: California State University, 1979.

Vazquez, Alexandra T. *Listening in Detail: Performances of Cuban Music*. Durham, N.C.: Duke University Press, 2013.

Vega, Marta Moreno. "The Yoruba Orisha Tradition Comes to New York City." *African American Review* 29, no. 2 (1995): 201–206.

Walsh, Bryan O. "Cuban Refugee Children." *Journal of Interamerican Studies and World Affairs* 13, no. 3–4 (1971): 378–415.

Warner, Michael. *Publics and Counterpublics*. New York: Zone Books, 2005.

Watkins-Owens, Irma. *Blood Relations: Caribbean Immigrants and the Harlem Community, 1900–1930*. Bloomington: Indiana University Press, 1996.

Waxer, Lisa. "Of Mambo Kings and Songs of Love: Dance Music in Havana and New York from the 1930s to the 1950s." *Latin American Music Review* 15, no. 2 (1994): 139–176.

———. *Situating Salsa: Global Markets and Local Meanings in Latin Popular Music*. New York: Routledge, 2002.

Weisman, Brent Richards. *Soldiers and Patriots: Buffalo Soldiers and Afro-Cubans in Tampa, 1898*. Tampa: University of South Florida, 1999.

Williams, William Appleman. *The Tragedy of American Diplomacy*. New York: W.W. Norton & Company, 1988.

Winsberg, Morton D. "Housing Segregation of a Predominantly Middle Class Population: Residential Patterns Developed by the Cuban Immigration into Miami, 1950–1974." *American Journal of Economics and Sociology* 38, no. 4 (1979): 403–418.

Zolov, Eric. Comments in response to panel on Culture and Society in Cold War Mexico. American Historical Association Annual Meeting, San Diego, California, 8 January 2010.

Index

Note: Photographs are indicated by *italic* page numbers.

149–51; Rizo and, 20–21, 35, 36, 38–39, 41, 55; on *Saturday Night Live*, 1, 221

Arnaz, Desi, Sr., 144, 145, 146, 147–48, 149, 190

Arres, Don, 110

Arroyo, José R., 136

Arsenio Rodríguez y Su Conjunto, 71

Arte Renovación, 47

Artesanos Cubano, 91

Arturo Benson y su orquesta Cubanacán, 200

Asociación de Artistas Hispanos, 179, 181

Asociación de Comerciantes Hispanos, 119

Asociación de Comerciantes Hispanos del Bronx, 139

Asociación de Empleados Puertorriqueños, 119

Ateneo Cubano de Nueva York, 61, 62–63, 75, 79, 82, *86*; Concurso de Popularidad de Artistas y Orquestas Hispanos de Nueva York and, 119, 139; Cuban independence and, 241 (n. 17); Cuban nationalism and, 91–92; Grito de Baire and, 87; Grito de Yara and, 85–86; Martí and, 84–85; Pan-American Day and, 96; race and, 88–89; 26 of July Movement and, 107; Virgen de la Caridad and, 99

Audubon Ballroom, 56–57, 90, 101, 167

Audubon Hall, 74

Auténtico Party, 105, 211, 215

Authenticity. *See* Musical authenticity

Avilés, Vitín, 197

Ayala, Gilberto, 70

Azcarraga, Lucho, 165

"Babalú," 2, 131, 164–71

Babalú-Ayé, 2

Baile del Mamoncillo (Dance of the Spanish Limes), 222

Ball, Lucille, 39, 141, 151, 218

Bandera, Quintin, 89

Baños, Alberto, 80, 96, 103

Baral, Luis A., 108

Barra Guys and Dolls, 18, 198

Barreras, Alberto, 147

Barretto, Ray, 221

Barrio. *See* Spanish Harlem

Baseball, 24–25

Bataan (film), 153–55

Batista, Fulgencio, 26, 60, 105, 106, 107, 130, 146, 179, 206, 215–17, 246 (nn. 73, 82)

Bauzá, Mario, 2, *42*, 265 (n. 68); African Americans and, 45–46, 47; Afro-Cuban genre and, 51–52; background of, 42–43; Club Cubano and, 89; on "colored circuit" in Miami, 213, 265 (n. 68); Cubanness of, 54; Cugat and, 27; at Gran Festival, 134; Guerra and, 69; on Harlem, 43, 45; later career of, 22; Machín and, 46; in Machito y sus Afro-Cubans, 20–21, 53–54, 55, 158; Machito y sus Afro-Cubans and, 137; mambo and, 53–54; in New York, 43, 45–49, 233 (n. 60); Palladium and, 172; as pioneer, 50–54; on race in Cuba, 43–44; relations with Puerto Ricans, 49–50; Marco Rizo vs., 20–21; Vilma Rizo on, 42; on Arsenio Rodríguez, 72, 77

Beachcomber, 196

Bebop, 163

Beer and Cracker-Eating Contest, 174

Benjamin Franklin High School, 68, 75–76, 181

Benson, Arturo, 200

Bergaza, Felo, 134

Beyoncé, 225

Birdland, 163

Bisbe, Manuel, 108

Blood drive, 181–82

Boada, Luis E., 124

Bodega, 47, 193, 195

Boggs, Vernon, 24, 50, 173

Bola de Nieve, 40

Popular music, 5–6; classical music vs., 41; Cugat on, 22–23; Curbelo and, 33; migration and, 21–22, 31–34; shifts in, 220–21
Portuondo, Emilio Nuñez, 242 (n. 17)
Portuondo Calá, Pedro, 94, 102
Powell, Bud, 163
Pozo, Chano, 101
Prado, Pérez, 53, 71, 72, 76, 77, 238 (n. 55)
Premio de Verano (Summer Prize), 177
Primera Conferencia Interamericana de Música, 209–10
Prío-Socarrás, Carlo, 92, 105, 211, 216
Pueblos Hispanos (newspaper), 26–27
Puente, Tito, 71, 75, 91, 139, 169, 173, 221
Puerto Ricans: Afro-Cuban music and, 50; in Concurso de Popularidad de Artistas y Orquestas Hispanos de Nueva York, 113–14; in Miami, 206–8; population of, in New York, 60; race relations with, 49–50; at Tropicana, 176–77
Pujol, Aida, 40

Quesada, Cayetano de, 99, 130
"Quimbara," 2
Quintero, Babby, 68, 134, 175, 179

Race: categories and, 11, 15, 17, 24, 44, 57, 59, 100; color line and, 11, 52, 159, 192, 213; consciousness and, 37–38, 50–52, 212; in Cuba, 9–11, 29–31, 42–45; Hollywood and, 152–55; Jim Crow era and, 5, 16, 58, 186, 192, 210, 212–14; Latin music model and, 24–29; Maceo and, 100; Martí and, 99–100; mixture and, 6, 14, 29, 44, 98, 100, 128, 228 (n. 5); segregation and, 37, 43–45, 154, 192, 212–14; silence of, 37, 61; "Trojan horsing" and, 213–14; U.S. military and, 153–56. See also *Nuestra raza*
"Race war" of 1912, 30
Racial discrimination: in entertainment industry, 46, 52, 67, 153; in public

spaces, 48–49, 207–8, 212–14; in social clubs, 88–89, 100
Racialization, 9, 11, 24–25, 98, 129, 193, 211, 214, 251 (n. 40)
Racial knowledge, 11
Radio, television vs., 81, 116–17, 239 (n. 69)
Ramírez, Carlos, 164
"Rapsodia Cubana" (Rizo), 40
Rebull, Reinaldo Fernández, 87, 102, 245 (n. 65)
Red Cross. *See* American Red Cross; Cuban Red Cross
Red Scare, 235 (n. 7)
Reina de *La Prensa* beauty pageant, 108–9
Reina del Desfile Hispano de Nueva York (Queen of the Hispanic Parade of New York), 203
Restaurants, in Miami, 194–95
Revueltas, Silvestre, 35
Reyes, Ángel, 85
Reyes, Eva, 118, 196, 206
Reyes, Raúl, 118, 196, 206
Rhumba, *187*
Riambau, Horacio, 24, 37–38, 176
Ricardo, Alice, 207
Ricardo, José, 207
Rich, Buddy, 162
Rico, Ricardo "El Rey del Merengue," 138–39
Rinconcito Criollo restaurant, 90
Ritmos de Otoño (Fall Rhythms), 74, 78–79
Rivera, José Martí, 200
Rivera González, Ramón, 200
Rivero y Conjunto, Facundo, 134
Rizo, Marco, *42*, 160, 169; Arnaz and, 35, 36, 38–39; background of, 230 (n. 22); Bauzá vs., 20–21; as classical musician, 40; in Cuba, 31–32; Cubanness of, 1, 29–31; Cuban roots of, 40–42; later career of, 221; in New York, 34–38; in World War II, 34–35
Rizo, Vilma, 41

Christina D. Abreu, *Rhythms of Race: Cuban Musicians and the Making of Latino New York City and Miami, 1940–1960* (2015).

Anita Casavantes Bradford, *The Revolution Is for the Children: The Politics of Childhood in Havana and Miami, 1959–1962* (2014).

Tiffany A. Sippial, *Prostitution, Modernity, and the Making of the Cuban Republic, 1840–1920* (2013).

Kathleen López, *Chinese Cubans: A Transnational History* (2013).

Lillian Guerra, *Visions of Power in Cuba: Revolution, Redemption, and Resistance, 1959–1971* (2012).

Carrie Hamilton, *Sexual Revolutions in Cuba: Passion, Politics, and Memory* (2012).

Sherry Johnson, *Climate and Catastrophe in Cuba and the Atlantic World during the Age of Revolution* (2011).

Melina Pappademos, *Black Political Activism and the Cuban Republic* (2011).

Frank Andre Guridy, *Forging Diaspora: Afro-Cubans and African Americans in a World of Empire and Jim Crow* (2010).

Ann Marie Stock, *On Location in Cuba: Street Filmmaking during Times of Transition* (2009).

Alejandro de la Fuente, *Havana and the Atlantic in the Sixteenth Century* (2008).

Reinaldo Funes Monzote, *From Rainforest to Cane Field in Cuba: An Environmental History since 1492* (2008).

Matt D. Childs, *The 1812 Aponte Rebellion in Cuba and the Struggle against Atlantic Slavery* (2006).

Eduardo González, *Cuba and the Tempest: Literature and Cinema in the Time of Diaspora* (2006).

John Lawrence Tone, *War and Genocide in Cuba, 1895–1898* (2006).

Samuel Farber, *The Origins of the Cuban Revolution Reconsidered* (2006).

Lillian Guerra, *The Myth of José Martí: Conflicting Nationalisms in Early Twentieth-Century Cuba* (2005).

Rodrigo Lazo, *Writing to Cuba: Filibustering and Cuban Exiles in the United States* (2005).

Alejandra Bronfman, *Measures of Equality: Social Science, Citizenship, and Race in Cuba, 1902–1940* (2004).

Edna M. Rodríguez-Mangual, *Lydia Cabrera and the Construction of an Afro-Cuban Cultural Identity* (2004).

Gabino La Rosa Corzo, *Runaway Slave Settlements in Cuba: Resistance and Repression* (2003).

Piero Gleijeses, *Conflicting Missions: Havana, Washington, and Africa, 1959–1976* (2002).

Robert Whitney, *State and Revolution in Cuba: Mass Mobilization and Political Change, 1920–1940* (2001).

Alejandro de la Fuente, *A Nation for All: Race, Inequality, and Politics in Twentieth-Century Cuba* (2001).